Why Europe?

Why Europe

The Medieval Origins of Its Special Path

MICHAEL MITTERAUER

TRANSLATED BY GERALD CHAPPLE

The University of Chicago Press   Chicago and London

MICHAEL MITTERAUER is professor emeritus of social history
at the University of Vienna and the author of numerous books,
including *A History of Youth*.

Gerald Chapple is a retired associate professor of German
at McMaster University.

The University of Chicago Press, Chicago 60637
The University of Chicago Press, Ltd., London
© 2010 by The University of Chicago
All rights reserved. Published 2010
Printed in the United States of America
20 19 18 17 16 15 14 13 12 11 10   1 2 3 4 5
ISBN-13: 978-0-226-53253-0 (cloth)
ISBN-10: 0-226-53253-4 (cloth)

Originally published in German as *Warum Europa? Mittelalterliche
Grundlagen eines Sonderwegs*, © Verlag C.H. Beck oHG, München 2003.

Library of Congress Cataloging-in-Publication Data

Mitterauer, Michael.
    [Warum Europa? English]
    Why Europe? : the medieval origins of its special path / Michael
Mitterauer ; translated by Gerald Chapple.
        p.   cm.
    Translation of: Warum Europa? (München : C. H. Beck, 2003).
    Includes bibliographical references and index.
    ISBN-13: 978-0-226-53253-0 (cloth : alk. paper)
    ISBN-10: 0-226-53253-4 (cloth : alk. paper)
    1. European federation—History.   2. Europe—Civilization.
3. Civilization, Medieval.   4. Europe—History—476–1492.
I. Chapple, Gerald.   II. Title.
D131.M5813 2010
940.1—dc22   2010005833

♾ The paper used in this publication meets the minimum requirements
of the American National Standard for Information Sciences—
Permanence of Paper for Printed Library Materials, ANSI Z39.48-1992.

To the teachers and students
at the Institute for Economic and Social History
at the University of Vienna,
in gratitude

Contents

Translator's Note

The translation of the title of this work—*Warum Europa? Mittelalterliche Grundlagen eines Sonderwegs*—needs a little explanation. The word *Sonderweg* is sometimes retained in an English text as a technical term; translated, it is usually rendered "special path." There is an argument to be made for "unique path," or "specific path," since "special" is so overworked, but because "unique" might be misconstrued as a plea for European exceptionalism, I have employed the word sparingly throughout the book.

I have several people to thank for all kinds of assistance. First and foremost, Michael Mitterauer for his conscientious reading of a late draft, countless suggestions, and patient explanations of textual difficulties. Without his energetic cooperation, at times under great stress, this English version of *Warum Europa?* would have been greatly diminished, if not impossible. Constantin Fasolt and Jonathan Lyon, both at the University of Chicago, read the manuscript all or in part, offering both corrections and encouragement. The text also profited from the careful scrutiny and extensive knowledge of George Thomas, my colleague at McMaster University, to whom I am most grateful. I am pleased to acknowledge different kinds of advice and support from other McMaster colleagues: Bernice Kaczynski, Virginia Aksan, Richard Rempel, and Gabriele Erasmi. Tim McGovern, Joel Score, and Rob Hunt of the University of Chicago Press were helpful in shepherding the project through its many phases. Special thanks must be reserved for Carlisle Rex-Waller for her superb copyediting, from which author, translator, and reader have benefited enormously. In spite of all this help, the responsibility for whatever translating flaws remain must of course rest with me. I would be grateful if any errors were pointed out, as well as English versions of foreign works listed in the bibliography that have escaped my notice. The notes and bibliography have been carefully revised.

Technical help from McMaster's Interlibrary Loan services was invaluable. Financial assistance came from the Canada Council for the Arts, which allowed me to take up a productive writer's residency at Villa Waldberta near Munich, made possible through the generosity of that city and Karin Sommer's able assistance.

Finally, I wish to thank Nina, my wife, for her unflagging support at all stages of the translation's composition. I dedicate this translation to her in gratitude.

Gerald Chapple
Dundas, Ontario, September 28, 2009

Preface to the English Edition

It is a great pleasure for me to see my book on the medieval origins of Europe's special path appearing in English seven years after its first German printing and after its Spanish translation. The circle of potential readers is widening, and the discussion of my thinking in the book can now proceed on a broader basis.

The task I set for myself in writing this book was not concluded at its publication. Much relevant material has appeared in the last seven years. It is impossible to work it into my text, so I will limit myself here to indicating some of the directions the book has taken me in my recent scholarly endeavors in comparative history.

Chapter 6, which explores the roots of European expansionism, has proved an important point of departure. Thus, in *Pisa: Seemacht und Kulturmetropole* (Pisa: Naval power and cultural metropolises), a volume I published with John Morrissey in 2007, I attempt to describe the reciprocal effects of economic, political, and cultural developments in an Italian maritime republic. The significance of these developments for the beginnings of colonialism has received scant attention until now. My concern with early modes of mass communication in chapter 7 of *Why Europe?* seemed to me even more relevant after I read the *Arab Human Development Report* from 2003. In my 2008 article "Schreibrohr und Druckerpresse: Transferprobleme einer Kommunikationstechnologie" (Reed pen and printing press: Problems of transfer in a communication technology), I focus on the issue of why the adoption of the printing press with movable type in the Islamic world had to wait for such an inordinately long time—surely a key question for the understanding of a specific cultural development in the history of religion. To further our knowledge of the specific political structures in the East and the West, in 2009 I followed up some ideas in chapter 4 in a little book on the important topic of Islam and democracy: *Parlament und Schura: Ratsversammlungen und Demokratieentwicklung in Europa und der Islamischen Welt* (Parliament and Shura: Councils and the growth of democracy in Europe and the Islamic world).

Two topics in particular have engaged me since the original publication of this book: the importance of the water mill for industrialization and the role of iron in Europe's special path. I take them up again in my 2007 study "Standortfaktor Wasserkraft: Zwei europäische Eisenregionen im Vergleich" (Waterpower as a factor of location: A comparison of two European iron-producing regions). In my 2009 article "Die Anfänge der Universität im Mittelalter: Räume und Zentren der Wissenschaftsentwicklung" (The beginnings of the university in the Middle Ages: Areas and centers of the growth of scholarship), I have tried to make up for a justly criticized deficiency in the present book— the all too brief treatment of the university as a specifically European educational institution. None of these references, now included in the bibliography, can replace for the reader what has been insufficiently described in *Why Europe*? But each emphasizes a scholarly context into which I feel my comparative studies can be integrated.

Seven years after the first edition of this volume is surely too early to take stock of the way it has been discussed. High praise has been matched by harsh criticism. It seems surprising that both positive and negative opinions have been so emotionally colored. One colleague wrote, "To begin a book on Europe with 'Rye and Oats' is no doubt a colossal act of aggression against whole generations and their thinking. We still expect 'Emperor and Coronation.'" My book's approach is surely an unusual one for a medieval historian to take. The emotional nature of many reactions probably has to do with current debates about Europe in which this book has played a part. Any argument over identity in the present always involves views of the past. Here is a leading scholar of the didactics of history: "Even Mitterauer did not consider all of Europe in a scholarly and analytical way but only the West. Aware of the threatening political risks of isolation or exclusion, he too fiddles a pseudo-solution for the East-West divide." Even if you are at pains to observe history analytically, you cannot avoid today's powerful current of history as identity politics. Any position opposing this view is readily suspected of Eurocentrism. Weber's introductory sentence in his essays on the sociology of religion—the starting point of my study—can easily be misinterpreted along those lines. This book's position in response to the issue should clearly counteract these suspicions.

A book lives by its readers. The fact that *Why Europe?* has prompted a vigorous reaction among its German-speaking readers is a gratifying confirmation that I have put something in motion. The hope for similar lively feedback accompanies this book on its way to an English-speaking audience.

Michael Mitterauer
Vienna, January 17, 2009

Introduction to the First Edition

This book is a response to a question with a very long tradition in history and social science. Scholarly debate over the last few decades, coupled with some recent societal developments, has made the question even timelier. It was classically formulated in Max Weber's preface to his *Collected Essays on the Sociology of Religion*: "Through what concatenation of circumstances was it that precisely, and only, on the soil of the Occident cultural phenomena appeared that nonetheless developed—at least as we like to think—in a direction that is universally significant and valid?"[1] Weber discusses this issue under the rubric "the special development of the Occident." Variations on his question appear in book titles like *The Rise of the West*, *The Rise of the Western World*, *The European Miracle*, or *Der europäische Sonderweg* (Europe's special path).[2] The concept of "the Occident's exceptional development" turns up in more recent research, showing a continuous link to Weber's terminology.[3]

Why Europe? The title chosen for the present book collapses Weber's question into a concise formulation. At the same time, it signifies a particular approach to the book's subject matter. The point is not to "provide . . . building blocks . . . for all those engaged in constructing Europe or expanding it."[4] That would be a problematic aim for anyone making a rigorous scholarly inquiry into the reasons for Europe's special path (*Sonderweg*). The point is "to interpret Europe," not "to build Europe." Historical scholarship has all too often been co-opted by the political interests of its day. And the threat certainly remains that new, Eurocentric images of history will usurp old, ethnocentric ones. The question this book poses regarding the special path developed in Europe is not so much concerned with the creation of an awareness of some special quality as it is with clarifying the specific processes that have led to past and present differences vis-à-vis other cultures. It is not a matter of identifying with a history felt to be exceptional but of interpreting historical and contemporary cultural phenomena by way of their genesis. This means comparisons are essential. Any comparison has to work with similarities and differences. The very act of evaluating those cultural differences involves risk. This is why treating Europe's special path from a comparative point of view is always open to a tacit devaluation of any dissimilar cultural phenomena. The present book's subtitle attempts to counteract any such negative evaluation. There are many *Sonderwege* in many cultures; Europe's path is but one among them. My analysis sketches out a few—Byzantine, Islamic, Chinese—in varying degrees of detail that are dictated by the topic under comparison. But the real *explanandum*—the question of Europe's unique development—will be dealt with more fully.

The book's title, with its emphasis on the "medieval origins" of Europe's special path, stakes out my position, which runs counter to mainstream research. The majority view in recent literature is that the decisive choice was not made until the modern period.[5] I side instead with the great anthropologist Louis Dumont, who is said to have told his seminar students, "By 1000 C.E. the basic work in Europe had already been done."[6] The present study examines some determining factors that can be traced back to the early Middle Ages and late antiquity. This stress on early preconditions of Europe's special path has emerged from a number of my studies preliminary to the present investigation. A description of these studies in more detail will serve as a useful introduction to the controlling concept of this book: It all started with a research project on the medieval Estates in the Austrian provinces that I began with colleagues at my institute in the late 1960s. By 1975, this work had led to a comparative survey of how medieval Estates were structured across Europe and of the factors determining their origin.[7] Building on Otto Hintze's research, I came to realize that there was something in the way European society had developed to this point that was unique in world history. And so the first components of Europe's special path that I encountered were parliamentarianism and democracy—not, as for many researchers working on the problem of special paths, capitalism or industrialization. This discovery probably dictated my approach to the subject from then on. In explaining this aspect of the phenomenon of Europe's special path, it became apparent that the defining roots of modern political authority were deeply embedded in the Middle Ages. The obvious next step was to look for early origins of other aspects of the special path. Chapter 4, "The Feudal System and the Estates: A Special Path of Feudalism," joined up with then-current research on European Estates.

My second approach to matters concerning Europe's special path also took me far back in history. It began with topics in historical research on the family, which I worked on in the early 1970s. Unlike the situation in Estates research, present-day issues were front and center. Here again, a comparative examination of structural differences across Europe led me deep into the past. The same applied to the emergence of the European marriage pattern that John Hajnal derived from twentieth-century data; the historical roots of this pattern were in types of agrarian systems found in central and western Europe, which differed from those in southeastern and eastern Europe. The organization of the medieval manorial system might well have affected the characteristic European family system. My grappling with Jack Goody's theses in his *Development of the Family and Marriage in Europe* took me into quite different corners of medieval research, where religious influences on the family and family relationships were paramount. Diverse determining factors came to light, such as the Frankish agrarian system and the Christian bias against basing families on genealogical descent. I also learned, when considering the roots of specifically European family relationships, how these two factors were linked with still others, sometimes reciprocally. For anyone attempting to reconstruct a multiplicity of determining factors like this, Weber's "concatenation of circumstances" makes a special kind of sense. For me, working on European family structures meant bidding farewell to any type of monocausal explanatory model. Chapter 3, "The Conjugal Family and Bilateral Kinship," is based on a number of my relevant preliminary studies over the last twenty years.[8]

A late stimulus, though a very important one for the conception of the present book, was my encounter with Jared Diamond's *Guns, Germs and Steel: The Fates of Human Societies*, which started me thinking about whether new crops might have contributed to the makeup of Europe's special path.[9] My early thoughts were articulated in a discussion paper in 2000, "Agriculture and the 'Rise of Europe': Jared Diamond's Thesis as a Stimulus to Research."[10] I followed the topic up a year later in "Rye, Rice, and Sugarcane: A Comparison of Three Medieval Agrarian Revolutions," adding the Islamic world and China to my area of investigation.[11] My first chapter, "Rye and Oats," builds on these two preliminary studies. The choice of this chapter to lead off the present study did not mean to imply that agriculture was the unequivocal *causa prima* of Europe's special path. As the interpretive models in subsequent chapters clearly demonstrate, my analysis is not based on any one-sided economic scheme. Within the "concatenation of circumstances" that shaped Europe's unique development, agricultural factors indeed rank very highly, primarily for the shift in the main area of developmental dynamics to the continent's northwest. Moreover, some of the later chapters of *Why Europe?*—on the manorial system and the feudal system, for instance—would be difficult to follow without knowledge of the prerequisites laid out in chapter 1. For the thesis that, when considering the revolutionary transformation in agriculture in the early Middle Ages, the point of departure must be new crops and not agrarian technology, I am indebted to Jared Diamond's seminal thoughts and the cross-cultural comparisons he inspired. The comparisons in chapter 1 involved cultures unfamiliar to me before I had read Diamond, and they required a similar expansion of my perspective in later chapters. I learned much in the process but am also aware that I have risked overstepping the boundaries of my disciplinary expertise. But there was no way for me to pursue these urgent cross-cultural comparisons without running that risk.

Although some of the other chapters in *Why Europe?* can also be traced to earlier and recent studies of mine, the effect of this previous work on the overall conception of the volume has been somewhat less. This applies to chapters 6 and 7, "The Crusades and Protocolonialism: The Roots of European Expansionism" and "Preaching and Printing: Early Modes of Mass Communication." The fundamental concept in both chapters was outlined in surveys written for a journal of continuing education for teachers, *Beiträge zur historischen Sozialkunde* (Contributions to historical social studies), but each has been greatly expanded thematically and geographically in its present version.[12] For the particularly difficult chapter 5, "The Papal Church and Universal Religious Orders," I had been assembling comparative material concerning studies in the history of religion for some time. But crucial for the ideas in this section was an invitation to write an article on religions for the survey *Historical Anthropology in Southeastern Europe*.[13] The religious communities in this part of the world—Islam, Judaism, and various Christian denominations—are many, and they differ greatly. To compare them from the standpoint of historical anthropology required a new analytical framework, one that proved to be very useful for the wider-reaching study in comparative religion in chapter 5. I am indebted to my colleagues in southeastern Europe for important assistance in this work, and—through the studies inspired by their kind invitation to collaborate with them—for the development of the present book.

I have regularly taken part for the past ten years in the annual "Winter Balkan Meetings" sponsored by the International Seminar for Balkan Studies at the Southwestern University of Blagoevgrad. Conversations there have reminded me more and more how ticklish it can be to argue about the historical phenomena of Europe's special path when comparing and contrasting western and central Europe, on the one hand, and western and southeastern Europe on the other—family systems are just one example. Certainly, it is on this point that dispassionate historical family research, historical demography, and historical anthropology will not only have to assess the powerful contrasts of past periods, but also those still operative in our own time. But it would be a gross abuse of scholarship to try to exclude southeastern European countries from "the construction and expansion of Europe" on the basis of these differences.[14] Political implications of this kind can only prejudice scholarly discourse. Contrasts are vitiated in advance if there is the merest suspicion that they might be used to exclude people from improving their lot in life. The experience I have gained from these discussions has also found its way into the present book; the ability of Europe's social and cultural space to change throughout the course of its history became an important guiding thought, as did differentiations within Europe itself.[15] Although the present study deals with Europe's structural borders, I do not consider them immutable. Indeed, I have first and foremost come to suspect the updating of historically developed spatial structures to serve political programs for the future. Studies of the regions on the continent that have been more or less historically shaped by Europe's special path cannot simply be deployed in political war games involving present-day coalitions.

Preliminary studies central to the concept behind this volume have had a bearing on my teaching as well. For several years I have held lectures and seminars on the general topic of the special path in the Middle Ages. My students had to produce independent work, so that my teaching gave me stimulating food for thought. Together with four students who had written exemplary papers, I put together an issue of *Beiträge zur historischen Sozialkunde* under the title, "A Special Path for Europe? Medieval Foundations of its Societal Development."[16] It focused on social forms that were specifically European but not on more general cultural phenomena, which the present volume emphasizes. I then took part in the series "Vorlesungen im Wiener Rathaus" (Lectures in Vienna's city hall) in 1998, with "The Development of Europe—a Special Path? Ideologies of Legitimization and Scholarly Discourse," which appeared in print in 1999.[17] This publication had twin purposes: First, to review briefly the state of scholarly research on the special path problem and to take a position on it based on my own work; to this extent it offers a concise preview of the interpretive models presented in more detail here. Second, I hoped to establish a clear-cut division between scholarly stances in special path research and ideologically motivated ones—not only on the borderline between scholarship and politics but especially in the everyday political rhetoric about "Europe." The principles set forth in this lecture also hold for the present book, but I cannot repeat them *in extenso*. This simple reference must suffice in support of my point of view.

––––––

Max Weber's formulation of the question of the special path is a highly complex one. For him the *explanans*—the fundamental explanation—lies not in one single factor but in a "concatenation of circumstances."[18] And even the *explanandum* seems many-sided. He wrote: "Only in the Occident is there a *science* [*Wissenschaft*] that has reached a stage of development we recognize today as 'valid.'" He adduces examples from theology, astronomy, mechanics, physics, medicine, chemistry, but mostly from jurisprudence. He sees similarities with art; with "rational, harmonic music"; with the rational utilization of the Gothic arch as "a constructive principle in grand monumental structures and in a *style* embracing sculpture and painting"; with "utilizing linear and atmospheric perspectives [as part of the 'classical' rationalizing], which our Renaissance created"; further, with the press and journals, universities and higher institutions of learning, and with "a professionally trained and *organized* bureaucracy." Then he names the "corporate *state*," parliaments, periodically elected representatives of the people, the state in general—"in the sense of a political *institution* with a rationally drawn-up 'constitution' [*Verfassung*]"; and finally, "the most fateful power in our life: *capitalism*," which he defines as "*bourgeois industrial, or enterprise*, capitalism [*bürgerlicher Betriebskapitalismus*] with its rational organization of *free labor*." Many scholars working in the *Sonderweg* field have reduced Weber's long list of distinctive Western "cultural phenomena" to the last-mentioned point, thus turning capitalism into the sole *explanandum*. This reduction of what needs to be interpreted to a single phenomenon is just as incompatible with Weber's conception as is a reduction of the interpretation to one possible factor. His view of this very complex question sees it proceeding on two levels—the "cultural phenomena" in need of interpretation and the determining factors that can interpret them, which are thought of as interconnected "concatenated circumstances." Any particular aspect of the object of our interpretation will dictate which particular package of factors we are to draw on from the whole mass of explanatory factors.

The present study follows along these conceptual lines. The list of particularly European cultural phenomena to be interpreted is congruent with Weber's list in part but extends it. Neither list can claim to be complete. The seven topics selected here have not been chosen at random, of course. Rather, their inclusion has been dictated by the assumption that we can derive from them a substantial number of things still seen as specifically European in more recent times. My analysis is limited to a detailed study of these phenomena in the Middle Ages. How they have affected later eras will for the most part be only briefly outlined. These subsequent effects are as a rule common knowledge—witness, for example, the references to parliamentary democracy, the separation of powers, and federalism that conclude the chapter "The Feudal System and the Estates." Many cultural phenomena that the present study leaves unexamined—and that characterize developments in modern Europe—can be effortlessly related to one or more of the seven main chapters because of factors influencing the origins of those phenomena. The concluding chapter broadens this spectrum by adding a few brief considerations. The attempt to answer the question "Why Europe?" does not imply that we can pursue every cultural phenomenon, in all its ramifications, that claims to be an interpretive model. It is not the width of the spectrum of cultural phenomena that is important but rather the plausibility of the interpretations themselves that makes it possible to understand essential, particularly European phenomena more readily. In light of the great number of phenomena treated and the factors determining them, even a complex model following in Weber's wake, such as the one chosen for the present volume, must place its emphases according to criteria of significance.

———

Anyone venturing an interpretation along the lines of Weber's question will inevitably make cross-cultural comparisons. This is the only way to comprehend what is specifically European, the only way to find the causes of divergent developments. The comparative method used throughout the present book involves only *aspects* of cultural phenomena.[19] I have selected a non-European cultural phenomenon only if its European counterpart is analyzed, a necessary reduction because a comparison of one aspect of European culture will as a rule bear on several non-European cultures. Any view based on cultural excerption may appear inadequate from the perspective of the particular cultures compared. But there is no alternative technique that is workable, and the exposition itself makes a broader contextualizing of the excerpted aspects quite difficult. Although the results of my comparative analyses are dealt with extensively only in Europe's case, they might also be profitably thought through for Byzantium, Islam, or China. Such a project would strain the boundaries of the present study, but my hope is that the comparisons demanded by this book will also open new avenues of research in disciplines studying non-European cultures.

My selection of cultural aspects is not the same in every chapter. But the cultures discussed in the fundamental first chapter have been taken into account in later ones whenever I felt it apt and possible. The rationale for deviations from chapter 1 emerges from the topics analyzed in each chapter. That is why Persia is addressed when the origin of a heavily armed cavalry is the issue, and Korea is examined because of the unique way it developed scripts and printing. The guiding principle is to keep the subject matter compared more or less on the same level. This principle also holds true within the European continent, where telling contrasts—involving Ireland, say, or the countries in the east or southeast of the continent—are also possible for the Middle Ages.

By restricting comparisons to individual aspects of cultural phenomena, I was able to limit myself to consulting the specialized secondary literature on non-European civilizations. This nevertheless runs the sizeable risk of building on an insufficiently large body of literature— and not just for my cross-cultural comparisons. It would be impossible to even come close to mastering the relevant scholarship, given the number of topics and the dimensions of the area under investigation. In view of this fundamental infeasibility, I have taken pains to make economical use of endnotes. This is also why I have documented the literature simply; that is, I have cited only the sources that I refer to positively. I do not deal with any scholarly controversies either in the body of the text or in the endnotes. Adding to the discussion of the huge number of interpretations of Europe's special path (let alone arguing over them) could fill volumes. If you do it once, you have to do it every time. Much of my knowledge of these controversies and the ideo-logical positions they espouse are present in the text by implication.

Steering clear of debate does not indicate a desire to avoid it in prin-ciple. Quite the contrary: the present book leaves so many questions open, so many assumptions still insufficiently backed up, and so many hypotheses that I feel they all need to be discussed further. I am aware that many of my conjectures are daring, many of my explanatory mod-els not completely supported. I have intentionally put forward thoughts that still need validating. The open nature of my models is intended to invite further elaboration, maybe even refutation. The present book does not mark the conclusion of a life's work. It does tie together many threads in my thinking and research over the years. In many ways it goes far beyond fields I have previously worked in. This is mainly true of the comparative studies involving non-European cultures, indis-pensable for locating the place of Europe's special path in history writ large. But these studies have led me into scholarly *terrae novae* where I expect competent experts will extend, modify, or criticize them.

———

This book appears in my forty-fourth and final year at the Institute for Economic and Social History at the University of Vienna. It is inextri-cable, for any number of reasons, from that community of instructors and students. Professor Alfred Hoffmann, who taught me much and whose assistant I later became, started me reading Max Weber, who was such a profound inspiration for this volume. Alfred Hoffmann's liberal and generous nature also allowed my scholarly work to follow along independent paths, some of which have led to this book. Studies on medieval Estates—where my work on Europe's special path began—were carried out jointly with Ernst Bruckmüller, Peter Feldbauer, and Herbert Knittler; our productive teamwork has had a long-lasting influ-ence on me. Among these colleagues I found an important sounding board for discussing Islamic issues in recent years—a fact that simply reflects the convergence of divergences that will always exist in the lively, ongoing development of an institute's work. Many of the pre-liminary studies for the present book first appeared in *Beiträge zur his-torischen Sozialkunde*—a platform for innovative scholarly approaches at the institute ever since some young assistants founded it in 1971. The list of all those who have been with me since the early seventies on many projects concerning the family would go on and on. As I have already pointed out, these projects led in special ways to cross-cultural comparisons—based on the history of agrarianism and of religion. Studies of this kind were important for the composition of this book. After the early 1990s, when my interests centered more and more on questions of Europe's special path, much of my teaching focused on this field. My lectures and seminars in this area seemed to have a special appeal for students. In any event, their papers were full of interesting ideas. I was able to pick up on some of them and carry them further. And so it is most appropriate that I express my thanks to students at the institute as well. To speak of a community of teachers and learners does not ring hollow—and never has—at the Institute for Economic and Social History in the University of Vienna. In times when university structures are changing, it will not be easy to keep this community sustainable. Be that as it may, I wish with all my heart that all those at the institute may succeed in preserving and improving the social foundation that nourishes their innovative scholarly work. With my good wishes for the future, I dedicate this book to the teachers and students at the Institute for Economic and Social History at the University of Vienna in deepest gratitude.

Michael Mitterauer
Vienna, August 15, 2002

One

Rye and Oats: The Agrarian Revolution of the Early Middle Ages

A geosocial component is fundamental to any inquiry into the historical roots of Europe's distinctiveness. The peculiarities of the regions where its distinctive phenomena originated are key to discovering the factors that shaped Europe's development. Congruencies between certain regions only reinforce the idea of a defining "concatenation of circumstances" for the continent, a concatenation that is the object of study in this book. Indeed, there is a consensus in historical scholarship that many of the developments typifying Europe's "special path" (*Sonderweg*) arose in the eighth and ninth centuries in the lands between the Seine and the Rhine, the heartland of the Carolingian Empire. This region was the locus of particular social evolutionary forces throughout the entire Middle Ages, the effects of which can be felt up to the present day. In contrast, in antiquity the marginalized provinces of Belgica and Germanica Superior and Inferior became the cradle of evolutionary dynamics in the *imperium Romanum*. These provinces were opened up relatively late by Romanization, urbanization, or conversion to Christianity. The most developed provinces, culturally speaking, were on the Mediterranean, where Rome was obviously the center of the western half of the area. A fundamental change took place in this geosocial constellation during the course of the early Middle Ages, when the gravitational center of so-

1

cial evolutionary forces shifted from the southern to the northwestern part of the continent. An elucidation of the factors that determined this shift can unquestionably contribute to our better understanding of why the area that is Europe emerged as it did.

A cross-cultural comparison clearly shows that the rise of new cultural areas was, from earliest historical times, tied closely to agrarian innovations.[1] Newly introduced cultivated plants opened up novel ways of increasing the food supply, making a new developmental dynamic possible. It seems amazing that this rudimentary explanation for the advent of European society is hardly ever advanced, and this is all the more surprising because rather fundamental innovations in agriculture were being implemented in the area between the Rhine and the Seine at precisely the time in question. Might there be a causal relationship between the new agriculture in this region and the particular developmental forces emanating from the Carolingian heartland during the Middle Ages? A comparison with other cultures will show that there is good reason to examine this working hypothesis more closely.

An American historian of technology, Lynn White Jr., is one of the few scholars who have attempted to account for the gravitational shift on the European continent from the South to the Northwest in terms of agrarian factors.[2] His argument appeared in 1962 but certainly not to universal acclaim. Although after forty years it doubtlessly needs modification, it still presents a useful starting point for deliberations about the agrarian foundations of Europe's special path. White and other scholars at the time and afterward wrote about an "agricultural revolution in the early Middle Ages," but only White argued that it had produced a fundamental shift in Europe's center of gravity.[3] The concept of "revolution" means something different, of course, with regard to economic development than it does in the political sphere.[4] We are not talking here of discrete events but of long-term processes, some of them spanning centuries. And so, by analogy with the later "industrial revolution," we can speak of an "agrarian revolution," a concept that with qualification can refer to earlier times as well. It has been applied to the period of European history customarily called the "early Middle Ages" and to developments in two non-European cultures: "the Arab agricultural revolution," referring to the Islamic world from roughly 700 to 1100, has become common coin among scholars, as has China's "green revolution" during the Song dynasty (960–1279).[5] With regard to Europe, we might stick with White's term, "the agricultural revolution of the early Middle Ages," in spite of the drawn-out nature of the process, but we generally prefer the term "agrarian revolution." The temporal overlap with quite different agricultural/agrarian revolutions in other cultures offers excellent points of comparison that will further our understanding of characteristics peculiar to Europe.[6]

White identifies agrarian technology as key to the social-dynamic shift in question. He lists the heavy plow, the use of horses in farming (because of the horse collar and the horseshoe), and the three-field system—the rotation of winter planting, summer planting, and fallow fields—as the crucial agrarian innovations.[7] He ranks the cultivation of recently imported crops lower. A comparison with other cultures, however, shows that the cultivation of introduced crops is the decisive factor in agricultural revolutions. This is clearly evident in the transformations in agriculture simultaneously underway in China and Islamic countries.[8] White's model therefore probably needs to be expanded. The enormous progress in paleobotanical research in recent decades has laid new groundwork for precisely this sort of broadening, from which we can deduce what written sources could not reveal: that the early Middle Ages also marked a phase of radical change in the types of crops cultivated in the Carolingian heartland. Two new grain species take pride of place as a result of this very complex process of change: rye and oats.[9] There is proof that these crops were cultivated before the utilization of the above-mentioned technical innovations. The connections between the two grains and the agricultural innovations becomes more plausible when we take into consideration the whole system of the new agriculture in the Frankish heartland and how it evolved as part of the medieval agrarian revolution.

————

Rye and oats do not belong to the "founder crops" of the Old World, such as emmer (*Triticum dicoccum*, two-grained spelt), einkorn (*T. monococcum*, one-seeded wheat), barley (*Hordeum vulgare*), and naked wheat (*T. durum/aestivum*), all of which came from the Near East, though it took a long time before they were cultivated in Europe.[10] Both grains started as weeds mixed in with the kinds of grain that were intended to be planted. Those traditional crops had likely been cultivated since the Bronze Age or the early Iron Age; then the climate apparently worsened, bringing cooler temperatures and increased rainfall. Given this changing situation, people in central Europe turned to two types of grain not planted until then. Rye is extremely resistant to cold and damp but also to heat and drought.[11] It depletes the soil less than wheat does, which is why it can be grown in consecutive years. It ripens quickly, so that

3

it thrives in cooler regions with a relatively brief growing period. It is not at all fussy as to soil conditions so is well suited for cleared land adjacent to better soils. Oats are also not particularly demanding as to soil quality, prefer a cool, moist climate as well, but are more susceptible to heat, winter cold, and frost. These particular characteristics may well have led to rye and oats becoming "second-generation cultivated plants" in central Europe long after they were brought from the Near East. They opened up whole new possibilities for increasing the scope of the food supply in Europe that were fully realized in the course of the agrarian revolution in the early medieval period.

A third "second-generation" grain, spelt wheat, played a temporary role in the agrarian revolution.[12] Spelt had been cultivated in central Europe even before rye and oats, beginning in the New Stone Age. It was surprisingly widespread during late antiquity and early medieval times, only to go into a rapid decline afterward. It held on in a few out-of-the-way pockets but was by and large replaced by rye. The specific characteristics of the two grains offer good reasons for this fluctuation. Spelt excelled because it kept particularly well in the central European climate. After being harvested, the spikelets were processed and stored. Spelt could be stored longer because, when the seed and harvested crop were cleaned, the ears were easily winnowed and sifted, protecting them from attack by parasites. It appears that in Roman times the border provinces north of the Alps were targeted for spelt cultivation. Grain for the army was stored either in camps (*castellae*) on the borders (*limes*) or on farming estates (*villae rusticae*) throughout the surrounding countryside. And we may assume that the Franks were similarly motivated to cultivate the crop, since they stored grain reserves at the royal courts. The decline in spelt farming was evidently tied to another peculiarity of the grain: processing spelt wheat in water mills involved additional, expensive procedures and incurred greater losses versus the milling of wheat and rye. This is why the rise of water mills pushed spelt farming into a decline. On the whole, the "milling revolution" led to the replacing of older spelt wheats by newer kinds of grain, rye being the most important among them.

Rye and oats were initially planted more intensively in the territory occupied by Germanic tribes beyond the Roman *limes*, but they were adopted on the other side of the border as well.[13] The increased cultivation of these crops in the border provinces could very well have been related entirely to the needs of the military, as has been assumed in the case of spelt. This prompted a rise in the number of cavalry units stationed in camps on the *limes*, which combined the demand for fodder with the need for bread. The border areas of the Roman Empire situated across from Germania Magna must have witnessed the first contact between Roman agricultural traditions and the cultivation of rye and oats in Germanic settlements.[14] But it was not until the post-Roman era that these two grains were to boom. Rye first appeared in Frankish northern Gaul at the end of the fifth century.[15] Even in south-central Europe, the diffusion of rye went hand in hand with Frankish expansion.[16] Gregory of Tours provides reliable evidence that oats were used as fodder throughout the Frankish Empire.[17] It was in their imperial heartland between the Rhine and the Seine that the foundations were laid for a thoroughgoing dissemination of rye and oats all over Europe north of the Alps. Beyond the borders of the Roman Empire, cattle raising had enjoyed precedence over agriculture. Now, under Frankish rule, a cerealization process got underway in those regions, with rye and oats playing a vital role.

———

The three-field system of crop rotation—with its sequence of winter grain, summer grain, and fallow fields—placed rye (the winter crop) and oats (the summer crop) in a closely structured relationship. Many other combinations were of course possible within the system, for example, wheat in winter and barley in summer. But the act of colonizing that propagated this system also opened up new arable land that was admirably suited to these two grains in particular. And it frequently happened that rye and wheat were grown together in a mixed field.[18] It is a still a moot point how old the three-field system actually is. The earliest documentary evidence confirms that it existed in the second half of the eighth century, but some historians believe that it emerged as early as the sixth or seventh century in the Alemannic region.[19] The assumption is that a merger took place there of the Alemannic structure of fence-and-farmland with the Frankish three-field system based on specifically northern grains: rye, summer barley, and oats.[20]

The three-field system offered many advantages over more ancient forms of the field-and-grass system of rotating grains and pasture.[21] First, the new system greatly increased farm yields, thereby expanding the scope of the food supply. Second, it allowed for a better distribution of farm work over the year—fallow fields would be plowed at a season when the other two fields put to crops would involve no labor. Third, it lowered the risk of losing a harvest to bad weather. Fourth, and most important, the new system of land use was integrated with cattle keeping. The sequence of planting phases left a great deal of time for pasturing animals on harvested or fallow fields, which produced the fertilizer needed for the more intensively exploited land. The keeping of horses and cattle could be substantially maintained in spite of more intensive farming. The link between raising livestock and agriculture enjoyed a very long tradition, mainly in northwestern Europe.[22] The three-field system was to cement this integration, even when cerealization was just being introduced, thereby initiating a special kind of farm economy. Raising livestock led to more work for draft animals: pulling plows and harrows in the field; drawing carts at harvest time, when cleaning out manure in the stables, going to market, or performing services for the lord of the manor. Furthermore, the amalgamation with raising livestock now provided further, special opportunities for dairy farming. Stable and barn—the essential farm buildings in this tradition—characterize this type of diversified farm economy.

———

The innovations in the technology of agriculture that emerged in the course of the early medieval agrarian revolution were obviously connected to a combination of newly introduced plants, new systems of land use, and new ways of integrating agriculture with the keeping of livestock. The key innovation was the heavy plow, which made it possible to till more deeply by turning the soil over.[23] Deep tilling was important for the root system of rye.[24] There might also have been a causal connection between the cultivation of oats and the introduction of the heavy plow.[25] This novel plowing technology helped open up the moist, heavy soils of the North that could be put to oats and rye along with other domesticated plants both old and new. The growing of new plants preceded the introduction of the heavy plow, but when and where it came from cannot be determined with certainty.[26] Archeological evidence points to several transitional forms between the older scratch plow (*Hakenpflug*) and the more recent moldboard plow (*Wendepflug*). On the other hand, evidence from historical linguistics regarding the various words for plow reveals that the moldboard plow was regarded as a special and novel agricultural implement. The derivation of the word "plow" shows it originated among the Germanic-speaking peoples in Belgica or Germania Inferior, that is, probably among a Frankish people.[27] The word and the thing itself must have reached the Slavic-speaking areas even before the Slavs split into three large linguistic groups in the later sixth century.[28]

The heavy plow required draft animals wherever it was introduced, and this meant having oxen or horses available. The work output of horses in agriculture was higher, and so, in explaining the intensification of farming, great importance must surely be attached to the adoption of the horse harness, which made this output possible. It was probably first used for harrowing, then for plowing later on.[29] The resultant growth in oat planting had a further effect on the keeping of horses. But the required "horsepower" had also been achieved with oxen and still could be. The rising value of the horse collar for the early medieval agrarian revolution is therefore probably not as significant as the emergence of the heavy plow.

The diffusion of the water mill, on the other hand, seems to have been essential, and there is broad agreement that it must count as one of the technical constituents of the agrarian revolution. The milling of grain in mills driven by waterwheels was already known in antiquity.[30] But in the Mediterranean area, the propagation of this technology—apart from a few favored areas—met with one difficulty: the water supply from streams varied greatly with the season and was often meager, which is why we frequently find mills in conjunction with aqueducts.[31] North of the Alps there were no similar hindrances to the water mill's adoption. A major advance in that region was the vertical mill wheel, later called the *molendinum Francigenum vel Gallicum* in contradistinction to the Mediterranean forms of the horizontal mill.[32] With rye, a new grain came to the fore in the North that was excellent for baking bread; unlike other grain types, it was almost exclusively consumed in the form of bread.[33] On the whole, the agrarian revolution brought with it a fundamental shift from spelt wheats to naked wheats that could be ground better, allowing the bread diet to become the favored one—a change that promoted the use of water mills.[34] As early as the sixth century the *Pactus Legis Salicae* took it for granted that the Franks had water mills.[35] There was already an exceptional concentration of mills in the heartland of the Franks by the eighth and ninth centuries.[36] According to Domesday Book (1080–86), England had no fewer than 5,624 mills in some 3,000 communities.[37] And so, with the agrarian revolution, the water mill gained ground over a broad front in Europe north of the Alps; milling with water became the most significant new trade created by the new agrarianism. Its widespread use shows that, in the course of this revolution, the water mill led not only to a process of cerealization but to a general rise in the bread diet. Now the "black bread" of the North was on an equal footing with the "white bread" of the Mediterranean.[38] Rye bread keeps for a significantly long time. The advantages of a bread diet over the older diet of mushy food constituted an altogether crucial force behind the agrarian revolution.

———

The water mill as a central structure in rural localities introduces us to the controlling social framework of the early medieval agrarian revolution: manorialism, the bipartite system dividing the land into lord's land and peasant's land.[39] The successful spread of the water mill in the Frankish Empire was primarily due to the lay and clerical manorial lords—above all, the king and his officials at the various royal courts as well as the cloisters surrounded by their own manor lands. Other key structures for the processing of agricultural products often lay in the lord's hands. This is true, for instance, of bake ovens, which were more widely diffused thanks to the growth of a bread diet, or of buildings for pressing wine or brewing beer. The bipartite manorial land system provided a framework favoring these processes of the division of labor, though it was not really indispensable to them. But the system was absolutely necessary for establishing the three-field rotation of crops that was adopted initially on the lord's land and only afterward on the peasant's. Had it not been for the lord's interventions, this fundamental reorganization would probably have been impossible to carry out.

"It is quite apparent that, except for the Mediterranean regions where wheat [*froment*] won out, rye prevailed almost exclusively over assarting, or land-clearing, and slash-and-burn [*essartage* and *ecobuage*] in the rest of Europe." François Sigaut's formulation summarizes the current state of research into the dominating position of rye in newly claimed land throughout all of Europe north of the Alps in the Middle Ages.[40] In a similar vein, Ulf Dirlmeier identifies rye as "a genuine discovery of the early Middle Ages."[41] The great diffusion of rye growing is often linked with other elements of the early agrarian revolution, but connections like these do not appear everywhere. In northwestern Germany, for example, the "everlasting cultivation of rye" based on plaggen manuring provided an alternative to the three-field system.[42] This deviation from the three-field pattern of the agrarian revolution spread out from the Frankish heartland, and it occurred within the substantial area that revolution encompassed. Outside this area we should mention one other context in particular: the increased planting of rye by the Slavic peoples of east-central Europe and eastern Europe. The expansion here linked up geographically with the rye-growing area in central Europe where the climate was similar, but it was in many ways carried out differently. This expansion thus relativizes any simplifying explanatory models based on the dominant plants under cultivation.

The specific determinants for the cultivation of rye in Europe, or for agriculture in the area generally, can be summed up by Europe's forest wealth.[43] This wealth explains the very important role of the burn-beating economy in the expansion of the Slavic peoples from the sixth and seventh centuries on (quite similar, by the way, to the case of the neighboring Balts). An indicator here is the Old Slavic calendar, which orients the names of the months according to the different phases of burn-beating cultivation: in the first month the trees were cut, the second was for drying the logs, the third was for burning, and so forth. In France, too, the names of the months reflected the most important agricultural tasks. Charlemagne took into consideration the shifts in these tasks resulting from the rise of the three-field system when he renamed June the "Plowing Month" (*Pflugmond*).[44] There is no reference to aspects of burn-beating in Frankish names for the months. As early as the Iron Age other forms of cultivation in central Europe might well have supplanted the burn-beating economy.[45] In the heavily forested area of eastern Europe, however, burn-beating played an important part throughout the entire Middle Ages and was to last in many regions up to modern times. In Carpathian backwaters an ancient species of winter rye called *kryza* was under cultivation until the modern age; it was sown in the ashes of a wood lot immediately after it had been burned, thereby obviating the need for soil treatment.[46] A special agricultural implement involved in burn-beating was the wooden plow (German *Zoche*, Russian *socha*) widespread in eastern Europe. It evolved from the scratch plow and was ideal for newly cleared ground still scattered with stones and roots.[47] The scratch plow itself could still be utilized for soils that had been cultivated for some time. It had appeared as early as the sixth century among the peoples of the Sukow-Szeligi group, between the Oder and the Vistula, the first Slavs to adopt rye as their principal crop.[48] The heavy plow was not found in this region until centuries later. In the wave of colonization of the East, it stood in stark contrast to the older Slavic forms of the plow.[49] Two different agrarian and social systems were now standing face-to-face. The pattern of the western agrarian revolution thrust eastward with the aid of the heavy plow, but it left the greater part of eastern Europe untouched. There *was* something from the West that was very significant for the rise of Russia: the cultivation of rye. But there it evolved in completely different economic, social, and cultural contexts.

9

There were also strong contrasts in the extreme northwest of the continent, in the British Isles. Whereas in England, parallels with agrarian developments in France could be found early on, particularly in its fertile southeast, the situations in Ireland and Scotland were vastly different. In England, wheat and barley had predominated in Roman times, but rye and oats had also been introduced, possibly to supply the army.[50] These two grains subsequently brought about the expansion of agriculture onto poorer soils, thus making an important contribution to the process of cerealization.[51] In Ireland there was no such development, even in the High Middle Ages; an animal-based economy was clearly predominant.[52] This is reflected in the variations in social prestige among different population groups depending on whether they raised animals or farmed. Oats took pride of place in grain growing, followed by barley, wheat, and rye, with rye, the new grain for making bread, coming last.[53] The bipartite manorial system—the social framework of the agrarian system—simply did not exist in Ireland. How very different from England, where the growth of the manorial system was analogous to the situation in the Carolingian Empire and its successor empires. The conservatism of the agrarian system in Ireland up to and through the High Middle Ages must surely be explained by social reasons as well as ecology.

Rye and oats are specific to the cool temperate climatic zones of Europe. Their expansion throughout the medieval agrarian revolution had scarcely any influence on Mediterranean agriculture. From the tenth century on, the growing of rye increased on the Iberian Peninsula in Catalonia, a region the Frankish Empire had influenced greatly.[54] But rye and oats also spread into Asturias and Galicia, where spelt had replaced wheat as the principal crop in the early Middle Ages. In the south of France rye established a permanent foothold, particularly on the poor soils of the Massif Central, where it had been grown in mountainous regions from Roman times.[55] (Pliny reported on the similar situation of the Taurini in Piedmont.) But it was wheat, as opposed to rye, that was generally predominant as the winter crop in the Mediterranean region. It was difficult to plant oats extensively because of the higher temperatures.[56] On the whole, climatic conditions hindered the planting of summer crops, hence the transition from the two- to the three-field system. The heavy plow, so well suited to the specific soil conditions and the heavier precipitation in Europe north of the Alps, was virtually useless in the Mediterranean region.[57] And other elements of the agrarian revolution coming from the Frankish heartland—haymaking, for instance—were limited in vast areas for ecological reasons. By and large during the early Middle Ages, the South was continually shut out from the dynamic agrarian developments in the continental Northwest.

Nor did significant new stimuli move in an opposite direction from southern to northern Europe, although horticulture may be regarded as a special case. In the Carolingian period, several places in the Frankish Empire imported numerous garden plants from Italy. To name but the main ones: onions, shallots, garlic, leeks, celery, carrots, beets, lettuce, parsnips, cauliflower, kohlrabi, and radishes.[58] These imports were first cultivated at royal courts and in large imperial monasteries; from there they later spread to peasants' gardens. We learn this from Charlemagne's *Capitulare de villis*, from the *Brevium Exempla*, from the statutes of Adalhard, the abbot of Corbie, and the Plan of the Abbey of Saint Gall, from around 820.[59] Apparently there was a deliberate policy of distributing useful domesticated plants around the greater empire, which confirms the role of agrarian policymaking in bringing about a total change in the agriculture of that time. The cultivation of new garden plants made a definite contribution to expanding the food base. But in the overall context and effects of the agrarian revolution of the early Middle Ages, horticulture played a rather minor role. We cannot count it as a key innovation like those that led to such profound changes in technology, the trades, the military, and the social order.

In the North, it was the climate that set limits on the introduction of plants from the Mediterranean region, where the cultivation of many kinds of fruit trees and grain had predominated for a very long time, which did not hold, of course, for central and eastern Europe.[60] The olive tree, so typical of Mediterranean agriculture, was a special component in the forging of Mediterranean civilization. Cultural requirements were a partial constraint on its cultivation even within that area, but transplanting it to the North was out of the question.[61] It was the same for other fruit trees, like figs or almonds. As a result, the elements of agrarian and social structures that were so typical of Mediterranean fruit growing had no impact north of the Alps.

Although the development of early medieval farming in the Frankish Empire veered strongly from Mediterranean agricultural practice, there were some essential basics common to them both. This was true to a considerable extent of two plants in particular, wheat and grapes. The reasons why this common, fundamental pattern was not merely maintained but strengthened are more cultural than ecological. The Eucharist—Christianity's central, communal, ceremonial ritual act—is celebrated with wine and with bread made from wheat, so that the two plants from which its elements derived assumed a position of indispensable significance.[62] Wheat and grapes became obligatory for agriculture as Christianity spread beyond the Mediterranean. This is best seen in the case of viticulture, which was pushed to its outer limits when Europe was being Christianized.[63] But wheat growing, too, with its more modest ecological demands, probably existed in many places only because of its high value, even above and beyond the ecclesiastical. Although its standing was probably connected to its religious significance in some mediated form, bread made from wheat also enjoyed a prestige that was class specific, and it was always ranked first among bread types.[64] In any event, thanks to the Christianizing of Europe beyond Mediterranean lands, the cultivation of two typical plants from the Mediterranean was expanded to the extreme limits of where they could grow. Wheat contributed to the cerealization process that had been launched in the same areas. Bread made from wheat stimulated the whole transition to a bread diet that was also based on species of grain other than wheat.[65] Along with the bread diet, so typical for the Mediterranean region in antiquity, the Mediterranean water mill migrated northward, to where ecological conditions were more favorable. The fact that other parallels crop up in these two so different agricultural zones in medieval Europe cannot be accounted for solely by their common root in classical Roman agrarianism. The influence of Christianity on crop farming might well have exerted a long-term, integrative force.

———

The eastern part of the Roman Empire in the early Middle Ages witnessed nothing analogous to western Europe's division into two agricultural zones or to the corresponding shift in its gravitational center. Agriculture in the Byzantine Empire had the same foundation as in the western Mediterranean, where the troika of wheat, wine, and olives replicated the traditional link between crop and fruit-tree cultures. Essentially, nothing was added to these three throughout the early Middle Ages. The advancement of viticulture for religious reasons is worth mentioning, which once again clearly shows how Christianity stimulated agrarian progress.[66] Rye and oats—the two new, important grain species in the West that made significant inroads into the Mediterranean region—had no role to play in the Byzantine Empire.[67] This was true of all the other innovations of the agrarian revolution as well. A three-field system based on wheat and barley would have been unprofitable and only increased the risk of a bad harvest.[68] Better manuring was not an option, and the tighter integration of agriculture with animal husbandry was equally out of the question, given the sensitivity of the agropastoral balance in the Mediterranean region.[69] Nor was there any rethinking of farming techniques. The scratch plow lent itself to traditional Mediterranean farming. Furthermore, the ecological conditions for a comparable expansion of the water mill for grinding grain were not right, at least for the vertical waterwheel that was typical of the Frankish Empire. And the seigniorial context of the bipartite manorial system simply did not exist in the East. All this basically arrested agriculture in the Byzantine Empire at the stage it had attained in late antiquity.[70]

Differences between eastern and western agrarian advancements were clearly evident even in late antiquity. By then, imported plants—primarily rye and oats, but spelt as well—had been adopted in the northwestern provinces of the Roman Empire, creating a new model in the Frankish heartland during the early Middle Ages that formed a base for the subsequent growth of the agrarian revolution—with a corresponding shift in the gravitational center to the Northwest. This process had no counterpart in the Eastern Roman Empire. In the border provinces there was no comparable synthesis of Mediterranean agrarian traditions and cultivated plants that would have been adaptable to more northerly climatic conditions. Neither within the Byzantine Empire nor in the adjacent areas to the north did a dynamic hub of agrarian development evolve similar to the western one. Byzantium had of course molded the religion and culture of the vast area of Russia, but Byzantine traditions do not seem to have influenced agricultural practice there in any way; they showed instead more congruencies with its Slavic neighbors to the west. Byzantium did not itself make any moves in the direction of agrarian colonization, nor did any similar actions take place in the areas it occupied. Not even the faintest beginning of an agrarian revolution could be found there during the Middle Ages. This consistency at the heart of the empire also shows the persistence of classical agrarian traditions in the eastern Mediterranean.

———

In asking why there was no agrarian revolution in early medieval Byzantium, we of course do not want to compare it exclusively with what happened in the Frankish Empire. A comparison with the contemporaneous situation in the Islamic region should prove just as interesting.

13

The "Arab agricultural revolution" covers large areas around the Mediterranean Sea, which already tells us something of what developed there.[71] The early medieval agrarian revolution in the Islamic world was distinguished by the unique variety of its cultivated plants. Wheat, barley, peas, and lentils—traditional Near Eastern and southern Mediterranean crops—were retained, as well as the olive and other long-cultivated fruit trees. Numerous foreign plants were added that were until then completely unknown in the region or else were grown only in its eastern part. A list of these new plants comprises sorghum, durum wheat, rice, sugar beets, cotton, oranges, bananas, coconut palm, watermelon, spinach, eggplant, taro, and mango, to name the most important. Most of them came from the tropics of Southeast Asia and had spread from India to Persia before being naturalized in the Near East and the southern Mediterranean. New agrarian techniques were needed for this assimilation process, especially for irrigation, which either expanded the amount of arable land available or utilized it more intensively.[72] Whereas traditional Mediterranean grains were sown before winter and harvested in the spring, the new plants could be grown in the hot, dry summer months. The importation and adaptation of Southeast Asian plants to the different climatic and soil conditions over the vast area stretching from Persia to southern Spain and Morocco was indeed one of medieval agriculture's most magnificent achievements.

The contrast with what happened in the Byzantine Empire is obvious. People have sought to explain this striking difference on two levels, both of them political.[73] First, the caliph, unlike the Byzantine emperor, had a religious duty to promote the construction of irrigation systems for agricultural use. Matters of irrigation were of religious significance in the Islamic world; Islamic religious law laid out the appropriate regulations. The second interpretive approach is connected to the first: it was the policy of Islamic rulers to tax improved land more favorably; the Byzantine Empire, on the other hand, taxed it more heavily.[74] A landowner would therefore show little interest in making any improvements. Other considerations might be added regarding this point. Unlike the caliphate, the Byzantine Empire did not have a great variety of regions with a diversity of agrarian structures that might have led to cultural exchange. The caliphate had brought a large area under one rule—a unity never seen before in history on such a scale. Communication within this large area was on a very high level.[75] Those groups who supported Islamic agrarian innovation were extremely mobile. The Byzantine Empire would have needed wide-reaching foreign contacts to have been able to import many of the plants the Islamic agrarian revolution brought in from the East. Even if it had the contacts, there would have been cultural barriers standing in the way.[76] Domesticated plants grown for food were as a rule particularly charged with strong connotations of "ours" and "foreign." The adoption of completely foreign cultivated plants did not seem to be a particular problem for Islamic culture, where new identities had been constituted with enormous force in the early historical phases of the new religion. But a comparable social dynamic did not exist in the early medieval Byzantine Empire. As a result, the Eastern Empire did not on principle utilize any innovations in farming that might have come from ecology or agrarian technology.

———

The peculiarities of the agrarian revolution in the heartland of the Frankish Empire become more apparent juxtaposed to the contemporaneous Islamic agrarian revolution than in comparison with the Byzantine Empire.[77] Although both the western European and the Islamic patterns built upon the common foundation of Mediterranean agriculture in Roman antiquity, they went in completely different directions. The process that emerged in the Frankish Empire and its adjacent and successive empires was cerealization; the key new plants were grains. In Islamic regions, the spectrum of newly introduced plants was much wider; new kinds of grain were not central to innovation. In the Frankish Empire and areas under its influence, the more intensive cultivation of crops led to an expansion of land clearance—a trend also seen in the transition from the two- to the three-field system. But in the Islamic world, new farming methods contained elements of an intensified horticulture. In the North, methods of working the soil were dominated by heavy farm implements requiring strong draft animals—oxen or horses—but above all by the heavy plow and the harrow. In the Islamic world, on the other hand, lighter implements handed down from antiquity, for which donkeys sufficed, were employed to work the soil. The central role in Islamic agrarian technology was played by irrigation: creating storage tanks, canals above and below ground, structures for transporting and distributing water—and regulating all of them.[78] Given the specific climatic conditions in Europe north of the Alps, however, it was not so much a problem of irrigating as it was of draining water away. The emergence of the heavy plow in this case represented a pioneering invention because water could run off in the deep furrows. Even the creation of terraced farmland—which in Islamic regions was

15

linked to irrigation—presented no particular problem for European agriculture as it developed during the early medieval agrarian revolution.

The relationship between agriculture and the keeping of livestock took on a very different form in each of the two agrarian revolutions. The connection between these two components appears to have been central to Europe's progress. This is why hay and fodder played such an important role. Livestock could be used to fertilize the fields but primarily to pull heavy agricultural implements; at the same time, draft animals would be available for transport. Apart from other farm implements, the cart was part of the equipment of the peasant economy. In the Islamic agrarian revolution, there was no comparable connection between crop farming and the keeping of livestock. On the contrary, these kinds of links with traditional Mediterranean farming in antiquity were eliminated. The raising of cattle declined—they were not needed for the new agricultural methods—and draft animals for heavy agricultural implements were no longer required. If the need arose, then donkeys could be brought in—and used for the task of short-haul transportation as well. In the Islamic world, thanks to improved saddle construction, a new animal became available for long-haul transporting: the camel. Cattle raising for the transport sector declined; the cart was neglected for centuries.[79]

In the Islamic world, then, the agrarian revolution was accompanied by a revolution in transport that was no less important for the growth of its society. It was based on a particular form of keeping livestock that was not in the least connected with new farming methods—whether through specific fodder plants or fertilizing methods or the use of draft animals to till the fields. The camel is a particularly efficient beast of burden. The early medieval Islamic world increased the raising of beasts of burden, the European world the raising of draft animals. In the early Middle Ages the camel became to some extent the "typifying, culture-determining animal" in Islamic regions. But in Europe, as far as the keeping of livestock was concerned, there was no domesticated animal that gained in significance during that time. Instead, with an eye to the process of cerealization, we could speak of specific "typifying, culture-determining plants." Of all the foreign plants cultivated in the Islamic agrarian revolution, not a single one stood out above all the others.

A very substantial difference between the European and the Islamic agrarian revolutions involved the ecological conditions for their expansion. Northern Europe had immense forest reserves in the early Middle Ages. Additional farmland was gained through forest clearance; the adaptability of the primary domesticated plants, rye and oats, allowed poorer soils to be tilled. The agrarian revolution triggered wide-ranging clearances, thereby promoting colonization within the homeland and outside it. As long as forests were still available, the new agriculture was able to expand. It was a very different situation in Islamic regions, where areas of enhanced farmland were not surrounded by woodland. Small, intensively exploited sites were sprinkled throughout enormous steppes and deserts. There was utterly no question of colonizing more arable land within the heartland or beyond its borders. The new plants the agrarian revolution introduced were of course not local, so that conditions had to be created artificially to facilitate their cultivation. The natural, topographical, and social conditions made it difficult enough to maintain any level of achievement for any length of time. The forcing of specialized plants led to soil exhaustion; maintaining irrigation systems was no easy matter, and successful farming was predicated on a stable political situation. From the twelfth century on, many areas in the Islamic world stagnated or even declined. The reasons for this are ecological rather than political or social: the destruction or neglect of irrigation facilities, the expulsion of highly specialized peasants, and the giving away of public demesnes to the military for tax farming in lieu of pay, which led to extreme exploitation. But these destructive social developments aside, the impetus to farming, so evident in previous centuries, was unable to keep up its momentum. People were up against their ecological limits. Stagnation or decline of the new agriculture brought the *première grandeur* of Islamic economic and cultural progress to a close.[80] It was not simply a matter of contemporary processes but of causally connected ones as well. Europe developed in a different way. The agrarian revolution of the early Middle Ages was less dynamic and did not involve as great an area, but it retained its continuity through to the late Middle Ages. It provided a base for far-reaching colonizing processes, expansion proceeding apace. This was how the early medieval agrarian revolution in Europe laid the groundwork for a stable agriculture capable of further expansion.

———

A comparison of Europe with a third culture—China—that witnessed an agrarian revolution at about the same time can further show how specific improvements to early medieval farming could dictate agrarian and economic development so powerfully.[81] The comparison is also interesting insofar as China's agriculture possessed several important

17

technological innovations that did not become important for European farming until later on, for example, not only the heavy plow with a cast-iron moldboard and the breast collar or the horse collar needed to employ horses as draft animals, but other innovations that never even existed in medieval Europe.[82] Unlike northwestern Europe, China already had a very progressive technology-based agriculture at the dawn of its agrarian revolution. Both parts of the world were developing in the same direction, and technology could have given China a considerable advantage. But this was not to be. The "green revolution" during the Song dynasty set everything on a different course.

The first important plant to be cultivated in the north of China—the leading region just before the Song dynasty—was millet, but it was shunted aside by wheat and barley. This followed the somewhat similar grain-growing pattern in the Near East and around the Mediterranean in classical antiquity. Rice-growing had long been dominant in the south of China, which is where the decisive changes throughout the agrarian revolution were played out. They began with the experimental wetland planting of new kinds of rice, the most important being so-called Champa rice.[83] The Kingdom of Champa in southern Vietnam had come under Chinese sovereignty in the early seventh century. In Champa there was a particularly quick-ripening variety of rice that made for two harvests a year. South Chinese peasants were the first to adopt and improve it; an imperial decree in 1012 ordered it to be planted in the lower Yangtze valley. Political expansion in China increased the potential for importing cultivated plants, just as it did in Islamic countries at the same time. But the difference was that one single plant came to dominate in the Chinese agrarian revolution during the Song dynasty: the quick-ripening wet rice from the South grown in wetlands became the definitive indicator plant. The other cultivated plants played a minor role by comparison. The intensified growing of wet rice took the development of Chinese agriculture in a very different direction than did the planting of rye and oats in Europe.[84]

Irrigation moved front and center in China's agrarian technology with the cultivation of wet rice. The parallel with the Islamic agrarian revolution in this respect is obvious, as is the contrast with Europe's revolution. Plowing, on the other hand, either declined in importance because of rice planting or became important in a different way. Deep plowing in wetlands is counterproductive.[85] The heavy plow for breaking up deeper soil was not utilized in China, nor could it evolve there—a further difference in the paths the two agrarian revolutions followed. The development of agrarian technology also affected the need for draft animals in various ways.[86] Oxen and horses were not found in areas where rice was intensively cultivated; high rice yields probably made it appear uneconomical to set aside arable land for pasture or fodder. The only draft animal in China was the undemanding water buffalo.[87] Integration of animal husbandry and farming did not occur in the Chinese agrarian revolution as it had in Europe. On the contrary, any initiatives in this direction were suppressed.

The development of Europe and China diverged with regard not only to their cultivation techniques but also to their techniques for processing cereals. Rice is not a bread grain; intensifying and expanding rice growing did not therefore lead to the diffusion of the water mill, as rye had done in Europe. The water mill was known in China very early on but did not undergo a boom during the agrarian revolution the way the mill did during the contemporaneous expansion in Europe north of the Alps.[88] Competition between mills and irrigation projects might well have contributed to slowing its development.[89] The differing attitudes of the respective authorities seem to have been symptomatic. In eighth-century China, there were repeated decrees ordering the destruction of water mills built by Buddhist monasteries and wealthy merchants.[90] At roughly the same time, the systematic building of water mills began in the Frankish Empire on clerical and secular estates, mills that were protected by a special law.

The Chinese agrarian revolution was more severely limited by natural and geographic conditions than the revolution in Europe was. Rice is a swamp plant by its very origin; because it was grown in wetlands, conditions for making it flourish could be created even high up in mountainous regions. And the peasant population of China went ahead and developed all kinds of systems to produce these conditions. Certain climatic constrictions, however, could not be overcome. Ultimately, the feasibility of wet-rice growing hinged on the summer monsoons. The "rice frontier" between the dry-field growing zone in the North and the wetland growing zone in the South turned into a quite clear line of demarcation.[91] It coincided with all areas having an annual rainfall of a thousand millimeters. The Chinese agrarian revolution of the Song era was essentially based on the enormous production of one plant in its previous farming areas: the fast-ripening species of rice from the South.[92] It took all sorts of laborious effort to develop variant strains that were viable in different soil conditions. This enabled the opening up of new arable land, an option that was largely realized as early as the Song dynasty. The large forest reserves so long accessible to Europe north of the Alps did not exist in China, at least

19

in areas suitable for rice growing. The thrust of the Chinese agrarian revolution had already reached its climax during the Song dynasty and was succeeded by a period of stagnation.[93]

————

The three agrarian revolutions that began in China, the Islamic world, and early medieval Europe did not just determine the course of very different, long-term, agrarian growth patterns in each culture, but they were also of considerable importance for diverging developments in other aspects of life. Specific emphases on agrarian innovations probably had important effects on the unique social paths subsequently traveled by the three cultures we have just compared. The different progress of the three agrarian revolutions certainly cannot be regarded as the *causa prima* of the different routes these three cultures took on their way to modern times. But the cross-connections between the agricultural sector and other areas are so numerous that they receive high priority in any analysis of the "concatenation of circumstances" we might carry out in order to understand these special paths.

Improved farming practices expanded the scope of people's diet in all three cultures and therefore stimulated population growth. Increased yields in China were far and away the largest because of escalating size of the harvests generated by fast-ripening types of rice. Even before these new strains were introduced, the population was very dense—compared with the other two cultures—and it increased substantially as the agrarian revolution progressed.[94] To be sure, the high population figures in the Song dynasty were unsustainable in the long run and were subject to great fluctuations during the following time period—a characteristic of China's demographic development that contrasts strikingly with Europe's much more stable development. Whereas China's population peaked in the Song dynasty and a few booms in growth were to follow, the burgeoning demographic revolution in the Islamic world that ran parallel to *its* agrarian revolution seems to have been a unique phenomenon.[95] In the event, population growth could not be maintained in Islam for long. Europe's early medieval agrarian revolution did not generate radical population increases like those in China. The rise in growth levels in the major areas of the continent is clearly congruent with the agrarian innovations introduced in the various regions. Western and central Europe were far in the lead.[96] The same holds true after 1000, when those innovations really started to bear fruit in most parts of the continent. The level that population growth reached during the agrarian revolution did not decline permanently in any of the areas it affected in spite of many dips. In this respect it seems that conditions in Europe were relatively stable, to the extent that we can explain any demographic developments by means of agrarian fundamentals. The agrarian revolution broadened a food base that incorporated not only all kinds of domesticated plants, but meat and milk products beyond that—a combination specific to the development of Europe.[97] To put it simply: the model of bread and meat as the two basic and indispensable foods in Europe was a creation of the early Middle Ages that united the ancient Mediterranean bread culture with the meat culture found north of the Alps.[98] The prerequisite for this lay in the innovating agrarian revolution, primarily and specifically by combining agriculture with animal husbandry.

The connection between agrarian revolutions and certain trends in the growth of the trades was a most important one. A broad spectrum of the trades involving refining and reworking processes resulted from the combination—typical of northern Europe since the early Middle Ages—of agriculture, animal husbandry, and forestry, because of the rich forest reserves there. The trades could, as a sideline for peasants, be related directly to the farm economy, or else—in a greatly more centralized form—they could operate as independent enterprises or workshops on the estate or around the main manorial houses. The bipartite manorial system, with its separate peasant and seigniorial economies, provided an excellent context for this. Once again, new stimuli to the growth of the manorial system came from a reciprocal relationship, the division of labor between decentralized and centralized production sites. The celebrated Plan of Saint Gall from around 820 lists the trade facilities at the manor house: a mill and a stamping mill—both water driven—a malt kiln, and an adjacent bakery and brewery run by monks. In the handworkers' building, tanners, shield makers, saddlers, and shoemakers were lumped together as workers in hides or leather processing, along with the fullers and smithies and wood turners and coopers, who formed the woodworking branch among the handworkers.[99] The *Capitulare de villis*, written shortly before, sketches out a plan for royal courts that was similar to the monastery's plan for an ecclesiastical manor's central area.[100] Here, too, we find a variety of trades connected with specific agricultural areas of production that were expanding throughout the early medieval agrarian revolution in northern Europe. The information in these two sources needs to be extended to include the textile trade that was also based on agricultural and animal products.

It must be said that the agrarian revolution did not initiate any changes with regard to the basic materials in those trades. It only influenced processing techniques indirectly, as, for instance, the flour mill did the fulling mill. Milling with waterpower was by far the most important trade the revolution contributed to the new European agriculture, as has already been mentioned; by the turn of the millennium every village had several waterpowered mills. The Champa rice revolution in China did not have a comparable effect on the development of trades; it was based on a single crop that in principle had no need of any further processing, such as milling or baking. Rice growing had no connection with the keeping of livestock or with forestry, so that what the peasants produced had no relation to the basic materials in many trades. The situation in Islam was similar. There was no linking of agriculture, animal husbandry, and forestry that would have corresponded to the interconnections typical of European peasantry. There was no real need to process the new plants grown in the Islamic agrarian revolution through the agency of a trade, with the exception of cotton and sugarcane. The sugar mill formed an additional connecting link between advances in agricultural and trade or industry. Conditions in the Islamic world were not conducive to the use of waterpower for mills.[101] Whenever waterpower rather than animal power was harnessed to process sugarcane, horizontal mills would be used.[102] Of the three early medieval agrarian revolutions, only Europe's can be regarded as having boosted growth in the industrial trades.

When it comes to the effects of the three agrarian revolutions on technical development, we must distinguish between direct and indirect forms. There was no innovation in Europe that even approached—let alone equaled—the grand, ingeniously designed, technical achievements of Islam, such as the construction of underground irrigation facilities, or of the tide locks constructed in China. In many respects, the caliphate and China in particular were technically far superior to Europe during the early Middle Ages. The agrarian revolutions in these two cultures led to impressive advances in irrigation technology. But if we take the long view of industrialization, these technological developments were not crucial. The European agrarian revolution had a greater indirect influence on technical advances—through new agricultural implements and animal husbandry—than a direct influence via the new technology of the agriculturally based trades. Absolutely critical in this regard was the water mill—and by this I mean exclusively mills powered by a vertical wheel, because they were the only form that could capitalize on the key device of the cam.[103] The mill was developed further in various directions and also processed nonagricultural products.[104] Mills could be classified according to the materials treated: flour, olives for oil, bark, gypsum, pigment, paper, powder, and ore; or according to the processing techniques applied: milling, grinding, stamping, fulling, sawing, pipe boring, polishing/sharpening, and crushing. Of all these, the fulling mills likely had revolutionary consequences for the textile industry.[105] The employment of waterpower that the mills made possible was especially beneficial to the mining industry: in iron production, for wheel and hammer works; in mining, for precious and nonferrous minerals by removing water from deep mineshafts, and in all mining industries, for crushing ore.[106] The progress of the European mining industry starting in the High Middle Ages appears to have resulted from a sort of multiple feedback from the early medieval agrarian revolution. In view of the extent of mechanization, and of the organization of labor in large enterprises, we may definitely speak of an early stage of industrial evolution with respect to mining in the waning Middle Ages.

Apart from the significance of the agrarian trades for mechanization, we must consider their role in the use of waterpower. Seen in the long term, they gave Europe's economic growth an important head start. In the world of Islam, water mills, where they existed at all, were relegated to serving the demands of irrigation.[107] The vertical mill offered more potential for the diversification of energy for the trades than did the standard model of a mill powered by a horizontal waterwheel.[108] China had already been employing water mills for centuries before they became widely diffused in Europe north of the Alps. The question is, why did China not utilize water as an energy source to the same extent? There do not seem to have been any ecological hindrances. I've already mentioned the competition between water mills and irrigation facilities for rice growing, along with the fact that the water mill was unnecessary for processing rice as a basic foodstuff—in contradistinction to the crops grown for bread in Europe. Clearly, there was not the same incentive for increasing the number of water mills and improving them. This applies to grist milling as well as to other processes that waterpower might have made possible, unlike the situation in Europe, where this energy source was readily available. Wherever waterpower could not be utilized, other energy substitutes were sought for the many kinds of trade and industrial enterprises that needed waterwheels. The windmill and the less important tidal mill marked efforts in this direction.[109] The decisive breakthrough in the search for a substitute for waterpower had to wait until the industrial revolution, which was essentially an energy revolution. Had it not been for the diffusion and enhancement of the medieval water mill, and for the cerealization connected with it, the road to Europe's industrial revolution would never have been taken.

———

No matter how powerfully the European agrarian revolution stimulated the growth of the trades, it had little effect on trade itself. Any excess production in a subsistence economy would go primarily to service local markets or the people in power locally. How very different was the Islamic agrarian revolution, where introduced plants and the products derived from them were almost totally destined for transregional markets.[110] The Chinese agrarian revolution occupied an intermediate position in this respect. The Song dynasty drew a distinction between provinces that consumed their total rice production themselves and those producing surpluses. To be sure, above and beyond the fast-growing rural population, provinces that consumed their own rice often had to deliver it to large urban centers. Any considerable surplus in a rice harvest in the many provinces would accrue first to the court and the army—the major consumers—and be used for transregional trade after that.[111]

As with long-distance trade, China and the Islamic world were well ahead of Europe in developing transportation. Agricultural irrigation systems in China promoted canal building, unlike the systems in the caliphate. The expansion of shipping routes was tied to organizing the supply of rice, a staple. By contrast, the agrarian revolution in China hardly generated any incentive for the advancement of overland transport; quite the contrary: it led to a decline in the keeping of draft animals. The contemporary revolution in transportation in Islamic countries came from the extensive use of camels, but it was not in any way connected with agrarian innovation. Initially, this revolution signified an essential step toward more intensive communication over a large area.[112] In the long term, however, the switchover to camels and the total abandonment of transport by cart had a negative effect on the advance of transportation. The progressiveness of the early Middle Ages contributed to backwardness in the modern age. In contrast, the European agrarian revolution presented constructive, long-term possibilities for the steady development of transportation by integrating draft-animal husbandry with agriculture. Introducing draft animals into farming pioneered their use for local and long-distance transportation. Labor that the lord required of the peasant in the corvée necessitated the keeping of draft animals. A transport system dependent on these animals needed, to a much greater degree, the cart and specific transportation structures, such as roads and bridges, in contrast to systems based on beasts of burden, as in the Islamic world. Conditions favorable to Europe's transportation infrastructure were already comparatively well established by the Middle Ages. And without the widespread use of the cart for land transport, the evolution of modern-day European vehicular traffic would probably not have occurred.

———

The various developments in the industrial trades, transport, and commerce that followed from the three agrarian revolutions left their stamp on settlement patterns. Population growth benefited large metropolitan centers in China but especially in the Islamic world. Many of these centers soon lost importance as rapidly as they had gained it, their rise and fall exemplified by several of their princely residences. No settlements in Europe even came close to having the dimensions of these large urban centers, either in early medieval times or afterward, not even into quite modern times. Medieval European settlement patterns were typified by a whole host of midsized and smaller centers. The well-developed trades linked to agriculture had brought about the early formation of predominantly trades-oriented settlements on the lowest social level and in small, localized areas. And the transportation sector that promoted local traffic though oxcarts and horse-drawn carts reflected the same organization of space. This hierarchical system of smaller settlements in close proximity to the surrounding farms proved to be extremely durable over time.

Turning to the military, we find that the advent of the heavily armored knight characterized the early Middle Ages as it had, to some extent, the period of late antiquity preceding it. The Frankish Empire developed a very specific form of dispersed settlement—and with it the social integration of knights in armor—because of the feudal and seigniorial systems. This military organization was founded on a substantial agrarian base. We should emphasize in this context first, the integration of livestock keeping with agriculture, and second, the increase in oats production that was so important for horse fodder—the two together were characteristic of Europe north of the Alps.[113] China

25

and Islam did not integrate the keeping of livestock during their more or less contemporaneous agrarian revolutions. And we cannot discern in either of these two cultures any direct influence of newly introduced crops on military organization. But in Europe we have a clear grasp of the connection between agrarian change and modifications in the military system, all within the framework of the feudal system and the structures deriving from it. The military system was to prove most effective in the history of Europe.

———

It is difficult to decide whether the agrarian innovations in Europe north of the Alps preceded manorial organization or whether they developed within a framework that system had already produced. Both the innovations and the system go back a long way in the Frankish heartland between the Rhine and the Seine; their full flowering in the Carolingian period shows how closely they were tied to each other.[114] And yet it is not only a matter of their congruence in time and space but of causal connections as well. The suite of agrarian innovations was fostered by the bipartite manorial system and the economic interlocking of the peasant's land with the seigniorial demesne. Secular and religious lords were the leading exponents of agrarian innovation. The tie-in with the manors was a principal difference between the European agrarian revolution and the one that Islamic princes and their officials carried out, or the one that peasant colonizers brought about in China. The close involvement with manorial lordship was why the European agrarian revolution—well above and beyond the military system—had such a great influence on the various social orders. It influenced kingdoms and countries by means of the princes' lordship, ecclesiastical houses and religious orders by means of monastic lordship, and peasant family farms through all kinds of lordship. Mediated by manorialism, the European agrarian revolution proved to have a most enduring effect.

The linkage between the agrarian revolution and manorialism points up problems of exposition in the interpretation presented here. The two phenomena together clearly form a "concatenation of circumstances" in the sense of the question Max Weber posed. They belong together by virtue of their substance. We must nevertheless discuss them separately, all the more so if we try to understand them by means of a cross-cultural comparison. For this purpose, they need to be detached from their "concatenation" and treated separately.

The European agrarian revolution, as analyzed in this chapter, is in itself a "concatenation of circumstances." The title of the present chapter, "Rye and Oats," is a condensation because it emphasizes two particular factors. Characteristic features of the European agrarian revolution were not apparent in every location where rye or oats were grown in early medieval Europe, as the contrasting examples of Russia and Ireland demonstrated. Even the joint appearance on the scene of the two crops in question, which we can trace back to Roman times and earlier, did not exhibit every single one of the agrarian revolution's defining features, either at the time or afterward. The "concatenation of circumstances" that constitutes the phenomenon of the European agrarian revolution stretches far beyond the combination of rye and oats. Although we have to take this broader connection into account, the highlighting of rye and oats is nonetheless legitimate—not only as a chapter title but as the explanatory model for which the title of the present chapter stands. These two new domesticated crops receive priority in the total ensemble of agrarian innovations because they were the first to appear. Moreover, we can trace subsequent key effects and connections back to them. And so—as is so often the case the world over—an explanatory model that attributes the special importance of the continent's agrarian foundations to newly domesticated plants seems to be the appropriate one for the special path Europe followed.

Two

Manor and Hide:
The Manorial Roots of
European Social Structures

It is obvious that an agrarian economy and an agrarian social system will influence each other. Agrarian revolutions leave all kinds of profound social changes in their wake that affect farming retroactively. The social orders in rural areas can certainly not be adequately accounted for by the agricultural economy alone; various other conditioning factors must be taken into account. Consequently, when we look at the organization of the manorial system that appeared at the same time and in the same place as the agrarian revolution of the early Middle Ages, we must ask how great the interaction was between agricultural innovation and changes in other spheres of life.

The "classic form of the manorial system" emerged during the Carolingian period in the heartland of the Frankish Empire.[1] French scholars refer to it as the *domaine bipartite*—the bipartite estate—a scholarly term that can tell us a great deal. German-language research prefers a concept from the language of its sources, *Villikationsverfassung* (from Latin *villicatio*). The so-called hide system (*Hufenverfassung*) was developed within the framework of manorialization.[2] This system connected early medieval manorialism in the Frankish Empire with later forms derived from it—*Bannherrschaft, Rentengrundherrschaft*, and *Gutsherrschaft*, which will be explained below.[3] The two concepts *domaine bipartite* and *Villikationsverfassung* draw

28

our attention to certain phenomena in the medieval agricultural system that were to become central to some developments unique to European society.

The term *domaine bipartite* expresses an elementary, essential characteristic of this form of manorialism: the land of a manorial estate is divided into two parts. On the one hand, there is the lord's manor house, or villa (*Fronhof, Herrenhof*), along with the properties belonging to it—farmland, meadows, gardens, and so forth. These are referred to collectively as the domain, or demesne (Latin *terra salica*, German *Salland*). Either the lord lives in the manor house or his steward does—the *villicus*, or *Meier*—who manages the domain and the servants living at the manor. On the other hand, there is a second category of people living outside the domain who also contribute to the manor's economy: the *mansi*, or hide farmers/peasants. The farms transferred to these peasants to be worked by and for themselves in exchange for services and corvée form the other part of the two-part estate.. The older term, *mansus* ("farm," from Latin *manere*, "to stay, remain"), is found from the sixth century on; the later term, *huba* (*Hufe*), comes from the second half of the eighth century. *Hufe* means the peasant's farm (*Hof*, which is derived from *Hufe* etymologically), but it also refers to a defined amount of service within the manorial system. Accordingly, the integration of the *mansi/Hufen* within the manorial system is called the *Hufenordnung* or *Hufenverfassung*—the hide system. Whereas the designation *domaine bipartite* addresses the division of cultivated land into lord's land and peasant's land, the German word *Villikation* (Latin *villicatio*) places a stronger emphasis on the social group working under a steward. The economic side of this unique interlocking of independent peasant farms, with a demesne and worked in common by peasants and villa personnel, occasionally is termed in the scholarly literature a *Betriebsgrundherrschaft* (roughly, a manorial agricultural enterprise).[4] But the early medieval *Villikation* was much more than a large farming enterprise. The word refers to a group of people having various social rights and duties extending far beyond economic cooperation. The term used at the time for those living at the manor or villa—the *familia*—graphically describes the high priority given to social relationships within the manorial system.[5]

If we look at certain concepts and the words used for them, connections seem to exist between the bipartite estate of the early medieval Franks and land ownership in the *imperium Romanum* of late antiquity. The Roman *villa rustica*, as a focal point of large agrarian enterprises, continued to survive through the *villicus* (steward) on the *villicatio* (estate). The Frankish manorial system preserved traces of the Roman villa in other terms and concepts. The concept of the *familia* established lines of continuity between the serfs domesticated in the villa in late antiquity and those who were domesticated in the early medieval manor. These are merely a few initial leads for a further examination of structural connections. But the simple juxtaposition of the villa of late antiquity and the early medieval *villicatio* will bring substantial differences to light. In essence, the rise of the bipartite estate represented a new beginning.[6] The question arises as to whether the changes in agriculture wrought by the agrarian revolution played a role in this new start.

The main difference between the late Roman *villa rustica* and early medieval *villicatio* was quite fundamental: the Roman system of land ownership was not a bipartite estate. In its classic form, the *villa rustica* had neither slaves on their own separate farms nor unfree peasants having to perform services at the villa. Originally, the Roman latifundian economy had no counterpart to the two main groups of *mansus* peasants in Carolingian times: it had *servi casati*—unfree farmers with their own house and property—and *coloni*, who were personally free, but tied to the land and obligated to provide services. In Roman times, a large demesne was worked principally by a villa's resident slaves. In late antiquity, this type of land cultivation on large estates was predominant in the provinces of Germania and northern Gaul, where Frankish rule replaced Roman.

How did it happen that this type of farming changed so fundamentally in precisely these two areas and within a relatively short time? Interesting clues can be found in two typical burdens put upon the early *mansus* peasantry that go back to the seventh century, maybe as far as the sixth: the *agrarium* and the *riga*.[7] The *agrarium* was a share of a tenant's grain harvest that was a due he owed his lord. This due indicated the preeminence of grain growing on independent farmers' holdings. The *riga* pointed in a similar direction but involved the demesne, where the individual *mansus* tenant was obliged to perform plowing service on certain "strips" (French *raie*, from Gallo-Roman *riga*).[8] These two services required of the *mansus* tenant indicate that the process of cerealization was underway during the early medieval agrarian revolution. This strongly suggests a connection between the creation of independent tenant holdings and the structural change in agriculture. The new form of the division of labor within the manorial system clearly signaled a rational use of labor. Grain production could not be increased merely by bringing in additional unfree slaves to the manor.

Apart from the fact that there were insufficient slaves available, it would probably have been difficult for the lord of the manor to keep and feed such a large number of workers at his house. It was the recategorization of unfree serfs as *servi casati* with their own farms that brought about multiple advantageous solutions to the problem: the lord saved himself the expense of feeding a large part of his labor force, and he himself did not need to keep the requisite number of animals for more intensively planted crops that came with the heavy plow—his economically independent *mansus* tenants, to whom he had granted sufficient land holdings, would do this. And his tenants had their plowing and wagon teams on hand at peak times to help with the plowing and the harvest; meanwhile they would be cultivating their own land. Moreover, the lord received a share of the produce grown on that land.

The leasing of land to personally free tenants—and the integration into the manorial household of free peasants required to perform similar services—followed the same economic logic as did the separating off of the *servi casati* from the lord's farm; it also had the same effect on the formation of the bipartite estate. These forms of dependency played an important part in the development of the manorial system. In central regions of the Merovingian Empire—around Tours, Le Mans, and Rheims, for instance—late Roman customs held on for a long time, for example, the levying of taxes.[9] Owners of large estates made certain to ensure sources of taxes from beyond their own lands. By means of the so-called *inspectio*, they practiced a system of services that made it possible for them to tie great numbers of freeholds to their own demesne and force the delivery of rents and services. This "system of duties" (*Abgabenherrschaft*) was probably a preliminary stage in placing the free peasantry under the control of large estate owners. A degree of dependency was a given for the *coloni*, despite their personal freedom, because of the leaseholds they had accepted. Dependency on their part had already become acute in late antiquity in many regions of the Western Roman Empire, for example, in North Africa and Gaul.[10] The evidence from North Africa is particularly early for dues or corvée exacted from small farmers on large estates. These obligations were a decisive step in making *coloni* and *servi* (serfs) equal; binding them to the land was a further step, a practice already widespread in late antiquity. Even at that time, the colonate appeared as a form of farm labor poised "between freedom and slavery."[11] The laws in Merovingian times—the *Lex Alamannorum*, say, or the *Lex Bajuvariorum*—drew few distinctions between the duties owed the lord by either *coloni* or *mansus* farmers. The quantitatively significant group of the *coloni* seems to have been

31

integrated into the manorial system. The indications of links between the colonate and newly reclaimed land are important.[12] As cerealization progressed, even marginally productive soils were cultivated. The growing land clearances that expanded outward from the Frankish heartland in the early Middle Ages could have provided some impetus for the integration of *coloni* into the bipartite estate. From this angle, the "classic" form of the manorial system seems to feed back from the agrarian revolution.

The answer to the question how far the Frankish manorial system represents a new kind of structure is not simply the combination of the persistence and modification of the Roman *villa rustica*. There are points of contact with other roots, for example, the so-called *gynaecea* often found on royal, ecclesiastical, and aristocratic manorial estates in the Frankish Empire.[13] These were houses for women at the manor, where bonded women and girls did spinning and weaving for the lord. The Greek root of the term points to antiquity. In Roman imperial times, the *gynaeceae* were textile workshops where women turned out cloth for the court or the military. In the areas settled by the Franks, we can say that the military was more likely to maintain continuity. Thus a line of development clearly led from the economy of the *limes castella* along the Rhine in late antiquity up to the manorial economy of Frankish times.

A blacksmith who died in the fifth century at a former *castellum* on the upper Germanic *limes*, left behind a hoard that included a plowshare—which represents to some extent the "missing link" in the development of the heavy plow. The hoard not only reveals that agricultural innovation was underway in the milieu of the *limes castella*; it also indicates how important the blacksmith's trade was for the Roman military economy.[14] Charlemagne's *Capitulare de villis* had put the blacksmith right at the top of the list of workmen every royal court administrator ought to have in his service.[15]

Extensive grazing land was necessary for the legions' camps along the Roman *limes*, especially for the cavalry's *castella*.[16] There is much evidence from royal Carolingian manors that clearly establishes a functional connection between manorial settlements and their stud-farm settlements; their original function lives on in place names containing the syllable *Mar-* (for "mare," from Old High German *marha*) or *Roß-* (for "horse," "steed").[17] The *Capitulare de villis* appointed special officials to supervise the stud farms.[18] Grain supplies for Roman legions' camps and the *castella* along the *limes* were kept in huge storehouses called *horrea*.[19] Still, a single camp would require 1,650 tons of grain for baking annually.[20] Besides the military granaries, large storehouse facilities were established at the *villae rusticae* as well. The barn economy of the Frankish manors was able to tie in with both kinds of storehouses. Many central features of the Frankish manorial system were able to blend in with the economy of the *limes castella* during late antiquity: workshops, farm buildings, workplaces for craftsmen. And there were further parallels in the requirements for many of the dues and services owed the manor. From the third century on, unpaid services for the lord's needs were increased, especially in the threatened provinces near the frontier. These included transporting military supplies, working on public buildings, baking bread, and tailoring clothing for soldiers.[21] All these services were part of the manorial system during the early Middle Ages. The needs of the army determined for centuries the economic life along the Roman *limes* and in the hinterland. This created institutions and structures that were plainly different from those in the tribal areas of Germania Magna. The Franks who moved into the border provinces as *foederati* were probably very familiar with the state of affairs there and may have integrated several of its features into those aspects of the manorial system they themselves had developed. At any rate, we may assume that this was the case for the royal manor, to which the former *limes castella* now belonged.

The frontier areas of the Roman Empire might even have felt the influence of more ancient manorial forms in Germania Magna in those instances where the Franks had brought them into their new settlement areas. When Tacitus wrote about the agriculture of the Germanic tribes in the twenty-fifth chapter of his *Germania*, he put it this way: "Suam quisque [servus] sedem suos penates regit. Frumenti modum dominus aut pecoris aut vestis ut colono iniungit." And so the Germanic tribes already had unfree slaves whose lords obligated them to provide rent in grain, animals, and cloth.[22] Tacitus saw that these services ran in the same line as those of personally free Roman *coloni*. He then contrasted the Germanic *servi* with resident slaves in the Roman *villae*, where there were both resident slaves and slaves who were employed in farming—some in the vineyards, others in the fields, still others in the stables. As a result, very different ways of using the labor force might have collided with one another on large farming estates in the provinces along the Rhine. Perhaps Tacitus meant those *servi* who, in his words quoted above, had control over "their own dwelling and their own household gods [*penates*]" and were precursors of the *servi casati* on manors in the Frankish Empire. But they were different from the latter in one very essential point. Tacitus spoke only of dues, not of serfs having to work

33

in corvée on their master's demesne. The plowing service that was such a vital part of the manorial system probably would not have existed in those earlier days. The resident serfs were probably more like the owners of smallholdings who might well have existed right from the outset on great Frankish estates, side by side with the *mansus* or hide farmers; they were later to form the basis of the population class below peasant farmers, such as cottagers, crofters, cabin- and hut-dwellers, and paid small farmers (*Seldner*). Tacitus's report is too skimpy for us to be able to discern any clear lines of development. But plainly apparent are the different organization of slave labor on the Roman *villa rustica* and the parallel with the colonate. We can probably speak here of different preliminary forms, compared to which the manor and hide systems of the Frankish Empire represented something fundamentally novel.

In the Roman imperial frontier areas on the Rhine, several elements might well have combined in late antiquity to forge a link between the agrarian revolution and the early medieval manorial system. The enormous demand for grain coming from the military units stationed there produced more crop cultivation and more large-scale modes of organizing farm labor. The Romans adopted spelt and oats—species that were new to them.[23] Subsequently, the Franks probably spearheaded the diffusion of these two grains into northern Gaul. They were one of the few Germanic tribes invading the Roman Empire to have promoted large farming settlements.[24] Their cultivation of new and different plants could have enabled them not only to reclaim land grown wild in the confusion of the Great Migrations but also to increase available farmland by clearing the land, which in addition allowed marginally productive soils to be exploited. We must assume that the expansion and restructuring of arable land was a prerequisite for the rise of the bipartite estate. The *fundi* (farms) of Roman *villae* could not by themselves have equipped the resident serfs and *coloni* bound to the soil—the people who worked the demesne lands so intensively—labor requiring special services, or corvée, that had no precedent in Germania Magna. In the late Roman Empire, these services were greatly expanded to meet military needs, especially in the outlying border areas.[25] In the early Middle Ages, we rediscover a term for the corvée, *angariae*, that originated in the public sphere and was revived in the context of the manorial system.[26] Whatever the lines of continuity may have been between the *munera* of late antiquity and dues and services in the early Middle Ages, the introduction of the corvée for working demesne lands was essential to the creation of the bipartite estate. These dues meant having draft oxen available for plowing grain fields not only on the villa but also on individual *mansi* or hide farms. In this way the integration of crop production with the keeping of large livestock that was so typical of the European agrarian revolution was placed on a firm footing both on the lord's farms and the peasants'. With the obligation on the peasantry to provide plowing service, the hide (*Hufe*) became a unit of the manor's productivity. As the basis for a completely farm-based existence within the hide system (*Hufenverfassung*), it outlasted the manorial system and its demesne economy, the labor needs of which probably constituted the original reason for its establishment.

———

The cultivation of arable land shows how the effects of the agrarian revolution and the emergence of the bipartite estate were linked. But this connection is also clearly visible in the way the key physical facilities on the manor evolved. Those at a Roman *villa rustica* in the northern frontier provinces as a rule included—the lord's manor aside—various kinds of stables, barns, drying kilns, an occasional wine cellar, ovens, smokehouses, and various types of workplaces and craftsmen's shops.[27] As antiquity waned, deurbanization led to a general rise in the number of tradesmen locating on large rural manorial estates.[28] Once again we may reckon that this trend was greater in frontier areas where the demands of supplying the military had a significant impact on economic life. Apart from the estates, whose job it was to supply the army, the *castella* themselves increasingly acquired similar key farm facilities. They merged with Frankish manors, which refined them further in important ways. The farming activities mentioned in the *Capitulare de villis*, for example, which were found on royal manors, went far beyond earlier attempts during late antiquity.[29] We may regard many of them as the fruit of changes wrought by the agrarian revolution. This is very true for the water mill in particular, the epitome of a key agricultural facility on the bipartite estate, although it did not always operate near the manor—its location being determined by the specific natural setting it required. Constructing a water mill was a costly affair that a single hide farmer could not have easily afforded.[30] Not only the building itself had to be built but also other structures necessary for exploiting waterpower. The builder had to own the water rights as well. A millstone was usually the most expensive item; it often had to be transported over some distance, which was the lord of the manor's responsibility to arrange. The mill served the lord *and* his dependent peasants. If the time came when the right of a trade monopoly (*Banngewerbe*) was exercised, this key service became a tenant's obligation to his manorial lord.

After the grist mill was introduced, other types of mills were to become central facilities of the manorial system. Many of them processed what had been produced on the manor itself—the fulling mill, for instance, or the sawmill. Waterpower was also harnessed for the malting mills that paved the way for a crucial activity in the manor's self-sufficient economy: brewing.[31] Breweries going back to Roman estates are found in what is today Belgium; in the Frankish Empire they would often turn up as adjuncts to large courts. Beer brewing could have been a tenant farmer's service, but beer might also have been an in-kind payment to his lord. The agrarian innovations of the early Middle Ages apparently did not influence brewing by growing barley—which had been cultivated for ages—but by creating the technology for processing it. The manor's brewery consisted of a brewing room with cauldron, cooling facilities, fermentation vats, and a room for storing the grain, drying it, and mashing malt. For this last process, waterpower could be employed, which promoted centralization. Later on, the use of the lord's tavern became obligatory (*Banngewerbe*) in the same way that the use of his grist mill was.

Not all of the main economic facilities on the estate processed what originated on the manor, as did the mill, the brewery, or the bakery, which was closely associated with the first two. The smithy, for example, took its raw material from elsewhere, but the agrarian revolution had made it indispensable for the economy both of the manor and of the individual hide farmers. It was essential for making plows and other agricultural implements; when horses came to be used, it was needed for manufacturing horseshoes, as it was for making iron wheel axles—a key piece of equipment in a vertical mill. The *Lex Salica* had already listed the iron wheel axle as having the same value as a steer.[32] As mentioned above, the *Capitulare de villis* put the blacksmith at the top of the list of trades on the manor. But wood, hides, leather, and meat were the manor-grown products that were more likely to be processed in situ. Of course all of these functions owed hardly anything to innovations in early medieval agriculture.

The case of animal husbandry presents a basically new configuration. The *mansus* farmer needed oxen for carrying out the services required of him. It was of course impossible for a farmer to keep a whole herd of animals. The solution to the problem appears to have been to assign the task of keeping stock bulls on the estates' principal farms. In this way important arrangements and services established many modes of cooperation between the peasants' and the master's farms. Who profited more by this kind of interaction is immaterial. The issue is, rather, the uniqueness of such a complex agricultural enterprise and, beyond that, the uniqueness of a rural societal form. Even though there were many prototypical forms that went quite far back, it was really the agrarian revolution of the early Middle Ages that made the phenomenon of the bipartite estate possible.

The estate's singularity lay not just in its nature as an organized farming enterprise; it was also unprecedented as a basis for organizing lordship within a large empire. This important function, acquired during the Carolingian Empire, produced some determinative elements of the estate system beyond the economic. The system was, to be sure, not integrated with the structure of the empire as a finished model but was constantly elaborated upon as the structure of lordship developed. In this way, the royal manorial system acquired the characteristics that differentiated it from the systems of the nobility and the church. The various forms of the secular and ecclesiastical estate systems had, as a matter of course, an effect on one another, but the leading role here was surely played by the ways in which the royal estate was organized.

The array of functions belonging to royal estates in Carolingian times was also apparent in the appurtenances of the royal courts.[33] These included the institution of agricultural features and objects of use—such as stables and barns, meadows and fields, orchards and vineyards, water and mills, beehives and woodlands—and other economically useful legal titles, such as iron mines and sources of salt, markets and market dues, or bridges and their tolls, but especially extraeconomic appurtenances such as ships or horses for royal transport and carting, properties with obligatory military service and the equipment for it, or royal proprietary churches, including their priests. These "add-ons" to the royal Carolingian courts went far beyond any type of agricultural enterprise. In such instances, significant functions of royal rule were tightly woven into the administration of the king's property. The king's dominion seems to have been underpinned by agriculture, and the exigencies of his dominion appear to have exerted an influence on how the royal manorial system was organized as much as on how agricultural innovations were introduced.

The shoring up of power on the royal demesne was connected to a specific way of utilizing lordship in the Frankish Empire. The king exercised his authority by riding from palace (*Pfalz*) to palace, from royal court to royal court, carrying out his official business on his travels through his empire.[34] This *Reisekönigtum* (peripatetic, or traveling, royal court) of the Frankish kings was fundamentally new. Whereas Merovingian kings often stayed at their palaces in old Roman cities, like Orléans, Paris, or Soissons, the localities in the country, such as Quierzy, Compiègne, Aix-la-Chapelle, or Ingelheim, claimed pride of place under the Carolingians. This corresponded to a shift of the central area of the king's lordship to less urbanized regions of the empire. The growing significance of the royal courts vis-à-vis urban residential palaces was reflected in the word for the royal household, "court" (*Hof*), which was to gain acceptance during the Carolingian period. The Carolingians definitely had their preferred palaces, where the rulers would quite often spend certain religious feast days or carry out particular official functions. Topographically speaking, this royal practice received support from a goodly number of larger and smaller royal courts, all of which had to be fortified in order to guarantee their provisioning for the king and his retinue should they stay for any length of time—a way of organizing lordship that was based less on money than on an in-kind economy. For all that, it was not in the least a primitive, or underdeveloped, form of support. On the contrary, this highly complex assembly of primary and secondary courts had thousands of dependent peasants under all kinds of obligations to render services and dues, as well as many different kinds of specialized appurtenances. The famed *Capitulare de villis* has provided a glimpse into the complexity of this organization.

The field of historical settlement research allows us to draw some conclusions about the emergence and structures of the Carolingian *villa*. A leading proponent in the field states:

I have introduced the concept of an early medieval "Frankish agrarian revolution" that is implicitly linked with the thesis that the . . . manorial village, field, and technical agrarian structures associated with this concept did not develop in Thuringia but were introduced as innovations—in a kind of "innovation package"—from the western heartland of the Austrasian part of the empire. . . . I have been able to determine that there were similar settlement patterns around royal palaces in the Upper Rhine area. I have already described how things proceeded in Thuringia from the middle of the seventh century on, where new, planned settlements, together with the restructuring and expansion of existing settlements, followed in the wake of Frankish-manorial agricultural reform. In light of these events, it now seems to me that subsequent settlement growth in those western areas was more likely spurred on by the use of long, extensive strips of fields than it was by the "Frankish state colonization" that I thought, until now, had taken place earlier, in the sixth century. I should like to reformulate my hypothesis thus: this type of agricultural reform was first put in motion in Austrasia around the middle of the seventh century, or somewhat earlier, under the Pippins, the majordomos of the Merovingians. They did this in the course of enlarging and strengthening their power base on the royal manors on crown lands around Merovingian palaces and royal courts. This innovation then caught on with nobles close to the king who in turn applied it to their own manorial estates. It would be most compelling to assume that the new model of the manorial hide system—with its *Hufengewannfluren* and its large blocks of land (*territoria*) that were farmed in long strips (*rega*)—was also put into practice in the new settlements that were laid out by and for the kingdom (at the discretion of the majordomos) along the lines of a "Frankish state colonization."[35]

He supplements his deductions about the history of settlements and fields with place-name derivations. Settlements could be found around those central royal courts bearing "schematic-appellative names," such as composite words ending in *-sta(d)t* (place, stead), *-hofen* (court), or *-heim* (home) that indicate some degree of "fiscal planning." We can gather that these names indicate settlements around stud farms or mills, for example, which were key facilities connected with royal courts. On the whole, the new format for organizing crown property can be clarified by examining the systematic settlements of colonized areas rather than older settled regions. These more recent establishments are where we observe in particularly graphic form the real importance of the organization of royal property for cementing royal rule.

———

The way in which the monasteries in the Frankish Empire developed had a lasting effect on the growth of the manorial system, as did the evolution of Frankish kingship. The royal manorial estates and those of the great imperial monasteries had much in common: they were organized on a large scale; they had a hierarchical structure, and they had similar obligations to serve the empire, such as guesting the king or serving in military campaigns.[36] These commonalities can be explained in part by the origin of many monastic estates as part of royal estates. But there were essential differences as well. The spiritual community of the cloister was nothing like a *Reisekönigtum*; it was dedicated to *stabilitas loci*, which fostered the high degree of continuity informing the peculiar character of basic monastic rule by virtue of its precise obligations. The obligation to pray stood front and center; prayers were offered for king and empire, in royal monasteries especially. Prayer was as much a *servitium regis* as were guesting the king and the obligation of military

39

service. In exchange for performing the service of prayer, monasteries were provided with royal estates. In this context, the grand basilica monasteries for relics of the saints of the empire, or for the interments of the kings connected with them, had particular commissions.[37] In addition, prayers had to be offered and commemorative masses said for a whole host of noble donors. Commemorating the dead was decidedly on the upswing during the Frankish Empire in Carolingian times, and this led to more generous donations.[38] The unique development of the commemoration of the dead in the Western Church resulted in a singular expansion of monastic manorial estates. That monasteries in the West had accepted the latifundian economy right from the outset in order to provide for their own subsistence was the prerequisite for the growth of monastic manorial estates from the donations of kings and the nobility.[39] This meant there was a basically positive attitude toward the cloisters' having an independent economy. Frankish monasteries were in many respects centers of agricultural innovation. This was surely the case for viticulture, which was indispensable for liturgical reasons. The many kitchen and medicinal plants that spread from Italy in Carolingian times might well have moved northward via monastery gardens. Even more important, newly domesticated plants and cultivation techniques appear to have been introduced on the estates of imperial monasteries at the same time as on royal estates. A preeminent role was played by monasteries in the diffusion of the water mill and by the increased use of waterpower generally in trade and industry. Cloisters played a pioneering role as well in the adopting of writing in the administration of estates. The polyptychs (account books, registers, and the like) of the great Carolingian monastic manorial estates provide concrete examples. The royal Frankish monasteries, as centers of agrarian innovation, made a definite, powerfully dynamic contribution to the growth of the "classic manorial system." The combination of Western monasticism with a self-sufficient economy (*Eigenwirtschaft*) was most important for bringing the imperial monasteries into the service of the Frankish kingdom.[40] This involvement with the tasks of lordship marked a qualitative leap for the monasteries and the monastic manorial system within the Frankish Empire.

As the "classic manorial system" of the Carolingian period continued to grow, it went through a many-sided process of restructuring and differentiation, whether by adjusting to particular soil and climate conditions or by changing the large, overarching determinants of society.[41] Among the latter, we can list the breakup of the independent economy of the manorial lords, which marked an end to the manorial estate system (but not to the hide system); the transformation of services into rents and of in-kind rents into payments of money; the obliterating of the distinction between free and half-free hide farmers, and much more. Most important among these transformational processes was the growth of the "immunities" of "banal lordship" (*Bannherrschaft, seigneurie banale*) that began in the tenth century.[42] This primarily involved the manorial estates of the nobility; ecclesiastical estates were referred to indirectly. Banal lordships of the nobility could practice jurisdictional and other rights of authority related to dues and services—including rights over subjects on ecclesiastical estates. The origins of these rights may have involved various forms of secular authority over imperial church property, such as lay abbeys (*Laienabteien*) and *Vogteien* (from *Vogt*, derived from Latin *advocatus*, "protector"), which we will discuss below.[43] Church people under a *Vogt*'s authority were subject to at least two masters: ecclesiastical lords of the manor and nobles with legal jurisdiction who, in turn, were themselves manorial lords over other subjects. Complicating the systems of dependency, additional forms of authority could supplement those just mentioned, for example, *Leibherrschaft* (control over the person of the peasant), or *Zehentherrschaft*, which meant paying tithes to yet another lord.[44] It appears that a banal lordship typically had a fortified castle (*Burg*) as its center. It might have been a *Vogtburg*, a castle built by a *Vogt* (as a noble who was a protector of a church) on church property or adjacent to it on newly cleared land—quite rightly, according to the views of the age.[45] Apart from churches, it was their lay patrons who were active in land clearance, creating for themselves an expanded manorial base— usually with more highly developed forms of leasing land (*Bodenleihe*) or of dues and services. The principle of the hide system as a way of organizing the units of labor determined by the lord was retained, however, even though the manorial system was to be reorganized later. The hide system was a lasting inheritance of the Carolingian *Villikation*, which it outlived by centuries as it expanded well beyond the area from which it had originally emerged.

To trace the expansion of the manorial and hide systems involves treating other, contemporaneous agrarian patterns throughout Europe that they either bordered on or replaced. It is possible to give only a few examples in selected regions inside and outside the domain of the Carolingian Empire and its successors. The area settled by the Frisians along the

North Sea coast is an interesting case from within the Frankish Empire itself. Manorial estates had not been established there—not by the king, the church, or the nobility—although the imperial heartland lay very close by. The reason for this may well be the ecological conditions that determined the economy.[46] The region was admirably suited for grazing, so that agriculture faded into the background. Sheep's wool formed the basis for a textile trade and cloth exports; wheat, on the other hand, had to be imported.[47] Natural conditions were lacking for the cerealization that had been implemented by Frankish neighbors. That a region in the Frankish Empire specializing in animal husbandry did not even begin to come close to establishing the bipartite estate confirms, *e contrario*, the belief in a connection between increased grain production and the rise of the manorial system. Nor was the agricultural system in Frisian settlements shaped later on by manorial structures. Very strong rural communal groups were established instead, placing the local nobles dispensing high justice in a precarious position.

The situation in early medieval Ireland can shed light on the interconnections between the predominance of cattle breeding and lordship over the land and its people. Structures analogous to the Frankish manorial *system* did not emerge there, but manorial *forms* certainly did. Irish lords distributed arable land to unfree, homeless people, the so-called *fuidri*.[48] In general, slaves and serflike unfree people were an essential part of Irish rural society. Unlike the *servi casati* on the Frankish estates, the Irish *fuidri* did not have to perform plowing service on the demesne; they did not possess the necessary draft animals, so they did not become plowmen. Grain was not grown in Ireland on a grand scale. The *fuidri* might be compared to the *servi cottidiani* of the Frankish Empire, who also kept huts on manorial land and became cottagers, small farmers (*Seldner*), hut dwellers, and so on.

The groups ranking socially higher among the dependents of a great lord were not given land as a fief but cattle, which they herded along with their own. There was no way a "classic manorial system," in the sense of a bipartite division of land, could have been established in an economy based on the loaning of livestock. Even if oxen for plowing happened to be included among the animals loaned by the lord, this did not also mean that the lord's land would be farmed.[49] Those who received animals in fief were classed as the lord's clients. A distinction was drawn between a base clientship (*dóer chéilsine*), and a free clientship (*sóer chéilsine*). Base clients had to provide their lord with dues from animal husbandry, such as meat, sausage, or bacon, as well as from crops.[50] They carried out farm labor, which was classified as servile. Free clients paid for loaned cattle with calves and assisted the lord further by building fortifications, taking part in military campaigns, and help-ing with the harvest—duties that apparently did not imply a lowering of one's status.[51] These patron-client relations did not generate a *familia* as they did on Frankish estates; social structuring was still maintained through kinship. It seems that mills and kilns were typically owned by kinship groups in common, and it was only at monasteries that these buildings were the key facilities on a manorial estate.[52] Given that a livestock economy was dominant, these facilities were much less sig-nificant in Ireland than even the rather anemic Irish crop production. In this respect, too, there were no institutions that would enable the bipartite estate to gain a toehold. Because of these agrarian contexts and the aligning of its social structures with kinship, the organization of power developed very differently in early medieval Ireland than in the Frankish Empire. "Cattle lords" and lower-level kings dominated the scene. No rudiments of a systematic organization of crown land as the basis of lordship could be found, and given the agricultural situ-ation on the Emerald Isle, Irish monasteries, too, simply lacked that drive toward a manorial system that marked the Frankish Empire.

The second half of the thirteenth century saw a radical change in the Irish agricultural system as a result of Anglo-Norman influence. Co-lonial settlement followed patterns very similar to those in east-central Europe at about the same time.[53] Here, as there, patterns were rooted in manorial structures that originated in the Frankish heartland. Ireland refused to give in to these influences for a very long time. This is all the more surprising because we discover quite early in England paral-lels to the Frankish manorial estate and the hide system. In the British Isles, two very different agrarian systems existed closely side by side for many centuries—a contrast that appears to be instructive.

In England, unlike in Ireland, we find an embryonic manorial system developing as early as the eighth century, which puts its origins almost as far back as the Frankish Empire's. We find mention—in the laws of King Ine of Wessex (688–726)—of a *gebur* (or *geburo*), that is, a peas-ant "outfitted" by his lord and obliged to perform plowing service on the demesne.[54] This service was to play an essential role in subsequent years on the manors of the Anglo-Saxon nobility.[55] We have learned from Frankish examples that this service was the key component of the bipartite estate because it determined the relation between the de-mesne and the peasant's land, along with the "outfitting" of the lat-ter with animals and tools. English manors belong to the same type.[56] There was also a counterpart to the Frankish hide system that emerged within the framework of the manorial system. The *Hufe* largely corresponds to the hide (*hid, hida, hidra*) in Anglo-Saxon-speaking areas.[57] There is evidence that the word "hide" is connected etymologically with arable land. The cultivation of crops defined the unit of a farming enterprise; as such, the endeavor had to be self-sustaining. The Anglo-Saxon hide had already been defined by the Venerable Bede (673–735) as a *terra unius familiae*, a term later applied to the Frankish *Hube*. Bede understood the family to consist of a married couple with children.[58] The hide had to provide a livelihood for a family so defined, and it became a unit of productivity, a measurable unit for tax purposes, and a unit of land measurement—exactly like the *Hufe*. Kings exerted a strong influence on these developments—yet another similarity with the *Hufe*. The hide played a major part in the military organization of Alfred the Great (king of Wessex, 871–99).[59] We come across congruencies even in settlement and field patterns that might well have been consequences of the hide system.[60]

Since many analogies can be established between manorial structures in the Kingdom of Wessex and the Carolingian Empire near the end of the ninth century, a plausible explanation for them lies at hand: the Wessex kings copied Carolingian laws, as other Anglo-Saxon kings probably did as well. But not much can be gleaned from this observation. Could the higher Irish kings of the time have done precisely the same thing? Certainly not. The economic and social conditions of their own land precluded these particular types of lordship. We must therefore ask why it was easier for kings in England to adopt Frankish models. Favorable conditions must have been created by parallel structures that go back much farther. Unlike Ireland, but like northern Gaul, Roman Britain was fashioned by Roman provincial patterns: by *civitas*, by rural *villae rusticae* and their latifundian economy, and by the economic requirements of provisioning an army stationed in a threatened frontier region.[61] The Angles, Saxons, Jutes, and Frisians did not of course come to Britain as Roman *foederati* as had the Franks when they entered northern Gaul, but some degree of assimilation with agrarian structures would have been necessary in Britain as well.

Their chief discovery in Britain was the existence of all the types of crops on which key agricultural innovations rested during the Frankish Empire of the early Middle Ages. The Anglo-Saxons were therefore able, right from the beginning, to follow the same path the Frankish agrarian revolution had taken, including the development of the bipartite estate that was based on increased crop production and the plowing services it typically required. And so, from the very beginning, the Anglo-Saxon kingdom—how very different from the Celtic peoples in the British Isles—shared the progressive farming practices from northwestern Europe that were being improved upon in the early Middle Ages. Although England never belonged to the Frankish Empire, its agricultural situation and agrarian system resembled it closely. The Norman Conquest of 1066 accelerated the process of assimilation. On one point, however, the English manorial system diverged from the continental one: banal lordship did not take hold in England. This important difference between the successors to the Carolingian Empire and other, contemporary European forms of lordship will concern us below, and more than once.

———

The most significant expansion of the model agricultural system in the Frankish heartland between the Seine and the Rhine took place toward the east. Its diffusion embraced almost the whole of central Europe and large parts of eastern Europe. The German term for this, *Ostkolonisation*—the "colonization of the East" (the *German* colonization of the East is what is understood here)—has suffered from the abuses of nationalist historiography; but if we leave these connotations aside, the word hits the nail on the head.[62] This great colonizing process, which transmitted Frankish agricultural structures and their accompanying forms of lordship, took off at the latest around the middle of the eighth century. Frankish majordomos or kings from the Carolingian house introduced manorial estates (*Villikation*) and the hide system (*Hufenverfassung*) throughout the royal estates east of the Rhine as well—in Mainfranken (now Middle Franconia), in Hessia, and in Thuringia. Research on German historical settlement refers to "Frankish state colonization" in this context.[63] The systematics and functionality of these new structures are particularly easy to grasp in regions where their diffusion was planned.[64] The eastern limit of the Carolingian Empire was for a long time an important dividing line between the expanding Frankish agricultural system and eastern European agricultural structures. When the push toward colonization continued with more force in the High Middle Ages, newer models of *Rentengrundherrschaft* predominated—but they were still founded on the hide system.[65] This pattern was consequently established over a wide area: in the Baltic, in large parts of Poland, in Bohemia, Moravia and parts of Slovakia, in western Hungary, and in Slovenia. Colonization established a line stretching roughly from St. Petersburg to Trieste.[66] We will come across this line again when studying European family systems and their diffusion. The sixteenth century witnessed the last great attempt to establish the hide system throughout an eastern European region when King Sigismund II of Poland tried it in the Lithuanian part of his empire in what is modern-day Belarus.[67] The eastward expansion of Frankish agrarian reform therefore spanned at least eight centuries. The basic model of the hide system was of course often modified over such a long period, but there was structural continuity nevertheless.

The more ancient agrarian economic structures of the East and the newer structures of the West stood in especially strong contrast to each other in the areas annexed by the colonization of the East. To take one example, in the early thirteenth century Duke Henry the Bearded of Silesia made a change in his schedule of dues and services. Grain was to be rendered after a certain point instead of the squirrel skins demanded until then.[68] This changeover was symptomatic of the structural transformations wrought by the colonization of the East; the age-old tribute of pelts that had been widespread in eastern Europe was replaced by rents in grain. Here, too, cerealization was the leitmotif of agricultural reform; it was accompanied by the three-field system of crop rotation, new agricultural implements—the heavy wheeled plow with a moldboard being chief among them—as well as the water mill for the processing of the swelling grain production.[69] These new economic methods found expression in new layouts of fields and meadowlands. The fields in long strips (*Gewanne*) were dominant, with the hide farmers receiving equal shares in the different "fields" of the village district. The ideas about new forms of settlement were reflected in the systematically laid-out villages—street villages (*Straßendörfer*), meadow villages (*Angerdörfer*), forest hide villages (*Waldhufendörfer*)—as the ever-growing number of hide farmers increased. These colonist villages were planned and laid out largely by settlement entrepreneurs from the nobility, who were no longer given villas but rent-free hides instead; these grants came with the hereditary office of village judge, along with its income and the proceeds from mill rights and beer sales.[70] Manorial estates were replaced by *Rentengrundherrschaften*. The rights of new immigrants were as a rule very favorable. They had their hide with the right of inheritance, were personally free, and paid fixed rents and tithing dues. The drastic deterioration of the legal status of east-central European peasants that occurred because of the agricultural structures of the manorial system came at a much later stage and was vastly different from the conditions prevailing during the period of colonization.

The piecemeal and intensive forms of manorial acquisition found over large areas of eastern Europe after colonization stand in stark contrast to older patterns in the region. The squirrel skins demanded by Duke Henry the Bearded point toward a particularly ancient model. Tributes in pelts were originally demanded collectively from tribal societies as a whole or in part. The inner structure of the societies ruled in this manner were completely unaffected by this system of duties. The expeditions Finnish lords made across Lapland, first on their own, then later, on a commission from the king of Sweden, represented an extreme and long-lived example of this type of tribute.[71] Tributes in furs were so important in northern and eastern Europe that a specific "fur geld" (*Pelzgeld*) based on them was created between the eleventh and the thirteenth centuries.[72] Tributary systems based on tribes were a long way from the arrangements established by the manorial system. According to *Nestor's Chronicle*, the districts requiring the services that the Grand Princess Olga of Kiev (945–69) had introduced in the northern part of her empire might have been connected to fur tributes like these, as later documents were to show.[73] The designation of these districts as *pogost* (Slavic for "guesting") indicates an additional element: providing the prince and his retinue with service for the table (*Tafeldienste*). Forms of guesting were found in various regions of Europe as an early form of organizing a royal manorial system, and they sometimes survived in later stages of development. Guesting and feasting generated all kinds of dues and services, thereby proving to be an important aspect of the history of the European manorial system.[74] Over the long term, of course, service for the table could not be equated with plowing service in its significance for the agrarian and manorial systems.

The same holds true for a third form of manorial service that can be identified in eastern Europe during the Middle Ages, the so-called service settlements. These settlements are traceable through place names like Kuchary ("cooks," cf. German *Köche*), Kowele (smithy), or Tokarzy (turner), established in areas around old castle towns (*Burgstädte*) that belonged to princes.[75] Obviously, specialist workers and servants had moved to these localities in order to provide services for the prince and his warrior vassals. These communities had certain parallels with so-called *Funktionssiedlungen* that were located around the manors of royal Carolingian courts. The service settlements of east-central European princes, which may have retained their importance into the twelfth century, can therefore probably be seen as an analogous effort to construct royal lordship over and above a royal manorial system. There is of course one crucial difference: the plowing services that were fundamental to the Carolingian manorial system did not exist in the East.

The organization of lordship in the East amounted to an agrarian economy, or an agrarian system, that was in existence prior to the critical transformational process of cerealization—a change not implemented in vast regions of eastern Europe until the hide system was introduced.

When we compare cerealization and the hide system to older patterns of the east European agrarian economy or system, we see that they both created radically different conditions. Why did the expansion of these two western innovations stop at the point it did? Pushing colonization farther eastward would have presented no difficulties, considering what the standard cultivated crops were. As early as the tenth century, winter rye was firmly established in most of the eastern Slavic principalities, as well as oats, which was planted in tandem with it as a summer crop.[76] The climatic conditions made it difficult to keep draft animals, but the breeds were tough enough to survive a winter of heavy snow without being stabled.[77] A further expansion of innovations eastward, then, probably would not have failed because of ecological obstacles. It may be that it did not seem necessary or sensible to switch over to different ways of increasing grain yields. The widespread slash-and-burn economy probably produced greater yields in the first years after a clearance than a three-field economy would have. Although the plentiful woodlands made these sweeping methods possible, from the perspective of the peasant population there would have been some question about the motivation behind such a radical change. Wherever agricultural innovations did get established during the colonization of eastern Europe, the initiative always came from the lords of the manors, be they princes, clerics, or nobles. Not all of them were in a position to do this in exactly the same way throughout the region.

———

It is remarkable that the medieval movement to colonize the East at no point crossed the boundary between Western and Eastern Christendom. Cultural models may account for this. It was the princes who, having fashioned themselves on the western organization of lordship, introduced the hide system on their fiscal lands. It was the noble vassals of these princes who came along right behind them. Above all, it was the great monastic orders of the Western Church, such as the Cistercians and the Premonstratensians, who disseminated western agricultural innovations on lands in the East that they had cleared. The Great Schism of 1054 set the course toward the ultimate split between the Western and Eastern Churches. The colonization of the East in the

High Middle Ages—wherever it did manage to get as far as the church's borders—was not able to climb that fence. The three-field system and the hide system were not isolated elements in a fenced-off economic sphere; rather, they were situated in a sociocultural context. As we have seen, their origins were influenced in a very particular way by Frankish kingship and Frankish monasticism. Even their later development seems to bear the stamp of persistent western structures. So it is no wonder that these two systems were only adopted by the empires sharing the culture of the Western Church.

––––––

The expansion of the manorial and hide systems that grew out of the Carolingian imperial heartland—or the later forms of the manorial system proceeding from them—played out very differently in the South than it did in the East. The situation in Italy seems particularly interesting in this regard. Rudiments of a bipartite estate had been adopted in the Langobard area even before the Carolingian Empire incorporated it, but it certainly stood under Frankish influence before then. The organization of the royal manor was not of primary concern in this case. Unlike the Frankish kings, the kings of the Lombards had a fixed residence, in Pavia. The great imperial monasteries might well have played a decisive part in the development of the manorial system. The monastery at Bobbio, in the Trebbia Valley, had been established in Arian times, in 612, although it was supported by the benevolence of the king and his Catholic wife; it was very closely allied with their kingdom for a long time.[78] Much of what we know about the ways agriculture was organized in early medieval Upper Italy comes from the enormous estate of this royal monastery. The same holds true for Nonantola, the imperial monastery founded in 752 by King Aistulf on the border of the Byzantine Empire.[79] With its extensive property of cells, hospices, parish churches, farmsteads, and all their appurtenances, the monastery controlled a network sustained by an estate that covered the whole of Langobardia. This structure was not found in Byzantine-controlled areas on the Apennine peninsula; the bishoprics there were very powerful, so that the Langobard rulers tried unsuccessfully to counterbalance them with their royal monasteries.[80] After Charlemagne conquered the Langobard Empire, imperial monasteries from north of the Alps—Reichenau, Saint Gall, Saint Emmeram in Regensburg, Fulda, Saint-Denis, and Saint-Martin in Tours among them—were granted holdings in northern Italy.[81] In this way, complexes of properties of considerable size were formed; the manorial system played an important part in their internal organization.

The bipartite estate was basically limited to Langobardia in Italy; it did not occur in Byzantine areas. The great landed properties were administered from urban houses, not from rural *curtes*.[82] The division into demesne and peasant tenancies—in Langobardia they were called *pars dominica* and *pars massaricia*—is exactly the same as the Frankish manorial system, but the economic backdrop to the agricultural system is different in several ways. Fruit trees, vineyards, and pasturing were frequently found on the demesne. A subject of a monastery obligated to perform the service of harvesting olives was in a very different position from a man who regularly had to perform plowing service. The latter service, which supplied the initial force behind the development of the Frankish manorial estate, most certainly did not have a similar function in Italy. Wherever the cultivation of crops with the heavy plow was not the priority, no plowing service was required. The peasants who kept large livestock were thus dependent on the specific nature of the dues and services demanded of them, as was the entire development of their independent farmsteads. Many of the farming cultures practiced in Italy were ill-suited for the introduction of dues and services because these called for a specialized labor force, for instance, for viticulture. So we must not assume that the bipartite estate in Italy grew out of local agricultural innovation. We should probably regard the crucial factor as being the transference of an organizing model of lordship that had been tried and proven elsewhere. Accordingly, Italian forms of manorialism were replaced relatively early by structures from other agricultural systems, especially by the system of sharecropping.[83]

The contrasts between Lombard-Frankish Italy on the one hand and Byzantine Italy on the other make it obvious that in the manorial and hide systems—to judge by the way they originated—we are dealing with something specific to northwestern Europe. Their roots went back in part to late antiquity, but in Italy they made an appearance as an import from the Frankish Empire and were, as a result, nonexistent where this influence was not felt. No comparable agricultural structures from Byzantium were adopted in early medieval Italy, an indication of a vastly different situation in the Eastern Roman Empire.

———

Throughout the eleven centuries of Byzantine agrarian history, periods of stasis appear to predominate over those of change.[84] This was as true of the agrarian economy as it was of the agrarian system. No agrarian revolution in the innovative, northwestern European sense occurred in the Byzantine Empire. Important new plants were not cultivated, nor were local ones transplanted to newly cleared land on a large scale. There was simply not enough land available for colonization of the kind. We do not come across the process of cerealization anywhere in Byzantine history, so there was no need for the plowing services of unfree peasants or *coloni* bound to the soil—services that had produced a new agrarian system within the manorial system that was so propitious for the development of the Frankish Empire. The tradition of slavery from late antiquity was continuously upheld in Byzantium, but there was no rationale for moving slaves onto independent farmsteads as *servi casati*.[85] And so a Byzantine counterpart to the *familia* on the western estate—the overarching household embracing many peasant households—never existed. On the whole, the lack of personal freedom was a minor factor in the Byzantine agrarian system. The assimilation process of the *coloni*—who were personally free but bound to the soil— with the *servi* was concluded in the East during late antiquity, but they did not form into the groups that were part of manorial estates.[86] A decisive feature here might have been the fact that the dues and services required of the *coloni* in Byzantium were primarily *angariae cum carrata*, that is, carting services that had been established by imperial decree in late antiquity as public services, and so they continued to be.[87] They included helping to construct streets, bridges, gates, fortifications, and the like. There is no indication that these state services were used by private citizens or broadened to include agricultural labor. The *coloni* by and large continued to be subject to state taxes, even though, since Diocletian's time, taxes were increasingly paid in kind rather than money.[88] Manorial social structures could not take root on this soil. In essence, the Byzantine agrarian system retained the traditions of late antiquity as far as services and dues from the peasantry were concerned. It was not until the High Middle Ages that a structural shift took place from large estates to the manorial system.[89] The *exkusseia*— identical in meaning to "immunity" in the West—first released landlords from taxes, then awarded them the power of jurisdiction. The *pronoia* system granted Byzantine lords either lands or the income from them, some for a limited time, others permanently. This brought about a situation similar to the western feudal system because it was a comparable form of lordship over land and people. In this way, a shift occurred in the Byzantine agrarian system from smallholdings to large properties. This did not cause a radical change in agricultural production. Neither *exkusseia* nor *pronoia* created a novel entrepreneurial system with novel ways of organizing farm labor—let alone of creating a group of people like the *familia*—as had happened with the Frankish manorial estate system. We are essentially talking about a power shift, not an agricultural reform.

———

The Byzantine system of *pronoia* has occasionally been compared to *iqta'* in the caliphate, and the Byzantine Empire is said by some to have followed the route taken by Arab states in this regard, rather than choosing the path of the European West.[90] Leaving aside the aptness of the comparison, the various forms of distributing land to dignitaries or of tax farming (*Steuerpacht*) that had existed in Islamic countries since the time of the Abbasids have nothing to do with the Frankish manorial estate and the forms of manorial lordship it spawned.[91] Creating these means of supply had no more to do with an agricultural reform than the Byzantine *pronoia* did. The *iqta'* and tax farming were not molded by an agrarian economy in any way, shape, or form. We certainly cannot consider them to be the results of an agrarian revolution the way we do the manorial system that was being born at the same time in the Frankish Empire. On the contrary, such means of supply were more of a hindrance than a help to an agrarian revolution because they would have jeopardized any initiative from the body of smallholders.[92] Unlike its counterpart in Europe, the Islamic agrarian revolution did not bring about any change in the types of manorial lordship.[93] Accordingly, nothing even came close in the caliphate to creating a power structure of lordship based on a royal manorial system like the one in the Frankish Empire or its neighboring or subsequent empires. The caliphate was—as was the empire of the Byzantines and the Sassanids before them—a state funded by taxes on agriculture, and it drew its resources directly from its peasant subjects.[94] This type of state was the rule during the Middle Ages in the great empires of the Near and Far East; the Frankish Empire was the exception.

———

The Chinese agrarian revolution during the Song dynasty did not bring about structural change leading to a type of manorial system any more than the Islamic agrarian revolution did. There was no counterpart—either in Islamic horticulture or in the new rice economy in China—to the productive, organized labor that coordinated demesne with tenancy and that was associated with the beginnings of the cerealization process. Corvées seem to have made little sense in a farming economy; they were certainly not suitable for wet rice cultures. But we nevertheless find stirrings of an embryonic manorial system during the Song dynasty. To rank this early development as a form of feudalism alongside French patterns under the Capetians would surely not be a clear distinction.[95] It would be more to the point to characterize it as "manorialism without feudalism."[96] Trends in this direction are visible in the binding of tenants to the soil, in the settlement of freed farm serfs, and in the exercising of judicial rights over independent peasants. This last example was occasionally put into practice but was not recognized in law any more than it would have been if an owner of a large estate had claimed for himself a tenant's dues and services that were actually owed to the state.[97] China never got as far as forming jurisdictions such as banal lordships.

Little is known about the structure of large estates in China. There does not appear to have been a system of stewardship or similar kinds of organization.[98] It seems remarkable that the courts of great landowners often possessed important facilities such as water mills and storehouses.[99] There were water mills in Buddhist monasteries, too, which were generally instrumental in initiating the growth of manorialism— although monasteries were to be dissolved later, in the Tang dynasty— not least because of the wealth of their property holdings.[100] A key facility was the granary, typically combined with a hall of ancestors and a school run by clans.[101] As social structures, clans and the manorial system are difficult to reconcile with one another. The colonization of the South as part of the Champa rice revolution led to a considerable increase in the clans' power in that region.[102] Very different forces competed side by side during the Song dynasty. Elements of the manorial system on large estates represent one such influence, but what is important is that they never became a determining factor in the long term. "Manorialism without feudalism" was merely an episode in the Song dynasty. In the long run, structures of direct state access to the dues and services of its peasant subjects were retained.

———

These cross-cultural examples of analogous, and markedly contrasting, agricultural systems illustrate the uniqueness of the manorial and the hide systems as they developed as components of the early medieval agrarian revolution in the Frankish heartland. The diffusion of innovations from the agrarian economy and the agrarian system very often took place in concert—as, for instance, during the great process of the colonization of the East. This was not true in every case, of course. The manorial system also expanded southward, following the Frankish Empire's specific forms of lordship and penetrating into regions where typical features of the Frankish agrarian revolution did not exist. A large, relatively homogenous area was created by these expansionist movements, which were characterized on the whole by identical or similar structures of the agrarian system and the social order it generated. Over against this "core Europe" was a "peripheral Europe" that did not acquire these structures until a relatively later date—or not at all. Here we can list Ireland, Wales, and Scotland in the West; the area of eastern Europe beyond the Trieste–St. Petersburg line that was unaffected by the colonization of the East; the entire Balkan region; southern Italy, which was formerly Byzantine, along with the southern part of the Iberian Peninsula that was under Moorish rule for so long a time. The political, economic, and social evolution of many regions in "peripheral Europe" took a different turn because of their clinging to other, traditional agrarian systems.

As Frankish models of the manorial system advanced through various parts of Europe, they met with quite diverse forms of social organization. In the North and East it was mainly tribal societies that were transformed by the new structures of the agrarian revolution. They could be organized in very different ways, as was evident in medieval Europe. When Germanic tribes settled on Roman imperial land—the Franks, Burgundii, Alemanni, and Bavarii among them—categories of descent as a basis for social order played a role, a role very different from the one it played in the thinking of Celtic tribes in Ireland or of Finnish and Baltic tribes around the Baltic Sea. Consequently, the resistance of the various tribes to manorial structures was highly differentiated from region to region. In many places these structures rapidly superseded more ancient types of tribal organization; in many others, not at all. We can say that the manorial system and the tribal system were basically incompatible at the social level of the peasantry. The economic rationale for an agriculture based on manorialism cannot be harmonized with dominant organizing principles based on kinship. That proved to be the case throughout Europe wherever the social organization of the manorial and hide systems supplanted tribal structures. In many non-European empires, the lack of such organizations might well have contributed to the local preservation of social forms based on descent in spite of the strong influence of a central state—for instance, in China and the Islamic world.

Not the least reason for the breakup of tribal societies resulting from manorial organization was the system's involvement of unfree people. The Frankish manorial system turned slaves into *servi casati* with their own farmsteads. Slaves and unfree laborers had a strong personal relationship with their lords, not with their kin. The manorial *familia* of the early Middle Ages formed a new grouping made up of unfree laborers, serfs, bondsmen, slaves, and peasants bound to the soil; there was no place for the legal concept of the slave as object (*sachenrechtlich*) that existed in antiquity. The basic distinction between freeman and slave became blurred as new forms of personal dependency emerged, after which, slavery was no longer a factor in European agriculture. It did not reappear until the period of early colonialism with its plantations—but then slavery was based on a completely different agrarian system and was found primarily outside the continent. The abolition of slavery from the agriculture of medieval Europe did not mean an absolute victory over slavery, although it was becoming increasingly restricted to the states on the European periphery.[103] Nowhere on the continent did it play a significant part in the organization of lordship equal to the role it played in Islamic countries, for instance. In Europe, it was not slavery per se that shaped the relationship with the lord; it was very probably the manorial subject's lack of freedom *deriving* from slavery that formed the relationship with his lord.

Special types of lordship systems arose from more ancient European tribal societies, but also from the social structures of the Roman Empire underlying the agrarian system of the Frankish Empire. Systems of lordship in which an elite was "outfitted" with manorial rights in return for military, administrative, or jurisdictional service are usually branded as "feudalistic." Although this concept originated in European forms of the feudal system, it is surely useful for a general typology of forms of lordship.[104] In comparative studies of feudal forms of lordship, the relationship between the prince and the elite has received, as a rule, most attention. The uniqueness of European feudalism will not become apparent, of course, until a cross-cultural comparison takes into account the special nature of manorial organization on which feudalism is constructed.[105] In this respect, the agricultural system that emerged in the heartland of the Carolingian Empire has had an abiding influence on European forms of lordship.

The manorial system of the Carolingian Empire was premised on the personal relationship of the lord with his *familia*. This principle continued to have a more or less potent effect on every form of the manorial system that grew out of it. Any and all lordship in this tradition was lordship over a group of people organized "as a family." Even royal lordship was no exception in this regard. It was underpinned by the manorial system—as were monastic lordship and the nobility's lordship—so that the king's lordship was directly over the land and its people within the more restricted area of the royal estate. Seen in a longer perspective, manorial features gained in importance because the evolution of the European state was rooted in them. The peasantry was tightly integrated in local corporations of different lordships. And these proved to be just as stable, over time, as were the mediating forces that incorporated them into larger imperial structures. The belabored phrase "feudal fragmentation" does not do justice to the conditions of lordship in the Carolingian Empire and its successors. On the contrary, the organizing features established at that time have shown themselves to be very long-lasting. The same is true for the regulating of rural areas as a result of the manorial and hide systems.

The ordering of lordship based on the *Villikation*, and on the estate systems derived from it, was markedly decentralized. This is apparent from the simple fact that the king would travel from place to place, supported in his royal authority by his royal estate. The courts (*Pfalzen*) of the Carolingians and their successors stood in stark contrast to the grand residential cities of the caliphate or East Asian empires, whose courts did not imply a weaker form of princely lordship, just a different one. Other decentralizing trends in the organization of lordship resulted from the disbursing of land to those noble lords obliged to give service as cavalrymen. That a nobleman was able to keep horses locally seems to have been a prerequisite for this service. Warriors on horse who exercised lordship over land and its people had seats scattered throughout the countryside. With the rise of banal lordship in the tenth century, these buildings were frequently converted to fortresses, so that they took on the particularly striking appearance of a seat of lordship. The numerous seats of noble and ecclesiastical lords demonstrated how decentralized the organization of lordship was—a pattern without counterpart in the formation of empires outside of Europe. The decentralized organization of lordship contributed in turn to a certain autonomous heft shared by the peripheral regions over against the center. This would promote federalist tendencies in the later history of Europe.

Manorialism and the hide system were just as significant for European social history on the macro level of organized lordship as they were on the micro level of household organization. Claude Lévi-Strauss has coined the term *société à maison*, which fits these developments in European society like a glove.[106] Households seem to have been a central ordering principle in this case. In a peasant society, at any rate, the primary social orientation was to one's house, not to one's relatives. This was an essential distinguishing feature vis-à-vis societies oriented toward descent; these kinship patterns were located around the periphery of Europe, but in the main they lay beyond Europe's borders. Belonging to a household was clearly a basic building block of the bipartite estate in the Frankish Empire. On the one hand, there was the villa, the lord's manor, or the steward's manor, with its resident labor force, the members of which were not tied to one another by kinship; on the other hand, there were the farms of the *servi casati*, that is, of the unfree laborers and their dwellings, as well as the *coloni* who were bound to the soil and therefore to a house. Together they formed the *familia*, an overarching household embracing several households. This system lived on in the hide system, whether it was based on *Villikation* or on *Rentengrundherrschaft*, which appeared later. The *Hufe* was defined exactly the way the English hide was, as a *terra unius familiae*. Affiliation with a farmstead of this kind was socially determinative, not the affiliation to a group through kinship. The hide system standardized the size of these farms, measured by what it was required to produce for the lord. The system became the crucial principle by which rural society was structured throughout the entire area into which the Frankish agrarian system spread. This was also true after the original units of production had long been fragmented into half- and quarter-hides, or after the growing number of cottages came to outnumber undivided hides. The household continued to be the defining unit.

Three

The Conjugal Family and Bilateral Kinship: Social Flexibility through Looser Ties of Descent

The concept of the hide as *terra unius familiae* solidifies a relationship between the family system and the agrarian system. The organization of the early medieval Frankish manorial system was, as we have seen, strongly, if not definitively, affected by new forms of agriculture. True, innovations in the agrarian economy inadequately explain innovations in the agrarian system. Nor is it any easier to interpret villa and hide systems as the sole determinants of new structures in family and kinship systems. Religion appears to have greatly influenced the organization of traditional family and kinship patterns the whole world over. It was precisely during the early Middle Ages that expanding religious communities created large-scale unifying trends in family life that manage to resonate to this day. This can also safely be said about Islam. In the Far East at the same time, there was a renewal of Confucianism and of its particular notions concerning the family in China, which were adopted in neighboring cultures. And we might ask as well how strong the effects were of early medieval Christian missionary work on family and kinship in Europe, particularly in places where a special social dynamism was at work. The family therefore seems to be an eminently suitable topic for an analysis of phenomena linking diverse causative factors in a cross-cultural comparison.

We owe a debt to the records kept on the great, emerging Carolingian monastic estates, which yield fundamental data for a relatively large population group on how peasant families were composed. The most important source is the so-called *Polyptichon Irminonis*, the property register (or polyptych) of the imperial abbey of Saint-Germain-des-Prés near Paris, dating from 825 to 828. It includes 1,378 peasant households totaling 7,975 individuals. An analysis of the makeup of the households brings interesting trends to light.[1] The vertical extension (that is, over generations) of the household is strikingly limited. Of the 3,470 women recorded only 26 were mothers of *mansus* peasants; among the male members of the peasant household there was not one identified as a father. Families extending vertically upward therefore played a minimal role. The same holds true for those families extending vertically downward: only two grandchildren of *mansus* peasants can be clearly identified. It is evident that this dearth of multigenerational families was intentional. The stem family was almost completely absent as a type, since the criterion of patrilineal descent was probably of no consequence for the family structure. The lateral, or horizontal, extension of the household was by no means restricted to brothers. It might have included a sister's spouse marrying into the family, but the people primarily involved were not related. We do not find a basic family composed of men related through patrilineage (these are also called agnates). Farmhands and maids who were not related to the peasant seem to have formed a significant group within the household. We may surmise that they would move between *mansus* and villa and also between smaller and larger *mansi* as well.

The organization of work was obviously a prime need that determined the makeup of peasant households. This is evident in the high percentage of married couples among farm owners. The two central roles of a peasant and his wife had of course to be filled, always. As the amount of arable farmland increased, the number of household members grew apace. To cover all the particular tasks was obviously the key criterion, not the coresidency of a descent community built on everyone's being related.

We can identify very similar family structures—where peasant families were tied to estates—in other regions of the Carolingian Empire in the ninth century. For instance, we know about Prüm Abbey in the Eifel from the *Prümer Urbar*, a property register that Abbot Regino drew up in 892–93, and we learn about Bavaria from an 820 *precaria remuneratoria* (remunerative donation) between Abbot Sigifrid von Engelbrechtsmünster and Saint Emmeram's Abbey in Regensburg.[2] It appears that we can generalize from these two cases. It was primarily the parent-child group that lived on the *mansi* and hides of the Carolingian *villicatio*, occasionally with servants or people who may or may not have been their relatives. This kind of grouping indicates a conjugal family structure.[3] From today's point of view, this type of structure does not seem worth emphasizing at first glance because it has become generally accepted in European societies. But there are past and present forms of the family where the primary relationship is not between spouses: the father-son relationship is the dominant element. Patrilineal family structures like this one are not evident in the sources for the manorial system in Carolingian times, at least not north of the Alps. And so we may surmise that the standard kinship system for the composition of family households was also not geared to patrilineage—to the extent that this system played a role in the estate-based peasantry. Clues for a bilateral pattern are found in the names of the *mansus* peasants and their family members that are listed in property registers. If, say, in Irmino's polyptych from Saint-Germain-des-Prés, a certain Gautsaus and a certain Faroildis had two sons called Gaudus and Faregaus, or a Rainordus and an Agenildis had a daughter Ragenildis, then we can clearly see that essential elements from both sides of the family were consciously meant to live on in the children.[4] This was not about a unilineal system of kinship but a bilateral one. Conjugal household organization and bilateral kinship system are correlated. Wherever the spousal connection is central, the genealogical lines of both parents will be more significant for their children.

———

We might well assume that, in later times, forms of the family that turn up in Carolingian property registers would have spread in tandem with the hide system. Strong evidence for this tie comes from the congruence of the frontier of the medieval colonization of the East with one of the most importance borders between two differing European marriage and family patterns.[5] In 1965, John Hajnal published his trend-setting article "European Marriage Patterns in Perspective," in which he worked out the far-reaching differences between marriage patterns east and west of a line running from Trieste to St. Petersburg, basing his findings on demographic data from more recent times.[6] No essential differences regarding age at marriage and marriage frequency showed up in a comparison of the East with the situation outside Europe; but in the West, the age at marriage and the number of singles were higher than average. In spite of factual and terminological criticisms of Hajnal's European marriage pattern,[7] we can say today that his thesis has been acknowledged in essence, even by his early skeptics.[8] Massimo Livi-Bacci has steered us toward special developments west of the "Hajnal Line"—which matches up with the colonization of the East—that have received less attention.[9] Historically, a relatively high frequency of marriage has been recorded in some border areas of the western pattern. This was mainly the case in southern Italy and Sicily (which was Byzantine for a long time during the Middle Ages), then in southern Spain (which was under Moorish control for many centuries), then in Ireland (which has often been referred to because of its unique development), and finally, in parts of Finland (although it lies to the east of St. Petersburg), which was powerfully influenced by eastern structures right up until the nineteenth century.[10] These findings strongly suggest that we look for the origin of the European marriage pattern in medieval times, while noting that the agrarian conditions created in the Frankish Empire were especially important. Medieval sources back up the assumption of an early origin of this type. Thus it was precisely the analysis of the family forms listed in Irmino's polyptich that have led us to suspect that conditions propitious for promoting the European marriage pattern were already present by the early ninth century.[11]

The cross-cultural comparison of the unique marriage pattern in Europe west of the Trieste–St. Petersburg line provides but a first piece of information about the special nature of family development in this area. Age at marriage and marriage frequency can be subject to a certain amount of variability according to time, space, and social stratum. Not all of these fluctuations should be seen as the result of particular processes of structural change in the family. But these family structures and their determining factors, which are persistent in spite of cyclical variations, are of prime concern for the question of a family development specific to Europe. John Hajnal later connected his European marriage pattern with the corresponding rules for household formation; Peter Laslett has worked out organizational trends in traditional European domestic communities on the same basis.[12] This typology was essentially derived from data from the eighteenth to the twentieth centuries. Only a few scattered quantifying sources have been analyzed that went farther back, which raises the question whether more recent structural features that are considered to be specifically European can identify lines of continuity from Europe's earliest times.

The correlation of marriage and family patterns by region on the European continent is different for Hajnal and Laslett. Hajnal originally juxtaposed "western" to "eastern," equating the former with "European," but he later restricted this pattern to northwest Europe.[13] He considers Scandinavia to be part of northwest Europe, including Iceland but excluding Finland, the British Isles, the Netherlands, the German-speaking area, and northern France. Laslett, on the one hand, speaks of a "Western family," while on the other, he distinguishes two large areas which he calls "Northern and Western" and "Southern and Eastern" and which he then subdivides into "West" and "West/central or middle" or in "Mediterranean" and East."[14] Two reasons could lie behind this terminological fuzziness. On the conceptual level, the two-track understanding of Europe as a physical geographically fixed continent and as a historically formed social and cultural space presents some difficulties. On the factual level, a problem arises in that, with regard to the patterns concerned, clearly defined borders similar to those in the East are not found the farther into the South we go. In the "West" there are transitional zones and areas of interference in the South that are difficult to categorize precisely, if at all. Both Hajnal and Laslett seem to see the northwest of the continent as the area where the "Western" or "European" pattern is centered. This fits in with the picture of a social dynamic emanating from the heartland of the Frankish Empire from the early Middle Ages on.

In his survey "Characteristics of the Western Family Considered over Time," Peter Laslett grouped specific characteristics of the European family into four areas.[15] His first point is that family membership "in the West" was confined for the most part to parents and children, the so-called nuclear family or the simple family household. Carolingian sources show that with regard to generational depth this form of the household was clearly dominant at the time. The prevalence of the two-generation family over the three-generation one is so apparent that we may suppose that two were desirable and three were in general deliberately avoided. Manorial labor policy within the *villicatio* system included the possibility of just that, especially where *servi casati* were concerned, that is, serfs/*servi* (*Unfreie*) who had settled in their own homes.[16] Individuals, divided families, or even whole ones could be moved around within the *villicatio*; once the sons and daughters of *mansus* farmers were grown up they could be required to serve in the manor itself or on the farms of other *mansus* farmers. Most important of all, the lord of the manor could influence the time when his subjects could marry. This seems to have been the key to the way *mansi* were settled, and it guaranteed the dominance of the nuclear family. Sons had to marry as soon as they took over their father's farm or any holding that was available. On the other hand, they were not allowed to marry as long as they did not run a farm independently. We know this from a way of handing down the farm (*Hoffolgepraxis*) practiced in later times, for instance, in central Europe.[17] This was an effective way to avoid having three-generation families, which would have been a particular burden on the peasant and would have impaired his ability to fulfill his duties to his lord. This restriction probably would have already been the practice in Carolingian times.

To marry only when the younger generation had become independent necessarily meant marriage at a late age. And now we come to Laslett's second point, which follows Hajnal's European marriage pattern: the relatively late age for mothers, which for Hajnal appeared to be particularly characteristic of Europe. We have but a few early medieval sources that enable us to calculate values for the average age at marriage. We can make a start in this direction with the 813–14 registry of the peasants who belonged to the Church of Saint Victor of Marseilles.[18] It records very high numbers of *baccularii* and *baccularie*, meaning unmarried people over fifteen. These people make up a percentage of the population that is clearly higher than that of children between the ages of two and fifteen, which can lead us to conclude that the marriage age of both sexes was a relatively advanced one. Sources of this kind are of course rare exceptions. We can see much more clearly the predominance of the parent-child group in practically all the regions of the Frankish Empire where the hide system was widespread. And this peasant family structure inclines us to believe that even then the European marriage pattern, organized around the establishing of a household, prevailed.[19]

Laslett's third characteristic of the "Western family" can also only be documented for the Carolingian period indirectly. He calls the minor age difference between spouses a phenomenon specific to Europe, particularly with regard to the comparatively high percentage of women who were older than their husbands. Irmino's polyptych for Saint-Germain-des-Prés mentions only 86 widowers and 133 widows among 8,000 peasant subjects. These are relatively low values, from which we can deduce that there was fairly strong pressure to remarry soon after entering widowhood. From the lord's point of view, this policy was obviously economically reasonable and rational. The *mansi* farmers could not carry out their prescribed dues and services until the two key positions in the household were filled. It was also in the lord's interest if a widowed peasant woman were to marry an able-bodied young man who could step into the deceased farmer's place. In European peasant societies, the comparatively high percentage of these second marriages where the woman was older might well have resulted mostly from this kind of influence by the lord. It is typical of regions where the hide system shaped agrarian structures.[20]

Laslett's fourth characteristic of the "Western family" is particularly important: the presence of servants who were not kin but were still fully recognized household members. These servants who were not related by bonds of kinship did not serve in one household throughout their lives but only from youth to marriage. This is why Laslett speaks of "life-cycle servants."[21] Life-cycle servants were people in the household who were different from the domestic slaves found in many cultures, and they were sometimes included among members of the family. They formed an element specific to the family structure that enables us to relate it to the hide system. As a matter of fact, these domestics were often found in property registers as early as the Carolingian period.[22] We cannot determine whether or not the servants mentioned in these sources were adolescents because no ages were given, but this was probably the case, since they were all single. The roots of this institution can probably be located in two moves concerning labor within the manorial system.[23] First, lords or their officials most likely took into the manor the younger children of their *mansi* farmers if their parents did not need them for helping take care of their own household—the children might have been young girls who could do some weaving in the *gynecaeum*. Relocations of this kind were most probable, given the close interconnections between manor and *mansi* in carrying out work because of *Robotleistungen* (compulsory work by the peasant on the domain). A second step seems to have been the labor arrangement agreed upon between the different *mansi* of a manor, or the hides, that involved servant labor. This kind of work, too, can be traced back to the ninth century. It probably originated with an initiative on the lord's part. There is no definite proof from the ninth century that children of *mansus* farmers would frequently move to other farms, something that was to become typical of servants in the hide system in Europe. But it does seem thoroughly consistent with the basic principle of the labor arrangement within the framework of the *villicatio*. The specifically European institution of servant work matches up with the manorial system in so many ways that it is highly probable that they shared a common root.

All four characteristics of the "Western family" that Laslett lists go far back in history. All four indicate the influence of the manorial system. All four can be connected with the hide system. All four point toward different facets of the conjugal family: In the simple family household, the conjugal couple were the nucleus. The uniquely advanced age at marriage was tied to the fact that marriage established the independence of the master or mistress of the house. The significance of remarriage can be explained by the necessity of having to keep the key positions of master and mistress of the house filled. Working as a servant was correlated with marriage at an advanced age. Until you could marry, you were kept in a dependent position that was essentially a child's role—if not at your parents' house then living as a farmhand or maid with a family unrelated to you. These four characteristics of the Western family can be supplemented by still others that similarly involve a strong conjugal family, that also have roots going well back in time, and that also display connections to the hide system.

———

The institution of the peasant's retirement especially distinguishes the rural family in the history of Europe.[24] It was by no means found in every major region where the manorial system played a formative role. And even where retirement was standard practice, only a minority of the peasant population made use of it. Nevertheless, it seems noteworthy because it exhibits essential elements of the family structure that are of broader significance. Retirement was based on the opportunity to relinquish the position of master of the house because of old age— not an obvious matter of course when compared with other cultures. After turning the farm over, the old farmer and his wife would continue to live there along with their successor, and they were entitled to have him take care of them. The new master—their son, as a rule— could now marry. The family was not reconstituted around father and son but around the new couple. A three-generation family was thereby created where the authority resided in the middle generation, not the oldest one. The obligation of caring for the older couple fell to the farm rather than to people. If the son who took over the farm were to sell it, then the new owner would have to care for the retired couple.

We can observe similar situations in modern times, which indicates that the origins of the peasant's retirement lay in the hide system. When this institution began, it was probably the lord who made the decision as to how and when the hide or *mansus* was to be passed on.[25] The heavy plow made special physical demands, and if the *mansus* farmer was no longer able to meet his plowing duties on the manor, or could not work his land, then he was replaced. As late as the modern age the lord's approval, or that of his officials, was required for regulating retirement. The farther back we go, the more we can expect to find the influence of lordship on issues of succession. In this regard, the *servi casati*, as well as the *coloni*, were certainly unable to regulate these matters on their own authority during the Carolingian period. Giving up the position of authority because of advanced age was a far-reaching intervention. Internal family arrangements by themselves cannot account for the institutionalizing of this break in the life cycle or the family cycle. The hide system, as an organized form of lordship, provides a plausible interpretive context for the institution of retirement.[26]

Above and beyond the regulation of retirement, the lord's right to decide matters of succession on his subject farms appears to have been important for the rural family within the European manorial system. In times and places where manorial influence on transferring the farm was strong, the peasant family structure could suffer from the diverse consequences of different retirement strategies. The peasant's rights of inheritance—which may have had the appearance of passing on the property according to standardized rules—were secondary, compared with the lord's strategic needs.[27] In spite of the great diversity of the lord's succession strategies, we can nevertheless begin with a commonality of certain principle interests.[28] In general, a lord would push for a single heir to the farm; its dues and services had to be maintained, something that would be jeopardized if several heirs were to take over. The resultant division into smaller properties might also have a negative effect on overall productivity. The hide as *terra unius familiae* should be retained if at all possible. Furthermore, it was in the lord's interest that the new farmer on the hide be able to work hard and well. The lord was primarily concerned with criteria of productivity and not of kinship. The most efficient successor might just as well be the eldest or the youngest or another son, or else a son-in-law, or someone outside the family who would then be the widow's new husband.

Given the lord's concerns, there were two consequences for independent peasant families: his interests promoted flexibility by working against strengthening certain rights of succession among kin, and they favored singular succession, that is, there was to be but a single heir. Here we can speak of "unigeniture," as long as it was the farmer's child who was taking over the farm. Unigeniture was only one variant among the many kinds of inheritance rights based on the lord's strategies for passing on the farm. And, in more modern times, it is more likely to show up in those areas on the margins of Europe that had adopted the manorial system earlier. It does not appear to have been preserved in the Carolingian heartland.[29] But unigeniture was probably originally found wherever the hide system had spread; it was most certainly a special characteristic of any part of Europe where the manorial system was established. The multiplicity of its later forms obscures the common features of its origins. As the influence of the manorial system declined, forms of the peasant's rights of inheritance arose that allowed for dividing the property and for singular succession—the latter permitted the transfer *inter vivos* (during the farmer's lifetime) or after his death, via primogeniture or ultimogeniture, and so on. Not only the male line played a role in all these modes of succession, but so did the female: the transfer of a farm to women marked a critical difference when compared to its opposite arrangement, the right of equal inheritance by all the males in the family that was found throughout eastern Europe.[30] These fundamental types of handing down ownership, along with the family forms related to them, were not restricted to the peasant's world: they characterized all of society. Only princely and noble houses occupied a special position in this regard.

The most important feature of the Western family is doubtless the fact that it was not constituted by bloodlines but was a house or household community largely free of kinship ties. English-language family research uses the very apposite concept of the "coresident domestic group" that is based on family contexts in more modern times but also fits medieval ones perfectly.[31] Living in a family that includes non-kin goes back a long way in European history. The hide system was probably key to this type of family life, but this will not have been the only source. Criteria for organizing labor were the leading factors in the composition of a household that farmed a hide. The life-cycle servant was the prototype of the non-kin coresident who would be taken into the family to augment the work force temporarily. We already find him listed in the polyptychs of Carolingian monastic estates in the early days of the manorial system. Other kinds of unrelated coresidents were added wherever the manorial system continued to develop in Europe: inmates, lodgers, guests, foster children, and elderly retirees and children left behind by previous owners who shared no bond of kinship.[32]

It was not only the need to supplement the labor force that was given priority when these people were taken in or allowed to stay permanently; other concerns were protecting and providing for all members in the household community. Compared to the farm's economic function within the hide system, these were secondary developments made possible by weakening the lineage principle. The hide as *terra unius familiae* was first of all a family operation, and the peasant couple was at the heart of the family enterprise's organization. All other forms of family enterprises in medieval Europe were modeled along these lines. The house or household was the prevailing structure that provided for interaction and a sense of belonging together. This is palpably mirrored in family names originating during and after the High Middle Ages. Wherever the manorial system existed on the continent, it was not the names based on descent that counted most, as in eastern Europe, but those derived from dwelling places.[33] The frequency of names like Maier, Huber, Hofer, Hofmann, or Lechner in German-speaking areas indicates to what extent this "domocentric" family—centered on the household—had grown out of the manorial and hide systems.

The domocentric family in those parts of Europe where the manorial system was in place very likely also influenced the kinship system. The focus on the married couple, the modest number of generations, the frequency of widows' remarriage, the taking of servants and other non-kin into the family group, and especially the handing down of the farm according to economic logic—all these must have worked against unilinear kinship patterns. As a rule, manorial and lineage structures are in conflict with each other, but this opposition alone cannot satisfactorily explain the profound changes in European kinship systems. These processes of change go back to well before the rise of the Frankish agrarian system; in spatial terms, they extend beyond that system's area of dissemination. So we must look for other determining factors that might allow us to understand why Frankish systems of agrarianism, lordship, and family could evolve in which lineage principles play so minor a part.

––––––––

Fundamental trends in the changing kinship systems in Europe can best be deduced from the modified kinship terms in various European languages.[34] Initially, terminological analyses will only yield very general clues that other indicators can differentiate and refine. Above all, these analyses cannot allow us to conclude anything about how some of the concepts used mirror a certain contemporaneous social order. Kinship terminology often outlasted by hundreds of years the conditions that gave rise to it. We frequently come upon phenomena of cultural lag when tapping this linguistic source in the attempt to learn about historical kinship systems, but that a change in a social situation must have preceded a change in vocabulary lies beyond the shadow of a doubt. Three major transformational processes illustrate this statement with regard to European kinship systems.

We can describe the first fundamental trend in the shifting of European kinship terms as the gradual appearance of the same, or parallel, terms for paternal and maternal relatives, which is best shown in the expressions for a parent's siblings. All the Indo-European languages of Europe originally distinguished between the father's brother or sister and the mother's brother or sister. Take Latin as an example: the father's siblings were called *patruus* and *amita*, and on the mother's side, *avunculus* and *matertera*. In Middle High German the terms were *Vetter* and *Base*, *Oheim* and *Muhme*. As the history of almost every European language evolved, distinctions between paternal and maternal relatives became neutral. And so French used *oncle* for both parents' brother (derived from the Latin word for a maternal uncle, *avunculus*) and *tante* for either parent's sister (following from the Latin word *amita*, a paternal sister). These bilaterally applied terms spilled over into other languages, for instance, English and German. Similar parallel nomenclatures developed that were based on kinship terms in one's own language, in Polish, for example. Greek was the first European language to eliminate the terminological distinction between the father's and the mother's side, a transition that began as early as between the fifth and third century BC.[35] Vulgar Latin in late antiquity was next. All the Romance languages derived from Vulgar Latin have the same terms for both sides of the family: Italian, Sardic, Rhaeto-Romance, Provençal, French, Catalan, Spanish, Portuguese, Sephardic Spanish, Aromunian, and Rumanian. This process was therefore complete by the early Middle Ages throughout the territory of the old Roman Empire.[36] The first Germanic language to undergo this change was English, beginning with the Norman Conquest.[37] Basically the same change occurred in German in early modern times.[38] There were two different developments in the Scandinavian languages. One tended to completely equate the father's and mother's siblings by using the same terms; the other did too, but formed compound words to differentiate the sides of the family. This was the case, for example, with *farbror* and *morbror* in Swedish, and with analogous forms in Icelandic and Scottish English.[39]

These descriptive compounds were fundamentally different from the completely independent terms for each parent's siblings in the early phases of Indo-European languages. It was not a matter of eliminating the opposition between the paternal and the maternal sides but of essentially equating them, as is apparent from the structure of the terms themselves. And in the majority of the Slavic languages, too, the process of parallelizing outlined above took place, first in Czech and Polish, relatively late in Russian.[40] The Slavic languages in the Balkans, on the other hand, have retained a differentiating terminology for kinship to this day: Bulgarian, Macedonian, Serbian, and Bosnian still have concepts distinguishing between a paternal and a maternal brother.[41] The same holds for Albanian, where even parents' sisters are differentiated. In this region the great process of transforming European kinship terminology, which emanated from southeastern Europe 2,500 years ago, has not yet reached its end.

A second fundamental trend in the transformation of European kinship terminology is the use of identical terms for blood relatives and in-laws. This paralleling process was also at work in Vulgar Latin during late antiquity. The term *cognati* at first referred to blood relatives who were not under the authority of the *pater familias*. Sometime around the fourth century, this concept underwent a substantial expansion: it came to include "affined" relationships (the Latin *affinis* refers to persons related by marriage). The word *affinis* therefore fell into disuse in late antiquity and was replaced by *cognati*. In-laws now became, through marriage, like blood relatives.[42] This sense of *cognati* survives in kinship terms in the Romance languages. The trend of using the same terms is even more pronounced in another terminological complex. French, Dutch, English, and German have a suite of concepts for relatives by marriage that is formed from compounds made from the designations for nuclear family members.[43] *Beau-père* corresponds to *schoonvader*," "father-in-law" to *Schwiegervater*, *belle-mère* to "mother-in-law." The same goes for *beau-frère*, *belle-soeur*, *beau-fils*, and *belle-fille*. All these related people had no names in Latin or Old High German that were in any way similar to the names for their closest blood relatives. Originally, the terms in all Indo-European languages for relatives by marriage were unmistakably different from those for blood relatives. This assimilation process poses the question whether there was a reevaluation of marriage at some time in medieval history and whether the terms for kinship produced in so doing were revalued along with it.

The third basic trend in the transformation of the European kinship terminology is unique by its very nature and therefore especially
instructive for understanding the whole process of change: the increasing number of parallels in the nomenclature of blood relatives and
so-called spiritual relatives.[44] A spiritual kinship was originally established by sponsorship at baptism. Then, in the wake of this model,
other relationships came into existence that were created around other
sacraments—relationships that eventually were regarded as kinship. In
general, ties that were instituted on a religious basis were conceived
of as kinship ties. Traditionally, spiritual kinship has no place in the
kinship typologies found in ethnology. This seems readily understandable because the typologies were, after all, drawn primarily from the
analysis of non-European kinship situations. But spiritual kinship is a
specifically Christian and European phenomenon that was essentially
propagated outside of Europe by Christian missionaries. Inside Europe,
it is found during the Middle Ages only in societies converted to Christianity. The new kinship terminology created by baptismal sponsorship corresponded to the system of relationships created by marriage:
parallel terms for kinship by blood were formed, with *patrinus* and *ma-
trina*, the godparents, juxtaposed to *pater* and *mater*, the biological parents. The terminology in most Romance languages followed the Latin.
The English terms are also very expressive—godfather, godmother, and
godparents—which have their counterparts in German. In Latin, godchildren were called *filiolus* and *filiola*, in parallel with the terms for
biological children, but the relationship between godchildren and biological children had no descriptive term that would indicate a sibling
relationship. On the other hand, the words for male and female godparents from the biological parents' point of view seem to have been all
the more important. In Latin they are *compater* and *commater*, that is,
cofather and comother, and their relationship to each other was *com-
paternitas*. We first meet a rudimentary application of blood kinship
terms to godparenthood terms in the fourth century.[45] Not until about
the end of the sixth century was there any documentation for *compater* and *commater* in the Western Church, from where they spread
eastward.[46] Spiritual kinship through sponsorship at confirmation or
witnessing a marriage played a minor role by comparison, but even in
these cases we can discover concepts analogous to blood kinship. It was
apparently significant that the priest officiating at the baptism and the
godfather could both be considered as a *pater spiritualis*. The idea of a
paternal role for the priest was not of course restricted to child baptism.

It belonged to the more general concept of spiritual kinship Christians had among themselves—one that was expressed above and beyond the physical relationship mainly by expanding the terms "brother" and "sister."

———

The decisive factor in this great transformation of kinship terminology in Europe was the influence of Christianity. This is more obvious in the parallel terms for blood and spiritual kinship than it is in the two basic trends discussed earlier. From an analytical perspective, we can distinguish three levels of influence: first, direct and intentional influence on kinship systems via canon law; second, indirect structural changes to fundamental elements of Christianity; and finally, the ramifications of traditions from classical antiquity that cannot be considered specifically Christian but that Christianity passed on to medieval societies.

The first type of influence incorporates first and foremost the church bans on marriage between relatives. These began in the fourth century and reached their zenith in the eleventh. The influence of these canonical norms is perfectly evident in the English terms for relatives through marriage such as "father-in-law," "daughter-in-law," and so forth. What is meant in these terms by the word "law" is canon law. Even though a "law" is not mentioned by name in similar, parallel terms, canon law is the motivating force behind them.[47] The basic principles guiding the changes in terminology, or the assimilation of terms, were exactly the same as those in Christian churches that prohibited marriage between relatives. The development of unions categorized as incestuous was a highly complicated affair in the various Christian churches and was in no way uniform at all times and in all places. But these unions share some basic tendencies: the equating of the paternal and the maternal lines, of blood kin and kin by marriage, and the inclusion of spiritual kin in the family. It was easily recognized from the relevant bans on marriage who was seen in the early Middle Ages as being related to whom from a Christian standpoint, and the bans were added to, step by step, right up into the High Middle Ages. We find it difficult to comprehend today just how preoccupied the era was with the fear of incest—and not only in the various Christian churches but in Jewish circles as well. Any explanation that it came "from upstairs"—for example, from the Church of Rome and its desire for possessions—can be dismissed a priori.[48] A foremost Christian source that fueled the ban on marriage between relatives was the principle of *una caro*, which, in the biblical formulation, held that married partners are "as one flesh."[49] It logically follows from this principle that the equating of relatives on both sides was as necessary in the parents' generation as it was in the next. The bilateral kinship system and the conjugal family were both based on this fundamental idea. A second basic Christian thought that significantly influenced the concept of kinship was the primacy of "being born of the spirit" over "being born of the flesh."[50] Seen against this background, the marriage bans applicable to "spiritual kin" are easier to comprehend. To put it in general terms: the value of baptism in Christianity appears to have been a deciding factor in the devaluing of lineage ties and in the upward reevaluation of spiritual relationships.

With the sacrament of baptism and its consequences for conditions of kinship, we come to the second level of interconnected effects: the structural elements of Christianity that indirectly influenced kinship structures and their relevant terminology.[51] A Christian joins a congregation through baptism; Christianity is a distinctly congregation-based religion. The most important religious acts are carried out within a congregation, especially the celebration of the Eucharist, but also the most important rites of passage, such as baptism, marriage, and burial, which do not take place within a descent group or household. Consequently, Christianity does not attach any religious significance to family and kinship groups.

Christianity is a religion of salvation. The relationship of all the great salvific religions to the family range from ambivalent to critical.[52] One aspect of this stance is individual justification. Salvation is a matter of an individual's act, not of the "merits of the fathers." And the individual cannot be charged with the "sins of the fathers." Lineage is insignificant as far as the salvation of souls is concerned.

Christianity is a missionary religion. It turns to all people without any restrictions as to their birth. It differs in this from tribal or ethnic religions, which by their very nature cannot venture beyond their real or fictitious lineage communities; Christianity works against thinking in categories of descent.

Christianity is a monotheistic religion; it is oriented toward a single god. Even when, in Christian history, the veneration of saints often jeopardized the monotheistic character of the religious community in practice, it never went as far as ancestor worship, which is why there are no Christian groups or actions based on lineage.

Christianity is a religious community organized on the basis of a hierarchical bureaucracy. Church offices are not inherited but passed on by consecration. The thought that charisma can be inherited is foreign to Christianity in principle—another fact reducing the importance of lineage.

Christianity is, finally, a thoroughly ascetic religion. The idea of a special holiness accrues to the monk and the priest who lives like a monk. The monk leaves his family and kin behind and renounces sexuality. All these factors running counter to thinking in lineage categories were part of Christianity from its earliest beginnings. Many of them can be attested by the sayings of Jesus in the Gospels.[53] These traditions led to a confrontation with clan and tribal societies in the course of Christianizing Europe from the early Middle Ages on, which in turn led to a radical transformation of kinship systems and terminology in those societies.

That the great transformational process of European kinship terminology must also have had pre-Christian roots is clear from a sequence of events over a long period of time. The rudimentary beginnings are found in the Greek language from the fifth to the third century BC, and it is very likely that broader conditions further influenced these processes. Traditional ancient Greek kinship terminology was probably transmitted just the way ancient Greek traditions were, by and large within a Christian context. The term "brother" can serve as a concrete example. The expansion of the concept of "brother" beyond blood kinship in several Romance languages led to the emergence of a new term for the biological brother.[54] This can surely be traced back to a Christian influence, but the phenomenon itself is not genuinely Christian.[55] In various Eastern religious communities, strangers became "brothers" by means of initiation ceremonies. The teachings of the Stoics spread the term even further. The use of "brother" in urban contexts for a brother in office or a fraternity brother goes back a long way. Hellenistic urban culture may be regarded as the social foil for this phenomenon, which, thanks to Christianity, continued to live and have an effect on medieval European societies. Similar causative connections must be considered from many angles to understand the changes to European kinship systems and their terminology.

———

The growth of European kinship terminology is a key indicator of fundamental transformations in the kinship systems of Europe. We can rarely decide precisely when these changes took place. Other ways of expressing kinship can yield more in this regard: naming a newborn child to give it its place in the family and among kin, forms of marriage, handing down property and the position of authority, burial customs, blood revenge and the surrogate of paying restitution, and so on.[56] There were, in all these areas, both a standardized order of things and concrete, individual cases that offer a preliminary basis for interpretation. These forms enable us to classify kinship phenomena according to time and space, to make class-specific differentiations, and to elucidate divergent and unique developments. The overall picture can be corroborated by investigating other kinship patterns: making paternal and maternal lines equal—and equating relatives by blood and marriage—as well as expanding our understanding of kinship as a whole. To put it differently, there was movement in a direction toward bilateral kinship and the conjugal family, both linked to looser lineage ties.

The assumption that Christianity was definitive in this development meets with a rather basic difficulty: the peoples of southeastern Europe, in whose languages the ancient pattern of Indo-European kinship terminology has been preserved to this day, have been Christian for more than a millennium. The situation was similar in Russia, where the transformational process came into play very late, although the new kinship terminology had already won out. Both in Russia and the Balkans, some aspects of strongly patrilineal kinship and family systems were evident quite apart from the archaic kinship terminology. In passing on a property, the common property shared by agnates or by equally inheriting male members of the family was dominant. The fundamental family structure was patrilineal, whether it was a complex, extended family or a simple one. In the western Balkans, we can find even today patrilineal descent groups or tribal groups subdivided into descent groups.[57] These relationships are far removed from bilateral kinship, the conjugal family, and less binding ties of descent.

The tension created by the family and kinship situation in the mountain regions of the western Balkans—but also in eastern and southeastern Europe as a whole—alerts us to the fact that monocausal explanatory models are inadequate. The situation can only be explained by the mutual interplay of economic, cultural, and religious factors, along with those of lordship. The circumstances on either side of the Hajnal Line provide a fine example.

A plausible argument can be made that it was the hide system that ultimately shaped family and kinship structures to the west of this line. The pattern of handing down the farm, the age at marriage, the use of servants, and other features mentioned earlier all point in this direction. On the one hand, the hide system presupposed an agrarian situation; it is not found where there is no cerealization—witness the situation in Friesland and Ireland. On the other hand, the hide system was located within a particular sociocultural framework: it could not have existed in a society with strict patrilineal family and kinship ties, for it required a complicated balance in the division of labor: between the manor estate and independent peasant farms, and between and within the individual hides throughout the family life cycle. If a lord's steward in the ninth century had to be careful about maintaining the basic patrilineal structure in every one of these domestic communities, then the manorial system would probably have soon broken down. Now there were most certainly other conditions obtaining at the time in the Frankish heartland, the cradle of this system. The *servi casati* were born into a complete lack of freedom, so that for them there was no kinship system to take into account. But no indications of patrilineal structures appear in the peasant population either, regardless of whether a peasant had free or half-free parents. It is difficult to ascertain which factor was preeminent here. Within the Roman Empire, the Frankish heartland stood under the centuries-long influence of a Mediterranean urban culture that on the whole resisted thinking in terms of lineage—an influence that involved Christianity as well, which had a special effect on this way of thinking. We can say that Christian social structures, to this extent at least, were a prerequisite for the creation of manorial organization within the Frankish Empire and for the family and kinship structures it influenced.

But what we can safely say about the origins of the hide system does not apply, even implicitly, to the diffusion of that system. During the course of its expansion it collided with societies in quite different agrarian and sociocultural situations. Ecological conditions might well have blocked the system's progress in Friesland and the North Sea coastal marshes. It is striking that those are precisely the areas where we find features—such as the clan system and most notably blood revenge—that typify societies strongly oriented toward lineage.[58] Blood revenge is rooted in a concept of kinship in which all men of a group are treated almost like a single person. The agnates together are considered to be the bearers of honor—and guilt. That is why the guilt of one relative can be avenged on someone else who had utterly no part in the deed. The idea of blood revenge is completely incompatible with Christian views of guilt and innocence. Nevertheless, the institution of blood revenge was still alive in several European societies even after they were Christianized, those in the North Sea marshes among them. Was Christianity so superficial in those areas that it did not adversely affect these traditional regional practices? Did Christianity perhaps somehow come to terms with them in spite of the apparently unbridgeable antagonism between them? Or was it the hard ecological and economic facts that prevented the transformation into a manorial system, thereby stabilizing the clan system and the code of blood revenge? These two, differing explanatory models were not, admittedly, mutually exclusive in any way, nor were they elsewhere in Europe.

During the colonization of the East, family and kinship patterns in the hide system were transferred to regions that very probably would have been organized differently before then. This can be assumed at least for the Slavic and Baltic tribes east of the Elbe that were incorporated into the western system during the High Middle Ages. There are many clues indicating that patrilineal structures probably used to exist in these societies. These include patrilineal, complex family forms and evidence of unpartitioned male inheritance, but also settlement patterns and burial practices.[59] Whereas changes in the makeup of the household, in the practice of inheritance rights, or in the organization of dwellings point to the influence of the new agrarian system, the shift away from common graveyards belonging to descent groups and toward community cemeteries implies Christian influence. The introduction of Christianity always preceded the introduction of the hide system throughout the entire area of colonization in the East—often by only a slight difference in time, but occasionally centuries earlier. The time sequence was never reversed, anywhere. The western agrarian system at all times found a state of affairs where Christian conversion had either relaxed or weakened older patrilineal patterns. This process had already paved the way for the transition to a bilateral system of kinship and the conjugal family.

This loosening or weakening effect vis-à-vis patrilineal lineage principles may be assumed in general for areas of Christianization to the east of the Hajnal Line as well—whether from the Western or the Eastern Church did not matter, because the Great Schism changed little on this point after 1054. To give examples from the three levels of causation discussed above: There was an attempt in eastern and southeastern Europe to implement church regulations for marriage, with their extensive bans on exogamy.[60] Then, too, the principle of the congregation dictated religious life even there. Finally, the idea of fraternity taken over from Hellenistic urban culture was still alive and well, thanks to the mediation of Christianity. There was nevertheless strong opposition in eastern and southeastern Europe that led to very long-lasting patrilineal descent patterns—varying in intensity in different regions but standing on the whole in marked contrast to the situation west of the Hajnal Line.

———

Turning to economic factors, we will begin by singling out two, which can be accurately called the "forest" ecotype and the "mountain" ecotype.[61] As we have seen in an earlier chapter, slash-and-burn economy had played a very important part in the history of northern Europe. It may well have been preeminent in more ancient times in many areas where the three-field system became dominant after its introduction as the East was colonized. The slash-and-burn economy's significance for family and kinship organization lay, on the one hand, in the necessity of having a gender-specific division of labor and, on the other hand, in the need for several adult males to cooperate. These needs were already taken into account by equal male inheritance rights and complex patrilineal family forms. Structural principles of this type were able to persist for a long time, even when their related economic form had long been abandoned.

The same is true of the second ecotype, which appears to have been typical primarily of the western Balkan region. A pastoral economy based on sheep and goat raising had defined people's lives there for thousands of years. And a rigid, gender-specific division of labor was a necessity for the region's pastoral economy, as was cooperation among several adult males. Accordingly, one could find complex patrilineal family forms, but beyond that there were patrilineally structured groups that, together, formed tribal communities.[62] The survival of these tribal relationships to the present day appears to be unique among European societies, as is the survival of vendettas within those very same structures.[63] Here is the extreme polar opposite of the developmental trends that led to the characteristic syndrome of bilateral kinship, the conjugal family, and less binding descent ties elsewhere in Europe.

———

Even though this diametric pattern represents but a thinly settled area in an out-of-the-way, mountainous region, the contrast makes it obvious which of the family and kinship patterns was possible for Christian Europe. And this opposition allows us to reach some conclusions about

causative factors and their origin. It was not only patrilineally structured family groups raising sheep by means of a strict gender-specific division of labor that defined the pattern; nor was it only property rights
based on equal male inheritance; nor only descent groups attending to
governance and military tasks; nor only villages divided into districts
by lineage groups, so-called *mahallas*—a division reflected even in the
location of the graves in the cemetery—all of these together were part
and parcel of the characteristic syndrome of family and blood relationships that were so powerfully centered on lineage.[64] A specific form of
ancestor worship in Christian guise was part of the same syndrome.[65]
The form is of particular importance because it qualifies the thesis that
Christianity is incompatible with ancestor worship, because it shows
that pre-Christian religious ideas continued to be significant for family
and kinship structures, and most of all because it is crucial for a comparison between Christian and non-Christian religions in regard to the
family.

The most concrete expression of pre-Christian ancestor worship is
the feast of the patron saint of the household in the western Balkans.
It is regarded as one of the most solemn feast days—if not *the* most
solemn—in the Christian year. Unlike Easter, Pentecost, and Christmas, it is not celebrated in the parish but in the home or together with
relatives. The feast day varies from home to home, and celebrating the
patron saint of the household is passed on from generation to generation. The tie with a lineage nexus is unmistakable. Indeed, persons
venerating the same household saints are often forbidden to marry lest
they be related through the patriline. It is important to have sons, because otherwise the Slava candle, which is lit on the patron saint's feast
day, will go out. It is clear from the liturgy for the feast day that not
only the saint is celebrated but also the patrilineal ancestors. The *čitula*
(the list of forefathers that is read aloud) plays an important part here.
The ancestor worship is strictly patrilineal and goes much further than
the Christian commemoration of the dead. This can be seen in the sacrifices connected with the patron saint's feast day. There are many regions where even the blood sacrifice of animals is found. Sacrificing to
one's ancestors means that they are expected to do something in return. Here we can still see the residual effect of the idea—typical of ancestor worship—that propitiating one's ancestors will induce them to
provide aid and protection in the lives of their descendants. When and
how ancestor worship came to be connected with festivals of Christian
saints cannot be unequivocally reconstructed, but we can take it for

granted that this religious component played a decisive part in the continuity of patrilineal descent forms in the western Balkans.

The social and cultural contexts of the western Balkan feast of the household saint broaches the question of broader connections: are there other eastern and southeastern regions in Europe showing links between patrilineal family structures, on the one hand, and practices of ancestor worship going back to pre-Christian times on the other? Ancestor worship is attested relatively well, through written documents and corroborating archeological finds, for the period before the eastern Slavs were converted to Christianity.[66] Vestiges of this practice have been found in folk customs up until rather recent times. The cult of the Russian *domovoi* (household spirit) displays many parallels with the feast of the household saint in southeastern Europe.[67] It is tied to lineage, not to place. It does more than simply commemorate ancestors: it sacrifices to them—and reciprocal actions are expected from them. The sacrifice is performed by the father of the house or the eldest man in the family. The Russian Orthodox Church fought hard and long against this domestic form of ancestor worship, as is shown in written documents stretching back into the early Middle Ages. Nevertheless, elements of ancestor worship were partly assimilated into church liturgy, for instance, through the celebration of "Ancestors' Days," or "Parents' Days," or "Ancestors' Saturdays."[68] The Eastern Church was more tolerant than the Roman Church regarding the syncretism of pre-Christian traditions. Orthodox Finns have likewise carried over remnants of pre-Christian ancestor worship into the present day.[69] It has been shown recently that the widespread cult of the house snake among Baltic peoples harks back to certain ideas from ancestor worship.[70] Elements of ancestor worship were common throughout areas of eastern and southeastern Europe up to more modern times. This appears to have been a significant determinant in the way patrilineal families and kinship were first organized, as well as in their tenacious survival.

A single factor cannot by itself account for the historical relationships of family and other kinfolk to the east of the Hajnal Line any more than it can to the west of it. There is also great variation within each of these two large areas. Socioeconomic and sociocultural determinants must be taken into consideration on both sides. In the example of the western agrarian pattern, it was the hide system in particular that encouraged trends toward the conjugal family, bilateral kinship, and the loosening of genealogical ties. But these developments clearly would not have been possible if Christianity had not been moving in the same direction for centuries. If we proceed from a multifactorial explanatory model for the East, then we can immediately discern that there was in its vast region no unifying colonization that might possibly have produced structural analogies with western kinship and family systems. Quite different forms of a subsistence economy seemed to have led to the region's characteristic social forms. To the slash-and-burn economy in the forests of the Northeast and sheep raising in the mountains of the western Balkans, we could certainly add several more types of subsistence economies. It might well be that a feature common to them all was the fact that they had existed for a long time within a tribal organization. The degree of urbanization in the East was relatively small, as were other socioeconomic advances that might have been capable of disrupting tribal structures.

Although as a socio*cultural* factor the adoption of Christianity did have this effect, the patrilineal organization of family and other kin was preserved, even in religious matters and in spite of the conversion of much of the East. This cannot be accounted for by differences of dogma between the Eastern and the Western Churches. The Eastern Church's greater degree of tolerance toward the pre-Christian traditions that did survive—a tolerance that led to a degree of syncretism—has already been mentioned. Another perspective might explain this East-West difference by pointing to the greater penetrating and integrative power of the Western Church in asserting its creed and ritual practices. However that may be, many pre-Christian forms of ancestor worship—especially in the domestic practice of worship—did live on in the East for a very long time after the tide of Christian conversion. This phenomenon cannot be interpreted as a dichotomous, side-by-side existence of two different religious forms; for those who practiced them, they belonged together. Elements of ancestor worship were fully integrated into religious practice in many regions of eastern and southeastern Europe. The tenacity of these patterns leads us to conclude that they played an essential part as a pre-Christian substratum. This was most assuredly not the case in the West. The verifiable forms of ancestor worship in the Greek tradition, which were even more powerful in the Roman one, had long disappeared by the time Mediterranean Christianity opened up the northwestern part of the continent. That ancestor worship can lead to patrilinearity has been observed everywhere, but these kinds of connections are difficult to track in the history of Europe. A comparison with non-European cultures will make the functional connections clear.

———

China is an ancient, advanced civilization shaped by ancestor worship in a special way: the practice has been called the "key to Chinese culture."[71] This is certainly also true of its family and kinship relationships. A scan through Chinese history suggests, however, that it was not self-evident that ancestor worship would exert a definitive influence in China for such a great length of time. Ancestor worship has been documented through divinations and sacrificial objects at least since the Shang dynasty (ca. 1500–1050 BC) and by textual sources since the early Chou period (1050–500 BC).[72] Confucian ethics embedded it in a philosophical-religious context: in the Han dynasty (206 BC–220 AD) Confucianism rose to become the state orthodoxy.[73] But strong competition was to follow, first from Taoism, then especially from Buddhism.[74] At the same time that Christianity was being established as the state religion of the Roman Empire in the West, Buddhism became the dominant religion in China in the East. Both religions are remarkably similar in their attitude toward family matters. Both are strongly oriented toward asceticism; they call for a person to leave the family—the Chinese phrase for "to become a monk" is *chu-chia*, "to leave the family" or "to leave home."[75] Leading a communal life with other monks is valued more highly than living with the family. Both are religions of salvation that strive for the perfection of the individual. Both give preference to moral behavior over descent.[76] Both hold to a view of a life to come that is incompatible with the belief that the dead live on in the grave or an ancestral shrine. It follows that both reject any thought of sacrificing to one's ancestors.[77] Buddhism in China inevitably had to come into conflict with Confucianism. Leaving one's ancestral family to enter a monastery was not the only bone of contention: a Buddhist monk would infringe upon a basic Confucian principle when he cut off his hair and his beard—the body was seen as a gift from one's parents, including one's skin and bones and hair; it was felt that to abuse this gift would demonstrate a lack of piety.[78] The monk would renounce his family name and take on a new one placing him within a continuum with his teachers or the Buddha.[79] He would be celibate, thereby refusing to carry on the male line of the family—in a society where even the premature death of an unmarried youth was regarded as an act offensive to one's ancestors, an especially grievous fault.[80]

Buddhism was preeminent in the early Tang dynasty (618–906).[81] Then Neoconfucianism began its ascent, bringing an anti-Buddhist reaction along with it. All Buddhist monasteries were disbanded between 842 and 845, and any monks and nuns in them were forced to join the laity. Incidentally, this measure affected not only Buddhist cloisters but those of the Manicheans and Nestorian Christians as well, that is, other religions based on the principle of salvation.[82] Neoconfucianism brought about the complete triumph of ancestor worship; its rites were now clarified, standardized, and canonized.[83] For its part, Buddhism continued to be an important factor in Chinese life and made some compromises with traditional views of the family.[84]

And so two developments in the history of religion—in western Europe and the Far East—that at first ran parallel ultimately went in diametrically opposite directions during late antiquity and the early Middle Ages. In the West, a Christianity inimical to the rights of genealogical descent maintained its supremacy. In the East, a Neoconfucianism supportive of genealogical descent won out. These divergent developments are significant not merely for the history of the family and kinship; taken together, they provide a key to our understanding of how two cultures and societies can develop so differently.

The quite substantial differences between Europe and China are more apparent if we take the terminology of relationship as a prime indicator of kinship systems. There is no Chinese counterpart to the paralleling processes discernible in Europe from antiquity on. Quite the opposite: an exceedingly complex system of kinship terminology was further differentiated and elaborated upon in China. Claude Lévi-Strauss speaks in this connection of an *"overdetermined system"* against which he counterposes the "marked tendency toward *indetermination*" in European cultures.[85] Historical dictionaries from after the second century BC list no fewer than 340 Chinese terms for the different relationships between kinfolk.[86] Typical examples of this differentiation are the terms for "uncle." The European languages have managed with one word since the great transformation in its terminology, whereas Chinese has five different words, depending on whether the father's older brother (*bo*) is meant, or his younger brother (*shu*), the mother's brother (*jiu*), the aunt's spouse on the father's side (*gufu*) or on the mother's side (*yifu*). This example also illustrates the four distinguishing criteria on which this terminology is by and large based: gender, relative age, the generation, and filiation. The strict separation of the paternal and maternal lines is particularly vital. A distinction is drawn in China and Tibet between "relatives of the bone" and "relatives of the flesh"; it also is found in a larger area stretching from India to Siberia and embracing the Mongolian and Turkic peoples of Russia.[87] What is meant by these terms are paternal and maternal relatives, respectively, with the former being given preference.[88] As this example demonstrates, the terminological distinction between an older and a younger brother is made only in the patriline, a differentiation that the Chinese system of kinship shares with many cultures in its extensive surroundings.[89] It occurs as far away as southeastern Europe, where Indo-European roots cannot even begin to explain this specific feature. In this case we might have to think about possible influences from the steppe nomads who came from the East.[90] Connections between kinship terms and practices of ancestor worship can be discovered in many of these neighboring cultures.[91] Age is a structuring principle where rank is determined by proximity to one's ancestors. Strict patrilinearity results from the necessarily unilinear carrying out of ancestor worship. In China, the further development of ancestor worship led to an elaboration of the kinship system. The heavily tiered system of degrees of mourning played a very important role here; mourning a relative in a society practicing ancestor worship looks quite different when compared to a religion based on salvation because of their disparate notions of life after death.[92] Nothing in Europe remotely resembles the peculiar nature of Chinese obligations regarding mourning, because its hierarchy is established by degrees of relatedness. The systematics of these regulations is reflected in the systematics of the terminology.

The traditional rules of marriage in China display the same basic outlines of a strict patrilineal ordering of kinship that is found in the terminology of kinship. From the Tang dynasty on, legal codes prohibited marriage to a woman from four classes of relatives: first and foremost, marriage to women with the same surname, then to widows of members of the same household, to women of another generation of fairly close kinship on the mother's side or by marriage, and finally to sisters from the same mother by a different father (half-sisters).[93] In China identical surnames meant in principle descent from the same patriline. The ban on marriage was valid even if the common ancestor was a long way back in the male line. The Chinese firmly held to these basic principles of exogamy, which can be found in many other cultures in Eurasia with an analogous kinship structure.[94] In early medieval Europe, far-reaching rules concerning exogamy were also established, but they were confined to certain degrees of relatedness.[95]

They mainly concerned the paternal and the maternal lines completely symmetrically. In China, on the other hand, the emphasis on the father's line led to crass inequalities when it came to enlarging the list of banned female marriage partners. The fact that marriage to one's sister from the same mother but by another father had to be expressly forbidden clearly shows that greater importance was granted to the father in determining kinship. The exclusion of women of a different generation points out yet again the importance of belonging to a particular generation, or indicates one's place in the hierarchy of age, or both. Marrying relatives from the mother's side was not forbidden in principle. In earlier times, marriage in China even between cross-cousins not only used to be permitted but was common practice.[96] Among China's neighbors it can be found up to this day as a preferred form of marriage.[97]

A second ban on marriage within a closer circle of relatives brings up a secondary phenomenon in China: the ban on levirate marriage, that is, when a widow marries her brother-in-law. This type of marriage was practiced among the Chinese peasantry as late as the sixteenth century, although it was forbidden in principle.[98] One of the functions of marrying a brother's widow—found in many cultures worldwide—is to produce sons for a man who has died without a male heir, in order to maintain the continuity of ancestor worship.[99] Posthumous adoption took over this function in classical China.[100] It may be that the levirate bond played a greater part in more ancient times in maintaining the patriline, but it was a form of marriage to a relative that Christianity attacked in Europe, fiercely and early on. In only one region has it survived to this day in spite of the church's bans: the Western Balkans.[101]

The basic principle of patrilineage that lies behind Chinese family and kinship systems is plainly visible in the institution of adoption.[102] In the age of Neoconfucianism, adoption was the preferred way of ensuring the continuity of the family and sustaining ancestor worship. Only someone with a son could become an ancestor after his death. Offerings made by the male descendants assured his forefathers' continued life. Anyone not receiving ancestral offerings would wander around as a "hungry ghost," bringing misfortune upon the people.[103] And so it was of the most vital importance—and also the supreme duty toward one's ancestors—to guarantee the continuation of the patriline. Whenever this was not possible through natural means, then one sought aid from nonbiological kinship. Posthumous adoption, a form corresponding to the levirate marriage, was an extreme example of the devices contrived for achieving this end.[104] In levirate law, the widow of a man who died without a son provided a male heir by marrying a younger brother or another agnate for religious reasons; the same procedure was followed if a widow adopted a son after her husband's death, after seeking his agnates' advice.

Adoption during a man's lifetime was more frequent than posthumous adoption. Men without sons were to wait until they were forty before adopting so as to avoid having adopted sons and biological sons at the same time. Forty was the recommended age for taking a concubine—another strategy to avoid being without a son.[105] An adopted son in China, unlike in other cultures, was to be an agnate of the adoptive father, his brother's son, if possible. According to this way of thinking, the patriline could only be continued by a member of the same clan. He should at least bear the same surname, which was understood as signifying membership in the same descent group.[106] The principle of keeping the generations separate was to be observed within the kinship group. An adopted son had to belong to the generation following his adoptive father's. As a rule, an agnate's younger son was chosen for this; the eldest son, of course, had to perform ancestral offerings for his own father. The adoption of sons-in-law who had married into the family, as was often the practice in Japan, for example, was not the custom in China.[107] By reason of the exogamy principle, a son-in-law would come from another clan. The principle of patrilineage was therefore very strictly adhered to in Chinese adoptions; its roots in ancestor worship are obvious. Of course there would have been deviations from these regulations in practice. There were other motives for adoption, not only the continuation of ancestor worship. The connection between these two phenomena was always maintained—on the normative level of Neoconfucian writings as well as on the practical level of performing ritual worship—and the principle of patrilineage was also preserved as the basis of family and kinship systems.

The institution of adoption grew in diametrically opposed directions in the East and West. To be sure, the Roman adoption process had its roots in ancestor worship, a function of no further interest to Christianity once it had turned against it.[108] There was no religious motivation, in the logic of Christian thought, to uphold the patriline. Sponsorship, which had evolved in the early Middle Ages as a specifically Christian form of artificial kinship, was in a completely different religious and social context; it was not, in the Western tradition, a manifestation of special significance accruing to the patrilineal principle but rather a manifestation of the principle's *in*significance.

In China, this principle did appear to have gained in importance during Neoconfucian times because of the increased impact of patrilineal descent groups, corporate lineages, and clans.[109] On the one hand, Neoconfucian texts propagated a mindset that thought in terms of lineages; on the other hand, colonization in the new rice-growing regions in the Southeast during the Song dynasty provided an opportunity to institutionalize lineage groups.[110] Southeast China is where clans are most firmly anchored to this day. Patrilineal lineage groups held land in common there, principally to serve the needs of a common ancestor worship.[111] Ancestral land was used for cemeteries and ancestral halls, and later for making offerings to one's ancestors. Particularly important was the layout of cemeteries according to the rules of geomancy (*feng shui*). A favorable siting of a grave was a way to encourage an ancestor's benevolence toward his descendants.[112] The lineage group's common land served other, nonreligious purposes as well; for example, a common granary could be built there.[113] The land was frequently used for clan schools that were intended to open the door to a career in the civil service. Any member taking this route would then benefit the entire clan. Land lying next to the undivided common land of a descent group was split among different branches and houses. Land division within the family was the organizing principle for new peasant farms in rural areas; divisions of this kind always occurred between agnates, brothers, or cousins in the same male line. The basic patrilineal household structure was the same after the division as it was before. In this way villages were created that belonged entirely to a single lineage group.[114] In this way, too, surnames turned into village names. Given these conditions, neighbors in a village were also related as agnates; they could perform the rites of ancestor worship either in larger groups or separately, household by household. Knowing this background can now help clear up a much-aired problem in Neoconfucian texts.[115] There were two alternatives for becoming the officiant at family rituals such as ancestor worship, marriages, and the "capping" ceremony for a family member coming of age: some saw the eldest male in the household—the father, uncle, or oldest brother—as the appropriate person, but others recognized the first-born male in the line of primogeniture, calculated from the great-grandfather on down (ancestors were commonly worshipped as far back as that generation). The tension between superior and inferior lineage groups was reflected in this debate, which was resolved in various ways in theory and practice. The patrilineal household by no means had to be the definitive structure.

The situation in western Europe stood in strong contrast to the circumstances in China. In the European hide system, it was not at all the norm for a neighbor to be a relative. To be sure, there were parallels with Chinese patterns in the eastern and southeastern parts of the continent, where equal male inheritance of land was operative. Villages, or districts within them, were founded according to the division of land among agnates.[116] In the western Balkans, we can find organized lineage groups founding settlement units. But there is no evidence in Europe, with few exceptions, of common religious institutions within lineage groups that were similar to the ancestral shrines of Chinese clans. Ancestor worship simply did not become the dominant form of worship anywhere in Europe. Its fiercest opponent among world religions won out instead: Christianity.

———

Along with Christian Europe and Neoconfucian China, there was a third sizeable area that exhibited trends toward the unification of kinship and family structures from the early Middle Ages on, and that was the Islamic world, which at the time still incorporated parts of the European continent. There can be no doubt that this homogenizing process was tied to Islam, which does not of course necessarily mean that it was specifically contingent upon religion.

A glance at the relevant factors concerning family and kinship in other religions can provide an initial orientation. Some possible religious determinants may be excluded a priori. Islam is not a tribal religion, even though it was from its beginning strongly linked to tribal traditions. It is, rather, a universal religion in which ideas of descent must be interpreted with reference to its different context. Moreover, it is not a religion of ancestor worship, which its strict monotheism precludes. The patrilineal structures in regions where it spread can therefore not be traced back to origins rooted in such religious forms. Nor is Islam a religion of ascetic monks as Buddhism is and, to a lesser extent, Christianity. The life of a celibate is rejected out of hand, whereas marriage and reproduction are highly esteemed. Finally, Islam is not a religion of sacraments. The concept of a spiritual kinship founded on the administration of sacraments is foreign to it. It does not have baptism, hence no baptismal sponsorship or any sacramental forms of spiritual affinity modeled on it. If we consider the sacrament of marriage to be a way of creating artificial kinship through religion, then it does not appear to have any counterpart in Islam, where marriage is of a different nature. In the absence of these factors, we can state that Islam represents a third path alongside the lineage-oriented religious forms of the Far East and lineage-unfriendly Christianity.

Various indicators show that patrilineal patterns play a far greater role in the Islamic world than in Christian Europe. The evidence from terms for kinship is clear. Here we must begin with the concepts from Arabic that have influenced other languages in this cultural area, Persian, for example, or Kurdish.[117] Arabic makes a sharp distinction between relatives on the paternal and the maternal side. The father's brother is called *amm*, the mother's brother *khal*. But the paternal great-uncle or a male descendant of the uncle or great-uncle can also be called *amm*; the term refers to a rather closely knit circle of agnates. There is no counterpart to this on the mother's side. The kinship system is therefore not seen symmetrically on either side of the family. Only grandparents have parallel terms. They are called *gadd* and *gadda* on both sides of the family. And so the system essentially corresponds to most Indo-European languages before the great transformational process took place. All it had in common with Chinese society, which was based on the cult of ancestor worship, was the bifurcation of the paternal and the maternal lines; there was no differentiation made as to generation or relative age. Furthermore, we can certainly not speak here, with Lévi-Strauss, of "overdetermination" in light of the relatively meager number of kinship terms. The set of Arabic kinship terms is more ancient than Islam itself.[118] This new, early medieval religion apparently did not cause any fundamental change in the kinship system, which was also true of its further development. There was no change in kinship terminology in the history of Islamic culture comparable to the one in Europe that was influenced by Christianity, as well as other factors.

Judging by these cross-cultural comparisons, the Islamic world possessed an extraordinary complex nomenclature that is a particularly good indicator of specific structures of kinship systems. Many components of names reveal fundamentals of patrilineage.[119] This is true for *nisba*, a term that originally referred to a tribe that situated an individual within a set of agnates whose obligations of solidarity went so far as to include the vendetta. In a secondary development, *nisba* came to indicate topographical descent. The word *nasab* slotted an individual into the sequence of his ancestors, just as *nisba* did into a lineage group. Its patronymic form included as a minimum the father's name—*ibn* (son) for males and *bint* (daughter) for females, the latter indicating that a woman's identity was marked in her name throughout her life by the relationship to her father and not to her spouse, even after marriage. The *nasab* can be extended beyond the father's name to include a whole string of forefathers, but only those in the paternal line—a pointed reference to the patrilineal nature of the system. It is unthinkable that Islamic societies would use matronymics as well as patronymics, as was the practice in many Christian cultures. Religious significance also accrued to the *nasab*. It was said that at the Last Judgment people would be summoned by both their *ism*—their given name—and their *nasab*.[120] So we are dealing with a crucial part of one's name here. Male ancestors with their *ism* live on in the *nasab*, that is, in their descendants. This system has no need to name children after their ancestors in remembrance of them, as was the custom in the Judeo-Christian tradition and in classical times. To choose the father's name for the son is not forbidden in Islamic societies, but it is unusual.[121] But in Chinese ancestor worship there is typically a strict taboo on the names of deceased parents and grandparents.[122] This element of the kinship system represents the opposite pole to Christian Europe, where naming a child after the father had been not only a permissible but a preferred practice since the early Middle Ages, even in areas untouched by classical traditions.[123] Islamic customs for designating given names fall between these two extremes.

The most obvious difference between components of Christian and Islamic names is the *kunya*, so characteristic of the Islamic world.[124] The *kunya* was originally a name given to men and women when their first son was born. It comprises the son's *ism* together with *abu*, the father, or *umm*, the mother. Over time, this name component was expanded. The original meaning of *kunya* showed how enormously important it was to have sons in this culture: assuring the continuity of the male line changed the position of husband and wife to such an extent that their given names were added to. The high value placed on sons fundamentally influenced family structure. The concern with having a son to survive his father resulted primarily in having women marry at an early age. Early marriage was necessary to ensure male descendants, for infants often did not survive and daughters did not count in the continuity of the patriline. The age when a woman was fertile had to be exploited as much as possible. Furthermore, the Islamic world forbade artificial kinships.[125] Muhammad had banned adoptions, so having biological descendants was crucial. This need explains a number of things besides early marriage, for example, divorce and remarriage if a first wife proved infertile, polygamy, and the legitimizing of sons conceived with slaves.

When all this is compared with the European marriage pattern or the conjugal family in Christian Europe, it becomes apparent that the latter structures were only possible in societies where the continuity of the patriline did not play the central role it did in Islam. In southeastern Europe we do find a similar interest in having sons, at times with similar consequences for the family structure.[126] We might begin the search for an explanation by examining relicts of pre-Christian thinking about ancestor worship. This would not be helpful in the Islamic sphere, however, where the sociocultural pattern of strongly patrilineal thought regarding lineage must have had a different root. This pattern would also mark a decisive difference compared with family and kinship relations in China, in spite of structural similarities between the two.

In the rules for marriage operative in Islamic societies, the importance of the patrilineal descent principle is easier to ascertain in the preference for marrying relatives than it is in proscriptions against marriage. The Qur'an (4:23, 24) bars a relatively small number of women from marrying certain relatives. It is forbidden to marry a mother, stepmother, daughters and sisters, aunts on either side of the family, a brother's or sister's daughter, a foster sister, a mother of a wife, stepdaughter, or a son's wife; furthermore, one cannot be married to two sisters at the same time. On the other hand, a levirate marriage—a typical indicator of patrilineal societies—is permitted.[127] The bans on marriage set out in the fourth sura of the Qur'an affect such a limited number of close relatives that a differentiation between the father's and the mother's line hardly seems possible. The high occurrence of in-laws on the list is remarkable. The ban on marrying a son's wife might point to patrilineal families that comprise several generations. The only case where an artificial kinship is cited is that of the foster sister, but there the point is that it is not a relationship originating in a religiously significant act, as is the case with Christian sponsorship.

Marriage preferences in Islamic societies were not stated in the Qur'an as religious recommendations, but the Qur'an does mention the most important among them: *bint amm* marriage with the daughter of a father's brother or of another agnate.[128] A recommendation would surely not have been necessary in order to make that type of marriage legitimate. Indeed, a prominent couple were wedded in this way at the founding of the new religion: Ali, Muhammad's cousin through his father's brother Abi Talib, married Muhammad's daughter Fatima. Clearly, *bint amm* marriage had been prevalent in Mecca before Muhammad.[129] As Islam expanded throughout a large area stretching from Morocco to South Asia, it was opposed by another massive area, Asia, with a long tradition of favoring marriage between cross-cousins.[130] From the point of view of a bilateral and European society, marriage to the daughter of a *mother's* brother appeared to be as near to a marriage to a close relative as was a marriage to the daughter of a *father's* brother. But where attitudes based on patrilineal descent prevailed, marriage between cross-cousins and between parallel ones were two completely different models. The one meant that a spouse was to be sought outside the descent group, the other, inside it. Any explanation for one marriage model can provide *e contrario* a context for interpreting the other. If, in China, the rule of exogamy—marriage *outside of* the descent group—was determined by modes of thought from ancestor worship, then it is difficult to use the same religious roots to account for the preference in the Near East for endogamous marriage *within* patrilineal descent groups. As a matter of fact, we find endogamous marriages in the latter part of the world in association with early monotheistic religions—it was particularly extreme in Zoroastrianism during the Persian Empire, but also strongly pronounced in Judaism.[131] Islam follows in the same line. Of course, this does not mean that monotheism basically favors marrying inside the clan, but it does remove obstacles that might stand in the way of such marriage practices, proscriptions derived from religious ideas found in societies practicing ancestor worship.

There is a scholarly controversy over the positive reasons for the spread of *bint amm* marriage that was present in pre-Islamic times and modified later by Islamic culture.[132] Perhaps the practice originated in the interest of keeping the blood line together, in strengthening the ties among agnates, and in preventing the expansion of affine relationships that would have impinged on the Bedouins unfavorably, given the special ecological conditions affecting them.[133] These explanations may all be correct, and they are not mutually exclusive; however, a comparison with other endogamous cultures in Near Eastern history puts something else into play: the principle of equal birth and the purity of the blood. The daughter of a father's brother can never be an inferior partner in a patrilineal society that does not differentiate between brothers; she in no way compromises the purity of the descent line. This is why endogamy has had a long tradition in the Near Eastern dynasties of princes and priests.[134] We find *bint amm* marriage particularly prominent in Sayid families, that is, among the putative descendants of Muhammad—the only nobility in the Islamic world—and in the families of high-ranking sheiks.[135] The principle of isogamy appears to be crucial for the practice of endogamy in these kinds of lineage groups. In early modern times, the princely houses of Europe also displayed a tendency to marry close relatives, reflecting a similar approach toward blood and equal birth. For more than twelve centuries the Christian Church in Europe fought mightily against marriage between close relatives, and even longer against it in the broader population. This battle made a vital contribution to the establishment of a bilateral kinship system in Europe, which it did not in China and Islamic countries.

In the rearview mirror of history, the two last-named regions reveal profoundly lineage-oriented cultures. The different causes of this go back to their different roots, but their effects were for the most part the same. Patrilineal structures meant that strong ties would organize the family, especially because the male line had to be continued. Christian Europe eliminated these ties by building upon the foundation of classical antiquity. This was overwhelmingly successful in the Mediterranean area, as well as in western, central, and eastern Europe, far more than in the East, where patrilineal traditions dating from pre-Christian times often survived in spite of widespread conversion to Christianity. The contribution of Christianity to the development of kinship and family in Europe did not so much put family life on a new religious footing as loosen traditional family ties. There is very little worthy of note in this regard except for the monogamous marriage of consent, which was elevated to the level of a sacrament. But the socio*economic* factors that were to aid in constituting the European family could not have become as vital as they did without the attenuation of those socio-*cultural* ties. For the broad mass of the peasantry, the framework of the manorial system determined peasant family structures. By and large, labor organization developed into a critical factor in family formation. An essential prerequisite for this process was the fact that Christianity had rendered traditional systems of family and kinship more flexible.

Some scholars, using differences in family and kinship systems as their point of departure, have attempted to characterize the nature of European and East Asian cultures by using catchy labels: "horizontal societies" and "vertical societies."[136] There was no ancestor worship in Europe, at any rate not since its conversion to Christianity. As a result, seniority and an age-based hierarchy were not among society's guiding principles. The comparisons drawn here have shown that the lack of religious ties to ancestors, together with the enfeebling of patrilineal descent ties, can elucidate many characteristics of Europe's special path. This is applicable not only on the microlevel of primary groups, and the place of the individual within them, but also on the macrolevel of more extensive social structures. The loosening of lineage ties created some leeway for striking up new social relationships beyond the family circle. Ties to people other than one's kin played an important part in European social history and made a major contribution to Europe's social dynamics. The weakening of lineage ties also meant a diminution in the way kin and family related socially. We can characterize the two aspects of this process as a trend toward individualization and toward singularization.

This trend had a particularly strong effect upon a certain phase of the life cycle: young adulthood. The European marriage pattern extended the phase of one's youth for a relatively long time, if we view it from a cross-cultural perspective. The pattern itself was determined by looser lineage ties: marrying late could only exist where there was no pressure to continue the patriline. Many people left home when they were young, primarily to work as a servant in another household. That, too, presupposed a relaxing of lineage ties. Working as a life-cycle servant in one of the many paths possible—as a hand or a maid on a farm, as an apprentice or journeyman in a trade, as a nobleman's page— seems to have been a defining experience for European youth. To work as a servant implied mobility, especially true in regional terms, but also in part in the sense of a change of social milieu. All this transformed the world young people lived in. Not only males were affected; girls too changed their surroundings by serving in another household. As a rule, the movement of servants from place to place wouldn't end with a return to the parents' home. The great mobility of young people— qualified by the institution of the life-cycle servant—was therefore an important precondition for European migration and colonization. Furthermore, working as a servant implied special training. Anyone moving into a stranger's household had to learn by knowing how to cooperate. This was particularly true for a trained tradesman but also for anyone serving at a prince's court or in a monastic community. Crossovers with forms of schooling were fluid. At any rate, service in a different household gave direction to one's life; it might complement the orientation in the parents' household or even provide an alternative to it. Finally, working as a servant implied a particularly radical form of separation from the home. The biological parents were often not the definitive socializing authority for the child from a very early age. The model of separating from one's parents acquired more significance in the history of European youth for young people leaving their family home to become life-cycle servants; it also became a common goal, especially for young males. The extended young adult phase of life in the time covered by the European marriage pattern, along with the increase in extrafamilial contacts during this time, seem to have been preconditions for making this phase of life in Europe a crucial phase of individualization.

The comparatively high age at marriage for men but mainly for women finds a counterpart in ways of looking for a spouse. There is little self-determination in this regard in cultures where marriage follows close upon sexual maturation. In Europe, the search for a spouse is a critical component of youth culture, which seems to be especially well developed there—probably because it is a characteristic of horizontal societies. Although the choice of a marriage partner was surely substantially codetermined by family interests and concerns in older European societies, we must not overlook the fact that, given the relatively large age gap between generations, the bride's or bridegroom's parents would no longer be alive in a high percentage of marriages. In addition, being employed as a servant took many young people far away from home. We can generally assume that a particularly high degree of self-determination in choosing a partner was to be found in the lower levels of society, where the age at marriage was especially high. The principle of marriage by consent, endorsed by the Christian Church, enhanced the trend to increased self-determination that was linked to marriage later in life. The Western Church's concept in the High Middle Ages of marriage as a sacrament was based on the view that each partner offers the sacrament to the other. The idea of consent is an essential, fundamental principle of the conjugal family, where the relationship between the couple is central, not ties of descent. What rested on the principle of consent—seen in the long term—was the ideal of marrying for love, but the obverse did as well: the particular vulnerability of a type of relationship based on personal inclination and the freedom to decide for oneself. And so, ultimately, phenomena such as the rise in divorce rates and the larger number of stepfamilies are products of the uniquely European development that led to the creation of the conjugal family.

The relative weakness of patrilineal descent ties in the history of Europe has affected the assessment of the number, sex, and birth rank of children. It seems remarkable, when looked at cross-culturally, that Christianity places no particular value on fertility in marriage; the issue of propagation is irrelevant for religious purposes, which is why religion does not push one toward marriage. On the contrary, celibacy was given a certain preference over marriage, one that was motivated by asceticism. The second element in John Hajnal's European marriage pattern—the low marriage rate—must be viewed in this light. We have already seen that his first point—the advanced age at marriage—can be accounted for by the lack of importance religion attached to childbearing. The low value placed on fertility in marriage is also demonstrated by the fact that infertility traditionally was no grounds for divorce in Europe, even when divorce itself was possible in principle.

In Christianity a son has no particular religious function, in contrast to societies based on ancestor worship; consequently the European tradition gave no preference to having boys over girls for religious reasons. If certain social classes happened to have a strong preference, then the reasons were different. The same applied to favoring the first-born son over his younger brothers. Unlike societies based on ancestor worship and other strongly patrilineal cultures, the European tradition did not deem it necessary to have as many children as possible in order to have at least one son survive his parents. Nor was childlessness discriminated against on religious grounds. As a result the attitude toward procreation was relatively flexible and allowed for changes in the social situation more easily. In modern times this flexibility applies particularly to the process of adaptation that scholars refer to as a "demographic transition." A continuing decline in the birth rate in Europe would demonstrate just how far back its root causes go.

The fundamental distinction that the terms "horizontal society" and "vertical society" attempt to make has to do mainly with the position of seniors in the family and society. In societies based on ancestor worship, those who are nearest their ancestors occupy a position of particular respect; in Christianity, there is no basis whatsoever for this kind of deference to age within the family or society in general. Seniority as a matter of principle is simply not a part of the European family tradition. If several generations are living together, the position of authority is not automatically awarded to the oldest one. The position of father of the house can be passed on during one's lifetime without any fuss or bother. The trend to the conjugal family correlates as a rule with the trend to neolocality—choosing to reside elsewhere rather than with or near either set of parents. In the history of Europe the problem of the elderly having to live alone was hardly ever an issue because of lower life expectancy and the greater number of children. This has become a problem in urban societies in the most recent past and the present. But in principle, the specifically European singularization of the elderly seems to be based on attributes peculiar to this culture.

The fundamental form of the European family is not the lineage group but the household. Its members do not necessarily have to be related through descent or marriage. This makes the system very flexible and adaptable in other situations. It was the needs of organizing labor first and foremost that led to specialized forms of domestic and household communities in agriculture, industry and the crafts, and trade. But other units of working and living in common were organized along the lines of the family as a domestic community, extending to religious communities: the manse, the bishop's palace, the abbey. And even the internal organization of a prince's court (*Hof*) can be understood as an all-embracing household where there were familial social relationships. The process of surrendering certain functions developed in and through the reciprocal connections between these very different household communities. Throughout the history of Europe, the functions of production, socialization, social welfare, and so on, were assumed by institutions that evolved from specialized types of domestic communities. Giving up functions in this manner further contributed to making the European family more flexible.

Looser lineage ties made it possible to form social relationships with people other than kin above and beyond the household unit. Important mediating factors here were the forms of spiritual kinship spawned by Christianity. Different kinds of ties in other areas of life could link up with these quasi-kinship relations that were founded on religion. We can distinguish between two basic types here: those based on equality and those on independence. The former are aligned with fraternal relationships, the latter on the relationship between father and son, or between the master of the house and its legally dependent members. The Christian concept of a fraternal relationship beyond one based on blood was more broadly embedded in the universal belief that Christians were God's children; this concept had a more specific origin in the fraternal model of the monastic community. The spirit of brotherhood that was originally grounded in religion acquired enormous significance in European social history. Guilds, associations, all sorts of cooperatives hark back to the quasi-kinship model of confraternity. Furthermore, the family was relieved of some of its functions through the same kinds of social institutions—in the area of social security, for example, through the so-called *Bruderladen* (benevolent societies of artisans and mineworkers) as early as the Middle Ages. The fact that Europe developed into a horizontal society can essentially be traced back to the influence of these kinds of cooperative social forms.

Here we must emphasize a quasi-kinship connection based on *dependence* that greatly influenced how European society developed: the feudal bond. Domestic law is one of its components—no question about it. Striking structural analogies indicate that there were probable connections with spiritual kinship via sponsorship. Wherever the feudal system took hold in Europe, it not only determined the relationship between the prince and the nobility, it also controlled the relationship between lord and peasant in the configuration of the manorial system. This is surely why the profound transformations in kinship and family systems in Europe were connected with the constitution of specifically European structures of lordship.

Four

The Feudal System and the Estates: A Special Path of Feudalism

"Representative government, which has left its distinctive stamp on political life all over today's civilized world, began with the medieval Estates system. This system in turn had its roots—though not exclusively nor extensively—in the most important countries and not least in the political and social conditions of the feudal system." Otto Hintze introduced his seminal work "Preconditions for Representative Government throughout World History" with these words; they are just as true today as they were in 1931.[1] That parliamentary democracy is a momentous, fundamental consequence of Europe's unique social development is also true beyond the shadow of a doubt. The medieval Estates of kingdoms and principalities (or territories), from which key elements of the modern parliamentary system have evolved, are specific to the historical social area of Europe; they find no parallel in any other culture.[2] And one form of feudalism in a general sense (*Feudalismus*) is just as exclusively European, and it gave birth to the Estates: a feudal *system* based on vassalage (*Lehenswesen*).[3]

Lordship systems defined by the feudal system prevailed in most regions of medieval Europe.[4] This was yet another development that arose in the central Carolingian region between the Rhine and the Seine—we have seen what a matrix of innovation that area was. There can be no doubt that the early medieval innovations it brought forth were interconnected. And so what was said in previous chapters about the determinants of agricultural developments in Europe, the agrarian system, and family structure may now act as starting points for understanding the feudal system as a special European form of feudalism in general.

———

In any systematic treatment of the feudal system, a physical component and a personal one are usually distinguished. The physical side concerns the fiefdom—the fief (*Lehen*, Latin *beneficiium*, *feudum*)—which gave us the general term "feudalism" for political systems in which military or civil officials or both were granted property. The personal component involved the social relationship between the liege lord and the feudal servant (called a *vassus* or *vasallus*); for the latter, the relationship was called vassalage.

Some of the distinctive features of these two components in Europe can be understood through their contexts. A cross-cultural comparison has shown that the bipartite manorial organization underpinning the Carolingian feudal system was a unique agrarian type that can only be fully grasped by taking into account the agrarian revolution of the early Middle Ages. The escalation of the agrarian economy allowed for an expansion of lordship. This holds true both for royal property, provided to ecclesiastical and temporal nobles alike, and for those nobles and clergy who possessed manors and would in turn grant fiefs to vassals. The unique bipartite manorial system and the way it was farmed tended to create hubs of local and regional lordship. Lordship in fiefdoms was, in other words, strongly decentralized—this would have an effect on the Estates later on. It has been demonstrated above that a peculiarity of the agrarian economy was the link between farming and raising livestock; cross-cultural comparisons have shown that there was nothing similar anywhere else, particularly as far as horses were concerned. The agricultural use of horses provided an economic base for western feudal knights to equip themselves; there was a buildup of a heavily armored cavalry at the beginning of the European feudal system. The emergence of lords and knights possessing castles (*Burgherrschaft*) in the tenth century marks a significant phase, which very nicely illustrates the decentralized nature of the lordship structure in fiefdoms. The lord's castle (*Herrenburg*) was as essential to the feudal system, as was service in the cavalry (*Reiterdienst*), which gave its name to chivalry (*Rittertum*). The castle is especially important because it was a distinctive phenomenon of European feudalism.

————

To this point, we have treated the personal side of the feudal system in the context of loosened lineage ties and the apparent kindling of new social relationships in Europe. Vassalage was one of the new, quasi-kinship bonds, and its orientation on family ties made it unique compared with other feudal relationship patterns. Although they were not related, the relationship between lord and vassal was familylike.[5] Its nature has been variously documented, especially in feudal law, and it is why a liege lord, if any of his vassals were to die, would have the right of wardship over their sons and the right over their daughters' permission to marry—rights that otherwise would lie with blood relatives. The quasi-kinship nature of the feudal bond is very evident in the practice of naming a vassal's children after his liege lord and his family.[6] As the feudal system became established during the waning of the Carolingian period, vassals would more frequently name their sons after princes, but this practice was more characteristic of later dynasties. Typical names were Heinrich, Otto, and Konrad in Germany, Hugo and Robert in France, William and Richard in England. Not much earlier, in the ninth century in fact, children were just beginning to be named after their godparents. Godparenthood was wielded as an instrument for creating close ties with one's lord. In the tenth century, the feudal relationship replaced the so-called baptism of submission.[7] A reciprocal relationship appears to have emerged between godparenthood and the feudal bond. The common background here was the weakening of lineage ties by Christianity—a typical aspect of European social development that was indispensable in constructing strong alternative relationships. A further aspect of the structural analogy between godparenthood and vassalage is worth mentioning: the principle of mutual obligation. The feudal bond was characterized by complementary duties: "to protect and preserve," on the lord's part, and "to give counsel and aid" on the vassal's.[8] This reciprocal relationship was essential to the European feudal system, and it was absent from other forms of feudalism. The lord's obligations were key prerequisites in the later development of the Estates system out of the feudal system.

————

More precise details and material can flesh out this outline of the origins of the feudal system, that is, the special form of European feudalism. The first priority is to provide more detail about the military's role. Until now, military issues have been examined only to the extent that they affected or were themselves influenced by parts of the agrarian economy or system. Our twin focus will now be on the army and fortifications.

The feudal system is first and foremost a phenomenon of military organization, and so our search must turn to the military sphere for the system's exact origins. An initial hypothesis might be that certain innovations in warfare produced the unique European form of feudalism.[9] To test this hypothesis, we need to compare different forms of early and later medieval military systems. The medieval feudal system was of course more than just a military phenomenon. If it had not affected the entire organization of lordship, then there would be no explanation for how the late medieval Estates grew out of it. Factors beyond the military must also be explored—factors mediated *via* the feudal system that were critical for the Estates in kingdoms and territories, as well as factors that had a *direct* effect on the genesis of the Estates. We will have to weigh each factor relative to another, but with an eye to the progression family → Estates → parliamentarianism, we can say in advance that the origins of European political systems were definitely shaped by organized military systems, even though few traces of this influence remain today. Any investigation of the origins of Europe's special path will have to look at the way the military was organized.

––––––

The arrival of the knight in armor can be regarded as the crucial military prerequisite for the feudal system's rise and subsequent growth, although this was a long, drawn-out process. We know that during the Bronze Age and early Iron Age there were mounted warriors in south-central Europe with helmets, armor, greaves (shin guards), lances, and shields; they have been called the "first knights," though that may be a bit of a stretch.[10] They were warrior chiefs, clad in all-metal armor, whose weapons differed radically from those of the people they led. It was a long way from those early armored knights to the knights in suits of armor who appeared on the scene toward the end of the thirteenth century and have informed our present-day image of the knight.[11] But we can discover phases of accelerated change and long hiatuses during this protracted development, most importantly during the flowering of the Carolingian Empire. The early phases of the feudal system are connected with this period both chronologically and causally.

The heavily armored Frankish knight rose to prominence in early Carolingian armies.[12] Unlike the Goths, for example, the Franks were mostly foot soldiers; Clovis employed them to expand his great empire.[13] The buildup of the cavalry shifted the emphasis to armored knights—a radical move away from the infantry. This change took place by order of Carolingian mayors of the palace or even of the kings themselves—Charles Martel, his son Pippin, and then, most notably, Charlemagne. An important gauge of this new military policy came in 755 when Pippin postponed the Marchfield—the traditional day for mustering the Frankish army—to the month of May (hence the new name of Mayfield). It was easier for horsemen to find fodder at that time of year.[14] Furthermore, the tribute the Saxons had to pay was changed from cattle to horses three years later.[15] The *fodrum*, a rent paid in horse feed, was introduced no later than Charlemagne's time and by the emperor himself; this was first documented in 792 or 794.[16] The entire Carolingian grain policy was probably a function of the new need to supply an army of armored knights.[17] Many references to an upgrading of the role of the heavy cavalry can be found in Charlemagne's capitularies; his military successes can essentially be ascribed to his massive deployment of these troops.[18]

Equipping an armored knight was a costly affair. His equipment included a lance and shield, a longsword (*spatha*), a shortsword (*sax*, or *seax*), a hauberk, or habergeon (*brunia*)—a coat of metal plates sewn on a leather vest—an iron helmet and iron greaves. The *Lex Ripuaria* from the Carolingian period records the value of a helmet at six solidi, a hauberk at twelve, a sword and scabbard at seven, greaves at six, and a lance and shield at two, the metal parts being by far the most expensive.[19] The total cost of the armament was worth the equivalent of about eighteen to twenty cows—the average *royal* farm at that time kept about forty-five cows.[20] The warhorse was yet another item in the cavalryman's armament.[21] Training to fight on horseback was long and tedious. The *dextrarius* (which gave us the English word "destrier," or charger) favored by the cavalry was very different from the breeds found in agriculture and transport. Packhorses were also counted in a knight's costs, along with their provisioning throughout the many months of military service. The traditional peasant-soldier could not afford these outlays. Charlemagne tried to solve the problem by alternating contingents of soldiers in which a mobilized peasant was equipped by several peasants who stayed at home. But these measures proved inadequate for his military expeditions, so he gave priority to deploying his vassals as armored knights. Army reform required expanding the feudal system, a practice continued by his successors. Within a relatively short time, this produced a feudalized Frankish army—the crucial foundation for an empire built on the feudal system.

This radical conversion of the Frankish army into an army of armored mounted troops has been termed *Verreiterung*, which defines the shift within a larger framework.[22] That is, the reform in the Carolingian Empire should be regarded as just part of a broad reorganization of the army. Many military powers of the time had instituted similar changes long before the Frankish kings did; Carolingian rulers were latecomers in this respect. Admittedly, their military reform initiated an especially long-lived evolution of the cavalry that subsequently affected European chivalry. The longevity of the phase dominated by the knight in armor is a notable phenomenon of Europe's special path. The "millennium of the heavy cavalry" was by no means launched in the Frankish Empire.[23] The beginnings of *Verreiterung* lay elsewhere and must be investigated in any analysis of the connections between cavalry armies and feudalism in general, and forms of the feudal system in particular.

––––––––

Numerous military powers in late antiquity and the early Middle Ages turned their armies into cavalry armies, a process begun by the steppe nomads of Inner Eurasia.[24] Simply put, this process boiled down to a structural problem, the root cause of which lay in some hard ecological facts.[25] The steppes of Inner Asia were not conducive to agriculture, but animal husbandry was generally feasible. Horse breeding was widespread for a very long time. The enormous steppes were bordered by farming areas with ancient, advanced cultures—China, India, Mesopotamia, and some Mediterranean urban civilizations. Again and again these regions were the targets of assaults from warlike steppe nomads. To counter them, the bordering countries had to organize their armies and adapt their weapons to be the equal of those possessed by their mounted attackers. This meant either training mounted troops themselves or hiring them. Every improvement in the nomads' military strike force prompted a reaction from their sedentary neighbors' military. In the Chinese Empire, this kind of ping-pong effect had a particularly long history and also generated new weapons technology different from the West's.[26] The great confrontation with nomads on horseback sparked the development of a trained heavy cavalry in both the Near East and Europe. Their definitive equipment consisted of a metal helmet, scale armor (or leaf mail) for a cavalryman—replaced later by iron (chain) mail—protective armor for horses, a lance and a longsword, bow and arrows, and their most recent innovation, the stirrup, which provided better footing to boost the horseman's efficiency in combat.[27] Many peoples with mounted troops were involved in the spread of these various innovations in military technology: Bosporans, Scythians, Sarmatians, Alans, east Germanic Gothic tribes, Gepids, Vandals, and most notably, the Huns.[28] The Avars had introduced the stirrup into Europe in the middle of the sixth century, and it spread rapidly. It first showed up in North Korea in the fifth century—an instructive example for how widely the European steppe nomads disseminated innovative military technology.[29]

Not one of the steppe nomad peoples who founded early medieval empires with powerful mounted soldiers ever set about building types of lordship similar to the feudal system. On the personal level, the feudal system meant eliminating ties of descent; the ruling warrior group of the steppe peoples, however, was still beholden to the rigid bonds of patrilineage.[30] On a concrete level, the feudal system still meant the possession of farm property, hence a close attachment to an agrarian base. But the steppe nomad empires could never, as a rule, progress beyond the widespread levying of tributes. And so their extremely advanced armored soldiers on horseback never created any feudal structures. On the other hand, some initial stirrings of such structures could be found beyond the Eurasian steppes, the most important example probably being the Persian Empire under the Arsacids and Sassanids.

There are striking parallels between the Sassanid Empire (224–651) and the later Carolingian Empire regarding their effective deployment of armored mounted troops. The Grand Monarch of Persia was a "prince-knight"—as were princes in the West—who officially appeared in armor and on horseback. He too granted heritable fiefs to nobles who fought as cavalrymen, the so-called *dekhans*. Paralleling European practices, these knights held jousting tournaments; novels of chivalry flourished in their circles; there might have been similarities in heraldry and banners.[31] Cultural analogues of this sort are obviously based on feudal structures going back to parallels in the military. There is no question in the scholarly literature that the Persian Empire was a "feudal state," at the very latest by the Sassanid era.[32]

A contingent of knights had long played a major role in the military during the Persian Empire. They were augmented particularly under the Arsacid dynasty from Parthia. The Parthians retained one of their Central Asian traditions: the knight and his horse were armored.[33] A knight's armor had originally been scale armor, like Scythian and Sarmatian armor; the mail shirt came later.[34] The main weapon of the "cataphracts," as the cavalrymen were called, was the bow, which eventually gave way to the lance. The Sassanids retained their predecessors' cavalry formation and actually improved on it. During the reign of the first King Khosrow, or Chosroes (531–79), a cavalryman's equipment consisted of body armor, breastplate, helmet, greaves and arm shields, horse armor, lance, sword, club, battleaxe, a quiver with thirty arrows, two reflex bows, and two replacement strings.[35] Apart from the longer-range weaponry, this is not so very different from what a European cavalryman would have had in the High Middle Ages.

Differences arise if we consider the military context of the Sassanid cavalryman, beginning with the situation of the cavalry within the army as a whole. Whereas the Carolingian cavalry became the dominant—perhaps the only—battle formation, the Sassanid cavalry was one element among many: a crucial role was also played by lightly armed knights and by foot soldiers as archers.[36] A Persian specialty was to deploy elephants as cavalry support.[37] There were differences as well in the economic situation. From the time of Khosrow's reformation of the army, the king had provided the Sassanid "knights" with horses, equipment, and money, if they possessed no assets themselves. An accurate accounting was kept of weapons, pay, and the condition of the horses;[38] the "vassals'" armor was stored in royal armories. Feudalization of the military was therefore limited.[39] The ruler provided armor for his nobles with fiefs in addition to what they themselves supplied. This had no counterpart in the Carolingian Empire and its successors, where the provision of weaponry was totally decentralized. Finally, there were differences in how the cavalry and other troops were paid, and the nature of the payment played a significant part in the Sassanid Empire.[40] Payment for service might have arisen because of the vast income from silver mines, among other sources.[41] In any event it, too, indicates an ultimately incomplete feudalization. A particularly important, long-term difference with the West involved the role of Sassanid "knights" in codetermination. We hear not a word about magnates giving counsel during a military muster, something we know happened at the Carolingian Marchfield.[42] To receive a fief did not grant the "knight" the slightest right to advise the ruler. And so, in spite of feudalization, the development of the Sassanid military followed a completely different route than did vassalage and the feudal system in Europe.

––––––––

Mounted troops were introduced into the Roman imperial army later than in the Persian; the former was not as extensive and had very different social repercussions. But the terminology for the cavalry was the same, which clearly shows the interconnections of the military buildup among rival powers in late antiquity. Heavily armored Roman horsemen were also called *cataphracti* and *clibanarii*; in the former case, only the horseman wore armor, in the latter, both horse and rider did.[43] The Roman army adopted both types of troops in the third century. Palmyra, Rome's ally, had made the switch to a cavalry of cataphracts earlier, which then helped them win victories against their common enemy. During the rule of the emperor Severus Alexander (222–35), Roman cavalrymen were apparently armed with weapons seized as booty from the heavily armored Persian enemy. The creation of a regiment of armored cavalry led to victory on other fronts—in fact, the adoption of Persian weaponry and military tactics proved on the whole to be a sound basis for reorganizing the Roman military in late antiquity.[44] Light cavalry formations were increasingly integrated into the army, diminishing the infantry's importance. The legionary, a foot soldier, had made Rome's military power great, but he lost his dominant position during this period. Doing battle with enormously powerful enemies and their strike force of heavy cavalry compelled the Roman Empire to make adjustments. The Romans were admittedly still quite some way from training an army of mounted troops, in the medieval sense, as a mainstay of their power—there was no consensus as to its military structure or the way the military's socioeconomic base was to be secured. The Romans were in this way essentially different from their Persian opponents, whose use of the heavy cavalry they had adopted.

The major reorganization of the Roman military in late antiquity was carried out under Constantine (306–37).[45] The army was split into a field army and a frontier army based in the *limes castella*. These heavily fortified Roman border positions grew in importance during late antiquity—an indicator of the increasingly defensive character of the army. The Romans garrisoned some mounted troops at the *limes castella* but not heavily armored ones. To some extent, these troops faced traditional modes of cavalry combat when they met in battle with peoples from outside the empire. The field army was not tied down to any one place and could be deployed in either defensive or offensive wars. This flexibility defined the heavily armored horsemen's key role, which was reflected in Constantine's creation of the rank of general. The position was filled by two men, a *magister peditum* for the infantry, a *magister equitum* for the cavalry.

The late Roman armed forces were by no means restricted to the army and fortified camps. The Roman Empire was also a sea power—in marked contradistinction to the Sassanid and Carolingian Empires. The navy under Diocletian (284–305) was 45,000 strong.[46] These facts are pertinent to any exploration of how feudal structures emerged from the military's needs for an agrarian base for its supply.

The cataphracts and *clibanarii* under the late Roman emperors were all mercenaries, which cannot be said of either the Sassanid armored cavalry or the later Carolingian cavalry. As a result, their new form of arming and armor did not produce a feudal system. The state supplied weapons and horses, but under some constraints because the change-over to combat on horseback drove up costs enormously.[47] The Western Roman Empire had rich iron deposits, allowing it to build state weapon factories;[48] stud farms for the army's horses were also state property—a form of centralization that also took care of fodder production. A heavy cavalry called for specific breeds, and horse breeding flourished in the late Roman Empire, particularly in the border provinces north of the Alps.[49] In this way, the late Roman Empire capitalized on favorable conditions for mounting a heavy cavalry force that was barely inferior to the resources of the Sassanids, who themselves had access to superb iron from India for manufacturing cavalry weapons.[50] But above all, the Sassanids had the horses best suited for armored cavalry combat. When the Chinese first tried to adopt armor, they were unable find proper horses until they managed to get hold of a breed known as the "Celestial Steeds from the Western End of the Earth"—horses raised in the Persian Empire.[51]

———

The Byzantine military structure was basically a continuation of the late Roman organization. There were hardly any major changes in weapon technology. The cavalry had adopted the Avar stirrup early on; beginning in the second half of the sixth century, the Byzantine cavalry as a whole was armed "in the Avar manner." A bow of Turanian origin formed part of their weaponry.[52] Once again, a superior opponent from the East prompted improvements to the heavy cavalry, or restructured it, just as the Sassanids had been doing since the third century. The Byzantine Empire did not, however, keep upgrading the heavy cavalry's armor; knights in the West continued improvements into the late Middle Ages.

A fundamental reorganization of the Byzantine military in the seventh century was touched off by external threats; the need was not for weapons but for provisioning. The so-called theme system (*thema*, pl. *themata*) converted mercenaries into peasant-soldiers.[53] Soldiers in the military unit of a theme would receive heritable property in their province in exchange for obligatory military service. These *stratiotes* were neither mercenaries nor *coloni* but free peasants with their own land, which enabled them to make a living and equip themselves with often very expensive military gear. The practice of paying soldiers in land had existed as early as the late Roman Empire for the *limitanei*—frontier troops who settled around the *limes*. The method was then applied to military troops of all kinds: infantry, cavalry, the fleet. When it came to taxation and granting landed property, soldiers in the navy were ranked below horsemen, but above the infantry.[54] This common method of securing the military agriculturally was typical of the Byzantine Empire as a dual power, on land and sea.

The theme system did not exactly lend itself to further improvements in the heavy cavalry. The land given to *stratiotes* was often insufficient to cover the cost of their equipment, so that they had to be granted larger properties.[55] In principle, the theme system bolstered a free, militarized peasantry based on smallholdings and with heritable military obligations. But it ran completely counter to the Carolingian army reforms a short time later, which ultimately eliminated the peasant-soldier. The theme system did not distinguish between a warrior nobility freed from a land-based economy and a demilitarized peasantry that did the plowing—both of which were typical of the feudal system in the West. Forms analogous to western fiefs did not spring up in the Byzantine Empire until *pronoia* holdings—lifetime grants of landed properties given for military and other service—were created in the eleventh century.[56] But these rudimentary steps towards feudalization in the Byzantine Empire were unrelated to army reforms.

How did the Byzantine and the Carolingian Empires happen to go in such different directions? If we proceed, on the one hand, from the theme system, and from the Carolingian army reforms on the other, then we should first consider the different goals of the two reorganizing models. The theme system had the primary task of holding and securing land and possessions against threats to the empire's very existence. The resettlement of peasant-soldiers was intended to strengthen regional forces; the basic thrust of the new system was defensive. Some have tried to ascribe a defensive posture to the new Carolingian military organization as well and have interpreted it as a reaction to Arab incursions, but this rather dated thesis has been abandoned.[57] The very nature of armies of mounted troops make them offensive weapons and ill-suited for defensive operations.[58] Charlemagne in particular used his levies of vassals this way, regularly keeping his army on the offensive.[59] Imperial annals take particular note if the emperor failed to go on a military campaign in a given year, expeditions that would take him right across Europe. Building and securing a large empire necessitated moving troops over great distances, something Charlemagne could not do with his contingents of peasant-soldiers; he needed mobile mounted troops completely unencumbered by the tasks of a land-based economy. It was during the crises of the late Carolingian period and afterward that armored cavalry troops demonstrated their ineffectiveness as defenders. The Hungarian, Saracen, and Viking invasions created a need for fresh ideas for the military—mainly the construction of fortified places, castles in particular. This building effort was then incorporated into the organization of the feudal system—a factor that produced important changes that will be discussed in detail below. But the erection of castles played no role at all in the substantial reform measures for the early Carolingian army.

We have already pointed out that Carolingian military reforms must be viewed against the backdrop of freeing soldiers as well as peasants from military service. The growth in farm labor resulting from the three-field system—thanks especially to the heavy plow—required at least one adult male to be continually working the farm. The hide system did not foresee the need for fraternal communities which allowed several men in the same family to share military service and farmwork. Here we have to take the entire relationship between the agrarian system and military reform into consideration. The Frankish feudal system grew during a stage of agrarian expansion that secured new forms of military organization economically and in a novel way. In the Byzantine Empire, however, there was not the slightest move toward an agrarian revolution during the period in question. The bipartite estate, one of the innovations of the Carolingian age, encouraged the distinction between the world of peasants and the stratum of lords and masters above it; there were not even the bare bones of a bipartite estate in the Byzantine world. The Carolingian agrarian revolution could encourage the massive cultivation of fodder crops within the three-field system, and hence the raising of horses—a must for a strong armored cavalry. In the Byzantine Empire, even climatic conditions were unfavorable for this.

The availability of iron ore benefited the equipping of armored troops in the Frankish Empire even as early as Carolingian times, but it is difficult to determine how great this advantage was. Significant technological progress in the manufacture of weapons has been documented from the early ninth century on.[60] The Frankish Empire's superiority over its neighbors is attested by the fact that the empire twice prohibited the export of swords and breastplates, in 779 and 805.[61] The Byzantine Empire was at a disadvantage vis-à-vis the West with regard to the mining of iron ore, as were Islamic countries.

If we compare the Byzantine theme system and the structures the Carolingian military reforms put in place, we must bear in mind that they were built on completely different foundations. The Byzantine Empire had a much more complex moneyed economy than the West: it was a highly urbanized state supported by taxation, and it had direct access to its subjects. In contrast, the Frankish Empire was built on the manorial system. To be sure, even in Byzantium, the theme system brought about a shift from a moneyed to an in-kind form of governance, blurring the division between the military and the civil spheres—a separation utterly central to the Roman tradition, but one that did not exist a priori in the Frankish Empire, whose military reforms consequently had a direct effect on its entire lordship system. Though the feudal system initially drew its rationale for its personal and physical basis from the military, right from the outset it affected political and judicial systems, too. The church's involvement also seems to have been vital here, a feature of the Frankish feudal system not found in other forms of feudalism.

In the history of the feudal system, the fact is virtually ignored that the military hegemony of the Carolingian kings and their German successors was to a considerable extent based on the large contingent of ecclesiastical vassals, at times amounting to two-thirds or three-quarters of the whole army.[62] Had the imperial church's aid not been enlisted, the upsurge of mounted armored troops would not have reached such dimensions. The Byzantine Empire was unable to draw on the church's resources for military purposes. In the Frankish Empire, the enlisting of church property began with Charles Martel's so-called secularizations. Then Pippin, Charlemagne, and Louis the Pious laid the definitive foundations of an imperial ecclesiastical system that was later fleshed out under the Ottonians and the Salians. The Carolingian regime saw to it that cathedral churches and monasteries were obligated to render certain services to the empire in return for grants of royal property and privileges of lordship.[63] Apart from prayers for the ruler, his family, and the empire, these services included above all *militia*, military service, as well as a donation of annual "gifts" in the form of horses and weapons—a sort of prototype taxation. The military obligations of bishops and abbots were not the least bit different from those of other vassals.[64] Prelates took an oath of fealty and looked upon the king as their *seigneur* just as much as temporal magnates did. The inclusion of heads of monasteries in the retinue can be traced back to the oath of loyalty Willibrord had sworn to Pippin, the mayor of the palace, in 706 on behalf of Echternach and his other monasteries.[65] The clergy was already represented, therefore, in the retinues of Carolingian mayors of the palace; the group of vassals belonging to the royal house was to grow out of these retinues later. Bishops and abbots formed an integral part of the Frankish feudal system and were to assume even greater importance in the empires to follow.

————

The buildup of the Carolingian heavy cavalry, which laid the groundwork for the rise of the European feudal system, represents a very late development in the process of *Verreiterung* set in motion by the steppe peoples of Eurasia. A few great military powers in previous centuries had structured their armies around an armored cavalry or integrated one into their forces, but none went so far as to create completely analogous feudal structures. Quite the opposite: the feudal system was a specific feature of the Carolingian Empire by virtue of its joining the *feudum* (as a real, in the sense of real property, component) with vassalage (as a personal component). The system can be further explained by the conditions encompassing the Carolingian military reforms. The new forms of lordship based on the agrarian revolution facilitated enough material provisions for the new armored mounted troops (unlike the Byzantine Empire). There was also recourse to imperial church property on a large scale—another situation found only in the Frankish Empire. The combining of high-ranking members of the laity and clergy with military and lordship structures created social rapports above and beyond those created within the lord's retinue—links that were to be vital in the later formation of Estates systems. With regard to both laity and clergy, the Carolingian system represents a unique path of feudalism in the broader sense that was indeed triggered by the development of a military system, which of course cannot provide a single and complete explanation for that path.

———

The spread of the feudal system and of the armored cavalry throughout post-Carolingian Europe progressed in lockstep. As a rule, modes of knightly combat would appear together with a culture of chivalry wherever the manorial system and bonds of vassalage existed. A new factor came into play in the tenth century: the castle as a fortified center of banal lordship (*Bannherrschaft*). The simultaneous dissemination of "Frankish weaponry" and the feudal system followed the expansionist territorial movements described earlier in the context of the growth of the agrarian system. Robert Bartlett's *The Making of Europe* sums up the situation in the High Middle Ages from the perspective of military technology:

[T]he most important distinction seems to be between those areas that had heavy cavalry and castles by around 1100 and those that did not. A sketch map of military techniques in non-Mediterranean Europe around the year 1100 would show three zones. The first would be the region already described, including northern France, Germany and England. In this zone warfare centred around heavily armoured cavalry, castles, siegecraft and, increasingly, bowmen. There were two other zones. One of them was the zone where footsoldiers predominated. This included Scotland, Wales and Scandinavia. Here men fought on foot with spears and bows, axes and swords. When the king of England imposed a military quota on the Welsh principality of Gwynedd in 1247 he expected 1,000 footmen and 24 well-armed horsemen. The proportions speak for themselves. The final zone was a region of cavalry, but of light, not heavy, horsemen. Eastern Europe, including the lands of the West Slavs, the Balts and the Hungarians, made up the largest part of this zone, but warfare in Ireland seems to have been similar, in its basic outlines, too. The Irish horsemen were notably the lightest in Europe, having neither stirrups nor true saddles and acting as mounted spearsmen or javelineers, but the eastern Europeans too employed a lighter cavalry than that of Germany or France.[66]

This thumbnail sketch of military systems around 1100 reveals a fundamental partition of Europe into a nucleus and a periphery, which we will return to in connection with the Estates system. Apart from regions molded by chivalry and castles, there were substantial districts with different forms of the military. Two issues arise from this split: First, which forms of authority were connected with the military? Second, were there alternatives to the feudal system based on those same forms? Some additional comment on Bartlett's portrayal might lead to further reflections of this kind.

The Irish situation is a case in point: mounted troops did not replace war chariots until about 1000, so that a very ancient form of combat hung on for a very long time.[67] The chariot had once been a technological military innovation, an agent of profound political and social change from China to the Atlantic.[68] It probably fell into disuse on the European continent during pre-Christian times; Caesar mentioned a chariot attack by the Britons (*Bellum Gallicum* 4.33). The war chariot required special virtuosity from the soldier riding in it, not to mention the charioteer; the interdependency of this team could engender a bond of trust that transcended age and class.[69] Chariot combat also promoted a strong champion-based culture. Hence the comparisons of the nature of combat between individual heroes in Irish and Homeric epics, since the latter were also produced in a chariot-based culture. The social milieu of Irish troops was a tribal system distinctly conscious of patrilineal descent ties and client relationships—not exactly fertile ground for transplanting descent relations based on feudal structures. Tenancy played a minor role in an Irish economic system dominated by animal husbandry. Castles and walled towns did not exist until after the Anglo-Norman invasion. After the Irish had engaged with chivalry and the feudal system, the newly imported military forms and organized lordship were rapidly established.

A promising alternative to the Frankish military was taking shape in early medieval Scandinavia. This was the only sizeable region in Europe apart from the Mediterranean where ships at sea played a crucial role in the military—and therefore in lordship formation. The equipping and manning of warships evolved along a completely different route from the way the Frankish cavalry was supplied. The system for planning and carrying out naval operations was called *Ledung* in Denmark, Sweden, and Norway.[70] The organization of *Ledung* was based on "ship-raising" districts where the inhabitants were required to equip and man a warship. A group of neighboring farms was obligated to recruit, arm, and provide for each *Ledung* man; this was done on a tightly cooperative basis. The head of a ship-raising district was the helmsman, who also oversaw the equipping of the ship, the muster, and paying of rents; he was the captain on naval voyages and had judicial authority over his fighting men. The right to mobilize a *Ledung* lay with the king, and the terms under which it was mobilized were subject to negotiation between the king and the peasants. The *Ledung*'s greatest military opportunities came with the Vikings. Foreign land forces with armored troops were no match for this new menace unless they could fall back on fortified positions. The seamen from the North made temporary and permanent conquests all over Europe. Wherever they established lordship structures, they never organized them along the lines of their own country's military system. Instead, the Northmen switched over to the feudal system wherever they happened to be—in Normandy, England, southern Italy. Even in Scandinavia, the *Ledung* system did not last in the long run. The war-based *Ledung* gave way to the tax-based *Ledung* in the second half of the twelfth century and in the thirteenth especially, when armies of feudal vassals and knights replaced it.

———

Why did the number of castles expand in the exact same areas where—by 1100 in Europe—the heavy cavalry had been established? The answer requires some contextualization. The word for castle, *Burg*, referred to a type of military fortification—a lord's castle under the authority of banal lordship, of *Bannherrschaft*. It was a distinct phenomenon in the growth of European fortifications and organized lordship. The castle emerged during late Carolingian times, a period when the empire was often menaced by threats from beyond its borders. It was found along with a second, older form of military fortification that contemporaries also called a *Burg*, although the term *Stadt* (town, city) eventually replaced it.[71] The evolution of different terms for the lord's castle (*Herrenburg*) and the fortified town (*Burgstadt*) is echoed in several Germanic, Romance, and Slavic languages. This pair of words reflects how two completely separate types of military fortification evolved from a single, older type, the so-called motte-and-bailey (*Motte*), which itself incorporated components of the nobleman's fortified house as well as the lord's castle.[72] The coexistence of *Burg* and *Stadt* is unique among fortifications worldwide. It is not just a peculiarly European design; it is also unlike anything else found in European settlement patterns and especially in European lordship forms.[73] Because it originated in the Frankish Empire, we might ask whether it had any connections with the feudal system. This requires placing it into other ninth- and tenth-century systems. Its special nature as a military institution will

115

of course need a more extensive comparison. The lord's castle, as a specific phenomenon of Europe's unique development, must be seen in the larger context of the history of fortifications.

Europe has always been blessed with many natural locations favoring the placement of fortified structures and installations. China, by comparison, was at a severe disadvantage in this respect; city walls in China were constructed of rammed earth and wood reinforced with stone, though wood was often in short supply.[74] Even the Great Wall of China was mostly built by this method. Wood and stone were less used in China until rather recent times.[75] In contrast, wood was available in abundance in Europe north of the Alps.[76] Stone masonry was prevalent in the Mediterranean area from the very beginning—the area from which the European method of building fortifications was disseminated. Mediterranean urban culture emanated northward into Celtic settlements.[77] The Mediterranean was where a particular type of preurban military settlement began to appear in the second century: the *oppidum*, which Germanic tribes also adopted to some extent. The *oppida* were settlement centers, like the Mediterranean *civitates* or *poleis*. They served as religious, political, and trade centers for the tribal community, either as a whole or in part.[78] Significantly, many names of Welsh tribes were given to urban centers *after* the tribes had been integrated into the Roman Empire. This kind of fortified center was found in the Roman Empire and beyond, spreading far into northern and eastern Europe throughout the early and late Middle Ages.[79] The *oppida* demarcate the growth limit of European fortifications that was to lead to the walled town.

A second track in the development of European military fortifications did not proceed from a fortified center but from the fortified frontier. The Roman Empire began laying out the *limes* in the first century AD. Severely threatened border sections were later secured by earthen walls, ditches, palisades, and stone walls, as well as wooden or stone *castella* and watchtowers. A permanent garrison was stationed in the *castella*. This building type was constructed on several frontiers ranging from Britain to the Near East and is typical of large, centralized empires. The Chinese and Roman Empires are perfectly comparable in this regard. The Great Wall of China has of course served its purpose far longer than the Roman *limes*. There were some attempts in Europe at fortifying the border, but they did not have any lasting influence on the essentials of European fortifications.[80] The organization of lordship in medieval European empires did not make long walls particularly useful for frontier defenses. Even certain features of the Roman *limes* that persisted into the Middle Ages belonged to defensive centers rather than fortified frontiers—though not necessarily to walled towns. These few first steps would eventually lead to the duality of castle and town.

After the Danube *limes* fell, new and different frontier defense systems were constructed in the provinces north of the Alps, later on in Italy.[81] They still relied on *castella* garrisoned by *limitanei* units, although there were no defenses connecting the string of separate strongholds. These *limes* systems were forever being modified to accommodate the continual shifts in the frontiers.[82] The Byzantines protected their Italian territories from the Lombards by erecting *castella* more systematically. The Lombards reacted by building a similar fortification system. On the Byzantine side, the same kind of military bases were still being built in the ninth and tenth centuries, when new themes were established in reoccupied territory.[83] It would be true to say that early medieval Italy was turned into a country of castles.[84] These were not seats of noblemen living in the manner of knights and lords; they were imperial army strongholds in the *limitanei* tradition of late antiquity.[85] The counterparts on the Lombard side were the castles to which the *arimanni*, warrior freemen, were allocated.[86] Although the *castella* functioned as a focal point for the surrounding land, towns rarely developed from them or other fortified settlements; they could, if anything, have been called "castle villages." This would correspond to the Greek terms *komopoleis*, *agropoleis*, and *astykomai*, some of which were found in the Byzantine Empire outside Italy as well.[87] The *incastellamentum* movement in Italy might well have linked up with these *castella* in the High Middle Ages.[88]

The fall of the *limes* in late antiquity, in fact the whole invasion of the empire by foreign forces, made it necessary to fortify imperial cities and towns once again. This affected more than frontier areas. The erection of walls drew attention to their defensive function, something long absent from the Roman Empire.[89] Towns were turned into castle fortresses. The military term *castrum* was used more and more, minimizing the difference between it and the *castellum*. The need to build and maintain the walls created a new obligation: every inhabitant of the empire was obligated to give the state and community free services, the so-called *munera*, in addition to his taxes.[90] Working on state buildings had already been part of these services; now, in the third century, came the added service of working on constructing town walls. The obligation to work on fortifications first appeared in the late Roman Empire and was to be of prime importance for European military development, as well as for building town walls and various types of castles.

It survived in the Byzantine Empire under the Latin term *angariae*. The immunity granted to *stratiotes* around the ninth century released them from work on fortified places, gates, bridges, and roads.[91] In Italy, the obligation in Roman law to erect military installations in Byzantine and Lombard territories was upheld. It came to apply to the members of a *castella* community as part of military service, defense, and the *wacta*, that is, guard duty in the castle.[92]

The Roman *munera* extended into the Carolingian Empire. The people in a *pagus* (the Carolingian shire) were generally obligated to help build, maintain, and guard the *civitates* and *castra*.[93] A document affirming an immunity that Charlemagne granted to the bishop of Metz mentioned the so-called *tres causae* that were rolled into one and that continued to be owed the king—military service, guard duty, and building bridges—the parallel with the Lombard and Byzantine empires is unmistakable. There was no corresponding obligation to work on castle construction, since there were so few threats from over the borders.[94] On the other hand, Charles the Bald, in the Edict of Pîtres in 864, emphatically underscored the duty to build *civitates novae*; military expeditions and the obligation to work on fortresses and bridges were called "a custom of other peoples" (*et aliarum gentium consuetudo*).[95] This could have applied as well to other empires in the late Roman tradition, and to the Anglo-Saxon situation, where we find an analogous trio of obligations repeatedly called the *trinoda necessitas*.[96] In England the labor service of helping to fortify county castle towns was maintained for a long time.

There is evidence from beyond the Carolingian imperial borders of a later general obligation to work on castles—combined as a rule with bridge labor—among various western Slavic peoples in Mecklenburg, Pomerania, and Bohemia.[97] Fundamental obligations within the framework of the *castella* system included the *aedificatio* or *reaedificatio urbium*, the *urbium excubiae*, the *reparatio viarum*, and the *aedificatio pontium*. There were parallels to all these duties in Hungary, Poland, Lithuania, and the eastern Slavic region.[98]

Basic changes in Carolingian lordship structures during the second half of the ninth century went beyond fortifying the *civitates* and *castra* that were county centers. The intensified construction of military installations beginning at that time was surely linked with new threats from foreign enemies.[99] But who built them and where can only be dis-

covered from the context of profound transformations in lordship organization. Later developments in the imperial church certainly played
a crucial part.[100] Bishops and abbots, as members of the Carolingian
retinue, had made substantial contributions to military organization by
assisting in the buildup of a strike force of armored cavalry. When the
time came to defend against foreign invaders, imperial church property once again proved its worth by providing a base for defense installations. Large ecclesiastical complexes were usually located outside
the county system beginning with the late Carolingian period. The
privilege of immunity increasingly released church lords from having
to provide *munera*, whereas royal officeholders were not exempted. The
munus of fortification work was now frequently carried out within a
new framework—a novel feature that varied greatly from region to region. It was not the same in the western Frankish Empire as in the
eastern, for example, where the imperial church was refined under the
Ottonians; it was different too in the empire's frontier marches than
in the empire's central areas. But under later Carolingian emperors
new castles sprang up all over. The so-called *Burgbann*, which allowed
the lords of these new castles to levy obligatory castle labor, was operative everywhere and became the nucleus of rights of authority that
defined a new type of authority: banal lordship (*Bannherrschaft*).[101] And
throughout the central region of Europe castles of the nobility could
be found next door to castle towns, which introduced a fundamental
change in fortification construction in Europe.

The involvement of the imperial church in castle building was extremely complex.[102] County rights transferred to bishops empowered
them to build defense installations, particularly walls surrounding
episcopal towns. Lay abbots of royal monasteries would be promoted
for recreating their cloisters as castles or constructing fortifications or
places of refuge on monastery property. Alongside the bishop or abbot
there now stood the *Vogt*—a high-ranking noble who was authorized to
build castles because the *Burgbann* belonged to his military authority.
For a *Vogt* to build his castle on imperial church property, or adjacent
to it, was not regarded as an act of usurpation if the church where the
Vogt was in authority had agreed to it. A church would often replace its
Vogt or appoint a different protector for an outlying group of properties. This created many opportunities for creating new castle lordships.
Conditions for castle building were very favorable in colonized regions.
As lay abbots had done before, good-sized dynasties of *Vögte* would
distribute church patronage and castle-building rights to members of
their retinue—viscounts, vice-domini, castellans, free noble vassals,

and (unfree) *ministeriales*. This practice was stopped in France before it was in Germany, where building castles on imperial church property continued into the thirteenth century. Wherever churches were able to get rid of their *Vogt*, the churches themselves would assume his right of sovereignty and construct castles to be their own jurisdictional centers.

The advancement of the imperial church system and the concomitant rise of the *Vogtei* were certainly not the sole causes of the wave of castle building in the center of Europe, and they cannot account for every new castle type. But the incorporation of bishoprics (*Hochstifte*) and monasteries into the system of royal government was undoubtedly crucial for the radical restructuring of Carolingian lordship during that dynasty and under subsequent kings—most notably for disbanding the county system and its castle town centers.

Beyond the Carolingian Empire's borders, the older type of lordship was much better preserved: in Hungarian *comitatus* (counties), Bohemian *castellaniae*, the fortress district systems of many Slavic peoples, but also in English counties, where church patronage was the king's prerogative, so that the *Vogtei* could never develop from the nobility.[103] This distinction between a core Europe and a Europe of the periphery will be helpful when it comes to understanding the different types of Estates systems.[104]

———

A new type of castle that appeared throughout the Frankish Empire near the end of the Carolingian period was located very differently because the lord reorganized the space around it. The old castle towns of the tribal, regional, or county-center type were focal points for the surrounding area in all spheres of life—as a fortified place of refuge, marketplace, judicial center, or place of worship. The Byzantine *castella* in Italy and its Lombard counterpart, together with later settlements surrounding this building type, became the central localities for their respective territories. A completely different and opposite strand began to develop with the emergence of the nobleman's "high" or "hill" castle (*Höhenburg*). Although monastery towns, created when lay abbots erected a town wall, may have functioned in several ways as the central point for the surrounding countryside, things were to take a different direction: the monastery was not about to become a castle as well. The division of duties between abbot and *Vogt*—who took over the military side of the monastery's lordship—reflected the topographic dual-

ity of the monastic settlement and the *Vogtburg*. On the whole, placing church property under protection—be it a monastery, cloister, or
bishopric—was not supposed to hamper the church. But protective
lordship started a trend that consigned any military installations that
the nobility might wish to construct to a location just outside church
property.[105] Land clearance favored this move, which basically led to a
physical separation: the church, as the center of a long-settled part of
the country that was often an ancient parish, now stood in contrast to
the rather out-of-the-way seat of a castle lord. People could choose to
go to market at either place. The nobleman's castle created by this pattern was a somewhat scaled-down focal point, since it had to compete
with other population centers. A castle would often be situated in a
lonely place in the forest, in stark contrast to the original locations of
castle towns. From the point of view of defense, an out-of-the-way site
could in fact be an advantage. Unlike the early medieval walled castle,
a thirteenth-century nobleman's castle was not expected to provide
refuge for the entire population of a settled area, including animals.[106]
It served as the seat of the lord, who was able to defend himself indefi-
nitely with a relatively small group of military retainers. Hilltop castles,
which did not have much of a "footprint," filled the bill admirably.

Levies of knights and the lord's castle both underwent a sustained,
productive synthesis in the military system in the kingdoms after the
Carolingian Empire.[107] If the heavily armored cavalryman brought
about this synthesis previously, it was the castle that now had the more
significant social consequences. Combats between mounted knights
did not lead to "lordship over property and people"—instead it was
the hundreds and thousands of fortified centers scattered throughout
those later kingdoms. The armored cavalryman—the key figure in the
army—had become passé after a few centuries; what remained viable
was lordship organized around fortified castles. The castle and the authority attached to it quickly dovetailed with the feudal system, which
had arisen with the early buildup of the Carolingian armored cavalry.
It was the great crown vassals, dukes, margraves, counts, bishops, and
abbots who pioneered castle building. And even lay abbots and *Vögte*
in the imperial church came from noble families of high-ranking vassals. This does not mean that new castles were always considered fiefs.
Quite the opposite: it was precisely the castles built by *Vögte* that were
often considered allods, especially if they were not located directly on
church property but on adjacent cleared land. The original connection
with imperial church property can often only be reconstructed today
with the help of subsequent ties of fiefdom.[108] Even castles of a *minis-*

121

terialis would not have fief status but would frequently be an *Inwärts-eigen*, an allod that could only be granted to other *ministeriales* within the unfree *familia* of a particular lord. How many vassals a nobleman could deliver to his lord in a military levy—if he could send any at all—hinged on the number of castle lordships he held sway over; lesser vassals or servant knights with their own fortified residences were very often aligned with a nobleman's central castle. The famed *Heerschild-ordnung*—the scale in medieval feudal law for determining a noble-man's particular estate—was calibrated by his degree of subjection to lordship and sovereignty rights accruing to the castle, not by any military criteria.[109]

The successive waves of castle building in central Europe into the thirteenth century affected the relationship between lords and their subjects for a very long time. New castles meant new services, new work, and new personal ties. This repeated restructuring probably influenced changes in manorial organization. These kinds of transformations were particularly involved with the overlapping and coordinating of lordship rights among the lords and other authorities responsible for the ownership of the peasant's person, property, and judicial affairs. The tension between church property and noble *Vögte* seems to have been a leitmotif in the differentiation among lordship rights. If we acknowledge that the manorial system's structure was a crucial component of the feudal system, then we must also recognize that the long-lasting imprint of the imperial church would typify the unique route of feudalism in the former Carolingian Empire.

The construction of fortifications from the late Carolingian period on produced something exceptional in western Europe. The lord's castle marked a new kind of military installation that stood shoulder to shoulder with the classic form of the walled town. This new building type spread rapidly, so that the term *révolution castrale* admits of some justification.[110] A tight network of castles was cast over empires and territories that frequently needed reorganization from the bottom up. A widely dispersed pattern of lordship centers sprang up that paralleled the development of the agrarian system discussed in earlier chapters. The owners of these castles and fortified noblemen's seats were, as vassals, directly or indirectly subject to a king or a prince, but this structure was not in the least a *unified* fortification system subject to a central authority. The castle's uniqueness comes into sharper focus when compared with the defenses of other great empires of the time—China, the caliphate, and the Byzantine Empire in particular, where the obligation to help build fortifications was a service owed the state, just like taxes. Byzantine *castella* continued to serve as army garrisons but did not become noblemen's seats. Differences in fortifications corresponded to differences in lordship organization. Large property holdings did indeed exist in the Byzantine Empire but banal lordships based on castles did not. Such differences had some fallout in the way the Estates were to develop later. The duality of vassals, with their own lordship rights, and princes was specific to the West, and the rise of the castle highlighted this dualism.

———

To comprehend the subsequent duality of the prince and the Estates, however, we must first investigate the various personal bonds forged within the feudal system. Even though these ties were not rooted solely in the military, they nonetheless go back to a component intertwined with warfare. Any military organization must solve diverse social problems; apart from the economic ones discussed above, these would include training and cohesion within the unit, although loyalty to one's prince would take precedence.[111] Vassalage offered a very precise solution to these problems: it created new social relations where traditional descent systems had proved unworkable. Vassalage produced new vertical bonds (to the feudal lord) and horizontal ones (among vassals); it eliminated the tension between centrally organized army actions and mounted troops who were not so organized. And so vassalage adapted to the economic and lordship realities peculiar to the Frankish Empire. A quick look at contemporaneous alternatives might make the uniqueness of vassalage clearer.

Around the time the Carolingians started to build up their vassal army, the army in China was undergoing a comprehensive restructuring. The country was moving from a militia-based to a professional army in 722.[112] At first, new mercenaries were stationed in the heart of the empire—the capital and its environs. The professional army's strike force was greater than what former militias could muster, but the all-important fostering of loyalty to the emperor and the government proved elusive. The mercenaries' first loyalty was to their commanders, many of whom were not Chinese. The army's political unreliability became all too apparent three decades later when a military governor attempted a coup using his troops, a perilous revolt against the dynasty that was only crushed because foreign auxiliaries—the Uighur cavalry—intervened.[113] As early as the twelfth century, the problem of disloyal mercenaries cropped up in Europe as well, when paid soldiers from Brabant—the "Brabançons"—were increasingly pressed into service. The Carolingians had not even entertained the idea of hiring mercenaries, so that the Frankish Empire had no previous experience with the questionable loyalty of hired troops. China, a highly centralized state run on taxation and a well-developed moneyed economy, was forced to face this issue when it went about recruiting a qualified professional army.

Shortly after the military reforms in China and the Frankish Empire, the caliphate made radical changes in its own military organization, switching to a completely different model of military relationships.[114] Early Islamic armies were basically tribesmen, who still played an important role under the Umayyads. If we compare Arab to early medieval Germanic tribal warriors—in the Frankish Empire, for example—we have to keep an eye on differences in tribal structure. But as to military organization, there was one common feature: tribal-based loyalties would crumble in large, new empires. In the ninth century, the Abbasid Empire adopted an extremely radical course by introducing slave soldiers, the so-called Mamluks. The first part of the century had witnessed some experimentation with professional slave soldiers in various parts of the Islamic world, from Spain and North Africa to Central Asia. Caliph al-Mutasim (833–42) later brought these soldiers into the heart of the empire itself. The slaves were all foreigners— Cherkassians, Turks, Slavs, and so on—and were meant to join the army's elite troops. They were purchased during puberty, or very shortly before, when their warlike talent could be assessed but they were still young enough to be molded into faithful Muslims and true followers of their lords and masters. After many years of intensive military training and religious instruction, they were solemnly released. Their group training developed a strong sense of solidarity. In this model, military loyalty was instilled by separation from their original milieu, by extreme dependency on the prince, and by a rigorous upbringing during their early years. The strong religious component in the Mamluks' upbringing appears to have been significant in the creation of a loyalty-based relationship. This recruiting system initially prohibited the siring of an heir, so one group of trained warrior nobles would last for that generation only.[115]

The military effectiveness of this system was exceptional—probably greater than anything the western feudal system ever produced. The Mamluks were an excellent instrument for augmenting the caliph's centralized power—but they were not to be contented with that. The Abbasid caliphs soon became the plaything of those same elite forces.

To be sure, some parts of the Islamic world were able to base stable lordships on Mamluk armies. The slave soldiers were probably not the cause of the caliphate's ruin. However that may be, it was never possible to achieve a stable power equilibrium between the ruler and his top military echelon. The Islamic institution of the Mamluks had no parallel in the feudal system or its laws.

Returning to the early medieval Byzantine military, we recall that the theme system was its most important reform, but there were few related changes in social relationships. The theme system marked a shift from a mercenary to a militia system, which stipulated that loyalties had to be local and regional. No doubt peasant-soldiers and newly resident *stratiotes* were sturdy defenders of their immediate environment. Bonds between neighbors were probably stronger as a result. The emphasis on regions meant that centralized power would be somewhat weaker. The theme's militarization of civilian forces was in perfect keeping with then-current trends in the West, but it did not promote any move toward feudalization. The Byzantine Empire carried on as a bureaucratically governed state run by officials. Had there been any glimmers of institutionalized codetermination, they would not have been associated with military and civilian administrative reforms within the theme system.

———

Social relations within the feudal system had a number of very different sources.[116] Vassalage had its roots in the retinue, which had in turn grown out of the household community.[117] The traditional, flexible, household community in Europe bred social forms that branched out beyond the confines of the physical house, even affecting the military. These forms established extensive lordship patterns; their distinctiveness frequently had a domestic or family origin.

The domestic origin of vassalage and similar forms of the lord-retainer affiliation are easy to recognize in some related concepts. The word "vassal" comes from Celtic *gwas* (servant), indicating a Celtic origin—as do many other terminological links—for the Germanic household retinue.[118] Particularly revealing is the pair of terms *hlaford* (lord) and *hlafoetan*, for "loaf giver" and "loaf eater" respectively.[119] The warrior retinue would eat at the lord's table, thereby joining the group of people who dined with his family. Domestic terms applied to warriors in the lord's retinue crop up again and again throughout the long history of the European feudal system. The *ministerialis*, for instance, when he finally left the domestic community as an unfree servant, might be granted something similar to a fief, an *Inwärtseigen*. Or take the similar case of the *Knappe* (page), who served the knight who was his lord. *Knappe* is one of several words referring to a young household member and is typical for the military system. Warrior retainers were bound to their lord's household early in their youth. Tacitus reports that a life-long oath of allegiance bound them to their lord. No matter what rites cemented that tie, spending one's youth living with the lord and his retainers created a strong basis for a permanent bond of loyalty. When retainers were "spun off" from the household to found their own household on a property the lord transferred to them, they would still be obligated to him in a familylike way, a bond that could be valuable for the military or for any other tasks the lord might assign.

The traditional European training of a knight in armor was basically a domestic affair. A similar pattern was sometimes found in a militia system. The father or an elder brother would often be the warrior-in-training's instructor. The importance of his training for the court of the retinue's lord, of the *seigneur*, of any other lord, appears to have been special to the feudal system. In the Frankish Empire, turning a peasant-soldier, now freed from working on the land, into an armored knight had made training a necessity because, for one thing, the technique of mastering efficient new weapons took long practice and constant physical training.[120] Learning how to handle weapons grew more and more complicated throughout the history of European knighthood, hence the need for a proper instructor.[121]

Training to be a knight was much more than being physically qualified for combat or familiar with weapons. The road taken by an early medieval armored knight was widened in the High Middle Ages by a later educational ideal embracing moral and religious values.[122] A vassal's loyalty to his liege lord was given an extensive religious reworking. Oaths of fealty to God and his liege came to be regarded as a unit. This grounding in religion of both military and lordship systems—their decentralized situation rendered them very vulnerable—must be kept in mind when reasons are examined for their astonishingly high level of stability. Here it is important that the prelates of the imperial Carolingian church were major supporters of this mode of organization, and their role grew even more powerful under the Ottonians.[123] Note in passing that the recruiting of high church officers from members of the clergy in the royal court chapel demonstrated from another angle how an education at a lord's court could help establish permanent ties of fealty. From a structural point of view, bishops coming from the royal chapel stood as another type of retainer: the "spun-off" household retainer.

The uniqueness of vassalage's social roots in a family or domestic community has already been demonstrated by some of the forms expressing it: a *seigneur*'s right of guardianship over a vassal's orphan son who was still a minor, his right to marry off a daughter in the same situation, and a vassal's naming a child after his lord or the lord's family members in the post-Carolingian period. Some additional terms refer to different times and places. An Old High German gloss translates the Latin *ultor* (avenger) as *mundporo* (patron).[124] In tribal societies, the obligation to take blood revenge applies to blood relatives who were usually in the same patrilineal descent group. The feudal system transferred this duty to all those bound to one another by the vassal relationship. The lord owed his vassals the same commitment, and the requirement was mutual. Tribal systems gave way to feudal systems that replaced descent ties with a new form of quasi-kinship. Vassals performed services in their lord's house. On certain occasions, the services would be obligatory even though the vassals might have been "spun off" from the lord's house long ago. A report on Otto I's coronation feast in 936 stated that the dukes of Lorraine, Franconia, Swabia, and Bavaria served at table because they occupied the domestic offices of chamberlain, steward, cupbearer, and marshal respectively.[125] Service at table was a typical domestic duty that vividly portrayed how one could belong to a family. But the magnates performing household services at the feast were the most eminent lay princes of the empire. That the regimen of domestic offices could survive at all in a feudal empire strikingly reveals the domestic roots of this aspect of lordship organization.

Armed service and serving at court were not a vassal's only duties; giving financial aid was a requirement as well, the result of a more recent development. In 1119 there were "four standard taxes [*tailles*]" on any fiefdom in Anjou: one for the lord's ransom if he were to be taken prisoner, one to celebrate his eldest son's dubbing ceremony, one for his eldest daughter's wedding, and one if the lord wished to purchase land.[126] The first three were generally recognized in feudal law. This may raise eyebrows today, given that they appear to be private or family matters, but the distinction between public and private did not apply to the feudal system. A major source of Europe's taxation system harks back to these auxiliary duties of a vassal to his prince. A comparative historical study of taxation reveals that this is a feature specific to

Europe. It establishes a connection between vassalage, which grew out of the household retinue, and the Estates, for whose development the right to assent to taxes became central.

———

The bond between lord and vassal that originated in the domestic sphere was an obligation built on reciprocity. This is plainly evident in the ritual establishing the relationship, outlined in Marc Bloch's classic depiction from *Feudal Society*:

Imagine two men face to face; one wishing to serve, the other willing or anxious to be served. The former puts his hands together and, thus joined, places them between the hands of the other man—a plain symbol of submission, the significance of which was sometimes emphasized by a kneeling posture. At the same time, the person proffering his hands utters a few words—a very short declaration—by which he acknowledges himself to be the "man" of the person facing him. Then chief and subordinate kiss each other on the mouth, symbolizing accord and friendship. Such were the gestures—very simple ones, eminently fitted to make an impression on minds so sensitive to visible things—which served to cement one of the strongest social bonds known in the feudal era.[127]

Bloch is portraying the act of a vassal's commendation. The commendation came from Gallo-Roman traditions; it confirmed a mutual, lifelong agreement for the lord and his man.[128] The commendation obligated the retainer to serve and obey, the lord to provide and protect. During the Carolingian age, the swearing of an oath of fealty was combined with the act of commendation that created a vassal. The oath goes back to the Germanic retinue, which also entailed elements of mutual obligation.[129] The oath was derived from the relationship between freemen; it improved the vassal's lot because the commendation's inherent subservience made him a close dependent. In any case, the oath was now a constituent of the feudal system's new social relationships that was to be vital for the military and the whole manner in which lordship was organized.[130]

Magnates in the empire paid homage to a new king through feudal rituals. Conversely, the Carolingian king was more and more constrained by certain bonds. In the coronation ceremony that became customary in the western Frankish Empire in the mid-ninth century, the king would swear an oath to the empire's magnates.[131] Under the church's influence, kingship was increasingly viewed as an office, which reinforced the crown vassals' role. The *consensus fidelium*—the agreement and cooperation of the vassals bound by an oath of allegiance—could be escalated to the point of having the right to resist the king.[132] The obligations of loyalty from fief holders were not unlimited. Even the king entered into obligations that he had to fulfill. Imperial magnates were banded together by an oath to ensure that their lord stuck to his obligations and to refuse him any support should he break them—as happened with the Strasburg Oaths of 842, for instance.[133] The vassals were banded together by a common oath. As early as the ninth century, some crucial checks on princely power were taking shape on which the duality of the princes and the Estates would be based. The feudal system's personal relationships provided the context for these mutual obligations.

The twinned concept *consilium et auxilium* took hold in the feudalized parts of Europe as the fundamental principle of a vassal's obligations to his liege.[134] The formula has been documented for the ninth century, and it meant that a vassal had to engage his whole person in giving his lord "counsel and aid." The term *consilium* referred to the vassal's obligation to carry out advisory, administrative, and judicial service at court (*Hoffahrtspflicht*), whereas *auxilium* meant, for the most part, service in arms (*Heerfahrtspflicht*). These two duties were a vassal's main tasks.[135] It is remarkable that this kind of dichotomy existed in the service expected from a vassal, and that the duty to give counsel—at least in the classic feudal formulation—was given precedence over military service. Probably both functions were there from the outset, but counsel was not the principal one. There was definitely not a contingent of vassals acting as a prince's advisory body. But the task of giving counsel in political, administrative, and judicial matters grew in importance and was separated off from military duties as the advice was implemented. Assemblies summoned for the service of *Heerfahrt* or *Hoffahrt* became segregated. The latter assemblies were to link up later with the imperial and territorial diets to form Estates assemblies, so that their connection with older aspects of military organization appears to have been mediated indirectly. However, the military's influence on shaping the whole structure of feudal lordship was strong enough to create some bonds. Just as vassalage ultimately could be traced back to the household structure, so too a similar organization survived in the lordship that underpinned the Estates system. This explains many of the system's features that are otherwise so difficult to grasp.

At the apogee of Carolingian lordship—under Pippin, Charlemagne, and Louis the Pious—there was a (temporal) connection between military assemblies and imperial advisory assemblies.[136] People obligated to provide military service and summoned to the Mayfield might also be asked for their counsel regarding imperial affairs. An assembly's decision to conduct a military campaign might at times be implemented immediately.[137] It is fair to say that this interaction between military and imperial assemblies ultimately did not have a future.

Other, simultaneous advisory assemblies were called variously *generalis communis*, *placitum*, or *synodum*, but they did not take place jointly with military assemblies.[138] Now and then they too would act like a synod, giving advice on ecclesiastical matters. There were no restrictions: discussions intermingled the spiritual and the temporal because of the assortment of advisors present: bishops, abbots, and counts, as officers of the king. This type of assembly has been accurately described as an "institutionalized congruency of imperial diet and synod," which reflected the structure of the Carolingian imperial church.[139] Bishops and abbots were *fideles* of majordomos or kings. Prelates were summoned to military or imperial assemblies, as were secular magnates. But it was impossible for high ecclesiastical authorities to summon a synod assembly separately and independently. Under the Carolingians, archbishops were not granted the ancient right of metropolitans to summon bishops in their archdiocese to ecclesiastical councils.[140] It was the king's prerogative to summon them, for the empire as a whole or in part.

The Carolingian Empire was not alone in making these kinds of political advances during the early Middle Ages: the situation in England was very similar. The Anglo-Saxon witenagemot was also characterized by the "congruency of imperial diet and synod." The king and queen, other members of the royal family, bishops, abbots, and abbesses participated, as well as ealdermen and thanes—magnates from the laity. Some believe there might even have been some Anglo-Saxon influence on the composition of Carolingian advisory bodies, because early Carolingian assemblies had been constituted on the church's advice after Saint Boniface's reforms—on which the Anglo-Saxon reform party in the Frankish Empire had great influence.[141] Be that as it may, the witenagemot was yet another *concilium mixtum* type of assembly and functioned like an episcopal synod, with lay magnates present and the king presiding.[142]

The synodal origin of early medieval imperial diets can be discerned more clearly in the Councils of Toledo, the capital of the Visigoth kingdom.[143] At least eighteen synods were summoned in Toledo between the waning sixth century and the early eighth century. They were obviously modeled on the ecumenical councils of the Roman Empire and by and large met without the king, who nevertheless set the agenda and had to ratify the councils' resolutions. Agendas were by no means restricted to religious affairs but increasingly included secular concerns, such as the election of the king's successor or taxation; consequently, secular magnates became involved. Here, too, a *concilium mixtum* was the outcome. The Eastern Roman Empire did not share in this development. The patriarch conducted a *synodos endemousa*, which was always to be a Byzantine ecclesiastical assembly independent of the emperor's secular advisory bodies.[144]

Resolutions in an ecclesiastical synod had to be ratified by a consensus of its members, which became custom in early medieval imperial diets and assemblies. This tradition merged with the right to advise possessed by the royal retinue and vassals, who in many cases held high ecclesiastical office themselves. Pippin wrote at the beginning of one of his capitularies, "cum consensu episcoporum sive sacerdotum vel servorum dei consilio seu comitibus et obtimatibus Francorum."[145] *Consensus* and *consilium* underwent a synthesis in the resolutions of the Carolingian imperial diets and in the capitulary legislation based on them.[146] The right of codetermination given to clerical and lay magnates in early medieval advisory and deliberative assemblies seems to have been strongly influenced by the modes of joint decision making practiced in synods and councils. These codeterminative arrangements were continued in the imperial diets of the High Middle Ages based on feudal organizations or the Estates assemblies that grew out of them.

The late and post-Carolingian periods witnessed a differentiation between royal assemblies and synods similar to the earlier division between imperial diets and military assemblies. Metropolitans or papal legates presided over synods, which the laity now no longer attended. The term "synod" was not applied anymore to an assembly advising the king; this was now called a *consilium* in compliance with the advisory duties owed by crown vassals, or else was referred to as a *palatium*, *domus regia*, or *curia regis*—a term that was generally accepted for *Hoftage* (royal court assemblies) in the eleventh century.[147] Terms derived from the royal court were by no means limited to the magnates present at the palace on every occasion. The king's "house" included all the magnates from the broader group of people associated with his house, that is, all the vassals who had received a fief from him directly but who could not carry out continuous, everyday services for their liege. But they were expected to appear for the larger *Hoftage*, which no longer occurred during military musters but on high church holidays instead, at Christmas, Easter, or Pentecost. The prince would consult with his clerical and lay magnates at these gatherings, hearing their *consilium* and *consensus* on important affairs of the kingdom. This event was also called a *consilium magnum* or a *consilium extraordinarium*—a great or extraordinary council. The former were to give rise to Estates assemblies later. These assemblies stood over against a permanent council, a smaller body of the court household that would attend the prince.[148] The boundary between these two types of council was rather porous. Various royal counselors would be called in to join the prince's permanent retinue, depending on where the king was residing at the time. In principle, every crown vassal was obliged—and entitled—to offer his king his counsel. Given the greatly decentralized structure of feudal empires, continuously attending the king was simply out of the question for anyone entitled or obligated to do so. The duality between the *Hoftag* as an extraordinary assembly and the prince's more restricted council sought to solve the attendance problem—a duality that continued on into the era of Estates assemblies.

––––––

The road leading from the high medieval *magnum consilium*, the *curia regis*, and the *Hoftag* to the late medieval and early modern imperial and territorial diets was characterized by various processes along the way: the sorting out—or relinquishing—of certain functions, and the taking on of new ones. But in principle the connections among the three institutions were never in doubt.[149] A cardinal right of all territorial assemblies in the German Empire—to choose the king's successor—was delegated to a very small circle, the electoral college; in Poland the imperial diet elected the king, with the entire nobility participating; in Flanders, on the other hand, the towns had laid joint claim to this right as early as the twelfth century.[150] It was extremely important for the development of the Estates in France that functions of justice were transferred to the Parlement of Paris—a court of justice that the king had recently founded—whereas Estates assemblies elsewhere long retained the character of judicial assemblies.[151] In late medieval Hungary and Poland, the old function of the military assembly was kept alive because participants in imperial diets continued to show up bearing arms—something the successors to the Carolingian Empire had already dispensed with.[152] Crucial functional changes occurred more often with regard to *auxilium* than *consilium*, both of which vassals owed their lord. *Auxilium* meant, in the first instance, serving in the army;

its political entitlement originally resided in the military service carried out by vassals. The military would of course be altered much more rapidly than would the lordship organization that it had founded and to which its political entitlement was still tied.

It would be superfluous to describe the dwindling importance of the late medieval armored cavalry in the same detail as its rise in the early Middle Ages. New weapons—like the crossbow and longbow—were part of the story, but so were the particularly important modifications to coordinating foot soldiers in battle.[153] Mercenaries had to be brought in, either to reinforce or replace armored cavalry. The more efficient new forms of military organization and fortifications were very expensive. Vassals had to cover this cost with some money even when their military duties were keeping them fully occupied.[154] The three or four cases where feudal law anticipated these kinds of financial *auxilia* have already been discussed. Unforeseen causes were also a factor, for instance, in connection with the Crusades. In principle, the advent of taxation was very closely tied to military needs. The territorial and imperial diets—as opposed to the princes—acquired new responsibilities, such as ratifying taxes.[155] Even the higher number of those invited to assemblies was related to the authorizing of taxes. This was especially true of the towns, a financially powerful group.

During late medieval times and through to the early modern period, the composition of the imperial and territorial Estates presented an enormously diverse picture that, at first glance, displays almost no common features. The Estates were divided into "chambers" and "curias" in quite a number of ways. Those present could attend by virtue of their person or by representing certain groups. High-ranking clerics would sometimes just happen to run into the highest nobles among the barons and would on other occasions mingle with clerics and prelates. The heads of certain religious orders would be present legitimately, others not. Some very important towns of a territory were often not invited, but minor ones were. High numbers of peasant communities would occasionally attend; another time, there might be absolutely none. The list of these obvious irregularities could go on and on. When it comes to trying to explain them, they seem arbitrary or insoluble. The problem really becomes intractable when we look at the representatives of various social classes attending territorial and imperial Estates, or if we try to connect these political Estates with particular social strata (*Berufsstände*), in the sense of the tripartite *ordines* structure: *oratores*, *bellatores*, and *laboratores*, as they were often called in the High Middle Ages and still are in the scholarly literature.[156] Imperial and territorial

Estates had nothing at all to do with this three-part division. We have Otto Brunner to thank for delimiting interpretations of imperial and territorial Estates as the superstructure of an economic and social order. In his words: "The ruler of a territory and the territorial Estates together make up the territory. They share authority over the totality of lordship rights in that territory. But at the same time, the structuring of the territorial Estates is determined by their relationship to territorial lordship."[157] This general statement on the composition of territorial Estates and, we might add, of imperial Estates, specifies that each territory would organize lordship in its own particular way.[158] Using this view of lordship as a point of departure, we can see a differentiated picture of persistent lordship structures emerging from the many types of Estates system—structures founded in the early and High Middle Ages. The Estates system is more than a characteristic feature of Europe's special path: it is an indicator of the rich variety of special paths Europe itself encompasses.

———

Any attempt to standardize European Estates systems can still essentially begin with their description in Otto Hintze's two great studies from 1930–31: the "Typology of Western Estate Systems" and the "Preconditions for Representative Systems throughout World History."[159] His first major point was that the diffusion of Estates systems was restricted to areas where the Western Church had spread. They did of course branch out farther—for example, to Serbia and Russia[160]—but there never was that characteristic duality of prince and Estates that was an independent corporate entity with the recognized right to codetermination. This disparity with the areas where the Eastern Church existed is understandable in the light of what was said above regarding the ecclesiastical roots of the *consensus fidelium*, the reciprocal obligations of vassal and liege, and the checks on a prince's power in the West. The Estates had no structural roots in lordship even in southern Italy, which was under Byzantine rule for a very long time. Imperial diets based on feudalism there were an Angevin-Norman import.[161]

Hintze's typology of the Estates within the Western Church's ambit drew a distinction between "peripheral countries"—England, the Nordic states, Poland, Hungary, and Bohemia—and "core countries," with France and the German territories as the chief exemplars: "Geographically speaking, the two types of Estate[s] systems can be separated according to whether or not they had once been part of the old Carolingian Empire."[162] Although territorial and imperial Estates were not fully formed until much later, Hintze saw that they were grounded in lordship patterns going back to the eighth and ninth centuries. Today, a modification of his two types of Estates—having either two chambers or two curias in one chamber—is overdue, as is his derivation of the Estates from the more or less powerful "disintegrating effect" of the feudal system.[163] Rudiments of a two-chamber system could be found in core countries as well. The tricurial structure was primarily typical of territorial Estates that existed only in former "core-country" Carolingian principalities. The main reason for the difference in lordship structure between core and peripheral countries was probably a factor treated above as a partial aspect of feudalism: the imperial church, which had its beginnings in the Carolingian Empire and kept evolving in Germany during the Ottonian and Salian periods. This structural element was not found in the peripheral countries of Europe, vital as it was for the growth of lordship in core countries.

The lordship established over church property in the Carolingian Empire had lasting effects, as was evident in the wave of castle building described above. In France, bishoprics as lay property and lay abbeys were major building blocks in the formation of principalities. In Germany, the *Vogtei*, as a diluted form of noble lordship over immune imperial church property, was equally important in creating territorial lordship. Bishops and abbots could be territorial princes either by retaining the rights of authority granted to them or by appropriating those rights through dispensing with the *Vogt*. The ecclesiastical prince of the empire, who was a member of the imperial Estates standing over against his own territorial Estates, was a typical phenomenon of the German imperial system. In imperial Italy, the bishop's lordship over the city was a preliminary stage in the move toward communal autonomy, which then emanated from the city. The liberation of urban centers by the granting of sovereign rights to the bishop signaled a key intermediate step in the emancipation of town communes on their path to self-government—a precondition for their representation in territorial and imperial Estates. The rights of rural communes to administer themselves were then formulated along the lines of autonomous town communes; these rights could just as well lead to political participation within the framework of Estates systems, as long as the rural communes had a relationship with the prince.[164]

In the kingdoms succeeding the Carolingian Empire, different forms of noble lordship over ecclesiastical property seem to have been crucial for more than just establishing a prince's territorial sovereignty;

they came to provide the basis for more and more novel ways of creating noble lordships in Germany right into the twelfth century—in the end this process included even the *ministeriales*, who were originally unfree. If a *ministerialis* possessed a castle with a *Bannherrschaft*, then his liege lord prince would have to tolerate him as an independent bearer of lordship. The *Vogtei* also played a significant part in the *Landstandschaft* (a person's right to appear at the territorial diet) of other bearers of lordship. Whoever or whatever was under a *Vogtei* directly connected to a territorial prince—whether prelates, towns, markets, or rural communities—might have extraordinary taxes levied on them, but they would by the same token have the right to take part in territorial Estates where those same taxes were to be authorized.[165] Certain features of the imperial church, such as immunity and the *Vogtei*, thus not only determined the rise of the territorial principalities limited to the successors of the Carolingian Empire—they also determined how the territorial Estates were to be constituted. The tripartite division into curias of lords and knights, prelates, and towns is an idealized, stereotyped, and standardized model that had all kinds of variants.

The existence of Estates systems on two levels—the empire and the principalities—was an attribute of countries in Europe's core. But in the peripheral countries, too, Estates were often determined by assemblies on two levels, though in a very different manner.[166] There were imperial diets on the transregional level corresponding to county, comitat, and wojwodship assemblies on the regional level, but these last-named assemblies now sat facing officers of the crown, rather than princes, as independent possessors of sovereign rights. They had a direct, unmediated relationship with the empire, which is why they could send delegates, usually elected, to the imperial diet. The classic exponent of the peripheral Estates was the English parliament with its House of Lords, where barons of the realm took their seat, and its House of Commons, for the delegates of the *communitates* of county knights and royal boroughs.

The situation in the core countries was totally different. The two Estates levels—regional and transregional—were not interrelated by an all-inclusive imperial diet. Each prince of the empire convoked his own territorial Estates; he did not represent them at the diet. It was not possible for the German king to summon vassals of his vassals to the *Hoftag* or summon to an assembly the nobility, prelates, or towns belonging to his imperial princes. The royal county system—through which the king could have involved noble *communitates* in imperial rule, as was done in the peripheral countries—had disappeared since the Carolingians, particularly thanks to the imperial church. What held for the German empire was also true for France—but there it was nevertheless possible to tie regional to transregional levels in a different way. The Capetian kingdom expanded its rule by systematically absorbing individual principalities within its lordship circle, all of which had territorial Estates. The French king summoned representatives of the regional Estates, which were now directly subordinate to him, as the États-Généraux. This represented horizontal integration brought about through expanding the assembly of barons with delegates from the counties, rather than a vertical integration, as in the case of the English parliament. This newer type of imperial diet based on the États-Généraux was of tremendous importance for the construction of lordship in the core countries of Europe.[167] It was restricted to kingdoms known as "composite states" because of the procedure used for constructing lordship.[168] The dukes of Burgundy successfully implemented the process. The Estates General of the Burgundian Netherlands have survived as the basis of its governance even to this day, whereas the Habsburgs were unsuccessful in their efforts to weld their territories together by this means.

The division of Europe, with its Estates systems, into core and peripheral countries is but a crude attempt to bring some order to its wealth of forms. From the point of view of historical origins, this dichotomy makes sense for descriptive purposes and as a starting point for interpreting certain differences. To be sure, in harking back to Carolingian lordship, it harbors the danger of an all too static reading. The history of European Estates assemblies presents a kaleidoscopic image bearing no resemblance to the structure of Carolingian lordship. The power relationships between the princes and those facing them were subject to constant change. Advisory assemblies were summoned—or not. Counsel was sought from those not entitled to give it, in spite of the Estates' opposition. New constituencies tried hard to gain admission to councils, with or without success. In the ebb and flow of political fortunes, certain lordship structures remained constant, and they had to be respected in spite of change: castles as centers of lordship, monasteries, and towns were inscribed in the landscape. Stamped by time well before the rise of the Estates, they gave the appearance of being permanent fixtures.

———

At what point can we begin to speak of Estates? Or of parliaments? The occurrence of certain concepts in historical sources cannot be the defining criterion, but the dominant functions and structures of those assemblies can. Lines of continuity bridge many periods but so did fault lines that created what Ernst Bloch termed a *Gleichzeitigkeit des Ungleichzeitigen* (the contemporaneity of the noncontemporaneous), so that conflicting phenomena existed side by side. It is difficult to refer to "progressive" or "archaic" features of a given Estates system. Even so, there are some developmental trends common to the Estates systems of Europe.

One significant trend was the increase in some aspects of representation that were ecclesiastical in origin; their later acceptance in the secular sphere may well have been influenced by canon law.[169] When the Estates began to evolve, exclusively personal rights and the personal duty to advise the prince were already present.[170] A crown vassal in the *consilium magnum* did not represent any group from the manor, not even his noble family or a religious community he might have led. The earliest modes of representation emerged among the lesser nobility, around the thirteenth century in territorial assemblies in southern France, perhaps even earlier with English county knights—if representation was predicated on certain particular requirements of the judicial system.[171] The *communitates* began to appear in thirteenth-century Estates assemblies; the fact that they sent delegates reflected acceptance of the principle of representation—for instance, in Castile, Aragon, and Catalonia by the thirteenth century, when royal castle and village communities were even then appearing along with royal towns.[172] Lombard cities sent delegates to the imperial diet at Roncaglia that Friedrich Barbarossa summoned in 1158—a very early example of how cities were represented in Estates organizations.[173] The line of development begun here was to be continued only for the cities of the Lombard League, not for imperial Estates.[174] Princes' towns were clearly the chief exemplars of the principle of representation in the Estates system, and their participation grew much stronger during the course of the late Middle Ages. But we must not overlook the part played by rural jurisdictional communities (*Gerichtsgemeinden*) in reinforcing some features of Estates representation. This was especially important in Alpine areas, for example.[175] Urban and rural communities occupied very different rungs on the ladder of Estates in the larger regions of Europe. All but a few Hungarian and Polish royal free cities managed to achieve codetermination in royal diets; Estates assemblies in these kingdoms were dominated by the nobility until well into modern times.[176] Flanders presents a contrasting model, where the *bonnes villes* were sole exponents of early forms of the Estates system by the twelfth and thirteenth centuries.[177]

Six, ultimately three—Bruges, Ghent, and Ypres—of the largest cities in the country shunted the nobility and the other cities aside. Along with the "Brugse Vrije," the autonomous district of Bruges, they formed the "Four Members [*Leden*] of Flanders" and were the sole representatives of the country vis-à-vis the count. An Estates system was therefore already formed in Flanders in the High Middle Ages that was based exclusively on having communities represented, that is, on the *principle* of representation. It is surely no accident that this example of a "progressive" Estates system leads straight back to the Carolingian heartland, which generated so much social dynamism—further examples being the very principle of representation in that system and the armored knight on horseback, who as a vassal was obliged to provide counsel and aid and who stood at the point where this whole development began.[178]

———

Probably one of the most vital movements emerging from the Carolingian heartland was the dissemination of the feudal system, which swept over the major part of the European continent. Europe as a historically developed social space was broadly identical with this "feudal Europe"; it was congruent with the Europe of the Estates system, the outlines of which are even clearer, as is its internal division into core and peripheral countries. Even today, some traditional structures of the feudal and Estates systems influence Europe's political and social organization, for all its internal differences.

The feudal system, as a uniquely European path of feudalism, owed its genesis primarily to a military innovation in the Carolingian Frankish Empire: the buildup of an armored cavalry based on vassalage. But in the long-term historical view, it was the system's lordship that ultimately flourished and not its military side. The creation of the great Carolingian Empire would have been absolutely impossible without the armored knight, but the cavalry was unable to secure the empire permanently; this would be the achievement of later dynasties that capitalized on constructing fortifications. Western and central European knights were certainly the most highly evolved type of armored horsemen that were originally found in much of the ancient world in late antiquity and the early Middle Ages. From a military point of view, knighthood would ultimately disappear, in spite of centuries of triumph. After the late Middle Ages, the future would belong to disciplined foot soldiers, firearms, and the fleet—the foundations of military domination by Europe's great powers, the building blocks of their future expansionism. Chivalry could not possibly have exploited this particularly problematic aspect of Europe's special path. Not to put too fine a point on it, chivalry amounted to a military dead end.

The lord's fortified castle (*Herrenburg*) was a much more significant military innovation long term, if we view it broadly as a defensive component of the feudal system. The combination of nobleman's castle and walled town is indisputably European. China, in keeping with its totally different forms of government, had devised a completely different defense system by constructing its Great Wall, from the third century BC until well into the Ming Dynasty (1368–1644). Neither system would have been feasible in the Islamic world. A cross-cultural comparison shows that Europe stood alone in achieving utmost security and stability by its tight network of fortified noble seats and towns. Central and western Europe were spared nomadic invasions after this system was concocted in late Carolingian times and afterward. Marc Bloch correctly viewed this as "one of the fundamental factors of European civilization, in the deepest sense, in the exact sense of the word."[179] Even the kingdoms created at the time proved to be relatively long-lasting. The construction of fortifications resulted in a continuous, progressive development; there was no break comparable to the demise of chivalry until modern times.

The nobleman's castle as the hub of banal lordship (*Bannherrschaft*) is a tangible expression of a lordship system having the military as an integrating factor. This is true of the feudal system as a whole; the functions of organizing armies, of the military system, the judicial system, the administration, and political codetermination are inextricably intertwined with the feudal system. From a comparative perspective on the history of political lordship, forms of lordship backed by fighting men are not exactly rare. And yet the difference seems remarkable if it is contrasted with earlier or contemporaneous cultures where military and civilian sectors were kept separate—the Roman Empire before its crisis in late antiquity, Islamic empires, and to some extent the Byzantine Empire. The contrast is particularly stark with China, where the tradition of appointing literary figures as officials was reinforced in the Song dynasty (960–1279) and the Confucian ethics of the Chinese state always asserted that the civilian sphere was superior to the military. These kinds of separations could only have existed in large, heavily centralized empires. Even in the extremely decentralized Carolingian Empire and its successors, the diametrical opposite of the Chinese Empire, inklings of a similar separation might have motivated distinctions between a vassal's obligation to serve at court or give military service.

Nevertheless, the group of people fulfilling these obligations remained the same for a long time. The feudal nobility and the political leaders who came from its ranks were still firmly anchored in both the civilian and military spheres. The military way of thinking and its value system had an influential afterlife in the political culture of Europe. The term "chivalry" is a perfect example of how an unbroken conceptual thread could extend from the warrior culture of the Middle Ages into the modern age.

———

Certain features of the history of the European feudal age are frequently termed "feudal disintegration." An appropriate response would be to stress the opposite idea of "feudal integration." Of course the modes of lordship in the feudal system generated small-sized structures, but the end result was a concentration of social bonds within and among those smaller constructs. Two fundamental thoughts guiding the present analysis are that vassalage was derived from household organization and was a bond of quasi-kinship.

Lordship was hardly ever based this way in any other world culture of the time, not in China, not in the Islamic world, nor in the Byzantine Empire. Japan was the only country with some parallels. Warriors (*samurai*) from the domestic retinue of great noblemen began to band together from the ninth century on; they were comparable to vassals and bound to their lord in a clanlike structure.[180] The Japanese form of feudalism deriving from this relationship possessed a high degree of integrative power—similar to European feudalism—but it was not conducive to forming Estates structures.

The flexible family system within the European sphere of influence unlocked lordship's potential to evolve differently. Quasi-family relationships bonded the king to his crown vassals, who in turn were tied to their own personal vassals all the way down to the manorial groups whose social relationships were also construed according to the feudal model. Lordship was organized in many tiers, with many kinds of mediating forces. But the bonds holding these constructs of small-scale lordships together were rigorous and lasting because they had been modeled on domestic, family, and kinship relations. To rule kingdoms with the help of "spun-off" house retainers was a principle of the feudal system that turned out to have a great future. The intense loyalties typical of European nation states in modern times were not formed in opposition to feudal relationships but had those relationships at their very foundation. The phrase "feudal integration" emphatically underlines this aspect of lordship's development as part of Europe's special path.

The most significant ramification for Europe, springing from the feudal and Estates systems, was without doubt the development of parliamentary democracy. The early modes of participatory lordship and representation outlined above were still a long way from the many forms of democratic codetermination today. The lines of continuity have occasionally been interrupted—the history of the English parliament is an exception, but even there, evolutionary phases alternated with revolutionary ones—but it is essential to realize that ancient traditions of codetermination existed on various levels across the whole area of "feudal Europe." Even centuries-long interruptions in the summoning of Estates assemblies were unable to bury the consciousness of codetermination as a right. The countermovement of absolutism was unable to suppress the principle that there could be legitimate checks on the prince's power. These traditions of codetermination were rather weak outside feudal Europe. They had no foothold in the larger states where the prince's power was unimpeded and strongly centralized state bureaucracies were in place. Feudal forms of lordship do not generally appear to have been a determining factor here, nor were forms of military organization akin to the feudal system. The path from feudal system to parliamentarianism via the Estates system constitutes a unique European development.

The duality of the prince and the Estates is the source not only of parliamentarianism but also of the power-sharing principle underlying conceptions of the state in modern European history.[181] To assign the three main functions of state power—legislative, executive, and judicial—to three different, independent state institutions would have been unthinkable if these institutions had not already existed in society. Medieval states can certainly not be called legislative, but they took care of many tasks that would devolve to parliaments later on. The prince himself, in concert with court officials and his smaller band of counselors, carried out limited functions that can be construed as executive ones. The prince and his vassals traditionally handled judicial concerns within the feudal system. The establishing of separate institutions came about early, compared to when Estates assemblies began acting as courts of law. State institutions independent of one another within the Estates system consisted, in the beginning, of the prince's government on one side and the Estates organized as a corporate body on the other. But without this institutionalized power splitting, the idea of a separation of powers might never have been conceived.

The trend to federative structures may be regarded as another long-term outcome of the feudal and Estates systems, elements of Europe's special path. The historical origin of federalism can have many different roots. Right from its beginnings, it seems to have had many connections to the way Europe developed: The Carolingian *imperium* and its successors were very decentralized; the "traveling court" graphically illustrates this structure of lordship. The king would rule without a fixed place of residence but with a mobile royal household, which he would take with him on his travels from one part of his empire to another. The *magnum consilium*, the progenitor of the Estates system, was a way of guaranteeing unity in this kind of decentralized imperial structure. This lordship system was radically different from contemporary kingdoms centered on a strong residential palace. In Constantinople, Baghdad, or Kaifeng there was no need to summon magnates to court to keep an empire together. But to achieve this same end, the German king had to insist on the duty of court service (*Hoffarhrtspflicht*), on pain of sanction. This strong, personal connection to the top exerted an integrating force on the diverse tribal areas and territories. The imperial diets and territorial diets provided a sort of organizing bond for the various scattered bearers of lordship autonomous in their own little sphere. This was how multiplicity could still be preserved. It was especially true for the emergence of more modern kingdoms through the accumulation of lands belonging to territorial princes, as was the case with Burgundian or Habsburg lands. There the territorial Estates were the leading proponents of independence and most conscious of being special and separate—and therefore supportive of federative structures.

Finally, Europe's special path of feudalism induced a unique development in the church that had an enduring effect on the growth of European Christendom far surpassing anything to do with its organization. Bishoprics and monasteries were enlisted in the service of the first Carolingian kings in a quite extraordinary way. The imperial church thus formed in Germany was consolidated further under the Ottonians and Salians. The Investiture Controversy was a conflict between princes and the pope over this very issue. The papal church took shape in the High Middle Ages, not because of any continuity with but by that very struggle over those imperial church traditions; there can be no accounting for the papal church if this episode in its pre-history is omitted. The papal church, given its unique position among Christian churches, is indispensable for an understanding of the genesis of Europe.

Five

The Papal Church and Universal Religious Orders: Western Christendom as a Highly Organized Religious Community

If we approach Europe's origins through its social space, one correlation in particular is conspicuous: phenomena specific to medieval Europe were to be found in all those regions where the Western Church was established. This applies to both imperial and territorial Estates, which, as we have seen above, were typical components of organized European lordship in the same way that Gothic or Baroque buildings were monuments of European art, or that universities typified the way European scholarship was organized, or that the system of polyphony marked the development of European music.[1] Given these social and cultural coincidences, it stands to reason that we attribute particular relevance to the development of Western Christendom as a contributing factor to Europe's special path.

As a social and cultural region shaped by the Middle Ages, Europe has never been under common rule, so that any elucidation of its relatively well defined social and cultural unity must extend beyond factors of lordship. The church's commonality seems a likely place to start. Because Europe's societies and cultures were already homogenous by the High Middle Ages, we can make an educated guess that powerful pervasive and integrating forces were at work. In fact, the Western Church was a highly organized religious community unlike other Christian churches or religious communities in the same part of the world.[2] Two of its organizational features deserve special treatment here: the papacy and universal religious orders. A cross-cultural comparison reveals that these two stand uniquely apart. Probing more deeply into their origins and growth might well help explain other specifically European phenomena. The papacy and religious orders are closely connected; the papacy promoted the rise of monastic communities, which in turn were vital to the integration of the Western Church under papal sovereignty. But we still must look at other, discrete determining factors, treating them either separately or in tandem.

To address the development of the Western Church as a determinant of Europe's distinctiveness is to broach the topic of the split between East and West. The long-predictable schism of 1054 left its imprint on very different aspects of culture and society that still affect us today. Culturally speaking, the Great Schism in the West from 1378 to 1417 did not even come close to producing the same polarizing effect. And even the Reformation did not call into question much of the common foundation of Western Christendom in the Middle Ages. These comparisons underscore the enormous formative power of the period in European history that created the papal church and international religious orders.

––––––

The papal church as a shaping force in European society and culture directs our attention back to Rome, the ancient center of the West. This might appear irrelevant in light of the shift in the center of gravity to the northwest of the continent, but that would be judging too hastily. The gravitational shift provided a vital link to the development of the Christian churches and—compared to non-Christian religious communities—to the uniquely positioned bishop of Rome during and after the High Middle Ages. Rome's marginal location, compared to newer centers, was precisely what allowed it to develop independently. The pope was *not* made bishop of the imperial court. This geographic constellation was a decisive precondition for the "productive separation" of secular and spiritual power that would be so vital to Europe's future course. To try to understand the papal church solely or primarily from its Roman roots would surely be shortsighted. Much of what contributed to the homogenizing of the Western Church during and after the High Middle Ages emerged from the dynamic core area of the Northwest. This effect was evident, too, in the beginnings of international religious orders, which will receive special attention here as a constituent of the Western Church, itself a highly organized religious community.

The realities of the social spaces that form the present chapter's point of departure are significant for the concepts we will use. There is much to be said for the term "Roman Church," considering the tendency to centralize everything around the pope's episcopal see; but in terms of historical genesis, the important contribution of the new European centers in the northwest would then have to take a back seat. To speak of the "Latin Church" would certainly capture an essential feature of Western Christendom in its entirety. Indeed, a critical unifying element was at work with the Latin liturgy, another factor distinguishing clergy from laity—itself a very specific structure of Western Christendom. Nevertheless, the term "papal church," which will have pride of place here, seems to render best the church's unique development throughout the Middle Ages. It is not only oriented synchronically along the contrast between East and West—as are, for example, the contrasting pairs, Roman/Byzantine, Latin/Greek, or Catholic/Orthodox—but it also aligns with particular structural elements that a diachronic comparison can bring to light. "Imperial church," "royal church," and "territorial church" are antonyms to "papal church."[3] The former accurately apply to the *imperium Romanum* in late antiquity and subsequently to the Byzantine Empire; to ecclesiastical organizations in the kingdoms that evolved from the Great Migrations, and to the so-called national churches in Eastern Christendom. The papal church in the West was not an imperial church but a social organization embracing a many-sided construct of principalities. Most of its specific characteristics can be connected, more or less directly, with this key trait.

————

Hans Küng described the papal church during the High Middle Ages as having five "characteristics of the Roman system": centralization, legalism, politicization, militarization, and clericalization.[4] These features promoted the unique development of the West within Christendom and hence replaced the "early church paradigm" with a medieval one; all five were concerned with particular ways of organizing the religious community. The most thoroughgoing organization in any of the Christian churches was by far that of the papal church as it evolved in the reform movement of the eleventh to thirteenth centuries. Relative to other religious communities, Christian churches in general reflected a high level of organization.[5] The characterization of the papal church as a highly organized social structure with a strong capability to integrate and penetrate allows for an extensive and wide-reaching comparison.

The Lateran Councils provide a particularly concrete example.[6] People from the whole area of Western Christendom attended, from the Iberian Peninsula to east-central Europe, from Sicily to Scandinavia. At the First Lateran Council in 1123 there were over three hundred bishops and a goodly number of abbots; at the Fourth Council in 1215, over four hundred bishops and more than eight hundred abbots and priors were in attendance, along with emissaries from most of the kings in Europe, princes attending in person, and representatives of municipalities, especially from Upper Italy. Secular lords were now attached to the body representing the papal church. The authority summoning this impressive array to the council was the bishop of Rome as the *episcopus universalis*. This differentiated the new "ecumenical councils" in the Western Church from those of late antiquity, convoked by the Roman emperor, not the church's hierarch. The Great Synod of Frankfurt in 794, which decided matters of dogma such as Adoptianism and the veneration of icons, was, in spite of its extensive claims of validity, in essence a Frankish imperial synod held in a royal palace—with papal legates present—and conducted by the Frankish king. The situation was similar for the Trullian Synods in the Byzantine Empire, held in the domed hall of the imperial palace in Constantinople that gave its name to synods. The very name Lateran Council signals a new type of church assembly. The councils took place in the Lateran basilica, the pope's ancient principal church as bishop of Rome; they originated with the synods for the bishops of the ecclesiastical province of Rome as a metropolitan seat. Church reforms expanded the number of participants from the middle of the eleventh century on. The morphing of the provincial synod into a general church assembly graphically reflects the elevation of the bishopric of Rome into a universal episcopate.

The organizational model of the general church assembly that twelfth- and thirteenth-century popes implemented in the Lateran Councils found striking parallels in contemporary religious orders. Even the great monastic associations were organized on a European scale and held assemblies on a transregional basis. The Cistercian Order was in the vanguard. The first version of the document constituting the order, the so-called *Carta Caritatis* of 1114, predated the First Lateran

Council. It stated that a chapter-general was to be the order's governing body and that it would meet every year on September 13 for seven to ten days, beginning with the vigil for the Feast of the Exaltation of the Cross.[7] All of the order's abbots were obligated to take part. The almost insuperable challenges this form of organization implied, given how difficult it was to travel at the time, were reflected in the privilege granted to the representatives of the Irish, Scottish, Portuguese, and Sicilian monasteries: they were required to come to the chapter-general only every fourth year. Orders founded afterward adopted and adapted the chapter-general model in different ways; the Fourth Lateran Council recommended it for all monastic communities in the Western Church. The council itself was preceded by an explicit regulation for representing the whole *populus Christianus* by delegates sent from the entire, vast area subject to the pope. Ecumenical councils in the High Middle Ages were not, in principle, an innovation. They existed in late antiquity, supported, to be sure, by the state infrastructure of the Roman Empire. The fact that popes and religious orders were now holding good-sized assemblies drawn from across the continent marks a qualitative leap in the Western Church's organization as a religious community.

The agenda of the high medieval papal councils shows which areas of life they regulated in the papal church's catchment area.[8] The First Lateran Council was above all supposed to solemnly ratify and proclaim the Concordat of Worms that the pope and the emperor had negotiated the previous year, which ended the Investiture Controversy that had so profoundly shaken the Western Church and set the fundamental course for the later history of Europe as to the relationship between spiritual and secular power. Other council decrees were handled like the Concordat of Worms; they confirmed rulings the popes had already made in the course of church reform: for example, regulations against simony and for assuring the canonical election of bishops; tighter regulations on the celibacy of priests, deacons, and subdeacons; measures against lay interference in ecclesiastical affairs; and decrees concerning the so-called Peace of God, indulgences, the protection of crusaders and their families, and of pilgrims to Rome. All these decrees, which sprang from religious concerns, increasingly reflected their respective social contexts. Thus, the agenda of the Second Lateran Council of 1139 would cover clerical dress, what the clergy were allowed to study, violence against clergy, jousting, arson and looting, a ban on usury, the abuse of the sacraments, the private houses of women leading a religious life, and prayers chanted by monks and nuns together.

Subsequent councils also addressed a very broad spectrum of topics: church union, the primacy of papal jurisdiction, the validity of consecrating bishops, disciplining the clergy, preparations for the crusades, condemning and combating heretics, drawing borders between bishoprics, the order of precedence within the hierarchy, modalities of electing bishops, and arranging the pope's election. These matters were extremely diversified, and the high medieval papal councils had to convert them into key regulations for the whole territory of the Western Church. The pope and the council cooperated in the decision making, but the pope played a leading role, of course, by planning for and conducting the council. A confrontation between the pope and the council did not actually occur until the waning of the Middle Ages—a struggle in which the pope ultimately gained the upper hand.

The creation of key regulations for all of religious and social life throughout Western Christendom was a particularly important aspect of the centralizing trend that so typifies the "Roman system." The pope possessed, by virtue of the papacy as it was elaborated in the High Middle Ages, the *plenitudo potestatis*.[9] To be able to exercise the power of primacy was what constituted the essence of the papacy, as codified in the statement, "Papa est nomen iurisdictionis"—"the pope is the supreme lawmaker." The pope had the authority to intervene in issues of canon law and church structure by issuing decretals—his written replies to individuals in questions of canon law and discipline. He was the supreme judge of the clergy, and not only in ecclesiastical affairs, taken in a very broad sense. The progression of the courts went from local church jurisdiction on upward to the head office in Rome as the supreme court. The pope was the high priest from whom all power to ordain emanated. An archbishop was unable to exercise his right to ordain within his ecclesiastical province if the pope had not conferred the pallium. The pope had the supreme authority in liturgical matters; he brought about great changes in unifying and ordering the Mass. He could exercise the prerogative of canonization. The Cult of Saints and the Blessed was no longer left in local church hands, which had its own local traditions and decisions. The pope was the highest doctrinal authority. As the incumbent of the *cathedra Sancti Petri*, he would decide what was consonant with the tradition of apostolic faith and what contradicted it. He was, finally, a ruler in a twofold sense: in the *patrimonium Petri*, the church state, and as the supreme feudal lord over secular princes, whom he claimed to outrank. Along with the miter that symbolized the high priest's office, he began to wear the tiara in the twelfth century as the *insigne imperii*. The many forms of the *plenitudo potestatis* exercised by the pope made the papacy unique, compared with other Christian churches and other religious communities.

It would be hard to find in the organizational structures of other religious communities any counterparts to the means by which the pope centralized the papacy. Apart from the papal councils, three other ways are worthy of mention. First, the Roman Curia must be understood as being specific to the papal church.[10] The papacy's fundamental reorientation from a primarily Roman and urban institution to the very peak of the Western Church—which resembled a monarchy—required more offices for its central administration. This led to an expansion of spheres of duties, to setting up completely new authorities, and mainly to an enormous increase in administrative personnel. The Curia had grown to about a thousand strong by the end of the thirteenth century. What was so remarkable about this extensive administrative staff was its domination by celibate clergy. To be sure, the Curia's personnel were hardly concerned anymore with their actual duties as priests. Their function lay predominantly in the chancellery, justice, and finance. Indeed, the great concern of a central office with the administration of a religious organization's finances was what made it into something almost certainly without historical precedent. The Roman Curia was the most elaborate administrative apparatus in medieval Europe; no secular administration could come anywhere near it. The Curia became the model for the beginnings of state bureaucracies. Wolfgang Reinhard got it exactly right when he called the Latin Church the "first Western state."[11]

A second feature of the papal church's organization was the office of papal legate, an institution begun in the mid-eleventh century. Whereas the Roman Curia strengthened the central authority of the Holy Apostolic See itself, the institution of the legate secured the pope's omnipresence, so to speak, throughout his entire sphere of jurisdiction.[12] By the agency of his deputies his effect was felt everywhere.[13] The *legatus Romanae ecclesiae*, or the *legatus apostolicae sedis*, essentially outranked the local episcopate; he could preside over provincial synods, carry out visitations, judge bishops, prepare and conduct crusades, or act on the diplomatic front on the pope's behalf, perhaps by recognizing royal elections or negotiating a peace. In a world where travel conditions were so primitive, this method of representation became most significant. The pope was firmly tied to Rome, the seat of his bishopric, because of his liturgical and spiritual duties; but the institution of the legate allowed him to exert his power of authority over a much greater area. This was how the legate became a chief vehicle for executing the pope's claim to supremacy in the entire Western Church.

Religious orders formed the third instrument for centralizing the high medieval papal church. They carried out special tasks on the pope's behalf: the military orders in the Crusades, for example, and the mendicant orders in fighting heresies or in missionary work. As special institutions in the Western Church, international religious orders were not creations of Rome's central authority; they developed almost entirely separately. The popes supported their independence—for example, by exempting them from diocesan organizational structures—and employed them in the interests of the papal church. The orders' infrastructure was an essential base for Rome's integration and penetration.

————

The papal church that took shape in the High Middle Ages differed from the paradigm of the early church precisely because of the growing significance of canon law in ecclesiastical life—what Küng meant by "legalism" (*Juridisierung*).[14] The changing situation was characterized by the arrival of "lawyer-popes," among whom was Innocent III (1198–1216), whose reign marked the high point of the papal church. For a leader of the religious community, legal training had now become at least as important as a theological one. And people well-versed in canon law were also sought after for posts in the Roman Curia's central bureaucracy. The enormous increase in papal legislation drove the entire process. It has been estimated that twelfth-century popes made more legal decisions for the whole church than all their predecessors put together. Through the collecting and interpreting of legal records a new branch of scholarship emerged: the scholarly study of canon law. This development placed canon law side by side with secular law, and the two would occasionally be in competition. A similar dualism came about in the administering of justice. Church jurisdiction at the regional level grew into an autonomous justice system with the right of appeal to the Holy See. This enhanced the papal church as an extraordinarily well organized religious community.

The legalism of the Western Church is best thrown into relief by the contrast with other Christian churches. In none of the churches of Eastern Christendom did the law ever play such a major role. In Judaism and Islam, two closely related monotheistic faiths, religious law was also clearly vital, but in a completely different way. Religious law for both of these religions involved the interpretation of a given sacred precept and not, as in the papal church's case, with fundamental norms freshly created by an absolute legislative authority.

———

The intense politicization of the papal church in the high medieval period compared to earlier eras resulted from its emancipation from lordship groups, which enabled the church itself to become an organized lordship of a certain kind. An imperial church, a territorial church, or a royal church were in no position to practice politics independently; only the papal church standing in stark contrast to those older social forms was able to do so. This presupposed the pope's independence as a secular ruler as well. His authority granted from the *patrimonium Petri* made him a prince among princes. But the politicizing of the papal church in the High Middle Ages was in no way related to his secular lordship over central Italy. More fundamental were issues defining the contentious relationship between secular and spiritual power in the whole vast area of the Western Church—a relationship that was not contentious, say, in the Byzantine Empire at the same time. The so-called Investiture Controversy, in which those issues came to a head, was not merely a quarrel between the pope and the German king but a conflict involving the whole of Europe. The Concordat of Worms in 1122 had been preceded by similar agreements with the French and the English kings in 1104 and 1107 respectively. The investiture of spiritual princes was a particular problem for the imperial church in northwest Europe. The settlement of the conflict by pacts, later termed "concordats," demonstrated that the pope and the king were partners on the same plane—a situation not found in any other Christian church. The subordination of Christian princes to the pope became a theoretical postulate, and the church's jurisdiction by canonical right in spiritual matters provided the means to put it into practice. The king—as a sinner—was subject to the high priest's power "to bind and loosen," that is, to grant or withhold absolution. To be banned from the congregation of believers would have unavoidable political consequences. In this way, the papal church fashioned a very specific instrument for political action. Only in the Western Church was administration of the sacraments politicized by ban and interdiction. A Christian prince's only counterstrategy was to call the pope's legitimacy into question.

The Crusades represent one obvious example of the pope's primacy in political affairs. Only the pope could proclaim a Crusade and thus initiate military action on the part of all Western Christendom. The reform of the church continued to refine this novel political instrument in the second half of the eleventh century—the papal church's crucial formative stage. Preparations for a Crusade necessitated a great number of political actions, not least the resolution of conflicts between the princes who had to be persuaded to take part—something that could only buttress the pope's role as the arbiter of Western Christendom. Preparation for the Crusades was a major point to be negotiated in the councils the pope summoned. This was not the least reason for secular exponents of lordship to participate in the councils.

––––––

The Crusades symbolized the papal church's move toward militarization. No other Christian church carried out large military campaigns headed by its supreme leader. The Crusades constituted the pope's war. The broad base of the population of Europe certainly provided all kinds of impetus to the crusading movement, but the constantly reiterated appeals to implement this type of "holy war" came from the popes. Rome's traditional struggle against the Saracen and the heathen—heretics, schismatics, and other such enemies—also fueled the growth of the crusading concept. The crusading movement produced a radical change in Western Christendom's attitude toward war, marking a turning point in the history of Western thinking. The Crusades unquestionably helped to forge Western Christendom into a highly organized social form. Preaching and tithing for them shifted the papal church's priorities with regard to communication and the moneyed economy, factors of integration and penetration within the huge area under papal influence. The military orders that were spawned to serve the crusading ideal expressed—if we compare them cross-culturally with other monastic forms of living—the uniqueness of the papal church's militarizing thrust. Hardly any other new religious order in the High Middle Ages was as tightly organized as they were.

––––––

The movement toward clericalization—Küng's fifth and final key characteristic of the papal church—was tied to Christianity's underlying social structure. The dichotomy between clergy and laity common to all Christian churches became in the experience of the papal church a unique split between the two estates from the High Middle Ages on. The enforcement of celibacy by the church reform has rightly been seen as the decisive factor in this separation: laymen were permitted to have families, but this was disallowed for clergy from subdeacons upward—very different from the policy in Eastern Christendom.[15] The laity and the clergy were put into two totally different categories as to how they were to live, with the clergy's way of life more highly valued. Sexual abstinence had been an obligation for religious ascetics since ancient times. It was typical of the unique development of the Western Church that priests were adopting a monastic way of life at the same time that more and more monks were being ordained as priests.[16] Celibacy was not the only obligation for the ascetic life; obedience and communal living were called for as well. The reform of the high medieval church worked to establish these three obligations for the clergy. As a result, the clergy became more closely knit, but the laity more firmly excluded. The Western Church was turning more and more into a clerical church, organized as a hierarchy and a monarchy with the pope at the top. Clericalization went so far as to equate the church with the clergy—still evident in the language today.

The clericalization process was not the sole reason for the intertwined development of the papal church and the Western monastic system. First and foremost, their transregional organization pointed to causal connections between the two. The *universal* episcopate of the bishop of Rome appears to be a phenomenon as unique as the spread of new monastic communities over the expanse of Western Christendom, which might well be called, by analogy, *universal* religious orders. Both institutions made their appearance at roughly the same time, in the period of church reform that began in the eleventh century, and stood in a reciprocal relationship.[17] This was especially true of the reformed papacy and the monastery of Cluny, probably the key large monastic organization in the early phase of the monastic movement. The same was true of the Cistercians—the oldest order in the narrow sense of the word—and the military orders, Franciscans, Dominicans, and many others. They supported the evolving papal church, serving in many ways as a model for it; but the papacy also encouraged their particular, transregional expansion, vis-à-vis the diocesan bishops in particular.

The distinctive organization of universal religious orders in the postreform Western Church is bound up with the distinctiveness of the tasks assigned to them. We can characterize Western monasticism as being essentially open to the world. This seems self-contradictory, in light of the world-shunning nature of religious asceticism. For all that the cloistered way of life turned its back on the world in Western

Christendom, monasticism's assumption of various social duties was a specific feature of the West's unique development. The Benedictine Rule rated the work of the *vita activa* equal to the *vita contemplativa*, and most of the later orders drew upon this rule when drawing up their own.[18] The reform orders of the High Middle Ages charged themselves with very specific responsibilities.[19] The Cistercians emphasized manual labor in agriculture and trades, apart from celebrating the liturgy. The Hospitallers concentrated initially on caring for pilgrims, later for the sick; the Antonites treated ergotism, also called Saint Anthony's fire, an illness caused by eating rye that had been attacked by a fungus. The military orders were assigned to fight the heathen in the Holy Land, Spain, and east-central Europe. Preaching stood front and center for the Dominicans and Franciscans; special priority was given to preaching against heretics, to propagandizing for the Crusades, and to missionary work. This kind of specialized division of labor does not appear in any other monastic system in the world. And to this extent, the universal religious orders that emerged from Europe in the High Middle Ages constituted a singular phenomenon.

The basis of Western universal religious orders was the monastery, a domestic community of monks living together like a family. Western monasticism was dominated by the cenobitic way of life, not the anchoritic one. The abbot was owed obedience, just as a Roman *pater familias* was. Obedience was the third of the monk's vows, taken upon entering the community along with those of poverty and chastity. To make a cross-cultural comparison, the obligation of obedience seems to be a trait peculiar to Western monasticism. When domestic communities were merged into larger monastic groups, obedience was transferred to higher bodies. Leadership of the order acquired particular authority, especially in the military orders with their military duties. On the whole, the vow of obedience was one factor that facilitated both transregional and centralized forms of organization. The principle was passed on from monasteries to convents (*Stifte*)—communities of priests or transregional units formed by merging several communities. As was mentioned above, the monastic and hierarchical structure of the papal church was generally geared to the monastic model of obedience.

———

Any attempt to explain why Western Christendom alone developed into such a highly organized religious community during the Middle

Ages has to draw comparisons on two levels—one between the various contemporary Christian churches, and a second between Christianity and other religions. Taking the second first, we must range far afield in both time and space, going back to developmental stages long before the time Europe's gravitational center was created in the continent's northwest. The comparison will help to bring general structural elements of Christianity into focus, and indeed some others that determined the Western Church's unique path. We must then of course pursue the differences of ecclesiastical organization between Eastern and Western Christendom.

———

Judaism, as the mother religion of Christianity, which adopted many of its structures at the very beginning, is a logical starting place for a comparison illustrating organizational features of the Western Church. Throughout its long history, Judaism itself has passed through a particularly large variety of organizational forms, so that we have a very broad spectrum of points of comparison. Although Judaism and Christianity are universal, monotheistic religions of scripture, the former was organized so completely differently in the Middle Ages that the contrast fairly cries out for an interpretation.

Paul Volz ventured a comparison of the older faith with Christianity's early stages of development in his *Die biblischen Altertümer* (Biblical antiquities, 1914):

After returning to Israel from exile, the situation there developed in ways similar to those facing the Christian Church during the first few centuries. The same things could be observed here as there: the widening gulf between clergy and laity, and the increasingly hierarchical structure of the priestly caste itself. We have already observed in pre-exile times the difference between clergy and laity, especially at the great sanctuaries. But then some events magnified that difference. One was the discontinuation of kingship and state autonomy. Formerly, kings had ruled over the priesthood. . . . The fall of kingship immediately altered the relationship between the king and the priests. . . . Now that there was no one who was superior to the priests . . . the temple had a unique significance that enabled the priesthood of Jerusalem to acquire a very special, holy quality. Clergy and lay congregation became two separate bodies; on Yom Kippur each had its own expiatory sacrifice. Throughout the centuries, as we have seen, the difference between clergy and laity hardened more and more, even affecting the planning of the temple precincts, until the laity were completely blocked off from the altar.[20]

Volz does not mean that postexile Jews were on the way to becoming a "papal church." He limits his comparison to the growing gulf between clergy and laity, as well as to the increasing hierarchical organization of the clergy. Other aspects of his comparative approach might well be taken further—perhaps the differentiation by rank when the priesthood is concentrated in one locality, or the elevation of the high priest after the kingdom disappeared. Both play a part in our understanding of the position of the medieval papal church. But here is a central point: the dichotomy between clergy and laity was connected with the significance of the cult of sacrifice—in postexile Judaism as in Christianity. The sacrificial mass in Christianity is very different in kind from the bloody sacrifice offered in the temple at Jerusalem, but the Christian form of mediation through sacrifice to God presumes a priest, who, as the one carrying out the sacrifice, is placed above the layman. The radical break in Judaism came in 70 AD when the Second Temple was destroyed. The sacrificial cult vanished, together with the sacrificing priest. Christianity, in contrast, used the celebration of the Eucharist, understood as a sacrificial feast, to create a religion that made the priest a necessity. The Eucharist, along with baptism, forms the nucleus of the sacraments administered by Christian clergy. Christianity, as a sacramental religion, needs to elevate the clergy above the laypeople. It is the only monotheistic world religion that has retained this structural element—and with it the capability of constructing a large clerical institution.

As stimulating as the parallels may be between the temple priesthood in postexile Judaism and the hierarchical clergy in Christian churches, their differences must be examined as well. To serve in the temple in Jerusalem—from the lowest positions to the dignity of the high priest's office—one had to be descended from certain families.[21] Postexile Judaism offers a prime example of a priesthood legitimized through hereditary charisma. Historically, the limiting of the priest's office to members of priestly dynasties is found in many religious communities and is particularly pronounced in Zoroastrianism, Hinduism, and Taoism.[22] The phenomenon was widespread in antiquity, as exemplified by the great oracular sanctuaries in Greece and Egypt.[23] Christianity broke radically with these traditions. Consecration was the exclusive qualification for priesthood. Preliminary moves in this direction were found in the Hellenistic mysteries.[24] Anyone who passed on something holy had to have some knowledge of the people from whom he had received it in his turn. In this model, spiritual forefathers replaced biological ones. Christianity latched on to these rudimentary beginnings via the concept of apostolic succession. Sacred continuity was forged neither by descent, as it was in religions based on hereditary charisma, nor by following a taught tradition—a pattern that occurred just as frequently—but by consecration. The power to consecrate was a fundamental structural element of the Christian Church. It was a key prerequisite for the pope's unique position that he gain control over the power to consecrate while obtaining jurisdiction over religious offices throughout the realm of the Western Church. Freeing spiritual offices from the framework of hereditary charismatic descent made them more available; Christian Churches took advantage of this availability, in which lay their particular organizational strength. The papal church knew how to utilize these offices better than any other Christian community.

The destruction of the Second Temple in 70 AD signaled the end of the priesthood for the Jewish religious community. A hierarchical clergy was no longer a cohesive factor and was not revived subsequently. Judaism's organizational structures developed along a very different route than did those of Christianity. Nevertheless, Judaism succeeded in achieving widespread integration in late antiquity and the Middle Ages, to some extent expanding into new territory. Judaism integrated without clericalization or a hierarchy and was by and large uncentralized. What centralization there was looked very different to Christian forms. A structural comparison of how these two universal religions developed differently may illuminate some controlling aspects of Europe's special path.

The scribes were the only ones left to provide leadership for the Jewish religious community after the end of the temple priesthood.[25] They did not perform any of the functions of a priest but owed their position to their scholarly expertise in Holy Scripture. These "rabbis" organized themselves into schools, the most important being the school of Hillel and his descendants, who ultimately settled in Tiberias.[26] The House of Hillel descended from King David, and through that ancestry legitimately possessed hereditary charisma. The patriarch from this dynasty, serving as supreme head of the Palestinian Jews, filled a role best described as "prince of scholars."[27] An advisory assembly from the academy he led was formed at the patriarch's side; although it was called the Sanhedrin, it was unlike the high council that existed before the catastrophe of 70.[28] After 138, Hillel's patriarchate attained the status of official representative of the Jews for the entire Roman Empire.[29] Further secular rights accrued, for example, the levying of taxes and jurisdictional rights. But state recognition also strengthened the patriarch's religious authority. He made doctrinal decisions, ordained rabbis, installed or removed heads of communities, and controlled the calendar, crucial for determining the dates of feast days.[30] Most important of all was the edition of the so-called oral Torah, the traditional religious law that needed to be established as binding. And so Mishna (tradition, teaching) was created and then Gemara (addition, completion)—together they made up the Talmud (teaching)—in a Palestinian version.[31] Trends toward centralization in Palestine came only in part from the Jewish religious community itself, in part from the constraints of the authorities around it.

The Jewish development in the Roman Empire was paralleled simultaneously in both the Arsacid and Sassanid Empires of Persia and after the advent of Islamic rule.[32] From the second century on, an exilarch represented the Jewish minority at the Persian royal court in Seleucia-Ctesiphon. He did not have any religious authority, but he did have political and administrative responsibility, with an emphasis on taxation and policing. Like the House of Hillel, the exilarch's family was descended from King David, their leadership hence legitimate according to the holy right of blood. The great Jewish centers of learning in Mesopotamia were promoted by the exilarch, who was nevertheless not their head. Two of these schools achieved exceptional significance: one was founded in Sura about 219 and the other in Pumbeditha after 259. The so-called Babylonian Talmud was written at these schools; it was to become the norm on which all of Judaism was based.[33] Jewish academies in Mesopotamia flourished longer than the ones in Palestine, most probably because of how culture and lordship were framed in the former, especially during the Abbasid caliphate. Even the extensive influence of the Babylonian Jewish Talmudic academies must be tied to circumstances affecting communications in the great empire centered there.

Neither the patriarchate in Palestine nor the exilarchate in Mesopotamia was able to be a centralizing force for very long in Judaic history. The same held for the great academies in these two key regions. The lasting achievement of integrating medieval Judaism did not originate there but with the writing down of the oral Torah, that is, the Talmud.[34] Through the Talmud, Hebrew and Aramaic gained recognition as written and literary languages in the entire Mediterranean and beyond. The Talmud brought about a "rabbinizing" process throughout the Jewish diaspora in the eighth and ninth century. Specialization on issues of religious law received an enormous boost because the law was now written down. The rabbi was (and is) neither a priest nor a clergyman separate from the laity.[35] His qualifications did not come through consecration but by study. A rabbi's authority was personal, residing in his learning, which offices and degrees of consecration could not hand down. The relationship of rabbis to one another was not the least bit hierarchical. Though schools played an important role, the office of principal did not lead to any higher rank. The medieval rabbinical synods in central Europe probably followed the Christian example. As structures, however, they were not binding on the organization of the Jewish religious community, never producing the right to summon and preside over an assembly that could construct a hierarchical relationship. The organization of the medieval Jewish religious community was in essence horizontal, standing in stark contrast to the vertical structures of Christian churches, particularly the papal church.

The pair of contrasting ideal types—"religion of the book" and "cult religion"—that Siegfried Morenz introduced into scholarly debate on religion can help us differentiate developments in Judaism and Christianity.[36] Both of these monotheistic world religions can be seen fundamentally as religions of the book because they are based on holy scriptures—to some extent on the same ones—whose particular character shaped them at different times in very different ways. Postexile Judaism possessed strong elements of a cult religion. The cult of sacrifice in the temple at Jerusalem was criticized by nonconformist groups in the community, for example, the Essenes, even before the catastrophe of 70. The loss of a religious center forced a radical redirection. The writing down of the oral Torah in the two versions of the Talmud took the route to a religion purely of the book to its conclusion. A wide-reaching integration of the religious community occurred that was anchored in the great significance of holy scripture and had no central institutions. In the great Christian churches of antiquity and the Middle Ages, the holy book scarcely had the same kind of cohesive function; elements of a cult religion seem much more firmly developed in those churches, along with the trend toward a separate clergy and laity.

Symptomatic of the differences outlined here are the respective reasons for divisions within the two religious communities. In the early Middle Ages, Judaism witnessed the secession of the Karaites, who refused to accept the authority of the Talmud. Acknowledging holy scripture was never an issue in the schisms of Christendom during antiquity and the Middle Ages. The main controversies concerned articles of faith, questions of cult, and problems of hierarchical organization, this last being especially prominent in the Great Schism of 1054 between the Western and Eastern Churches. Such questions never even arose within the Jewish religious community because of the particular way it was organized.

After the emergence of academies and scholarly centers, typical of religions of the book, Judaism showed some stirrings in the direction of centralization, or transregional integration. About the same time that schools of Judaism were being established in Palestine and Mesopotamia, the monastic universities of Nalanda and Vikramasila were becoming intellectual centers of Buddhism. Around 500, they were joined by schools in Nisibis, in the East Syrian Church. Not until the twelfth century were the first Western universities established in Paris and Bologna—and not, significantly, in Rome. As transregional teaching institutions, new universities in Europe needed authorization from the pope and so fell under his jurisdiction. Thus they were rapidly incorporated into the papal church system, but they hardly played a part in founding it. The organizational forms of the papal church did not emerge from the organizational forms of religious book learning.

———

In the spectrum bridging religions of the book and cult religions, Islam can indisputably be categorized as a religion of the book. There were no eucharistic liturgies, no sacraments, and consequently no priests or any cultic authorities acting as intermediaries between God and mankind.[37] Therefore, a split between laity and clergy like the one in Christendom could not exist in Islam, so it did not construct any hierarchies. Islamic religious authorities had no priestly functions. They were scholars of religion, befitting Islam's nature as a religion of the book. The word *alim* (plural *ulama* or *ulema*) means "the person who knows." The *ulama* became a class of religious scholars who interpreted the Qur'an, who had learned the Prophet's sayings and practices (*hadith*) that had been handed down, and who from that knowledge could give information to simple believers about everyday religious issues.[38] Their tasks, dress, and social role were very similar to those of Jewish rabbis.[39]

We can find other striking parallels with Judaism if we understand Islam as a religion of the book. Just as Judaism had a second written source besides the Torah, the Talmud, Islam had, besides the Qur'an, the Sunnah, a collection of the sayings and practices of the Prophet and his Companions. The concept is the same: just as the Talmud summarizes the oral Torah in writing, so too, the Sunnah summarizes the "unwritten revelation" of Islam.[40] In the ninth century, this written record of the oral tradition became, next to the Qur'an, another written source for the system of standards and duties to which Muslims must adhere. Just as the codification and dissemination of the Talmud throughout the Jewish diaspora led to "rabbinizing," the writing down of the tradition established the importance of the *ulama* in Islam.[41]

The recording of the *hadith* collection led to a process of juridification in Islam. Islam, like Judaism, is a religion of law. The western branch of Christendom did not become a religion of law until it developed canon law.[42] The *ulama*, as learned religious men, were mainly concerned with legal issues, often acting as judges. The juridification of the Islamic religious community led to very little centralization or hierarchy formation, if any. Unlike the situation in Christendom, religious authority continued to be distributed over a wide array of people. In the papal church, the making of laws and the spiritual jurisdiction of, and over, priests were tied in with a system already established by the consecration of priests, which thereby reinforced the system. This preestablished situation did not exist in Islam. Beginnings of a hierarchy were created in the *madrasas*, Islamic advanced schools, where religious scholars of different ranks educated the *ulama*'s recruits.[43] In the ninth century, Islamic religious scholarship crystallized into four great schools that were to be of lasting importance: the Malakites, Hanafites, the Shari'ites, and the Hanbalites. But these great schools never developed any organizational structures. There were no principals heading the schools, no highest teaching authority, no advisory councils. Solidarity was forged by a school's founder and especially by the teacher-student relationship that became significant for the authority of the teaching tradition. Owing to the principle that a law could originate with a consensus of believers, or at least of legal scholars, and not just with legal written sources, centralizing trends could not even materialize.[44] The belief that the Muslim congregation could never agree to anything that was an error did not lead to the formation of institutions like the synods and councils found in Christendom.[45] Islam never went so far as to generate large, widespread, and permanent organizational forms for the *ulama* as religious authorities.

Interactions among the many kinds of *ulama* groups historically involved the relationship of this class of religious scholars to the head of the religious community, the caliph. The relationship was occasionally conflicted, and for a long while rather distant and not very clearly or formally organized. The caliph's position was at first defined by his succession to the offices that the Prophet Muhammad held when he died in 632. Caliph comes from *halifa* (deputy). It is not absolutely clear whether the first caliphs understood themselves to be God's deputy or merely the deputy of God's ambassador—a question that was to become significant in later conflicts.[46] At any rate, as Muhammad's successors they filled a role that—to our current way of thinking in separate categories—comprised both secular and spiritual functions, that is, political and religious ones.[47] When Islam was founded, a specific way of organizing lordship was established, something that did not happen in Christianity. Islam was also radically different from medieval Judaism. The caliph was the leader of the *ummah*, the community of believers, which was a religious community and a state body at one and the same time. The caliph had to lead Friday prayers and conduct governmental business; he had to head up the army during a war that was basically considered to be a jihad, and he had to distribute any money that was the booty of war. The question of the caliph's specifically religious authority was hardly raised at this early stage, but it became increasingly important with the recording of the religious tradition and the rise of the *ulama* as qualified interpreters of religious law. The opposition between the caliph and the *ulama* grew most acute under the Abbasids.[48] The *ulama* considered themselves to be the guardians of the holy law independent of state power; the caliph claimed to be Allah's deputy *and* the highest political and religious authority besides. The conflict came to a head under Caliph al-Mamun (809–33). The caliph decreed that certain religious views be banned, proclaimed the dogma of the created nature of the Qur'an, and ordered an oath to be sworn on this dogma. A kind of inquisition was instituted to persecute dissenters. There was broad resistance to these measures, not only from the *ulama*. They had to be rescinded a few decades later, which seriously limited the caliph's authority. He was not empowered to interpret religious laws, let alone make new ones. The *ulama* were still the only ones qualified to interpret the law, and that meant independently of the caliph or the superiors who relieved him. Religious authority and political power went their separate ways—and of course in a very different form compared to Christian Europe, which produced the highly organized social forms of the papal church alongside the principalities.[49]

Hereditary charisma played a crucial role in the leadership of the Islamic religious community, just as it did in early Judaism—but in striking contrast to Christianity.[50] A great conflict flared up over issues of the lawful succession based on bloodlines, which led to the permanent split into Sunnis and Shi'ites.[51] This was a very different conflict than the clashes over holy scripture in Judaism—the Talmud—or over issues of dogma, cult, and ecclesiastical organization in Christianity. The

Shiat Ali (the party of Ali) argued that only the Prophet's direct descendants were entitled to succeed him, and descent derived only through his daughter Fatima, the wife of his cousin Ali. Extreme Shi'ites believed that divine inspiration would continue to come to the direct descendants of Muhammad.[52] The different Shi'ite factions fought over which line of Ali's descendants (the Alids) were his rightful successors and over how to find the legitimate one among them. The leadership of the religious community by virtue of heredity was undisputed during the two great dynastic caliphates of the Umayyads (661–749) and the Abbasids (749–1258). The special legitimacy of the Abbasids was founded on their descent from Abbas, Muhammad's uncle on his father's side. The Umayyads opposed them; although they belonged to the Prophet's clan, they were more distant relations.[53] The caliph's office came to be seen, at any rate, as basically belonging to the tribe of Koraish. There was some sort of election process in the appointment of the first successor to the caliph's position. Omar, the second caliph, appointed his own elective council to choose his successor—but this did not become an institutionalized regulation.[54]

But in the Christian Churches, only at their beginning were there any intimations of hereditary charismatic elements. The Jewish-Christian congregation in Jerusalem was first led by James, the brother of Jesus. Similar, but later, occurrences were exceptions, and they only turned up in fringe groups, such as the so-called Mountain Nestorians around Mosul, the remnants of a once-significant Assyrian (or East Syrian) Church that had collapsed under Tamerlane's rule.[55] Legitimation by election, not heredity, was the dominant factor in the appointment of a supreme head of a Christian church. There were other patterns as well; for example, a predecessor could designate his successor or a ruler might appoint one, a modality typical of the imperial church. The principle of election was operative in the papal church. The decisive step taken by the eleventh-century church reform, to have the College of Cardinals elect the pope, conclusively established and cemented the principle, defining he papal church's uniqueness as an organized religious community.

The way the supreme head of a religious community received legitimation marked his relationship with the places where those communities were located. The caliphs started to change their place of residence early on. Only the Prophet's first two successors resided in Medina and were buried there. Soon many Mesopotamian cities got into the act as the caliph's place of residence. The Umayyads were centered in Damascus, the Abbasids in Bagdad or Samarra. The leaders of the *um-*

mah had no particular need to tie themselves to Mecca and Medina, the two holy cities of their religious community. A pilgrimage to the holy cities was of course a duty, but the caliph had nothing to do with this religious act. Otherwise, there were no central religious institutions that required his presence; as far as his position as the religion's leader was concerned, the caliph was in principle free to move from place to place. Nor were there essential religious institutions in his respective residences. Even when Caliph al Mansur founded the new capital of his empire in Bagdad in 763, this did not create a new center for his religion. It was surely expected that the design of the caliph's residence would express his sacred quality as God's deputy, but Bagdad did not become a religiously important place because of it. A Friday mosque where the caliph could carry out his obligation to lead the faithful in prayer—that could be located anywhere. A mosque specifically for the caliph that would be given preference before others simply did not exist. This was of a piece with the caliph's other religious functions as the supreme head of the *ummah*. The lack of central religious institutions wherever the caliph resided, and in the holy cities of Islam as well, draws our attention to basic organizational differences compared to Christianity, especially vis-à-vis the papal church. There was no equivalent to the Roman Curia, either in Mecca or in Bagdad.

The pope, as bishop of Rome, was tightly bound to the city, following the Christian principle that tied a bishop to his local church. When the pope's episcopate became universal, nothing essential changed in that regard. The pope, from the twelfth century on, often took up temporary residence outside his episcopal city—in Anagni, Orvieto, Viterbo, and so on.[56] The pope's stay in Avignon from 1303 to 1378 raised serious doubts about whether Rome was indeed the center of the Western Church.[57] Leaving aside the political motivation, there appears to have been a rational argument for the move, given the location of the new residence.[58] Rome was on the periphery of the area belonging to the Western Church, whereas Avignon had a much better, more accessible situation. Ultimately, however, a more favorable geographical location counted for little. It says a great deal about the nature of the papal church that the pope's new residence in Avignon had to be given up and that he returned to Rome. The pope's legitimacy as the *episcopus universalis* was based on his succession to Saint Peter. The *cathedra Sancti Petri*, the *sedes apostolica* on which he founded his authority, was tied to Rome. The pope could not simply build a new city for his palace whenever he wanted to, which is what the caliph did in Bagdad and Samarra. The Avignon experiment went awry. After the papacy's return, the popes created the Vatican, a palace district where their holy isolation as the supreme religious head found expression in a manner similar to the caliph's residences.[59] But the palace was situated on the edge of the episcopal city of Rome and immediately next to the basilica built over Saint Peter's tomb. The structure of the papal church, which is so very much centered on Rome, cannot be grasped without its connection with the episcopal city and the tomb of Saint Peter. Contexts like these are of no interest to the Islamic world. Although the burial places of caliphs, imams, and the Prophet's Companions are venerated as places of pilgrimage, they are insignificant for the leadership of the religious community.

"Suffer not monks in Islam!" was the Prophet's express demand, apparently to draw a line between his religious community and neighboring Christian groups both near and far. He frequently condemned celibacy, and with harsh words.[60] Given these unambiguous instructions from the religion's founder, we cannot expect that forms of monastic organization would be of the slightest importance for the internal structure of Islam. It is all the more surprising that ascetic movements, with their idiosyncratic social forms, did indeed develop in medieval Islam, and were described as "orders," using the term in the broad sense.[61] They are certainly to be taken into account in any comparison between organizational forms in different religious communities.

Very soon after the Prophet's death, tensions arose between world-conquering rulers and pious people who were profoundly swayed by the Qur'an's threat of judgment. A further cause of tension: with the juridification of Islam into a religion of law, the inwardness of religious practice had declined. Mystic and ascetic movements drew their dynamics from these tensions; practitioners were later known as "Sufis" and often opposed the caliphate as well as the *ulama*. There were many models for their way of life in the religions around them, especially in the Iraqi and Syrian regions, which witnessed the earliest beginnings of Islamic asceticism—probably on account of Christian, Manichaean, and Buddhist influences.[62] They had some fundamental principles in common: the ideal of poverty ("fakir" and "dervish" mean "a poor man," "a door-to-door beggar"), fasting well beyond the requisite time period, and prayer, also performed outside of the prescribed times. The only exception in Islamic asceticism was the principle of celibacy. The early mystics were often artisans or plied some other trade. In the early stages there were probably masters surrounded by a circle of disciples, but permanent forms of organization did not develop until the twelfth century, when followers of the great ascetics formed brotherhoods constituting permanent religious communities.[63]

The social basis of Sufi orders was not the cloister, as it was for Christian orders.[64] Nor was it a question of spiritual domestic communities forming a transregional association. The organization was based on the relationship between master and disciple. The *sheikh* or *pir* had virtually unlimited power over the *murid* ("the committed one"). Absolute obedience was required.[65] The master supervised the disciple's development, until accepting him, through an act of initiation, as a part of the chain of a spiritual tradition stretching back to the founding *sheikh* and through him to the Prophet. This so-called *silsilah* was the constitutive organizing principle of the community; it created a spiritual "lineage," so to speak, that was based on descent through doctrine—a concept also found elsewhere.[66] Other regulating factors might be added to this essential organizing principle of Sufi communities—sharing a domestic life together was one—but it never resulted in a unified model.[67] The *sheikh* might live with his disciples—with or without his family— either temporarily or permanently. The *sheikh*'s house of instruction could be a regular meeting place for the brotherhood's members. His family could be so closely drawn into the life of the brotherhood that the directorship and the house of instruction would be handed over to a son.[68] This had precious little to do with the monastic life, whether compared to Christian or other forms. The Sufi orders founded very strong religious traditions on these social structural models. Many of them were active in distant areas of the vast Islamic region. To the extent that they can be so understood, we might very well speak of them as universal communities belonging to a religious order. The principle of spiritual genealogy according to which they were organized gave them a high degree of stability. But this foundation never led to the construction of organizational forms based on a principle of representation spanning huge areas. The Sufi orders had no chapter-general and did not elect a grand master. In the papal church, the root model of the spiritual domestic community seems to have been crucial to the growth of these organizational forms in the church's universal religious orders. Differences of this sort are significant over and above the purview of monasticism and asceticism. It was only the specific composition of the universal orders in Western Christendom that enabled them to give the papal church lasting support.

In Sunni Islam, the sectors of religious organization were relatively disconnected, which was so different from the papal church with its homogenous, highly centralized organizational structure incorporating an immense area. There was no bracketing of the *ulama* and the Sufi orders as happened with the secular and the religious clergy in the Western Church. Neither group of religious experts was dependent on the supreme head of the religious community, the caliph. True, there were legal scholars in the administration; Islam did not differentiate between spiritual and secular law. But the *ulama*, as the repositories of religious authority, were independent of the caliphs—and especially of the rulers who succeeded them after the decay of the Abbasid Empire. This process of making legal scholars independent cannot be interpreted in the European sense as a separation of spiritual and secular powers. Nor did the process produce a secular state entity—quite the opposite: politics and religion have hardly ever been as closely allied in any culture as they were in the Islamic world. From its very founding, the *ummah* was simultaneously a religious community and a sovereignty association (*Herrschaftsverband*).

Considering how loosely connected the various social forms of organization were, it is astonishing that a cultural area as large as Islam became so tightly unified. This was true as well in the linguistic sphere. Whereas Latin, the sacred language of the papal church, is no longer a living language, the holy tongue of Islam is spoken by hundreds of millions. This has to do primarily with the different positions the holy book occupied in Christianity and Islam. The Qur'an is an "Arabic Qur'an," as it itself literally says.[69] The divine word is closely tied to Arabic through its revelation in the holy book. The Qur'an, as the "inlibration"—the "bookification"—of God's word is considered to be untranslatable, which is not the case with the Bible. Accordingly, the Arabic language and script, together with the Qur'an, spread throughout all of Islamic culture, resulting at the very least in bilingualism.[70] The sacred language was more likely to be accepted in regions dominated by orthodox *ulama* Muslims, but it was not adopted in its entirety everywhere. Wherever heterodox thinking had its followers, the more ancient vernaculars survived. This was also true of places Islamized by Sufi orders, the different communication systems of the two groups crystallized in language use. Arabic was of course not only disseminated in Islamic culture as a holy language; it was also the language of an imperial administration and several of that empire's successor states—and the two functions were inextricably intertwined. This was the complete reverse of the situation in Europe, where the papal church and principalities faced each other as two discrete systems. Even using language development as an indicator reveals profound differences in the ways Islamic and European cultures regulated lordship and religious communities.

————

The problem of how to regulate lordship and organize religious communities is fundamental to all universal religions. "Universal religions" have been defined in contrast to the type "ethnic religions"—a somewhat unfortunate label.[71] The latter term refers to the religions of individual tribes, peoples, or kingdoms; in other words, these religions claim no validity beyond their immediate social groups. But universal religions claim exactly that, and so their problem is to tie their own structures to those of an established lordship alien to them. The problem may arise from very different situations: the religious practitioners may be persecuted and suppressed minorities or minorities with a recognized status; they may have a problem with a dominant imperial church or an imperial church claiming exclusivity. Islam occupies a special place among universal religions in that the expansion of religion and empire went hand in hand, and so scarcely any parallel structures of lordship and religion developed. Rather, the caliphate assimilated the older universal religions under the all-embracing conditions of its lordship; practitioners of monotheistic religions of the book were recognized minorities, distinct from persecuted polytheistic groups.[72] In this respect, the caliphs carried on the religious policy of their Sassanid and Arsacid predecessors in the Persian Empire. The example of the Babylonian Jews, led by the exilarch and with academic centers spreading beyond the borders of the empire, showed that these conditions of lordship could produce an elaborate organizational structure, even for a minority.

This point holds even more for the Nestorian Church,[73] which constructed a tightly knit ecclesiastical organization based on a hierarchical clergy headed by a catholicos or, later on, a patriarch residing in the imperial capital of Seleucia-Ctesiphon. The weakening of its broader ties to Christendom in the Eastern Roman Empire, which the Persian kings demanded but which also reflected internal decisions, did little or no harm to the creation of a strongly centralized Christian church in an empire controlled by non-Christians. The Nestorian Church's mission extended well beyond the borders of the Persian Empire and later of the Islamic Empire, even as far as China. The Nestorian Church had the largest catchment area of any medieval Christian church—and it never became an imperial church.[74]

Of all the great universal religions, it was Buddhism that was subject to a great many different influences from the varied forms of organized lordship that framed its context. Although its organization as a non-hierarchical monastic religion did not in the slightest preordain its becoming the state religion of several Asian kingdoms, it did indeed become just that, although not a religion that the state specifically endorsed—in Sri Lanka, Japan, but especially in China.[75] For the last, the Toba Wei dynasty (386–534) of the early Middle Ages is illustrative.[76] Monks and monasteries were brought under state control. The emperor appointed a monk as supervisor, an "imperial teacher" who was given a role in the conduct of the empire—a new form of organization in Buddhism that contradicted its own traditions. Rulers founded monasteries, donated lands to them, bestowed money upon them, and financed the translating of sacred texts. In return, the monks had to pray for emperor and empire—paralleling in many ways the functions of Frankish imperial monasteries. But the construction of a Buddhist imperial church in China was, as it turned out, only an interlude. Buddhist monasteries were disbanded in the ninth century as part of a Neoconfucian reaction—at the same time, by the way, as institutions of other universal religions were disbanded, for instance, those of the Nestorians and the Manicheans.[77] The Chinese empire's attempt to protect itself from the influence of universal religions had a lasting impact upon the cultural region, as we have seen in the preceding chapter in connection with the family. The development of an organized church was restricted to indigenous Taoism.[78]

The relationship between the regulation of lordship and the organization of a religious community changed often throughout the history of Christianity as well. The fourth century was clearly definitive, establishing Christianity as the imperial religion of the *imperium Romanum*. The extensive assimilation of the imperial church into the structure of the Roman Empire started during the Council of Nicaea convoked by Emperor Constantine in 325.[79] The Roman Empire in late antiquity was an intensely hierarchical and bureaucratic construct. As a consequence of its assimilation, the Christian Church adopted the same organizational forms. Every *civitas* was to have a bishop. The bishop of a capital of a political province was given special rights. The metropolitan was to convene provincial synods, preside over them, approve the election of bishops, and oversee the religious and disciplinary life of his province. Special rights accrued to the bishops of Rome, Constantinople, Alexandria, and Antioch, from which foundation the concept of the Pentarchy was born: five patriarchs when Jerusalem was added. The honorary primacy among them fell to the bishop of Rome, the oldest imperial capital; the bishop of Constantinople ranked second. This status had nothing to do with the right to summon synods at the imperial level, which the metropolitan could do on the provincial level; *that* was the exclusive right of the emperor, who traditionally claimed sovereignty in religious matters as well. The organization of the imperial church in the fourth century, retaining the structure of the Roman Empire, was supposed to be permanent. From the standpoint of its assumptions regarding lordship, that is why the universal religion of Christianity acquired such a hierarchical order. But hierarchical does not necessarily mean centralizing. The development of the papal church into a highly centralized religious community for cultic matters, for doctrine, jurisdiction, and administration, was not preset in the Roman imperial church. The comprehensive conditions of lordship played an important part in it as well.

The systems of lordship with which early medieval Christian churches were implicated developed very differently in the East and the West. There was continuity in the East that lasted over many centuries. The Byzantine Empire carried on the tradition of the eastern half of the Roman Empire. The patriarch of Constantinople was secure in his official seat next to the imperial palace, but he was also dependent on the emperor. The power relationship between the emperor and the patriarch kept changing; the patriarch essentially held the position of a court bishop. It was completely different in the West. Rome had lost its role as the imperial residential seat even before the Western Empire came to an end. The congruency of the bishop's seat and the ruler's seat therefore ceased to exist sometime before 476. The end of the Western Roman Empire put the bishops of Rome into a precarious position. True, Justinian's conquests had once again brought Rome and the lands around it under imperial lordship, but there was no guarantee of lasting protection. The menace grew larger when the Langobards invaded Italy. The very existence of the Roman Church was threatened, particularly in the sixth century.[80]

This critical time, however, created some opportunities for development. Many local lords in the Italian regions, who were still nominally dependent on the Byzantine Empire, took over the protection of the population, thereby earning a measure of autonomy. Even the bishop of Rome acquired secular rights of lordship during this time.[81] The amalgamation of secular lordship within the environs of Rome and spiritual authority over the city's larger encompassment would give the popes some backing when they later laid claim to the universal episcopate. But from the start, their relative independence under Byzantine sovereignty made a particular kind of development possible. The pope was part of the Byzantine imperial church, of course, and until the eighth century he would notify the emperor of his election; compared to the patriarch of Constantinople, however, he enjoyed far greater independence. It was the papacy's particular good fortune to be able to establish its position at a point on the empire's margin and not at its center.

The same principle lay at the heart of the papacy's relationship with the second great medieval European power, the Frankish Empire. The popes in the eighth century asked the Carolingian kings to protect them from the Langobards, who although distant were nevertheless very active in Italian affairs. After Charlemagne conquered the Langobard kingdom, the bishop of Rome's see was once again on the periphery of a large empire. The pope in the Carolingian Empire ran little risk of sinking into the dependent position of a court bishop. The marginal geographic location of the papal see on the empire's edge thus appears essential to understanding the papacy's singular development.

However, the alliance that the popes concluded with the Carolingian kings was based on terms very different from those grounding its relationship with the Byzantine emperors. In reciprocation for protection, or for the granting of regional authority, the popes legitimized the new dynasty by anointing Pippin in 751 and again in 754, along with his sons, and ultimately by crowning Charlemagne emperor in 800. This produced a brand new configuration of lordship. Anointing or crowning a ruler had, as it were, sacramental character. The model of the high priest as mediator of grace conferring the Christian office of ruler redefined the relationship between spiritual and secular powers. This understanding of lordship would afterward gain acceptance throughout the Western Church. It opened up new ways for the church, especially the pope, to intervene in the regulation of authority. It was an important step in the development of the papal church into a structure that was to be the equal of, but also superior to, the princes' authority.

The reorganization of the Frankish imperial church was another result of the alliance between the pope and the Frankish king.[82] Ecclesiastical organization was just underway in large areas of the empire, so that the potential for exercising influence was particularly strong. On the whole, Carolingian church reform largely aligned itself with Rome.[83] This was true not only of ecclesiastical organization in the narrow sense but also of the liturgy, the administration of the sacraments, the veneration of saints, and many other aspects. An important indicator of Romanization was the exclusive use of Latin as the liturgical language. It can be said that this reform created a new type of imperial church in which the pope occupied a special position. The reformed Frankish imperial church was to be an important foundation stone for the papal church in the High Middle Ages. It was predicated on a completely different structure of authority than the Byzantine Church was. In the latter, the bishops held an almost bureaucratic post, whereas in the former they were incorporated into a feudal system in which their duty to the king included even military service.[84] The imperial church under the Carolingians was based on manorialism and the feudal system and was further elaborated upon in the Ottonian and Salian eras. The tensions inherent in this system, primarily those around the appointing of bishops, led to the great eleventh-century conflict that would direct the relationship between spiritual and secular powers in Europe: the Investiture Controversy. The Eastern Church never experienced a similar conflict because it lacked the requisite lordship structure. In the West, the Investiture Controversy, and the preceding *Libertas ecclesiae* movement as well, created essential structural elements for a papal church in the process of freeing itself from lordship ties, ties that were also unknown to the East.

––––––

The constellations of lordship within which the papal church was developing interacted repeatedly with doctrines that the papacy was generating concerning its own position. This does not mean, of course, that the papal church's advance can be accounted for primarily, let alone exclusively, by the elaboration of these doctrinal theories. Theoretical claims all too often blatantly contradicted the political and social realities. But no doubt the concept of the pope's primacy—which had been worked out in theory long before it was actually realized—contributed to the very possibility of a phenomenon unique in the history of religion. Three stages in the growth of this concept will serve as illustration.

The reign of Pope Damasus I (366–84) was a critical period in the enlargement of the claim to primacy. The Roman emperor had assigned special authority to the pope. Emperor Theodosius stated in 380 that "all peoples are to follow the faith given to the Romans by Peter, which is now represented by his deputies, Pontifex Damasus and Bishop Peter of Alexandria."[85] Two years earlier, the emperor Gratian had declared the bishop of Rome to be the court of appeal for proceedings against bishops in the Western Empire and made him also the sole legal court for similar proceedings against metropolitans in his part of the empire. Rome thereby became the jurisdictional center of the Western Church. The claims of Pope Damasus himself went much further.[86] Drawing support from the New Testament promise to Peter (Matt. 16:18), he was the first to articulate the doctrine of the pope's universal episcopate. He said that Peter was granted the power to loosen and to bind, which was tied to the *cathedra Petri*. Furthermore, all of his successors as bishop of Rome were to occupy the *cathedra* and would thus be the successors to all the power of the office granted to Peter. This doctrine of the *sedes apostolica*, the Apostolic See, formed the basis of the pope's claim to primacy.

Following the alliance with the Carolingian Empire, a second, very important phase in the papal church's progress produced the *Constitutum Constantini*, the so-called Donation of Constantine, a crucial document for the theoretical underpinnings of the papacy.[87] The document was a forgery that originated within the pope's circle, probably in the third quarter of the ninth century. The papacy's actual power at that time was hardly impressive; its attempts to interfere in Eastern Church affairs had failed. The Donation recounted the legend of Pope Sylvester I's conversion of Constantine and grounded the transfer of his ruling seat to Constantinople on the argument that the earthly emperor should not reside where the deputy of the heavenly Emperor had his seat. The document appears to reflect full awareness of the opportunity to consolidate power from a position on the periphery. According to the Donation, the pope as the supreme head of the universal church was to receive imperial rank; the emperor serving in this elevation by presenting him with what was later called the tiara, along with other honorific insignia, and granting him the right to ride on a white horse, just like the emperor himself. Finally, the emperor was to give the pope sovereignty over unspecified lands and islands in the West. Making the claim to primacy dependent on having secular rights of lordship, however limited, was obviously intentional.

The claims articulated in the Donation of Constantine played a leading role in a third and ultimately deciding phase in the establishment of the papal church: the Investiture Controversy. Gregory VII's *Dictatus Papae* in 1075 built on the Donation of Constantine, completely working out the papal church's program, as can be seen in the first twelve (of twenty-seven) statements of the *Dictatus*:

The Church of Rome has been founded only by the Lord.

Only the Bishop of Rome is legitimately called universal bishop.

He alone can depose or reinstate bishops.

His legate presides over all bishops in council even if he is of lesser rank, and can pronounce the sentence of deposition on them.

The Pope can also depose those who are absent.

Among other things we may not even live in the same house as those who have been excommunicated by him.

He alone is permitted, if the age requires it, to decree new laws, establish new bishoprics, transform chapters of canons into monasteries and vice versa, divide rich sees and combine poor ones.

He alone may use imperial insignia.

All rulers have to kiss only the Pope's feet.

His name alone may be named ceremoniously in the churches.

This name is unique in the world.

He is permitted to depose emperors.[88]

The principles in the document quite openly displayed the major bones of contention of its time. In part, they summarized *faits accomplis*, in part, claims that were never realized. Gregory was far from achieving them, at least for his own reign. To interpret the creation of the papal church from the development of the primacy doctrine alone would certainly be one-sided, improperly discounting the great variety of controlling factors in its emergence. Another pertinent fact remains:

no other Christian church even began to consider instituting a similar program to make one bishopric supreme and advance it with such consistency over hundreds of years.

———

In areas where missionary work was being carried out, new structures evolved that were key in turning the papal church into a centralized and highly organized religious community.[89] Significantly, some of them started in the small Anglo-Saxon kingdom of Kent, part of Europe's Northwest so crucial to the dissemination of an extraordinary developmental dynamics in the period that followed. Gregory the Great dispatched missionaries to the court at Canterbury in 597—here the pope was acting as a leader in the missionary field.[90] The Roman emperor had carried out this function, and secular lords in the territorial and imperial churches had taken it over a very long time ago. The mission was based on a comprehensive plan. All the Anglo-Saxon kingdoms were to be organized into twelve dioceses, with archbishops' seats in London and York. The mission did not have any lasting success except in Kent, so that Canterbury became the center of the ecclesiastical province. Augustine, the mission's head, received the pallium—a newly introduced insignia of exceptional importance.[91] It symbolized how closely the young Church of Kent was bound to headquarters in Rome. Any new archbishop's power of consecration was dependent upon his being granted the pallium; before being awarded, this ring-shaped stola lay on Saint Peter's tomb. This gave the person wearing the insignia a share in papal governance—an exceptional contemporary expression of Rome's supremacy. The close organizational ties with Rome led the Anglo-Saxon Church to adopt the Roman liturgy, Roman rites, the Roman festal calendar, and so on. This kind of tie between a missionary region and Roman headquarters was not a matter of course in those days; quite the opposite, it was the exception. Irish missionaries were very successful at the time in the Anglo-Saxon kingdoms as well as on the continent. The Irish Church—itself a product of missionary work—had not the slightest connection with Rome; there were essential differences in matters of cultic practices and the ecclesiastical system.[92] In 664, at the Synod of Whitby, the Anglo-Saxons had to choose between a Christianity that was linked to Rome and that of the Irish Church, which was not; they chose the former. The clinching argument was the Petrine tradition in Rome, because Saint Peter unlocks the heavenly gates.

The model of the Anglo-Saxon mission was critical for the Romanization of the Western Church and for the selection of Rome as its center. The crucial, overriding point was the model's adoption in the Frankish Empire—by Anglo-Saxon missionaries.[93] There was a direct line leading from Wilfried—a leading proponent of the 664 decision at Whitby in favor of the Roman observance and a later missionary to the Friesians—through Willibrord (d. 739) to Winfried, later Saint Boniface (d. 754), the great reformer of the Frankish imperial church. All three men went to the pope in Rome to receive their charge as missionary. Willibrord was consecrated archbishop there for the region he was about to convert. When Boniface was consecrated bishop during his second stay in Rome in 722, he swore an oath of obedience to the pope on Saint Peter's tomb, which until then was only customary for suburban Roman bishops. His act acknowledged the pope to be his immediately superior metropolitan. He received the pallium in 732 and with it the right to create new dioceses and to consecrate bishops in them. He was ultimately named papal legate for Germania during his third stay in Rome in 737–38. The plenipotentiary powers of papal authority that were granted to Boniface were new instruments of an ecclesiastical organization dependent on Rome. His explicit goal, too, was to bring about "unity and submission to the Church of Rome."[94] The aim of the principal territorial church in the West was realized with the reform that Boniface had initiated for the Frankish Church. And so missionary work, or at least the new structural elements the church had evolved from the seventh century on, was a crucial tool for integrating the older territorial churches, with all their many liturgical and disciplinary regionalisms, into the centralized papal church.

Inherent in any mission is the tendency to link newly opened-up regions with old centers, to create a centralizing effect. This inclination does not generally lead to the expected consequences, as the results of the pope's Anglo-Saxon mission demonstrate. In the fourth century, Patriarch Athanasius of Alexandria consecrated the missionary Frumentius as bishop of Ethiopia.[95] For centuries afterward, the Ethiopian Church was then required to have its catholicos consecrated in Alexandria, with the result that the office might remain vacant for long periods and high rents often had to be paid to the patriarch as well as to the caliph.[96] This burdensome obligation continued to exist into the twentieth century. Nonetheless, Egyptian influence on the Ethiopian Church was slight, which allowed it to develop independently in every respect. The liturgy was probably originally under strong Syrian influence; the Alexandrine liturgy of Saint Mark was scarcely known.[97]

177

There was no question that the patriarch had the least jurisdiction over the Ethiopian Church.

The work of conversion created more, and ultimately independent, territorial and imperial churches. As a rule, the connection with an original missionary center soon weakened, often recognizable only by virtue of its last remains. In the eighth century, the Georgian Church managed to have the patriarch of Antioch relinquish the consecration of the catholicos, whom the clergy and people had elected, and to have him give it over to local bishops.[98] Only the consecration with Myron oil—the ointment required for sacramental acts—still took place in Jerusalem, a clear indication of how significant Christendom felt matters of continuity to be. These symbolic references to old missionary centers did not have any influence at all on the independence of ecclesiastical organization. Even in the catchment area of the patriarch of Constantinople, missionaries created national churches that were largely independent; the first was in the empire of the Bulgars in the ninth century, the second was in Kievan Rus' in the tenth—both used the Old Church Slavonic instead of the Greek liturgy.[99] None of the Eastern patriarchates sent forth missionaries to build up ecclesiastical organizations that even came close to those the papal Church created.

Important factors molding the papal church into a highly organized religious community can be found in some ritual practices specific to Western Christianity. Aspects of a cult religion were decidedly on the increase during the Middle Ages. Indicative of such practices was the Feast of Corpus Christi (*Fronleichnam*), a high feast celebrated in the medieval Western Church. It had no counterpart in any other Christian church and no place whatsoever in the Christian calendar of high feasts that marks the celebration of significant stages in the act of salvation. The mystery of the feast was situated in a completely different context. In 1209 a nun, Juliana of Liège, had a vision that revealed to her the need for a feast venerating the Blessed Sacrament of the Altar. The bishop of Liège introduced just such a feast in his diocese in 1247. A Liège prelate—having become Pope Urban IV—prescribed the feast for all Christendom and equated it with the highest feasts in the church year by celebrating the octave as well.[100] It was therefore a rite derived from the culture of piety in a part of northwest Europe; Rome adopted it at one remove—an example of the reverse flow of influence between the two centers of the Christian West. The nature of the feast referred to two interrelated directions in the development of ritual. The feast indeed celebrated the Blessed Sacrament of the Holy Eucharist—not in the sense of communion or of receiving a sacrament but as the worshipful adoration of the real presence of Christ believed to be in the sacrament.[101] The message of salvation transmitted through seeing something holy was the focal point, as it was in the contemporary cult of relics. The festival's name, Corpus Christi (the body of the Lord), itself referred to the connection between the piety shown toward the body of Christ and the veneration of relics.[102] The Feast of Corpus Christi thus marked a dual trend in the course of Western Church ritual—a growth in the importance of the sacraments and of the cult of relics. Both were found as far back as the early Middle Ages.

There were no great differences between the Eastern and Western Churches on fundamental matters of sacramental doctrine.[103] There was nevertheless some drifting apart—mainly in questions of receiving and administering the sacraments. Acts that the East combined in baptism were in the West separated out into baptism, first communion, and confirmation, according to one's age. The sacrament of penance was individualized, restructured, and made a requirement for receiving the Eucharist. The doctrine of transubstantiation helped establish the concept of the Eucharist as the Blessed Sacrament of the Altar, which led to the introduction of the Feast of Corpus Christi. The ordination of priests was revalued upward by making it, too, a sacrament. The number of sacraments was not fixed at seven until the Council of Ferrara in 1439, but administering and receiving the sacraments were a major topic in council deliberations and for papal legislation throughout the High Middle Ages. Setting the number of sacraments at seven distanced them from sacramentals—acts that mediated salvation—which likewise acquired greater significance in the medieval Western Church. Nor were there differences of principle between the Eastern and Western Churches concerning the veneration of relics. That this ritual form developed somewhat differently in the East probably had to do with the veneration of icons.[104] Being able to venerate the saints via the medium of images exonerated the veneration of saints via relics. In the West, relics were thus of greater religious importance; the cult of images had not caught on there the way it did in the Byzantine Empire. The administration of the sacraments and the cult of relics had a heavily material component. Religious elements of this kind may have accommodated the mentality of the largely illiterate peoples in Europe north of the Alps who were converted to Christianity in the early Middle Ages. That might be one explanation for why Western Christendom promoted the more widespread adoption of elements from cult religion when it expanded—or shifted its center of gravity—to the northwest of the continent.

The greater significance of the sacramental enhanced the clergy's importance in the papal church. The more important the administration of sacraments, the more significant the position of the man administering them. Around the middle of the twelfth century, Gratian, the "Father of Canon Law," wrote:

There are two kinds of Christians. One is concerned with the Divine Office and dedicates himself to meditation and prayer; these are the clerics, those consecrated to God, or converts. The Greek word *kleros* means in Latin "being chosen." That is why those people are called clerics, that is, the Chosen Ones. They are kings, that is, they have command over themselves and others by their virtues, and so they have their authority from God. And that is what the "crown" on their head symbolizes. Laymen make up the second kind of Christians.[105]

The "crown" means the tonsure, cutting one's hair to create a bald spot. It originally signified the ascetic life and submission.[106] In Western Christendom, it became a sign of having entered into the estate of the clergy. Consecration was permitted only to the man who received the tonsure from a bishop or abbot. There were eventually seven degrees of consecration in the Western Church, more than in all other Christian churches: four lower ones and three higher—subdeacon, deacon, and priest. The bishop and pope were superior to them and hence comprised a separate level of consecration. Clergy of all degrees were distinguished by a certain "divine office," to use Gratian's phrase. Religious authority in the Western Church was in principle attached to an office. This did not seem to have been taken for granted in any way. Jochen Martin has drawn our attention to the very different development in this regard in the eastern and western parts of the former Roman Empire.[107] Whereas only religious authority tied to offices was valid in the West, people in the East other than those holding ecclesiastical office could have religious authority—for example, theologians, monks, living saints. This difference between the Latin West and the Greek East can be discovered in traditions that go back a very long time. It was the Latin-Roman tradition that remained in effect in the papal church and its offices.

The nature of offices in the papal church was as strictly hierarchical as it had been in the Roman Empire. The *cursus honorum*, according to which a man would move through offices in a prescribed sequence, had its counterpart in the ecclesiastical career ladder.[108] There were no preconditions for this hierarchy in the origins of Christian offices. The deacon's functions were very different from a priest's. It was not necessary for a man to have been in one office in order to move up to another. But the original functions of many church offices that were part of the degrees of consecration disappeared or were diminished in importance. Cooperation between offices became crucially dependent on cooperation in the liturgy of the officeholders.[109] The papal liturgy was to become exemplary in this regard. And so things went from a horizontal division of labor among ecclesiastical offices to a vertical gradation of clerical ranks. Participation in ritual acts, and especially the assignment of specific duties in administering the sacraments, effected a clericalization that established a hierarchy at the same time.

The evolution of the sacraments in the Western Church also had many consequences for further centralization. The development of the sacrament of penance reserved for the *sedes apostolica* the particularly difficult cases requiring absolution. Indulgences for eliminating earthly punishment for one's sins also made Rome into a central authority. The concept of marriage as a sacrament transferred to headquarters in Rome the competence for the dispensation of obstacles to marriage; many matters of matrimonial jurisdiction were similarly passed on. The ordination of a priest—the sacrament that granted the administering of the sacraments—had a remarkable centralizing influence. We have already discussed the binding of the pallium to an archbishop's power to consecrate—and with that, the entire process of ordaining the clergy had now become concentrated in Rome. To the contemporary way of thinking, the pallium received its power from having lain on Saint Peter's tomb for several days. This tomb acquired great significance as a unifying factor in the papal church. No other Christian church had command over a comparable power center. And moreover, the West's recapture of Jerusalem during the Crusades precluded any competition for the pope as Saint Peter's successor and bishop of the church where the saint lay buried.

———

Rome, the site of Saint Peter's tomb, was at one and the same time a place of pilgrimage and the seat of the church's supreme head. That combination was in no way self-evident from either a religious or a topographical point of view. The popes knew how to exploit this twin function. We have already seen in connection with the Anglo-Saxon undertaking that missionaries on pilgrimage to Rome received their commission from the pope. Great numbers of pilgrims from England—even kings—were to come to the tomb of Saint Peter afterward.[110] Boniface was the first non-Italian bishop to swear obedience to the pope at the tomb. The granting of the pallium, its power believed to have been enhanced at Saint Peter's tomb, was often linked to the appointed bishop's journey to Rome and with time became obligatory.[111] The higher clergy would as a result keep in personal contact with the pope over great distances. The same held true in the secular sphere because the coronation of the emperor was tied to Rome. The penitential pilgrimage and thus the whole nature of pilgrimage experienced a boom because of changes in the practice of penance.[112] The apostles' graves in Rome were among the pilgrims' prime goals. Indulgences granted for pilgrimages produced a pilgrimage system centered on Rome through the introduction of Roman jubilee years.[113] These kinds of measures in the popes' pilgrimage policy cannot alone account for Rome's significance as a center of pilgrimage. Pilgrims from all over Europe would not have been attracted if they had not believed that relics possessed the power to mediate salvation. Rome's growth in importance as a primary place of pilgrimage can probably be explained by a general increase in piety toward relics. This made Rome the papal church's focus for organizing countless pilgrims and at the same time a center for experiencing sanctity. The papal church's position in this dual function, too, made it unique among Christian churches of the time.

The rise of the crusading movement was interconnected with the pilgrimage boom. The peaceful pilgrimage to Rome preceded the armed one to the Holy Land.[114] The Crusades were yet another crucial precondition for the rise of the papal church. The popes' contributions have already been explored. Their summonses would not have generated so much action if they had not resonated at the grassroots level, a further example of the interplay between "upper" and "lower" that is worthy of more consideration. The masses of Christian knights who heeded the calls for Crusaders did not have their mindset formed in Rome. The Carolingian Empire and its successors had produced a new social type, the *miles Christianus*.[115] His two contexts of lordship were the feudal system that came from the heart of the Carolingian Empire and the imperial church in the empires thereafter. And so Roman and Carolingian traditions merged in the Crusades—another factor in the papal church's formation. The new centers in the northwest of the continent had a major influence on the nature of Western Christendom by militarizing it. Without this influence, the contribution of the Crusades to the papal church's centralization and particular form of organization would be inexplicable. And it must be reiterated: no other Christian church in the Middle Ages displayed such propensities.

———

The Roman pontiff ruled over two hierarchical systems at the climax of the high medieval papacy's growth—the secular clergy, who belonged to a diocese, and the regular (or "ordered," "regulated") clergy, who belonged to a monastic community or a religious order. The mere fact that we can speak of a regular clergy as early as then presupposes an important clericalizing process: the vast majority of monks were no longer laymen but priests. The background for this fact can be found mainly in cultic rites and rituals. The celebration of Mass gradually became "the sacrifice of the Mass."[116] In this interpretation, the Mass could be employed for a variety of purposes. The salvation of the souls of the dead grew more significant from the motivating factor of the "sacrifice" of the Mass. More and more masses were donated with this stipulation, and also because the specifically western belief in purgatory was beginning to emerge.[117] Priests leading the monastic life were considered to be particularly propitious officiants at the sacrifice. The idea of the "service of the pure hands" made monks the preferred performer of rituals.[118] More and more monks were consecrated as priests. The number of altars in monastery churches grew apace in order to keep up with the huge number of masses donated. But priests were increasingly required to live the celibate life, like monks, so that they could perform the "service of the pure hands." After the reforms of Gregory V (1073–85), celibacy was an obligation for all clergy from subdeacon and above—a development peculiar to the Western Church.

Requiring priests to live like monks encouraged tighter means of organizing the clergy. Unmarried religious had no descendants to inherit their benefices, and so the nature of their office was preserved—an important tenet of the Roman ecclesiastical tradition, as discussed above. The monastic way of life also involved a *vita communis* for priests at the same church, for example, the cathedral clergy and the bishop, or the canons of a convent *(Stift)*—another feature unique to the West. Life in common required regulations, and the Western monastic tradition ranked obedience highly once the Benedictine Rule came into effect. The assimilation of the monastic way of life thus meant more rigid ties of obedience for the secular clergy. At the Lateran Synod of 1059, as church reform was getting underway, Pope Nicholas II prescribed for the entire secular clergy an amalgamation of their pastoral office with monastic discipline.[119] The assimilation of these two types of religious had precedents of varying strength in the different districts of the Western Church during the reform. In England, for example, some bishoprics had, from missionary times on, so-called cathedral cloisters where clergy lived like monks; this was probably an offshoot of Irish influence.[120] In the Frankish Empire, Carolingian reform attempted to establish the *vita communis* for religious in cathedrals and all secular clergy.[121] Forms of monasticism for the secular clergy were more deeply rooted in northwestern Europe than in the Mediterranean region. There was disparity in the Western Church in these matters between the old and new centers, which had to be eliminated in the era of reform. As monastic principles gained acceptance, the secular clergy became increasingly dependent, which reinforced the church's monarchic and centralist structure.

The two systems of clergy in the papal church can be seen in contrast: The secular clergy were neither as homogenous nor as unified structurally as the regular clergy were. There was a plethora of universal orders, and not all monasteries were organized as monastic associations by any means. In terms of the whole papal system as a highly organized religious community, we may view the regular clergy as a manageable, collective structural element. It is crucial for fitting the two clerical systems into a typology that they be seen as standing side by side in the papal church and as being related in a number of ways. The papal church was not a monastic church, nor Western Christendom a monastic religion. In monastic churches and monastic religions, the forms organizing asceticism were the foundation for the forms that structured their religious communities—this was the case in Buddhism and Jainism, for instance, and to some extent in Manichaeism.[122] Some medieval Christian churches made a few starts in this direction, for example, the Egyptian Church, the Ethiopian Church, but primarily the Irish Church.[123] The special nature of Irish monasticism might well be traceable to earlier connections with Eastern Christianity, but primarily to the social structure of early medieval Ireland with its dearth of cities—a society ill-suited for the way early Christian bishoprics were organized. Perhaps Irish monastic communities were one source of universal religious orders in the Western Church.[124] But those communities were in a very different position. The church was organized primarily along the paradigm of the bishop's church of late antiquity. Monastic communities and universal religious orders came along as secondary forms of organization. How this happened and why they became exceptionally vital to the papal church merit particular elucidation.

The papacy's most significant contribution to the rise of universal religious orders was the exemption given to monasteries and monastic communities, that is, the privilege of being free of the bishop's authority. The Council of Chalcedon in 451 had decided (in canon 4) that monasteries fell under the jurisdiction of their local bishop. The bishop would keep a sharp eye on the monastic way of life, appoint abbots, and, in particular, consecrate clerics in monasteries.[125] Adherence to the Chalcedon decisions was the main reason that the Eastern Church did not develop transregional monastic communities.[126] This marked a change from earlier stages of Eastern monasticism.[127] The Irish missionaries in Gallia and Upper Italy were the first in the West to demand a break with this tradition. Saint Columban claimed the right to combine leadership of a monastery with the power of consecration, as befit an Irish convention. This was granted to him in 628 when he founded the monastery at Bobbio. A similar papal privilege was granted to the monastery of Luxeuil a short time later.[128] Irish monasteries on the continent were now able to use their own consecrating authority to bind their clergy and their dependent churches to themselves, bringing them all together into their own "mini-diocese" so to speak. Any consecration of people and things—altars, bells, cemeteries, and so on—always signified a linking with the consecrator.[129] The power to consecrate as a central structuring principle in Christian church organization—and not, for example, the tradition of teaching, as in other religions—is clearly visible in the principle behind the papal exemption. It spread from Irish monasteries but had not really made an early contribution to the formation of orders because traditional Irish monasticism could only preserve a limited foothold on the continent. The exemptions the pope granted in the tenth and eleventh century for the groups founding the reform monastery of Cluny were decisive: when Cluny was founded, it was placed directly under the pope.[130] The monastery received the pope's permission in 931 to accept any monk whose monastery refused to be reformed, and it could take over any monastery wishing to be reformed—thereby taking the first step toward a reformed congregation. The pope then awarded a crucial exemption in 998 granting unlimited freedom from the authority of the bishop of Mâcon, who had until then resisted the privilege to the point of deploying military force. Freedom from episcopal authority was extended in 1024 to all abbeys and priories under Cluny. The monastery of Cîteaux no longer had to cope with similar difficulties: it was given an exemption when it was founded.[131] It was the same with military and mendicant orders and many other communal orders that sprang up in the High Middle Ages. Removal from the bishop's power was by then taken for granted; it weakened the bishop's church to the benefit of the papal church.

The interests of monastic communities in an alliance were countered by the papacy's interests in taking monasteries and monastic communities under its wing. Some of these interests would exist simultaneously or alternate. One of the earliest outcomes of this was to band together for the purpose of memorializing the dead. Prayer leagues (*Gebetsbünde*) were set up in monastic communities, but not exclusively. The prayer league of Attigny in 762 was particularly historic; it was agreed upon at a Frankish imperial synod of seventeen abbots, five abbot-bishops, and twenty-two bishops.[132] The initiative came from Archbishop Chrodegang of Metz, Boniface's successor, who has been called the "architect of the Frankish imperial church."[133] There were obviously political motives at work, but the object of the agreement was a religious one. The confraternity promised that a brother's community would assist a brother when he died—by saying a hundred masses and psalters for bishops and abbots, thirty for clerics. The commemorative Mass and the (liturgical) remembrance of the dead, with the corresponding ideas of purification in the next world, were motivating factors behind the founding of these associations. The leagues' supporters all came from the Carolingian heartland between the Rhine and the Seine, proving the region to be an innovative center in matters of ritual as well.[134] At the Synod of Dingolfing in 770 a similar prayer league was created by Bavarian monasteries and bishoprics (*Hochstifte*); the two great Swabian abbeys of Saint Gall and Reichenau did the same in 800. The confraternities reached their high-water mark with the monastery of Cluny, which was divided into groups that were integrated differently—there were priories on the property of the main monastery, and affiliated houses (*Tochterkloster*), and loosely associated reformed abbeys. The common bond for the whole association was the remembrance of the dead, which, however, was no longer the constitutive element in Cluny for forming the association.[135] Remembering the dead had played a role in earlier forms of the order; however, it was most certainly but one factor among many, and not the most vital one at that. On the whole, memorializing the dead in the Western Church became very significant for the way the religious confraternity developed and expanded into secular confraternities. Remembrance of the dead evolved quite differently in the East.[136] There was no commemorative Mass, no belief in purgatory. It appears that commemorating the dead was left up to the monasteries there as well, but monastic communities did not create any associations on this basis.

One of the monastic communities' greatest concerns was the reform of monastic life, which was to lead to the founding of monastic associations. Reform could of course mean very different things at different times; in the Carolingian Empire the main point was universal establishment of the Benedictine Rule.[137] Benedict of Aniane began the job with a "reform from below."[138] His founding of Aniane near Montpelier eventually produced a great monastery, just as Cluny achieved later thanks to its reforming spirit. He dispatched monks to reform other monasteries in the subkingdom of Aquitaine. He himself undertook visitations and held instructional courses for monks from other countries. This did not induce monasteries to amalgamate quite yet, but modes of communication between convents were set up that were crucial in later monastic reforms. But to teach monasteries of the same observance how to apply the Benedictine Rule came first and foremost. Benedict continued his efforts in a "reform from above." Louis the Pious commissioned him to reform the monasteries in the whole Frankish Empire and built him a model Benedictine monastery, Cornelimünster, near the imperial palace at Aachen. The imperial synods of 816, 817, and 818–19 dealt with monastic reform; the emperor proclaimed their decisions to be law. There was no mention of the pope anywhere during this period of monastic reform in the Frankish Empire. The Frankish king was the supreme head over imperial abbeys. Benedict of Aniane was his *missus monasticus*, visiting monasteries at the king's behest. This could only be understood as creating an organization in the broadest sense of the term.

But Carolingian reform did have one outcome vital for the future: the monasteries of the empire now followed the Benedictine Rule, and it was uniformly applied. Consolidating the monasteries would only be possible if the rule were the same everywhere. It was the Benedictine Rule that, according to medieval belief, cemented God's bond of salvation with the monk. A tenth-century author expressed the rule's significance as follows: "[God] added a fourth stage of revelation to that of Nature, of Moses, and of the Law of Christ—a stage that was to strengthen the perfected Law: the Rule of Saint Benedict."[139] An opinion of this kind would have been completely unthinkable in the Byzantine Church or any other church in Eastern Christendom.

Achieving freedom for the monasteries provided the strongest motive in the eleventh century for banding monastic communities together—

the most significant stage in the rise of affiliated monasteries. The envisaged *libertas* had, on the one hand, to do with independence from secular lordship—from lay abbots, proprietary church lords, or monastery *Vögte*. In this respect, the movement was a typical phenomenon of the vast region of northwestern Europe where in Carolingian times the feudal system had been established and subsequently the *Bannherrschaft*, based on the imperial church system. But, on the other hand, *libertas* also meant freedom vis-à-vis the bishop's authority. Monastic communal life could not be lived according to the ideals of the age unless it was independent of both secular and ecclesiastical power—and to implement monastic ideals was ultimately what it was all about. The Rule of Saint Benedict offered general guidelines for realizing this goal. Special supplementary *consuetudines* came from individual reformed monasteries as well. Other monasteries gathered around them, taking them as their model. The forms by which they organized themselves were vastly different. The influence of Hirsau, a most important reform center in the German-speaking area, extended to 120 monasteries. They were held together by common ideals and a shared commemoration of the dead based on fraternal prayer leagues.[140] The reform center of Gorze went even further. It sent out monks to be abbots in monasteries wishing to ally itself with Gorze's observance; it expanded its main monastery into a center of education, but it also founded autonomous priories on the abbey's land, together with its affiliated monasteries.[141]

These modes of organization approached the most successful and tightly disciplined monastic community of the time, the *ecclesia Cluniacensis*. Cluny was secularly and spiritually autonomous. Its founder had renounced his right to appoint abbots so that they were chosen without any constraints. The popes had granted the abbey an exemption from the Diocese of Mâcon, as mentioned above. This context enabled Cluny's monks to put an extensive reform program into effect. Cluny was such a magnet of reform that a great number of monasteries were donated to it or subjected themselves to it, in addition to new monasteries founded on its lands.[142] This substantial monastery was still, formally and legally, a single abbey with a single abbot; dependent monasteries had only priors. All monks taking their vows placed them in the hands of the abbot of Cluny.[143]

There were at least two earlier forms for this type of organization. There is proof that some abbots had previously presided over two or more abbeys, lay abbots in particular. And there was already a traditional system in which monks, individually or collectively, settled down in affiliated manors on large monastic estates.[144] But the combination of these different organizational forms and their employment in a radical reform operation was novel, giving rise to a totally new kind of centralized monastic association ruled like a monarchy. As its religious, cultural, political, and administrative center, the monastery of Cluny was on a par with the administrative headquarters of the papal church, which in many ways was its model. The construction of Cluny as a monarchic, centralist band of monasteries was a challenge taken up by the founding of the Cistercians—a democratic, decentralized religious order—so that now the religious order had developed fully as an organizational form characteristic of the Western Church. Around 1200 Cluny consented—not least as a result of papal pressure—to a constitution for its order modeled on Cîteaux, which prescribed annual chapters-general and apostolic visitations to the provinces of the order.[145]

The uniqueness of what Cluny instituted in the direction of universal religious orders becomes especially apparent when we compare this monastic center of the Western Church with the monastic center of the Eastern Church—the "holy mountain" of Athos. The two had several things in common. The first monks began to settle on Mount Athos in the mid-ninth century—not long before Cluny's founding; the Great Lavra—the main monastery on Athos—was founded in 963.[146] In both cases, the eleventh century marked their most significant expansionist phase, and in both cases, freedom from secular and spiritual authority played an essential part in the autonomous development of their respective monastic ways of life. The first imperial privilege, which granted the monastic community on Mount Athos its constitution, dates from 972. Athos was later released from episcopal jurisdiction—an exceptional event in Eastern monasticism—and placed directly under the patriarch of Constantinople. Athos was a center of reform just like Cluny. The Great Lavra was founded in the spirit of Theodoros Studites's reform movement. Further essential impetus to spirituality came from the monks of Athos, although they took a very different direction from Western Church reform and were not guided by issues of the monastery's constitution.

The contrasts between Cluny and Athos are of interest here as examples of tendencies toward divergent modes of monastic organization in Eastern and Western Christendom. The *ecclesia Cluniacensis* was a closely knit monastic society of transregional scope, stretching from Spain to Flanders and from England to central Italy.[147] In 936 its *princeps*,

Alberich, made Abbot Odo the archimandrite over all the monasteries of Rome and the regions along the borders of the area of his lordship— significantly, his title was that of a Byzantine hierarch of the Eastern Church.[148] The "holy mountain" Athos had a transregional catchment area, too, on an extraordinarily broad scale. There were monasteries for Greeks, of course, but also for Caucasian Albanians, Armenians, Georgians, Bulgarians, Serbs, Russians, even South Italian Amalfitanians who were under the jurisdiction of the Roman Church.[149] Athos had lively contacts with all these places. Pilgrims trailed after the monks, with many returning to their own countries as heads of monasteries.[150] But all these connections were kept informal; they did not manage to create a transregional social group, something that was lacking anyway in the monasticism of the Eastern Church.

The *ecclesia Cluniacensis* was a domestic community composed of domestic communities. It was nominally a single large monastery with a single abbot-father at the top.[151] But it was a de facto household embracing hundreds of individual monasteries, each led by a prior, the abbot's deputy. The organization was based on a monastic family living together as cenobites, a way of life that had dominated the Western Church for a long time and that was to provide a foothold for the rise of universal religious orders. This was at variance with the Eastern Church, where anchorites played a far greater role; Athos was settled by ninth-century hermits.[152] A third monastic way of life was practiced at Kellia, where a small number of hermits led a loosely organized communal life.[153] The Grand Lavra, too, had anchorite origins.[154] The *vita communis* was less developed there than in Western monasteries. Many kinds of ascetics on Mount Athos lived in very different types of monastic organizations, but the bonds among them were relatively weak. There would be an annual gathering of the hermits from Kellia, eremites, and abbots, who represented the monasteries. A monk, called a *protos*, would sit in judgment over various legal matters.[155] "A colony of monks" best typifies the organization on Mount Athos.[156] There were "colonies of monks" on holy mountains elsewhere as well. The organization of communal life on Mount Athos proved to be tenacious in the long run in spite of the rather relaxed ties among the ascetics there.

Although the Cluniacs put the liturgy at the center of their communal life, they took on many tasks outside monastery walls—pastoral care, attending to pilgrims, church politics. At its height, the abbot's scriptorium at Cluny was writing more letters than the papal chancellery was. Cluny was at the center of a Europe-wide communication system, and the orders of the Western Church followed in its wake, with very different emphases. In Athos, on the other hand, the monastic colony's out-of-the-way location was itself an indicator of the direction its monastic life took. There were no activities outside the colony; monastic life there turned inward.[157] The *vita contemplativa* was in the forefront, not the *vita activa*, which meant prayer, fasting, and manual labor. The contemplative aspect was intensified on Mount Athos and branched out into the Eastern Church during the Middle Ages. Whereas monks in the West went into the cities to preach to the masses, monks in the East intensified their inwardness. Hesychasm is emblematic of this trend, with its striving to experience divine light through regular repetition of formulaic prayer and through breathing techniques reminiscent of yoga.[158] These major conceptual differences over religious asceticism in East and West caused the two forms of monastic organization to grow farther and farther apart.

————

Organizational structures put their stamp on spatial structures. The density of the transregional organization of the universal religious orders in Western Christendom had a long-term impact—as did the papal church—on the way society structured its relation to space. As we saw in the comparison between religious communities earlier, such a high degree of organization was the exception and not even close to becoming the rule. The intensive transregional organization of the papal church and universal religious orders created excellent conditions in Western Christendom for social and cultural expansion and integration. We will sketch out the geographical context for these processes because it was the foundation for the further growth of European societies.[159] And the geographical context of the most important conditions to be analyzed—those that produced the specific organizational structures of Western Christendom—were most significant for Europe's unique path.

The geographical range of the medieval papal church was much greater than the area encompassed by the European agrarian revolution. This was mainly true of its southern expansion. But we have seen in eastern Europe as well that the new agrarian system at no point jumped the border between the Eastern and Western Churches, and in fact hardly ever got that far. There have been attempts to invoke the diffusion of the manorial system to explain this, especially the spread of monastic manors. The geographical range of the papal church in the Middle Ages was also far greater than the area where the manorial system was established in Europe. The feudal system developed when it joined up with the agrarian and the manorial systems. The scope of the medieval papal church went beyond "feudal Europe." If we pursue the chain of specific and mutually conditioning features of Europe's unique path, then we find the lands occupied by the imperial and territorial Estates were the first to overlap geographically with the papal church. It was stated earlier that the Estates had specifically ecclesiastical roots, as well as origins in agrarian and defense systems. Our brief survey of factors involved in Europe's unique path showed that the papal church was the most sweeping geographical area of all, and processes of diffusion played out over more or less extensive regions within this area. Many of these processes saw the light of day in the Carolingian heartland, that is, in northwestern Europe, where factors that helped form the papal church and religious orders also originated. But the papal church was ultimately a social space centered in Rome, which brings a Mediterranean catchment area into the picture. The papal church, together with the Frankish Empire, began settling people in many places, resulting in a new north-south integration. It also simultaneously created a regional polarization that was to become a huge source of tension as Europe later moved along its unique path.

Another, older, axis was the one linking Rome and the Anglo-Saxon kingdoms; it was no less important than the later one between Rome and the Frankish Empire central to the creation of the papal church. This axis was to Romanize the Carolingian Empire in matters of ritual and ecclesiastical organization. It was modeled on England's ties with Rome. Anglo-Saxon missionaries in the Frankish Empire assisted in the creation of similar ties there. But England was also the jumping-off point for the integration of Ireland and Scotland into the papal church; church expansion there would receive important support from the spread of the manorial system. The same thing happened in regions Christianized by missionaries from the empires that followed the Carolingian *imperium*. The Carolingians in Germany pushed well beyond their eastern frontier in the tenth century and incorporated the areas they conquered into the imperial church. In the eleventh century, the Christianizing of the Scandinavian and east-central European countries made use of forms powerfully dependent on Rome. When Hungary and Poland opted for the Western Church, and Bulgaria and Russia chose the Eastern Church, the papal church's eastern border was essentially confirmed. After Byzantine rule was pushed back along the Adriatic coast and in southern Italy, the pope seized the opportunity to revamp the parameters of the church's situation and make those areas directly dependent on Rome. The same was done for the areas regained from Islamic rulers in the western Mediterranean, for Sicily, Sardinia, Corsica, the Balearics, and especially Spain after the Reconquest. A similar reorganization was attempted in the regions the Crusaders conquered in the eastern Mediterranean: the Holy Land and former Byzantine districts. In both areas a "Latin" episcopate was instituted under the pope's primacy. But the papal church was to give up these regions—apart from a few residual strongholds—when it lost the Crusader states and the Latin Empire of Constantinople.

In this way the borders of a vast area were established by the thirteenth century at the latest, an area that was permanently shaped by papal church structures. It retained many common features in spite of the fragmentation of lordship and the religious split. This was the Europe of the Renaissance and humanism, the Reformation and Counter-Reformation, absolutism and the Enlightenment, princes with limited power and Estates, social disciplining (*Sozialdisziplinierung*) and individualism, universities and secularized science, and the Latin language as it was written and spoken. All these examples are confined to Europe as a social space. And they all had their provenance—in a more or less mediated fashion—in the papal church of the Middle Ages.

Six

The Crusades and Protocolonialism: The Roots of European Expansionism

It goes without saying that the globalization processes shaping advances in today's society had their origins in Europe. Any cross-cultural comparison that does not examine the roots of these processes very closely pays insufficient attention to Europe's particular evolution. European expansionism is a fundamental feature of Europe's special path.

"European expansionism," a term now more and more accepted in scholarly circles, means more than just "colonial history."[1] And if we go back to the beginnings of this expansionism, we cannot confine ourselves to traditional period terms such as "the Age of Discovery and Conquest."[2] The significance of certain early medieval developments has been foregrounded ever more conspicuously in the scholarship on European territorial expansion outside the continent.[3] Two strands of these developments will be given closer scrutiny: the Crusades and early expressions of the Italian maritime republics' colonial policy, which we will call "protocolonialism." They produced two completely different influences crucial for European expansionism: religiously motivated military action and a profit-driven economic policy. Their origins must be treated separately, but the interplay of these influences in the ebb and flow of history generated similar causative factors in European expansionism.

194

The Crusades and protocolonial processes tended to diverge so frequently during their development that we must briefly outline their variant models. In the Mediterranean basin an Islamic expansionist phase, first on land, then by sea, preceded the age of the Crusades from the seventh to the tenth centuries. A common ninth- and tenth-century concern in repelling the Saracen threat forged an alliance between supporters of the subsequent Crusading movement—spearheaded by the Roman popes—and those Italian cities that possessed a fleet. Around the turn of the millennium, an offensive phase followed this defensive one, earning the ambitious maritime republics dominance in the western Mediterranean.[4] There were still common aims in this phase as well. But the Crusade of 1096–99 was to reveal disagreements. Until the pope applied massive pressure, the maritime republics were reluctant to send their fleets to the Holy Land—Venice waited until about 1100, after the fall of Jerusalem—so that they would be in a position to secure their trading outposts.[5] Commercial interests had made the republics think twice about participating in the Crusade itself. They had meanwhile entered upon so profitable a trade with Islamic countries that they had no inclination to put it at risk.[6] These interests continued to color their ambivalent attitude toward crusading exploits. A fuller engagement in the Holy Land might have troubled their Islamic partners elsewhere. There were repeated violations of the trade embargoes imposed by the pope or the councils, and Venice was a major culprit. On the other hand, new trading centers were formed in territories the Crusaders conquered, including bases in colonies supplying raw materials that had to be defended. The ideology behind the Crusades provided an underpinning for military action of this kind. And the maritime republics were indispensable for backers of the crusading movement; they were the only naval powers, or the most important ones, that could guarantee the transport of troops across the Mediterranean or the delivery of provisions to the Christian states in the Holy Land. And so the popes made every effort to stay on good terms with the maritime republics. Warring with "enemies of the Christian faith" and a concern for profitable trade with them seemed in principle to be irreconcilable. But convergences nevertheless materialized from these conflicting motives, creating an area of tension around the protocolonialism of the Italian maritime republics. The crusading movement continued to affect European expansionism through this kind of protocolonialism, although the movement to some extent kept its distance.

There was no equivalent outside Europe for the protocolonialism of Italy's maritime republics and the simultaneous rise of the crusading movement. Culture-specific roots of this sort in medieval Europe may lead us to assume that European expansionism as a whole possessed the same unique character. Although many later facets of expansionism were to evolve in modern times, its decisive pathways had been laid down in the Middle Ages. We must keep in mind that, over and above their significance for the rise and growth of European expansionism, the Crusades and protocolonialism also triggered other specifically European trends, so that together they constituted one key factor, broadly speaking. Examining the dynamics of their genesis will take us to the heart of the debate over special paths in general.

––––––

A comparison of the different medieval Christian churches shows how unique a phenomenon the Crusades were in world history. A crusading movement did not emerge in any of the Eastern national churches, nor in the Armenian, Georgian, Nestorian, Coptic Churches, nor in the Syrian (or Syriac) Orthodox Church. Most conspicuous was the absence of a crusading movement in the Byzantine Church. The Byzantine Empire was initially and more powerfully menaced by Arab invasions than the West was. It fought bitter wars against the Muslim conquerors with varying success; the battle for the holy sites in Palestine became increasingly important. The emperors attempted to imbue this particular battle with the sanctity of religion. They argued that it was a battle for the fame and glory of Christendom, a struggle to free holy sites and crush Islam. The vocabulary of crusading rhetoric in the Byzantine Empire had been fully worked out by the second half of the tenth century. Nicephorus II Phocas (963–69) proposed an imperial decree stating that all soldiers killed in fighting the Muslims would have died a martyr's death; when he tried to enlist the support of the patriarch of Constantinople for this, the supreme spiritual head of Constantinople withheld his approval.[7] The Eastern Church's view was that murder was not entirely excusable, even if committed during the exigencies of war. And public opinion supported their supreme pastor's ruling. That is why the Byzantine emperors' "holy wars" lacked a crucial element of a Crusade: that a warrior's participation was tied to the promise of salvation. The Byzantine Empire did not mobilize any Crusades.[8] Just the opposite: it fell victim to a Crusade itself in 1204. Among the many variously configured Christian groups in the medieval world, the Crusade was an institution restricted to the Western Church.

The close link between the medieval Crusades and Western Christendom can be interpreted by a very simple causal connection: the Crusade was the pope's war. This may sound provocative; on the surface, it contradicts the "grand narratives" that have drilled an image of the Crusades into our heads from our schoolbooks on: Western kings and princes fighting for Christendom's holy sites in the Holy Land—a Godfrey of Bouillon, a Richard the Lionheart, a Saint Louis IX. The pope never used to appear in those narratives. That is certainly right and proper. But it was not the battle for the holy sites that made a Crusade a Crusade; it was the summons of the pope, who—to his own mind—was proclaiming God's will. Without the pope there was no Crusade. Only the pope could summon one; only the pope could dispatch preachers of a Crusade to Western Christendom's farthest reaches so they might motivate knights to take the Crusader's oath—"to take the Cross," as the eloquent formula of the age had it. Most important of all, only the pope could promise the gifts of grace associated with a Crusade and that constituted, in the religious sense, its special character. Not until the armed pilgrimage was joined with the promise of religious salvation did the crusading movement in the West become such a resounding success.

The fully realized crusading paradigm can best be understood through Urban II's call for a Crusade on November 27, 1095, and through the council decrees that followed.[9] The pope's speech whipped up enthusiasm by demanding a "just war" against the Muslims—the people kept interrupting him with cries of "Deus lo volt!" (God wills it!). The Crusaders, he said, would be carrying out "the work of God, and God would lead them. For those that died in battle there would be absolution and the remission of sins." This was precisely the assurance of salvation that the patriarch of Constantinople had refused to give. The council then passed decrees modifying this key point. A general decree granted remission from secular penalties for the sins of all those who would take part in the holy war with pious intent. Moreover, the worldly belongings of all participants were to be placed under the protection of the church while their owners were gone to war. Their surety would be the local bishop's responsibility. These important secular guarantees originated with the Truce of God movement. Every person taking the cross was bound by an oath—a religious requirement for executing such a novel military undertaking. In Clermont, for example, a churchman, the bishop of Le Puy, was nominated to lead the expedition. He was a papal legate, and as the pope's representative he unambiguously expressed the pope's supremacy over this ecclesiastical military enterprise.

Spain and Italy had already witnessed crusading prototypes for the expedition to the Holy Land that Urban II created at the Synod of Clermont in 1095. In Spain, the fight against the Saracens started early and was to drag on for a long time. The whole crusading panoply was present at the battle for the Aragonese city of Barbastro in 1064—more than thirty years before the so-called First Crusade.[10] Barbastro was unequivocally a religiously motivated war, unlike earlier military conflicts when Christian and Moorish leaders would cooperate time and again—El Cid is a typical figure from this earlier time. The knights in the battle for Barbastro did not come from the immediate surrounding region; contingents from various Spanish kingdoms as well as Aquitaine, Burgundy, Normandy, and the Capetian territories were involved. An international army of volunteer knights bore the brunt of the Barbastro and later Crusades; they served in the battle against the heathen quite apart from their feudal obligations. The international composition of the army seems to have been typical of the Crusades and a noteworthy exception in the era of the feudal system. It would enable the pope to lay claim later to a military leadership that exceeded the claims of any feudal organization. The pope was crucially—and characteristically—also involved with the Barbastro Crusade. When knights were gathering in southern France for the Spanish expedition in 1063, Alexander II granted all participants a remission of all secular penalties for sins. This was the original Crusade indulgence, which was to become standard procedure for all undertakings the pope would initiate or approve, in 1095 and after. Alexander II had also probably authorized the Crusade by giving one of the leaders the *vexillum Sancti Petri*, the banner of Saint Peter, another attribute of the Crusade that marked it as "the pope's war." A legate to the Crusades with papal plenipotentiary powers might also have taken part.[11] On the occasion of the Barbastro Crusade, the bishops and princes of Catalonia—but not the pope—proclaimed the Peace of God, which was to protect the people left behind at home. Urban II's summoning of the Crusade in 1095 at the Synod of Clermont also featured the Peace of God—but that time the proclamation originated with the pope himself. Even before Clermont, in 1089, Urban II's actions clearly signaled the Spanish origins of the crusading concept: for the reconstruction of Tarragona, a city on the Moorish border, he had granted an indulgence as substantial as could be earned for a pilgrimage to Jerusalem. In the latter instance, the combination of carrying out penance together with military service, so typical of the idea behind the Crusades, seems to have come into effect. The attractiveness of a pilgrimage to Jerusalem was apparently deflected toward other efforts—in the interest of the papacy. Novel religious and military models of these kinds would not have been feasible without the pope's authority, and the authority ascribed to him, to dispense a release from penance.

Direct prototypes of Urban II's Crusade turned up in Italy as well. The Pisans, along with the Genoese, Romans, and Amalfitanians, undertook a naval expedition in 1087 against Mahdia (or al-Mahdiyya) and Zawila, two major seaports in Islamic North Africa.[12] This enterprise may have been coordinated with a simultaneous campaign in Spain against the Berber Almoravids. In any event, the operation was carried out entirely as a Crusade. Victor III passed on the banner of Saint Peter to the troops and granted them an indulgence. The Pisans used the booty to enlarge their cathedral and erect a church dedicated to Saint Sixtus—the deciding battle had been fought on his feast day. A poem composed soon afterward depicted the whole enterprise as a battle of Christ against God's enemies. The justification for the venture was the freeing of a great number of Christian prisoners, rather than the rescue of holy sites or the reconquest of former Christian territories. Contemporaries felt this was reason enough for a Crusade. One source reported that the naval expedition of the maritime cities was preceded by the pope's call for a war with the Saracens to almost all the peoples of Italy. If this is correct, then it gives us yet another initiative comparable to the one Victor's successor, Urban, carried out and that would lead to the so-called First Crusade eight years afterward.

The Norman conquest of Sicily—a papal commission carried out around the same time as the Barbastro Crusade in Spain—also exhibited features of a Crusade.[13] The granting of the *vexillum Sancti Petri* to a Norman leader at that time was the very first record of the banner of Saint Peter, a clear indication of the nascent militarization of the papal church.[14] Twisting the usual sequence of events, Count Roger did not make contact with the pope until *after* the deciding battle. Believing he owed his victory to Saint Peter, he sent a portion of his booty to Alexander II.[15] The pontiff responded by saying that he would grant all soldiers absolution—but not an indulgence—and in the name of the Holy See he sent a banner to accompany the Normans, now trusting in the protection of Saint Peter, into battle against the Muslims. The pope was now revealed as a special patron of a war in which religious pardons had but a secondary connection. His religious patronage linked his authority to this new type of war—a novel constellation in the history of warfare. The fact that many Christians in Sicily were living in bondage was thought to be a sufficient religious basis for the pope's intervention.[16] Particular emphasis was placed on the fact that Sicily had been a Christian country before the violent intrusion of the Muslims. This motivation was in essence no different from what Urban II had enunciated at Clermont. The liberation of holy sites was by no means the dominant motive in the early phase of the crusading movement.

Pisa engaged in similar methods during the conquest of Sicily. It won a naval victory over the Saracens in 1063 and pushed on into the harbor at Palermo, the capital, a year before the Normans besieged the city. As the inscription on the façade of the cathedral they began commemorated: "Six great ships laden with treasure fell into their hands. This building was erected with the avails of this treasure." Was the Pisan enterprise paralleling the Norman conquest of Sicily a Crusade too? The use to which the booty was put offers meager support for this hypothesis. We hear nothing of an appeal from the pope or of promises of salvation. Pisa had been taking part in many naval ventures from the ninth century on, even leading some of them. Not until their North African expedition in 1087 do we find the first unambiguous characteristics of a Crusade, basically lacking in Pisa's most significant naval action, the victory over the emir Mujahid al-'Amiri in 1016, when the Pisans operated in concert with Pope Benedict VIII.[17] Mujahid al-'Amiri had attacked and occupied the Tuscan city of Luni, whereupon the pope summoned "all the leaders and defenders of the Church . . . to attack the foes of Christ [with him] and slay them with God's aid." This does have the ring of a general summons to a Crusade, and it came from the supreme ecclesiastical authority—without the spiritual promises, to be sure, that were to become a component of the Crusades a few decades later. But there was no mention of granting indulgences or of other promises regarding religious matters. Moreover, the pope did not bring this initiative to a conclusion while heading up a great army of Crusaders; instead, he entered into an alliance with the maritime republics of Pisa and Genoa, which, by defeating Mujahid al-'Amiri, freed Italy and its outlying islands in the western Mediterranean from the Saracen menace. This step was basically no different from the many anti-Saracen alliances entered upon since the ninth century to which popes were major parties—admittedly as secular authorities, in the main, and not as dispensers of religious grace. There were as yet no tools for dispensing grace; the indulgence—regarded as the remission of secular punishment for sins—was a later innovation.[18] The indulgence had to do with changes in the way penance was practiced in the

Western Church. The distinction between eternal and temporal punishment of sin remained undecided with regard to the sacrament of penance, of expiation after absolution, which was for the church to decide. Indulgences reflected changes in the Western Church's sacramental practice that ultimately forged the link between penitential practice and military service that was to give so much impetus to the crusading movement from the end of the eleventh century on.

———

In contrast to Spain and Italy, there were no models comparable to the Crusades to guide the fight against the Saracens in the East. A search for the roots of the crusading movement in the most important areas where the Crusades took place would not yield any major finds. In the quarrels between the Byzantine Empire and its Islamic neighbors, forms of warfare were obviously influenced by religious differences. Witness the cult of knightly and warrior saints that arose no later than the tenth century—Saints Demetrius, Theodore, Sergius, George, Mercurius, and Procopius, to name only the most noteworthy.[19] As the Crusades progressed, Westerners also greatly venerated some Byzantine warrior saints as auxiliaries in battle, particularly Saint George. But the veneration of these figures produced no fundamental changes in the nature of warfare, nor did they spur Crusaders on to battle. The campaigns against the Muslims were begun and led by the emperor and his commanders as a matter of principle. It would have been completely unthinkable for the patriarch of Constantinople, let alone authorities in other areas of lordship, to call for campaigns of this kind. The situation of lordship was fundamentally different in Eastern and Western Christendom, as was the relationship between religious and secular power. It took a unique social construct like the papal church in Western Christendom to make the equally unique phenomenon of the Crusades possible. In a nutshell: no papal church, no Crusades.

———

Because a long period of Islamic expansionism preceded the expansionism of the Crusades in the Mediterranean basin, it is reasonable to look for early forms of the Crusades in the jihad, the Muslim holy war.[20] Parallels indicating possible connections between the two are few and far between. Essentially, only one religious idea appears common to both sides: the achievement of redemption by those who fall in battle. The

Muslim who dies in a jihad is, as a martyr, assured of Paradise.[21] The emperor Nicephorus II Phocas apparently would have welcomed this idea for his Byzantine soldiers and might have propagated it by decree, as we have discussed. But the patriarch of Constantinople blocked him, insisting on the early Christian view that dying in warfare had nothing to do with martyrdom.[22] The Roman popes were less reluctant in this regard; when the Saracen threat to Rome put Leo IV (847–54) in an extremely precarious position, he said, "He who dies in this battle will not be denied the heavenly kingdom, for the Almighty will know that he died for the truth of our faith, for the salvation of the *patria*, and the defense of Christianity."[23] When John VIII (872–82) found himself in a similar thorny situation, he reiterated this promise of salvation. Leo IX (1049–54), one of the first reforming popes, elaborated on this promise in a special way.[24] When battling the Normans in central Italy, he deployed a small band of German knights from over the Alps. He promised them impunity for their crimes, remission from penance, and absolution from their sins. After the papal troops were defeated, the slain Germans virtually became cult figures. Their deaths in the battle of Civita were considered a Christian martyrdom; the dead were included among the saints of the Roman Church. Contemporaries recognized this as a notable innovation. And so the view that those killed in battle were martyrs offers at least one parallel with jihad; we might perhaps even speak of an influence here.[25]

That said, the cult of martyrdom cannot be interpreted by circumstances like these. Islam simply does not recognize anything similar to the Christian cult of the saints. In regard to the idea of religious war, any points of contact between these two world religions—often in violent conflict at the time—were merely ephemeral. Full absolution, and not a martyr's crown, was foremost in the pope's guarantees. Crusade and jihad—so strongly divergent from the beginning—were to go their separate ways even more radically as time went on.

Differences in principle between jihad and Crusade far outweigh any congruencies between them. Jihad arose from the specific conditions of life for the nomadic clans and tribes of the Arabian Peninsula.[26] Repeated mini-wars, raids, and forays were the order of the day. The Prophet's community, which had migrated to Medina, joined these conflicts as part of their struggle against the Meccans, which became a religious obligation. There was no distinction between spiritual or secular wars in subsequent campaigns of conquest, when the Islamic *ummah*—the community of believers—grew so strong. Islamic doctrine on holy wars expressed the fundamental aim of extending the Muslim community's rule externally.[27] Jihad was supposed to turn infidels into tributaries first and converts second. Even overthrowing a state could serve the greater glory of Allah and was therefore holy work. If anyone who was taken prisoner converted to Islam as a result, that was merely an outcome of war and not the war's immediate aim. The rapid expansion of the caliphate in the seventh and eighth centuries extended Islam's borders relatively quickly.[28] Within the newly acquired area, jihad could theoretically no longer exist—even after the area disintegrated into several power centers—because it was a type of holy war forbidden among Muslims.

Unlike Islam, Christendom did not evolve in a milieu of warring tribal societies. Unlike the Islamic *ummah*, the Christian religious community kept its distance from state power for centuries. Unlike Islam, too, Western Christendom developed a religious authority, via the papacy, that took its place beside the exponents of state rule, providing the structural context in which the connection between religion and war would develop in a singular way. Islam never had a problem with legitimizing war and from the very beginning seemed to take the likelihood of a holy war for granted. This was an extremely difficult process for Christian churches because of their respective traditions; the process worked differently in each of them, most radically in the Western Church. It was no accident that the Crusades—a new military institution legitimized and in fact led by the church—started up precisely as the papal church was expanding under a reforming influence beginning in the mid-eleventh century. We have seen that militarization was a constituent of this new social formation. The Crusades promoted the rise of a centralized, bureaucratic, and institutionalized church that was to employ holy war as a device for consolidating its power. The new papal church of the High Middle Ages and the Crusade as the pope's war fall within the same time frame. The evolution from a war against the "foes of Christianity" into "the pope's war" against *his* enemies is probably the most striking difference between jihad and Crusade in their respective historical manifestations. Unlike the Islamic jihad, the Christian Crusade was perfectly able to turn into an instrument for dealing with conflicts within the religious community. The "pope's war" took this turn very early on.

———

Urban II had initiated his crusading enterprise to the Holy Land as a model venture in 1095–99. Paschal II (1099–1118) got embroiled right away in a military escapade that starkly contrasted with his predecessor's idea.[29] Prince Bohemond of Tarentum-Antioch, one of the great leaders of the Crusade that concluded with the capture of Jerusalem, was able to persuade the pope that the real enemy of the Latins in the East was the Byzantine emperor Alexios. When Bohemond traveled on from Rome to France in 1105, he was joined by Bruno, a papal legate who was preaching a "holy war" against Byzantium. Bohemond and his "crusading army" crossed from Apulia to Epirus in 1107 in an effort to seize the Byzantine fortress of Dyrrachium. The attempt went awry, and the adventure came to a miserable end. Steven Runciman, the great historian of the Crusades, reduces the result to this: "The Crusade, with the pope at its head, was not a movement for the succour of Christendom, but a tool of unscrupulous western imperialism."[30] He continued: "This unhappy agreement between Behemond and Pope Paschal did far more than all the controversy between Cardinal Humbert and Michael Caerularius to ensure the separation between the eastern and western Churches." This wrangling had led to the schism between the Western and Eastern Churches in 1054. Schismatics were now equated in principle with infidels, against whom a Crusade was possible. A century later this policy took the logical next step. The campaign that historiography has labeled the "Fourth Crusade" was rerouted toward Constantinople at the instigation of the Venetians.[31] The old capital fell in 1204 under the Crusaders' onslaught. Its capture led to a huge bloodbath. Innocent III, the Crusade's initiator, did of course condemn these events, but in the end, he approved of the newly created power arrangement. The phrase "unscrupulous western imperialism" seems to hit the mark yet again.

The measures against Christian schismatics that Innocent III ultimately sanctioned in 1204 were the same as those he began, on his own initiative, to implement against Christian heretics in 1208. The Albigensian Crusade in the south of France lasted more than twenty years and was pursued with exceptional cruelty by a crusading army from all over western Europe. The Crusade was continued by the Inquisition, which had been instituted simultaneously to combat heresy. Other antiheretic Crusades then targeted opponents as varied as the peasants in the North German community of the Stedinger, the followers of Fra Dolcino in Piedmont, the Bosnian Church, and the Hussites in Bohemia—the last-named assailed by an enormous horde of Crusaders from the whole of Europe.[32] Crusades against heretics had a greater and longer-lasting effect on Europe's history than Crusades against the schismatics did; they symbolized a whole tradition of excluding, stigmatizing, expelling, or wiping out dissenters and dissidents—a fundamental contribution to Europe's construal as a "persecuting society."[33] Many other cultures have been spared this inward-turning holy war. Even the Islamic jihad was never to take such a turn.

Crusading wars against Christians and those against non-Christians both had a long history. Apart from schismatics and heretics, the pope's enemies were principal targets, even if they could not be accused of straying from the faith. The history of the Crusades is often described as if they developed from the campaign to liberate Jerusalem, a Crusade considered legitimate because of its objective. In this interpretation, the Crusades against heretics, schismatics, and the pope's enemies—seen as *not* being legitimate in the same way—simply grew from this basic model as a secondary form, as a later abuse, so to speak, of an initially just cause. This presumed priority is hardly defensible. The pope's holy war against his enemies within the church predates the Jerusalem Crusade. Every element constituting the Crusades, including fighting against Christians, appears to have been completely worked out before Urban II made his call.

A key figure in the mobilization of holy war against Christian enemies was Leo IX (1049–54), a reforming pope.[34] His belligerent personality made him no different from many of his predecessors. But he was the first pope to justify his wars on the basis of religion, setting new criteria for them as soon as he assumed office. He did not fight the dethroned Benedict IX and his followers with the usual methods, with raids and ambushes; instead, he quickly summoned a reform synod after his consecration. The previous pope and his followers were condemned as simonists and heretics, then anathematized; the Roman militia was mobilized to fight these *perfidi*. Leo's Crusade against the Normans, which was really about who would seize the town of Benevento, has already been mentioned. A plenary indulgence and the remission of all sins was granted—long before Barbastro and Clermont—to the German knights who fought on the pope's side; any who fell in battle were to be venerated as martyrs. The pope justified his enterprise ex post facto by charging the Normans with "pagan godlessness," although they had been Christian for a long time.

Hildebrand, the monk who was to become Gregory VII (1073–85), was one of Leo IX's collaborators and continued down the pope's path with a vengeance.[35] Even under Leo's successors, he was frequently involved in the pope's affairs that furthered the "holy war" against external and internal enemies of the Roman Church. His pontificate then played a major role in militarizing the papacy. He has been called the "most bellicose pope who ever occupied the See of Saint Peter." Most important in the evolution of the "holy war" against external foes was his plan for a Crusade to the East, on which Urban II's later venture in 1095 was undoubtedly patterned. Gregory had already honed his tools for a "holy war" against the papacy's Christian enemies in the fight with Henry IV. When he solemnly granted the followers of the anti-king Rudolf absolution from all their sins, it was the same device in principle that Leo IX had used against the Normans—now in a world-historical clash of much greater dimensions. Both Leo IX and Gregory VII preceded Urban II in granting an indulgence for a Crusade.

A papal synod in Pisa decreed in 1135 that the same indulgence given to participants in the "First Crusade" would be granted to anyone fighting forces hostile to the pope. But this was really nothing new.[36] The converse could also have applied: those taking part in the "First Crusade" had received an indulgence promised for the first time to those who fought forces hostile to the pope. The great era of Crusades against the pope's Christian enemies did not arrive, of course, until the thirteenth century. Innocent III preached a Crusade in 1199 against Markward von Annweiler, the powerful Staufen imperial *ministerialis*. The pope's crusading campaign against the Staufen and their party in Italy dragged on for many decades. Other crusading campaigns were designed to regain the papal states. Even the popes' straightforward, private wars, such as Boniface VIII's feud with the Colonna family, were legitimized and financed under the rubric "Crusade." The inflation of these crusading actions automatically devalued the promises of salvation for those who took part in them.

Accordingly, there were many types of Crusades, and Crusades aimed at very different adversaries. The number of Crusades against "unbelievers" could be inflated to include those against the Wends, Mongols, Turks, and other peoples, as well as those against Christians, or the various military ventures against Italian city states. At any rate, the total picture is far more complicated than the canon spelled out in research and teaching that lists seven or eight "great" Crusades, whose closed system has been reinforced by a chronological listing.[37] Their common denominator was supposedly established by having the holy sites of Palestine as the intended or achieved goal. But some of the "great" ones never even got there. Others did go as far as the Holy Land but are nevertheless not counted. Consequently, the canon of numbered Crusades yields a skewed picture overall. Crusading activity is solely or primarily defined by the establishing or preserving of lordship over the holy sites of Palestine. This allows us to see only a specific and partial segment of the Crusades, with the result that we can interpret them only in part. The question of the causes of the papal church's militarization in the wake of church reform leads to larger contexts. The Crusade, if taken to be "the pope's war," opens up a much wider horizon.

———

The fact that Europe everywhere was drifting toward militarization during the ninth and tenth centuries can be explained by the intimidating scene at its borders. Saracens were pushing in from the South, Normans from the North, Magyars from the East. In the face of such threats, it was logical to invent new military institutions, as well as novel forms and techniques of military organization. These boiled down in principle, however, to conventional modes of fighting, like those practiced in the adjacent Byzantine Empire under similar threats. Around the middle of the eleventh century—as church reform was taking shape—a new reality held the stage: the Crusade, a military venture that the pope initiated, supported, and religiously prized. It would have been totally beyond the realm of imagination for the patriarch of Constantinople or other heads of smaller churches in the eleventh century to undertake a Crusade of that kind on their own; in point of fact, it would have been impossible. The patriarch of Constantinople's residence was close by the Byzantine emperor's palace. It was the emperor himself who attended to matters of war. The bishop of Rome was in an entirely different situation. The German king and the Roman emperor were far away. Under the emperor's nominal protection, the pope was in control of his own territory; granted, he often turned to the local military for assistance. The fundamental conflict between pope and emperor, between spiritual and temporal power, flared up in the West during the period of church reform. It ended with the former gaining independence from the latter. The militarizing of the church was a reasonable, but not a necessary, price to pay for the *libertas ecclesiae* that this conflict secured. The Eastern Church, and the other medieval Christian churches, never witnessed an equivalent controversy between spiritual and temporal power.

The papal church had developed into a large social organization during the reform of the church. It had control over church assemblies, where clergy from all over Europe would confer on business arising from the Crusades. It had control over the best communication system of the time for disseminating a call for a Crusade throughout the whole continent and for sending out preachers to recruit for it. It had control over the institution of the legate, who more or less established the pope's presence throughout Europe—as a recruiter of princes for the Crusades, as a negotiator between conflicting powers, as a person accompanying the Crusade itself. It had control over finances—thanks to tithing for the Crusades and taxing its prebends—which safeguarded the economic side of so enormous a venture. It had control over core troops as a strike force that was permanently at the ready, thanks to bases the military orders had established throughout Europe. Finally, it had control over the gifts of grace—through expanding sacramental power—that promised salvation, gifts that were a motivating factor of the Crusades. No other medieval Christian church had control over the same material and nonmaterial resources as the papal church, which successfully maneuvered the crusading enterprise to augment its own resources. The uniqueness of the papal church as a social megaorganization both offers an explanation for and in an extraordinary way was underscored by the unique nature of the Crusades.

———

Any interpretive model for the Western Church's militarization in the era of church reform and the Crusades would come up short if it relied solely on the growing papacy by way of explanation, for change was encouraged not only by the head of the church but also by a shift at the grassroots level. This can be better understood by examining novel organizational forms in the Western Church, along with its exemplary religious figures. Military orders provide an example of the first, the ideal of the *miles Christianus* of the second.

Universal religious orders were peculiar to the Western Church, with no equivalent in any other Christian church, as has already been shown. They made robust progress, particularly during the period of reform, with the thrust coming from the grassroots. Pilgrimage and crusading movements were reflected in the military orders the same way that the *libertas ecclesiae* movement was in the Cluniac cloisters and the poverty movement in the Franciscan and Dominican mendicant orders.[38] The oldest of these communities arose from the conjunction of charitable work with the care and defense of pilgrims; the orders did not actually engage in combat with enemies of the faith until later. Caring for pilgrims was often still an obligation. The military orders of the Knights Hospitaller of Saint John, the Knights Templar, the Teutonic Knights (*Deutschherren, Schwertbrüder*), as well as many communities founded in Spain, were examples of warrior monks, something completely new to Christendom. We can find parallels here with East Asian and Indian asceticism. A particularly noteworthy analogy was the Islamic institution of the *ribat* in North Africa and Spain, which originated in the eighth and ninth centuries. This military settlement assisted jihads, functioning as both a defensive fortification and a base for launching attacks. It was garrisoned by volunteers who in fulfilling their religious and military duties led the life of a soldier-ascetic.[39] But as striking as the congruency is, we cannot entertain the thought of a direct Christian imitation in this case.

Hospitaller communities, in fact, wherever pilgrims were cared for— that was where early forms of Christian military orders were more likely to be found. Pilgrimages increased in number enormously during the eleventh and twelfth centuries, not least because of new penitential practices and their attendant promise of salvation.[40] The popes approved and sponsored military orders, deploying them to further their interests. But the popes did not found any orders themselves. We can only appreciate their origin and evolution against the unique background of the religiosity of the Western Church in the age of the Crusades. A mass movement in the twelfth and thirteenth centuries created hundreds of houses, castles, and commanderies of the great military orders along the length and breadth of Europe. It produced major achievements of lasting value—in fortifications, in the logistics of transporting the military, but mainly in banking and finance.[41] Enthusiasm for military orders declined during the late Middle Ages, along with crusading zeal. The warrior monk was an ephemeral phenomenon in the history of Christian monasticism. Yet he was a fascinating, shining figure for the age of the Crusades, indicating how deeply anchored the movement was in the European populace.

––––––––

The example of the military orders created during the crusading movement must be considered within the context of all models of Christian chivalry at the time. The term for a Christian knight, *miles Christianus*, or *miles Christi*, appeared in the eleventh century and originally meant something different: it had been applied to apostles, monks, and Christian ascetics for almost a millennium. There was a clear distinction between the *militia Christi*, the unarmed fighters for the faith, and the *militia saecularis*, whose service required the bearing of arms. The term's conceptual change in the eleventh century corresponded to a change in society. Throughout the entire early Middle Ages, the training of a young soldier did not have the slightest religious significance. Surviving collections of liturgical formularies that appeared in the tenth century and especially the eleventh—first in Germany, then in France and England—incorporated texts for the *consecratio ensis* and the *benedictio novi militis*: the blessing of the sword and the dubbing of the knight.[42] A widely distributed version implored a blessing upon the new knight's sword, "that it be a defense and shield for the Church, widows, and orphans, for all the servants of God against the rage of the heathen, and that it instill fear and terror amidst the foe." And so the church charged the young knight with specific obligations to society that had no parallel among more ancient knightly ideals. We can see reflected in the ritual of the blessing of the sword and the dubbing ceremony a process of raising the knight's status in the West that reached its climax in the thirteenth century. Specific rites of passage, such as vigils, bathing, and new clothing, symbolize this process of transformation. The Christian knight, the *miles Christianus*, is the representative of a new estate for which the church tried to stipulate a specific ethos of virtue. The "monastic warrior" of Christian chivalry was the counterpart of the "warrior monk" of military orders. These were identifiable trends in the church's programmatic aims.

The program was quite concretely apparent in the veneration of saints. Warrior saints had been foreign to the Western Church for a long time. The Byzantine Church had a head start in their veneration.[43] Some were adopted in the West during the tenth century, such as Saint George, who was to be so very significant for the Crusaders; other soldier saints were added, like Saint Mauritius and Saint Sebastian. These early warrior saints were augmented in the tenth and eleventh centuries by completely different saints, whose lives fused chivalry with monastic asceticism. Among these monastic knights were Saint William of Gellone, Saint Otger, and most notably Saint Gerald of Aurillac. A central theme in their *vitae* was the juxtaposition of great monastic deeds with great military ones. The *vita* of Saint Gerald of Aurillac that Abbot Odo of Cluny wrote in 925 or shortly thereafter offered a new image of a knightly saint and at the same time new guidelines for how a nobleman was to live his life.[44] The reform monastery of Cluny in southern Burgundy in general played an important role in the propagation of this new prototype, which brings us to the Cluniacs and the reform of the church. The new ideal of the *miles Christianus* appears to have been closely associated with the *libertas ecclesiae* movement, so that it made an essential contribution from below to the militarization of the papal church during the era of church reform.

The origins of the *miles Christianus* model can be traced a little farther back, to the south of France, where the Truce of God movement surfaced in the tenth and eleventh centuries.[45] This marginal area was barely kept under control by the central authority; feuding among the nobility was particularly excessive. Bishops took the initiative in opposing the violence, and church synods promulgated decrees to restore and guarantee the peace. The nobility had to swear an oath on holy relics that they would honor these conditions and would take military action against those who did not keep the peace. On the one hand, acts of violence were placed under sanction; on the other, constructive goals were set out for the militant nobility. Obligations to defend the church, widows, orphans, and the entire defenseless population—mentioned above as duties of the *miles Christianus*—were spelled out for the first time in these alliances for peace initiated by the church. In practice, these Truces of God often meant "warring against war"—which took place under religious leadership. Even the Truce of God movement harbored elements that would lead to militarizing the church.

The *miles Christianus*, as conceived by the eleventh-century Western Church, was an ambiguous figure. The above-mentioned blessing of the sword points up the model's inherent ambivalence: defending the church, widows, and orphans was "balanced" by fighting the heathen and striking "fear and terror" into the enemy. The noble warrior, who was seen as a hero not merely for killing the heathen but for thereby performing a religiously meritorious deed, marked a definite break with traditional moral values. When combined with the idea lying behind the Crusades, this reevaluation had dire consequences that have influenced Western Christian and secular attitudes toward war up to modern times. It seems paradoxical that this swing toward militarizing the Western Church took place precisely during a reform phase, even more, that it was a cause of the church's very renewal.

———

The Crusades' various, persistent consequences for Europe's special path cannot be traced in full here, but we can shed at least some light upon their ties with European expansionism. The heavily formalized concept of "expansionism" is ambiguous. We will first treat its many different aspects before attempting to work out its particular European form.

Robert Bartlett, in his *The Making of Europe*, calls one of the first forms of the expansionist crusading movement the "aristocratic diaspora":

One of the more striking aspects of the expansionary activity of the tenth to thirteenth centuries was the movement of western European aristocrats from their homelands into new areas where they settled and, if successful, augmented their fortunes. The original homes of those immigrants lay mainly in the area of the former Carolingian empire. Men of Norman descent became lords in England, Wales, Scotland and Ireland, in southern Italy and Sicily, in Spain and Syria. Lotharingian knights came to Palestine, Burgundian knights to Castile, Saxon knights to Poland, Prussia and Livonia. Flemings, Picards, Poitevins, Provençals and Lombards took to the road or to the sea and, if they survived, could enjoy new power in unfamiliar and exotic countries. One Norman adventurer became lord of Tarragona. A Poitevin family attained the crown of Cyprus.

This period of aristocratic diaspora coincided with the great age of the crusades, and, for many, migration began with the taking of the cross. Nevertheless, this is not the whole story. In some places, notably the British Isles and the Christian kingdoms of eastern Europe, the settlement of aristocratic newcomers took place without a crusading umbrella.[46]

The thesis is stimulating but in the final analysis much oversimplified. The various manifestations of post-Crusade aristocratic power were certainly related to other contemporary processes of power formation. But there is a great difference between the aristocratic colonizers of Bohemia, Poland, and Hungary, on the one hand, and aristocratic subjugators in the regions of the Reconquest or the Holy Land on the other. But the underlying idea of the above quotation relates to the enormous population changes in the upper strata of the nobility during the age of the Crusades, which led to a unique intermingling of the leading noble families. It was not for nothing that they went by the blanket name of "Franks" at the time of the Crusades.[47] The majority of the Crusaders did, after all, come from the heartland of the former Carolingian Empire. This merging process attracted many nobles from the North to the Mediterranean. But even northern Italy—a second, dynamic region linked with the Crusades, especially by the participation of the maritime republics—sent people out into newly opened-up areas in the South. On the whole, the prosperous areas in the Northwest and the Mediterranean drew noticeably closer during the Crusades. From this perspective, it is probably true that this process provided some impetus to the integration of Europe. As a part of Europe's expansion, it meant more mobility and more colonizing activity in a cultural area that had grown larger.

The question of what the essential features of European expansionism actually were varies from one area occupied by Crusaders to another. In a move paralleling the Saracen Crusades in the Holy Land and
Spain, Pope Eugene III, at Bernhard of Clairvaux's instigation, called for
a "Wendish Crusade" in 1147 against the heathen tribes in the north-
eastern part of the empire—the first case of sanctioning an armed mission as a crusading goal. Later, in 1245, Innocent IV approved a permanent Crusade for this region as a unique privilege, one that would
no longer require special approval.[48] Until the end of the fourteenth
century, knights from far and wide would make a "Prussian journey"
in order to fight in the summer and winter campaigns of the Order of
Teutonic Knights (*Deutscher Orden*).

The Order of the Teutonic Knights, founded in 1189–90, settled in
Prussia in 1225, after brief interludes in Cyprus and the Burzenland
district of Hungary, where they fought the heathen inhabitants.[49] In
1237 they occupied the territory in Livonia established by the Order
of the Brothers of the Sword, which provided fertile ground for the
construction of an independent state with a particularly progressive
administration. Here, post-Crusade expansionism meant extending
lordship through conquest, through the employment of methods applied in neighboring territories during the colonization of the East, and
through the use of compulsory conversion of those they conquered.
There was no indication of a trend toward colonialism of any kind.

The Crusades brought expansionism to the Holy Land, where it took
on different, many-faceted forms. The move to the cities was very significant, whereas settlement in rural areas was secondary.[50] Conquered
areas were not expanded further, something that could have promoted
agrarian colonization. From the point of view of lordship in Outremer,
we can hardly speak of colonial structures. The Crusade's leaders themselves ruled territories they either conquered or were granted. Even if
some, like Bohemond of Antioch, held lands at both ends of the Mediterranean Sea, those territories were never interdependent.

The possessions the Italian maritime republics owned in the Holy
Land presented a different case. The republics simply owned, as a rule,
factories, roads, residential streets, quarters, and districts in trading cities, where a tie-in with the home city was a foregone conclusion.[51] But
Venice's acquisition of territory around Tyre in 1124, where sugarcane
fields and sugar mills had stood in Islamic times, represented an exception.[52] The Venetians planted much more sugarcane on land near the
coast and farmed it themselves, managing the plantations with cor-

vée, slave labor, and paid work. As a result, a colonial enterprise based on commercial agriculture had emerged by the second quarter of the twelfth century, that is, soon after the end of the "First Crusade." The maritime republics were to copy this exemplary precursor in their initial colonization of many Mediterranean islands, producing a direct link between the independently operated sugar plantation economy and later types of colonial plantation economies. Sugar plantations were modestly sprinkled throughout the lands of Outremer within a quite differently structured lordship and economic system. But their model character has earned them an important place in world history, creating an essential line of expansionist development that was distinctively European.

––––––––

The regions occupied during the "Fourth Crusade" in 1204 lay *oltra mare*, as had the Holy Land for the crusading powers. This constellation is significant for the connection between the Crusades and European expansionism. Distant possessions accessible only by sea were more easily positioned to be dependent colonies than conquered neighboring areas were, where lordship and settlement could be seamlessly and continuously extended. Unlike the Crusader states in the Holy Land, the lordship structures created after the fall of Constantinople in 1204 may best be considered to have resulted from a Crusade only in a formal sense. That Crusade, which the Venetians hijacked against the pope's will, was aimed at destroying the Byzantine Empire and was intended to maintain the Republic of Saint Mark's economic hegemony around the Aegean and the Black Sea—an early misuse of the crusading concept for commercial interests that was the first of many similar abuses during the Crusades' history. The phenomena of expansionism in evidence there should for this reason be categorized more as the results of protocolonialism, not so much of the Crusades. It was the secular magnates from the Crusaders' ranks who built up the smaller and larger territories, as had been the case in the Holy Land; here, too, the colonies were not dependent on their area of origin. The maritime republics were now more heavily represented[53]—particularly Venice, but increasingly Genoa, which the triumph of the Venetian Crusade had pushed into the background. Venice extended its lordship indirectly to many Aegean islands by handing them over to grand patrician families. But it also banked more and more on economic colonies in the narrow sense—on Crete, say, where the commercialization of agriculture was carried out in the home city's interest on a far grander scale than it had been in Tyre. The colony of Crete was administered directly from Venice after the island's economic and social transformation.

The situation was different for Genoa's most important colonies in the Aegean. The island of Chios was ruled by the so-called Manoa, a chartered company of major Genoese capitalists. The republic found the island economically significant for its nearby alum mines, which were centrally important for the dyeing industry in Europe; the island was also essential for a unique monoculture: the mastic tree or shrub, which produced a very valuable resin or gum. Finally, the island was important because of its excellent location as a trading hub. The founding of trading bases in the region was one of Genoa's priorities. Galata on the Bosporus and Kaffa in the Crimea were essential bases at the end of the great Silk Road to East Asia. There was precious little crusading activity in these expansionist trends. The "schismatic" inhabitants of the former Byzantine districts were allowed to keep their faith. Missionary work, especially from bases in the Crimea, was carried on mainly by Franciscans and directed at non-Christian areas. As so often, when missionary work followed in the wake of trade, it was independent of lordship.

———

The Iberian Peninsula offered the most conspicuous connections between the crusading movement and European expansionism.[54] The panoply of tools for this particular kind of Christian holy war was developed there particularly early—in the Barbastro Crusade of 1164—and it was there that the Crusades enjoyed a special legacy, both in spirit and in practice. At a very early stage, Urban II placed the Spanish Crusade on the same footing as the Palestine Crusade. The same remission of sins and the same heavenly reward would be granted Spaniards who fought the foe on their native ground. The makeup of the crusading armies was as international on the Iberian Peninsula as it had been in the Holy Land. The only difference was that the army was under a king's direct command. There were religious military orders on the Iberian Peninsula just as in the Holy Land; they were located on the border with the Moors and brought with them something of a permanent belligerent mood. Southwestern Europe knew nothing of the institution of continuous warfare found in the Northeast, but there was a similar situation de facto. The bull promulgated for the Spanish Crusades had a time limit, but beginning with Gregory XIII in 1579, it was renewed every six years. This meant that the war with the Moors would always be religiously sublimated. The century-long readiness for a holy war, supposedly willed and rewarded by God, was transferred to new opponents after the loss of the old hereditary enemy.[55]

The Portuguese subjugation of Ceuta in 1415 typified the interplay between the elements of the crusading movement and those of European expansionism in the waning Middle Ages. Renate Pieper has put the future consequences of this conquest in perspective: "The beginning of Europe's integration with worldwide trade in general started with the 1415 Portuguese conquest of Ceuta on the Northwest African coast. This founding of a new colonial base in Northwest Africa was followed by the conquest and colonization of the Atlantic islands of Madeira, Porto Santo, the Azores, Cape Verde, and the construction of trade and shipping bases along the coast of West Africa, all before 1460."[56] But the campaign in Ceuta had definite retrospective aspects as well.[57] The Portuguese expedition was mounted conjointly with the pope and conducted as a Crusade, amassing an international army of Crusaders. It set out on July 25, the Feast of Saint James the Apostle, a key date in battles with the Moors in past centuries. The city fell within a few days; on August 25 the mosque was converted into a church, where three of the victorious king's sons were dubbed knights: Duarte, Pedro, and Henry, who was later known as "the Navigator." Ceuta was elevated to a bishopric and placed under the archbishop of Braga in Portugal. The diocese of Ceuta would include the African kingdom of Fez, which was yet to be subjugated, as well as bordering areas. The ecclesiastical and colonial organization of space, then, preceded the secular one—a theme that can be traced back to the tenth and eleventh centuries as the basic pattern of European expansionism.

Henry, the infante of Portugal, dubbed a knight in Ceuta, was to become the symbolic figurehead of European expansionism.[58] As the grand master of the Order of Christ, which was formed from the disbanded Order of Knights Templar, he stood squarely in the tradition of the crusading movement. He put the wealth of his order into voyages of discovery and erecting an economic empire on the islands of the Atlantic. He was swayed by ideas about wars of religion as much as he was by capitalist trading interests, both as a knight of the order and as an entrepreneur. Straddling two worlds, his personality displayed lines of continuity that were not so apparent elsewhere, and perhaps knew no equal.

There has been no debate in current scholarship about the fact that European colonialism in Atlantic regions, beginning with the fifteenth century, followed seamlessly from the older colonialism of the Italian maritime republics in the eastern Mediterranean. Wolfgang Reinhard, in his history of European expansion, has put it this way:

Basic forms of colonial organization and of financing colonial enterprises, of distributing land and of its peaceful use were created in the Crusader states, the Italian colonies in the eastern Mediterranean, and last but not least on Venetian Cyprus and on Genoese Chios and in Kaffa—forms that were to serve in good stead and persist in the Atlantic area for centuries. Apart from the implementation of initially very popular feudal lordships, we also find prototypes of the various colonizing and trading companies of the seventeenth and eighteenth centuries. Plantation economy was in the forefront—sugar was the preferred product—and the slave economy along with it, as the two of them were in Palestine and Cyprus. The plantation economy then moved via Valencia and the Algarve to the Atlantic islands and ultimately from West Africa to America.[59]

The connection between the Atlantic and older Mediterranean forms is obvious—but why were the roots of this early colonialism located in the eastern Mediterranean, of all places? We might harbor the tacit notion that this somehow started with the Crusades—surely an untenable supposition. The Crusades presented an opportunity for founding colonies insofar as they acquired new territories that Italy's maritime republics deemed appropriate to colonize. But the fact that the territories became colonies can be chalked up, not to the Crusades, but to the policies of those very maritime republics instead—where our quest for the early stages of protocolonialism must begin.

Italy's maritime republics employed a policy based on controlling trade in the eastern *and* western Mediterranean. We can therefore safely assume that they created the first phase of colonization in the West as well. Parts of this phase appear to go even farther back than in the East. We will pay close attention to Pisa's situation on this very point. But first we have to go back a step: the expansion in the western Mediterranean that Pisa and other maritime republics initiated was in reaction to the expansionism emanating from the southern coast of the Mediterranean. For almost a century, from 888 to 973, an Islamic stronghold was situated near Saint Tropez on the Provençal coast. The

La Garde–Freinet of today, it used to be called Farakhshanit in Arabic and Fraxinetum in Latin.[60] Subject to the caliph of Córdoba, it was important economically because of the slave trade and as a supplier of wood for shipbuilding. Wood was in short supply in the Islamic Empire, a fact that placed Islamic mastery of the sea in constant jeopardy. From their stronghold at Fraxinetum, the Saracens controlled Provence, the western Alps, and Liguria; a network of smaller bases surrounded this central hub. Fraxinetum appears in the older literature as a "pirate colony."[61] But was this Arab settlement on the Provençal coast fundamentally different from, say, Portuguese trading bases in West Africa? Leaving the question of Eurocentric interpretations aside, we will have to ask whether and how the Arabic principalities in the Mediterranean executed their colonial policy during the time of their maritime hegemony.[62] We cannot of course expect to discover a direct continuity with the policy of the maritime republics of Italy.

————

The large islands of the western Mediterranean aroused the same interests in the maritme republics as the large islands of the eastern Mediterranean, for example, Crete or Cyprus. Islands could be naval bases for trading expeditions, furnish vital raw materials for trade or a city's wants, and generate profitable trading goods if agricultural production were switched to a particular monoculture—probably the most thoroughgoing change in a ruling colonial power's interest. And so control over the islands was hotly contested in the western Mediterranean as well.

Iron-rich Elba was particularly important among the islands with abundant raw materials in the western Mediterranean during the Middle Ages. Of all the iron ore deposits exploited, some as far back as antiquity, those worked mainly in medieval times possessed a high mineral content that yielded a tough iron, resulting in a mining boom in the eastern Alps and Lombardy, but especially on Elba.[63] Pisans worked the iron mines there, as has been documented from the eleventh century on, but they might have started earlier. The mines were frequently leased to wealthy city merchants. Some of the specialized skilled workers, such as miners and blacksmiths, were brought in from elsewhere, mainly from Lombardy. In winter, these *fabbri* mined the ore on the island and smelted it on the nearby coast; in summer they manufactured iron tools and weapons in the city of Pisa.[64] Elba was ruled by the commune of Pisa from the eleventh century, but it is unclear how this came about.[65] In the early Middle Ages, Elba belonged to the territory of Populonia, in the south of Tuscany, and was under the authority of its bishop. It did not become part of the diocese of Pisa until 1138, so that its ecclesiastical alignment came *after* changes in lordship. We will see that the reverse sequence was possible when it came to Sardinia and Corsica, where lordship was established after the issue of church control had been regulated. At any rate, Elba's ecclesiastical alignment in 1138 was a further indicator of its dependence on Pisa.

Pisa's leading source of income in the twelfth century was selling iron from Elba.[66] Accordingly, it went to great lengths to keep the island dependent. It defended the island against numerous Saracen raids that were most likely prompted by interest in the sought-after metal; the city also had to ward off competition from Genoa. Pisa fortified what it felt was an all-important territory, the longest-held of its island possessions.

Can we consider Elba to be a Pisan colony from the eleventh century on? The question concerns an overseas possession that was heavily reliant on Pisa politically, legally, and, last but not least, ecclesiastically. There also seems to be an element here of "targeted transformations in economics and a society geared to the needs of the metropolis."[67] These changes did not, to be sure, take place in the same way they did in the Venetian and Genoese colonies in the eastern Mediterranean, which occurred because of the demands of stepped-up monocultural farming. On Elba, the working of a valuable mined product proved to be the economic force that dominated everything. We will have to pay closer attention to mining colonies, which comprised a second major type after those early colonies based on commercial farming. If we are looking for the origins of protocolonialism, perhaps mining is, broadly speaking, the one that goes back the farthest.

———

Mining helped to make Sardinia dependent on Pisa, bringing another large western Mediterranean island under its early control. From all of Sardinia's mineral wealth, silver most captured the attention of foreign powers. Control of Sardinian silver mines enabled Pisa to introduce its own coin, around 1150—it was one of the first minted by any municipal community and was at the same time a very early example of the new grosso coins.[68] But the island was rich in other potentially exportable products, wood, fish, wool, cheese, and grain among them.[69] Sardinia was declared Pisa's *caput et sustentacio* in 1309. The amount of the *sustentacio* could be quantified a short time later: about 40 percent of Pisa's revenue originated in Sardinia.[70] The economic exploitation of the island was well organized. The locals were excluded from mercantile trade, which remained in the hands of merchants from the governing home city.[71] The merchants established a *commune portus* in many squares on the island, each headed by two consuls, one on Sardinia and one in Pisa—a system also instituted in Pisa's trading bases in the East, although they had different duties.[72] The consuls in Sardinia were the agents of Pisa's colonial policy safeguarding the trade monopoly of Pisa's merchants.[73] The system was modified in the thirteenth century when Sardinia came under direct rule—to the extent that it could be controlled from distant Pisa—by some of the city's noble families, such as the Viscontis and the Gherardescas.[74] No matter what type of economic control was in effect on the island, a yawning social gap was created between the Pisan merchant elite and the Sardinians, who were working to some extent under conditions of quasi-bondage. The saying, "citizens in Pisa, kings on Sardinia," foreshadowed much of the racial arrogance that generations of colonial masters would demonstrate later in the protocolonial era.[75]

Unlike colonial rule on Elba, Pisa's lordship on Sardinia was not grounded in sovereign rights, if we set aside the later phase of direct rule by the city's noble families over certain jurisdictions. Pisa basically governed Sardinia as a protectorate, aided and abetted by the pope. Sardinia belonged *de jure* to the Byzantine Empire in the early Middle Ages.[76] The Saracens routinely invaded it between the eighth and the early eleventh centuries. Four jurisdictions were created from what was left of Byzantine administrative units; the island's petty kings were able to acquire a modicum of autonomy. But they were quite helpless against the Arab navy. When Mujahid al-'Amiri, the emir of Denia in the Córdoba caliphate, conquered Cagliari and other parts of the island in 1015, Pope Benedict VIII seized the initiative and counterattacked. He felt empowered by the forgery known as the Donation of Constantine. He enlisted Pisa and Genoa in a joint naval expedition, one of many anti-Saracen alliances of the time that were already beginning to assume, by fits and starts, the nature of a Crusade.[77] The enterprise was most successful: the Arabs were driven off the island. The victorious naval powers felt afterward that they were its protectors, and Pisa-led naval expeditions in the western Mediterranean reinforced this attitude.[78] The pope stepped in once again when Urban II elevated the bishop of Pisa to archbishop, simultaneously making him papal legate for Sardinia and metropolitan bishop of Corsica.[79] This appointment was significant not merely for the internal workings of the church; it confirmed the predominance of the maritime republic in one of its acknowledged spheres of influence. Similar examples solidify this interpretation. Ceuta has already been mentioned, though in the context of a later time. Among earlier noteworthy examples was the elevation of the episcopal see of Amalfi, the oldest maritime republic, to an archbishopric about 987, together with four suffragan bishoprics, including the island of Capri. The bishopric of Naples—another leading sea power of the time—had probably been elevated to a metropolitanate earlier and Ischia subordinated to it.[80] At the consecration of the reconstructed Barcelona Cathedral in 1058, the bishop's sphere of jurisdiction was extended to include the taifa (that is, the Muslim-ruled kingdom) of Denia as well as the Balearics, an act which laid express claim to the conquest of these areas.[81] Barcelona was also an ambitious sea power, and the Balearics must have been absolutely critical for its naval policy. In 1133, Innocent II would resolve a conflict between Genoa and Pisa over spheres of influence in Corsica by making the bishop of Genoa archbishop and granting him two suffragan bishoprics on the mainland and three on Corsica: Mariana, Nebbio, and Accia.[82] There could be no clearer demonstration of how colonial politics were carried on and modified through ecclesiastical jurisdictions. These actions also confirmed indirectly that by granting Pisa a primate in 1092 the pope had legitimized the city's colonial rule on Sardinia.

———

Corsica, of all the large islands in the western Mediterranean, was the most coveted on account of its forest wealth. Important tree species crucial for shipbuilding were in abundant supply, especially holly oak (or live oak) and pine. As a consequence, many naval powers made an effort to gain access to the island or to control it. This had been going on since the fifth century, since the Vandals. When Arian kings condemned Catholic bishops to cut down trees on Corsica, it was most likely they had to cut timber for the navy.[83] Wood was in particularly short supply for the Islamic territories in the southern Mediterranean who used to plague the island from the seventh century on. After Saracen dominion over the Mediterranean faded away in the eleventh century, a quarrel broke out between Pisa and Genoa over access to Corsica's forests.[84] The two maritime republics needed enormous quantities of wood for naval construction. The popes had transferred the guardianship of Corsica to Pisa in the eleventh century. The Genoese landed on the island in 1124 and challenged Pisa for the right of possession.[85] Innocent II brokered a compromise in 1133 that did not last very long. Genoa eventually gained control of the whole island. Boniface VIII got involved in 1297 and brought Aragon into play as a new colonial power on the island, resulting ultimately in its division. In the fifteenth century, Genoa handed over its ruling authority to the Casa di San Giorgio, a merchant bank that formed a state within a state.[86] It was unique in the Middle Ages for bankers to be lords over an independent foreign possession. In short, Corsica fell under many varieties of colonial rule. Compared to the eastern Mediterranean, these types of rule had a longer history on Corsica, as they also did on its large neighbor Sardinia and on Elba.

Overseas possessions that were rich in raw materials and strongly dependent economically represent only one aspect of Pisa's and Genoa's medieval colonial empires in the western Mediterranean. A second encompasses a far-reaching network of trading outposts in the Christian Mediterranean and well beyond. A project for assembling a similar trading empire that was never realized yields instructive insight here.[87] When Frederick I was planning a campaign to destroy the Norman kingdom of Sicily, he promised vast territorial gains to the city of Pisa in 1162 as a preliminary move. The privilege involved expanding the territory around Pisa itself by awarding absolute lordship over the seacoast between Portovenere and Civitavecchia; no port would be built in this area without Pisa's agreement. Furthermore, if the Normans were conquered, Pisa would receive the ancient port of Gaeta as well as Mazara and Trapani—the latter two strategically situated on the west coast of Sicily—half of Palermo and Messina and Salerno and Naples, and a street in every other city in the Norman kingdom. All in all, the size of Pisa's share of the hoped-for Norman booty would have been something like three-eighths of the Byzantine Empire—the amount that the Venetians had stipulated would be theirs in the "Fourth Crusade" of 1204 and that was to become the foundation of their colonial empire in the eastern Mediterranean. The thinking behind the Venetians' good-sized deal seems to have been anticipated decades earlier by the privilege granted to Pisa in 1162. It is significant that a series of trading posts was given priority. No one sought to acquire additional colonial lands like the ones the parties already possessed.

The twelfth-century trading posts of the Italian maritime republics extended far beyond the Christian-controlled countries of the Mediterranean. It seems paradoxical that at times when all Europe was being summoned to a Crusade against the Islamic kingdoms, merchants of the maritime cities were concluding treaties with the same kingdoms, establishing trading posts and organizing far-reaching systems of trade.[88] Pisa signed most of its treaties with Egypt and Tunis, the Genoese with the Almohad kingdom.[89] An Italian merchants' fixed trading post, or factory, in Islamic countries was called a *fondaco*, from the Arabic *funduq* or the Greek *pandocheion*, which means "inn" or "hostel." These *fondachi*, operating under a special privilege, consisted of large complexes of living quarters and warehouses, often with a Christian church, a bakery, and a bathhouse.[90] The merchants living in the trading centers often stayed in touch with their home city through various organizations. This is why Pisa instituted the two-consul system there as well—the elected consul (*consul electus*), chosen by Pisans living in the trading settlement, and the professional consul (*consul missus*), who was under the Ordo Maris, the presiding authority in the home city.[91] In this way, tightly structured novel forms of authority organized a wide-reaching colonial and trading empire.

———

Colonial empires of this size and structure may rightly be deemed protocolonialist and therefore seen as an early colonial stage that shaped a more comprehensive European expansionism. But why did this protocolonialism develop only in Italy, and why was it limited to just a few maritime republics there? Pisa, which has been treated in some detail above, was essentially eliminated from the race after Genoa defeated it in 1284, so that only Venice and Genoa were still in the running. The question concerning the rise of Mediterranean protocolonialism requires us to go far back in time. Three determining factors appear to merit most attention: the emergence of navies sponsored by maritime cities; the (relative) independence of those cities, and finally, the dominating position of trading interests in the cities' political leadership.[92]

Mediterranean cities in late antiquity did not have navies. The Byzantine Empire organized its navy along the lines of the *imperium Romanum's* fleet. Naval, trading, and fishing fleets were under separate commands.[93] The theme system introduced in the seventh century elaborated on and modified this structure, but it stayed in essence the same and continued functioning in the Byzantine regions of Italy. It is remarkable that Roman-Byzantine naval bases seldom became bases for the Italian maritime republics. This is true of Venice, Amalfi, Gaeta, and Genoa. All of them were settlement centers in the early Middle Ages for people from the surrounding lands who were seeking refuge.

223

Favorable shelter was crucial for siting a base—in lagoons for Venice, on mountain slopes for Amalfi, on a spit of land in the Tyrrhenian Sea for Gaeta. This turned out to be the most important factor in the volatile centuries after the fall of the Roman Empire in the West. When cities created their navies afterward, continuity with antiquity did not enter into the picture. Of all the great medieval maritime republics in Italy, only Pisa merits consideration as possibly having a link with the ancient empire. The city served as a port from the late imperial age up to the beginning of the seventh century, without a break, as has recently been documented as well for the ninth century and beyond.[94]

There were a variety of prerequisites for constructing and maintaining a municipal navy. To take the environment first: a navy could only be built up by coastal cities that had the good fortune to have a fine harbor and access to forests for the raw material required for shipbuilding. Thus Pisa, for instance, had a special advantage thanks to an excellent hinterland rich in forests.[95] Furthermore, shipbuilding was an enormously capital-intensive business.[96] The arsenals found in Italy's maritime republics were among the largest industrial complexes of the day. Only cities grown wealthy through naval wars or trade were in a position to afford navies on a grand scale, possession of which would further improve their competitive edge. Constructing a naval fleet was, after all, an extremely risky business. Threats from natural forces were a minor problem. Corsair raids jeopardized their gains, naval battles with political opponents or trading competitors even more so. Unlike land battles, naval warfare tended toward total material destruction because that was the most effective way to hit the enemy. Pisa knocked out Amalfi in 1135 and 1137 in a war of annihilation—by wiping out the city and burning its ships in port—but then Pisa was itself eliminated from competing for the rule of the seas when Genoa inflicted a devastating defeat in the battle of Meloria in 1284 and subsequently blockaded its harbor.[97] Under these conditions we can appreciate why, in the end, only very few Italian maritime republics grew into trading powers that encouraged development of early forms of colonialism.

The initial stages of early medieval shipbuilding in western Mediterranean cities were minimally affected by long-distance trade. Saracen ships were masters of the Mediterranean. A city could ward them off with their own ships, or maybe even go on the counterattack. Mariners in the northern end of the Tyrrhenian Sea turned out ships as privateers right from the outset.[98] Their galleys were built for quick attack and retreat. Piracy was their primary purpose, not maritime trade. Pisa had a particularly long tradition in this respect. As early as 828, Margrave Boniface of Tuscany led a naval expedition, mostly of Pisans, to the coast of North Africa. Large-scale pillaging raids became more frequent and continued in a combined campaign with Genoa against the cities of Mahdia and Zawila in 1087. Matters had gone well beyond privateering, as ships were now setting out to sea to conquer well-fortified cities.[99] The maritime republics could draw on highly developed siege techniques. Their expertise in shipbuilding probably stood them in good stead when it came to constructing siege engines.[100] These plundering ventures allowed Pisa to accumulate enormous wealth—no little portion of which went into building magnificent churches. Cargoes from ships in Palermo's harbor were seized as booty, to become immortalized as part of the façade of Pisa's cathedral. The Pisan and Genoese pillaging mentality may have stayed alive as long-distance trading became paramount for them. Something of the kind was evident in their behavior toward economically dependent areas. In any event, it must be recognized that protocolonialism in the western Mediterranean was rooted in this tradition.

———

There were major maritime trading cities in Italy and the Mediterranean that did not rise to the rank of colonial powers. Thessalonica in the Byzantine Empire or Palermo in the Norman kingdom would be on the list. Naples was on track to becoming a naval power like Amalfi, Pisa, or Genoa until it dwindled in importance by 1139 at the latest, after its incorporation into the Norman kingdom. And Amalfi seems to have lost its position after coming under Norman rule, even before Pisa ultimately pushed it out of contention.[101] To put it differently: only coastal cities that were not directly ruled by a prince had any hope of becoming a colonial power by building their own navy. Early medieval Italy was a propitious place for ambitions of this kind. Relatively autonomous lordship structures were able to flourish on the margins of large kingdoms because they were not under the tight control of central authorities. Venice was part of the Byzantine Empire for a long time in name only but was to all intents and purposes independent from the eighth century on. Amalfi, Naples, and Gaeta owed their independence to a slow process of disengagement from the Eastern Empire. Pisa and Genoa were part of the *regnum Italiae*, which placed them under the German king, but his actual influence in the two communes was relatively weak. They stood up to him in the twelfth century, more as allies or political partners than as dependent imperial cities. Clear indicators of their de facto sovereignty were the trade agreements they concluded with North African Islamic rulers without consulting the court.[102]

Italy's maritime republics—communes with their own highly developed administrations that were almost independent of the princes—were unique in comparison with the cities around them. Italy was one of two sizeable areas in Europe where the communal movement originated in the High Middle Ages. A crucial criterion for a city's self-rule was its ability to defend itself. Coastal cities with their own navies were better at this than the rest were. Naval power, which none of the princes could draw on for protection, gave them military status that was also apparent in their lack of dependence on external authority. As a result, the maritime republics came up with early, particularly powerful forms for organizing communal autonomy. Thus the formation of Genoa's system of consuls in 1099 appears to have been associated with a naval expedition.[103] The maritime republican model had an effect on the constitution of other urban communities. Conversely, the communal movement in medieval Italy was the matrix for an emergent self-rule that would enable some coastal cities to build colonial empires.[104]

The third precondition for the rise of protocolonialism—the dominating position of trade—is closely connected with the first two, for naval supremacy and urban autonomy were its prerequisites. But if a city deployed its ships mainly for plundering and privateering, it could not possibly create colonies, either as trading bases or sources of raw materials, nor would it have any reason to. Colonies made no sense unless and until they were integrated with organized, long-distance trade. That is why Pisa's and Genoa's exploitation of Sardinia as a colony could commence only after the military phase of pillaging was over. And the next stage—the integration of a colonial economy into the system of long-distance trade—also turned out to be a gradual process. What held for the dominance of long-distance trade had to hold for municipal government as well. Very diverse social groups were involved in the development of communal autonomy in Italy. A vital intermediate step in several cities was the lordship of its bishop. The bishop or the archbishop played a key part in running municipal governments in Pisa and Genoa, and as we have seen, these lords saw no conflict between ecclesiastical and commercial interests. Ultimately, however, cities under episcopal control never came to rule a colony. And so we find that one precondition for protocolonialism was to have the representatives of trading interests in autonomous communes making the decisions.

———

Our exploration of the three factors shaping the origin of protocolonialism in the Mediterranean followed the threads of protocolonialist development and the crusading movement back in history and showed that the two converged. The territorial situation in early medieval Italy offered fertile ground for both. No single, strong central power could gain a foothold—neither the Byzantine nor the Carolingian Empires nor their successor kingdoms. One of the most obvious factors in this case was the shift in Europe's center of gravity to the Northwest, discussed many times above. A multitude of small, fragmented, loosely dependent lordship organizations sprang up, which were by and large left to their own defenses against the Saracen menace; as a result, they sought out their own ways to assert themselves.[105] These small, fragmented lordships were chiefly located along the lines of the old Roman urban districts, or of similar territories around settlement centers well positioned for defense. This pattern did not sustain the autonomous communities of Roman citizens from the classical imperial age, but the tradition of having a community elect its magistrates was still an important reversion should the monarch's central authority fail; the office of the bishop, which still was an elected one, might then be the first to bridge the power gap. These fragmented lordship territories rooted in antiquity developed in completely different directions in the early and later Middle Ages. Maritime republics with their own navies, on the one hand, and the *patrimonium Petri* as the secular basis of papal lordship, on the other, marked the two extremes of lordship in Italy created as the Western Empire declined. Both contributed to expansionist trends in their own ways. The bishop of Rome needed a protective force, guards who would be granted every religious pardon the early reforming popes had given to those who came to their aid against the Saracens. The Crusade as the pope's war coalesced these elements into a universal, expansionist institution. As for the maritime republics, the implicit expansionism of their naval forces kept developing: from self-defense to pillaging expeditions and long-distance trade initiatives, and finally including various aspects of early colonialism.

The expansionism of the crusading movement and protocolonialism led to rather profound changes in the configuration of Europe's space.

The territories it added after the Wendish Crusade in the Northeast were of minor importance. The constant colonization of the East would probably have absorbed that region even without murderous crusading campaigns and violent "missions of the sword." And the group of states in Outremer established by the "First Crusade" was short-lived; its reintegration into the Islamic cultural sphere has been ongoing to this day. The crushing of the Byzantine Empire in the "Fourth Crusade" rendered any rapprochement between the Eastern and Western Churches out of the question and entrenched the antagonism along the schism's borders. At the same time, the empire's defeat laid the groundwork for the Ottoman sweep into southeastern Europe, thereby making an outer limit to Europe more precise. The Reconquest on the Iberian Peninsula, which was inspired by the crusading ideal, permanently integrated areas of expansion, something that Spanish and Portuguese colonialism was to carry on. Internal shifts in importance were every bit as significant as the redrawing of distant boundaries. The Mediterranean area grew in importance for Europe as a result of the crusading movement as well as protocolonialism. Large areas of overland and maritime traffic were more closely linked—not only by military action and the burgeoning exchange of goods but by religion and culture, thanks to political ties. The maritime republics expanded during the High Middle Ages into cities of a magnitude virtually unknown in Europe before then. A blossoming landscape of cities in northern Italy now stood next to the one that resembled it in northwestern Europe. And urbanization kept growing along the corridors connecting these two core areas. But there were also losers; for instance, the large Mediterranean islands were the first victims of European colonial politics within the continent.

That the Crusades were a specifically European phenomenon without parallel in other cultures has already been explained from within its own context: the unique nature of the papal church. The protocolonialism of the Italian maritime republics was equally exceptional. Autonomous cities controlled by merchants with their own navies are historical rarities. Wherever the Hanseatic League operated—it was the second-largest maritime trading region in medieval Europe—it could only take halting steps in this direction. Cities of this kind simply did not exist in large, centralized, bureaucratic empires where the navy was in state hands and urban self-rule was unheard of—for example, in the Byzantine Empire, the caliphate, or even China, where the merchants' lack of social prestige made it completely unthinkable that they would ever come to power. We would have to go far back in time to find any parallels.

Phoenician cities had begun to establish Mediterranean trading posts in the eleventh century BC, which evolved into colonial empires.[106] Then Greek cities built similar trading outposts from the eighth century on, but their colonizing efforts only partially accomplished what the Phoenicians had. These early colonial forms were later absorbed into the greater empires of Hellenism and the *imperium Romanum* respectively. It is an astonishing fact that the Italian maritime republics were able to hold out for so long against the princes of Europe, and that those very principalities rather seamlessly carried on with early republican colonialism. Lying behind this continuity was the interplay between several maritime republics and monarchies interested in colonial ventures—which allowed earlier practices to continue under new leadership.

Genoa and Pisa were engaged in the politics of trade on the Iberian Peninsula and North Africa as early as the twelfth century. The Genoese maintained their *fondachi* in Valencia, Denia, and on the Balearics, later in Bugia, Ceuta, Tunis, Tripoli, Salé on the Atlantic, and Morocco.[107] The Genoese colony in Portugal constantly featured in the empire's early colonial history. King Dinis promoted the Genoese Emanuel Pessagno to be his admiral in 1317 and gave his family the right of succession—an act symbolizing the cooperation between Genoa and Portugal.[108] Five more members of Pessagno's family were to follow him in this leadership role. The Genoese had reached the west Moroccan coast by the twelfth and thirteenth centuries and pushed on to the Canary Islands in the fourteenth century, driven by their interest in dyes, pelts, tallow, and other commodities.[109] The Portuguese, too, moved southward along the west coast of Africa, at times in concert with Genoa. Genoa's primary role was to put up the necessary capital for these expeditions, but they also contributed shipbuilding technology, nautical know-how, and essential colonizing techniques. Portugal was in a preferred position among the kingdoms of the Iberian Peninsula because of its aptitude and readiness for maritime expansion. The Atlantic Ocean was part of its very nature. Trade with northwestern Europe moved through Portuguese coastal centers, which required the designing of more seaworthy ships. Unlike other kingdoms on the peninsula, Portugal's royal house was receptive toward trading and inclined to favor expansionism; as we have seen, this was sustained partly by conventional motives in the crusading tradition, but surely more powerfully by hopes of economic gain. The Aviz dynasty that came to power in 1385 turned for support against the higher nobility to the bourgeoisie and merchants, therefore to the Genoese. The Aviz kings have properly been called "crowned capitalists."[110] So the two partners complemented each other very well indeed. Genoese colonialism went ahead in the West under the Portuguese flag. This did not diminish the republic's income; Genoans exercised their function as bankers more and more. Portugal was the first European princely power to become active on the colonial-expansionist front. Others were to follow and eventually take the lead.

Whereas the protocolonialism of Italy's maritime republics— exemplified in our brief sketch of the Genoa-Portugal connection— flowed directly into expanding the growth of the great European powers from early modern times on, the same cannot be easily said about the crusading movement.[111] There were certainly occasions where the two strands of development came together—witness the conquest of Ceuta in 1415. Generally speaking, the Crusades of the waning Middle Ages and early modern times did not have any role to play in colonial expansionist ventures. The catastrophes the crusading armies suffered fighting against the Turks at Nicopolis in 1396 and Varna 1443 obviously contributed nothing to expansionism. But the naval battle of Lepanto, fought under the Crusaders' flag in 1571, did indeed safeguard the colony of Crete for the Republic of Saint Mark.[112] Yet this did not mean that anything had changed. The victory the army of Crusaders won over the Turks before the gates of Vienna in 1683 launched a phase of Hapsburg territorial expansion toward the Southeast that could hardly produce colonial structures, at least during the late seventeenth and early eighteenth centuries.

Although the crusading movement was now of little consequence as far as concrete ventures were concerned, the power of the Crusade as an idea would have a centuries-long influence on the mindset and behavior of people in conflict situations. As an idea it could legitimize a religiously dictated image of one's enemies; it could raise levels of preparedness for military battle; it could help devalue one's opponents by arguing first from the standpoint of religious opposition and then, in more general terms, from a political or cultural point of view. The ideology of the Crusades must certainly have induced Europeans to deal with foreign cultures aggressively. It could very well be used in expansionist ventures to exacerbate conflicting positions. Although it had an intensifying and aggravating effect, we probably cannot deduce the real root of militant European expansionism from this line of development. That honor surely goes to colonialism.

The multifaceted phenomenon of expansionism, as formally and generally defined in this chapter, presents religious, colonizing, political/governmental, and commercial/economic aspects. Religious expansionism is inherent in all universal religions that claim authority above and beyond a tribe, a people, an empire. All proselytizing religions are expansionist in this sense: Buddhism, Jainism, Manichaeism, even Christianity. The crusading movement was originally uninvolved with this kind of universal, missionary-driven expansionism. Its function was not to spread the faith but to reclaim Christian territories, especially Palestinian holy sites. A first synthesis of missionary expansionism and land acquisition appeared in campaigns like the Wendish Crusade, a type the pope legitimized in 1147. This was where the "mission of the sword" was born, the compulsory conversion of the "heathen" by Crusaders—which ran contrary to Christian tradition. Saint Francis opposed it in his sermon to the caliph by countering with an ideal of conversion based solely on the power of religious conviction. Francis's argument marked a significant start, but the fateful alliance of land acquisition and compulsory conversion remained the legacy of certain crusading traditions. Missionary work came to be a factor in legitimizing expansion rooted in economic or lordship interests. As medieval protocolonialism grew, economic motives appear to have been the mainspring of European expansion. The fallout from economic motives was evident in the different modes of enlarging lordship, such as the system of trading bases the Portuguese favored, or the extensive Spanish vice-regal kingdoms. Genoa's cooperation with Portugal demonstrated that enterprises could also be profitable in the waning Middle Ages without any form of direct rule at all. There was no model worldwide, during the decline of the Middle Ages, for an expansionism geared to the commercial exploitation of foreign territories. The Italian maritime republics were the only influence in the Mediterranean area to launch initiatives in this direction. They owed their exceptional position to a unique constellation of lordship. It was only in those republics that merchants controlled a maritime power, and they had been in control for hundreds of years.

Seven

Preaching and Printing: Early Modes of Mass Communication

Europe took the road to the information society relatively early on: its beginnings date from the Middle Ages. Historically, other societies of course developed media of mass communication at an early stage. But from a worldwide perspective, it was the evolution of media from Europe that won out. If we speak of globalization today, we refer to communicative processes that originated in Europe. Early, exclusively European forms of mass communication were of course localized within that culture for a very long time. And so their cultural, social, and economic effects appear to be determining factors for Europe's special path. Preaching and printing—two significant phenomena of mass communication involving orality and literacy—will receive special attention in this chapter.

The sermon cannot really be considered a broad form of mass communication in medieval Europe; the number of appropriate criteria is too small.[1] Mass communication presupposes an anonymous and heterogeneous audience. The communicator has no idea about the recipients' particular expectations because they have no shared group experience. As a rule, the Christian sermon in medieval Europe would probably have been a form of *group* communication, not mass communication. The preacher's audience was of a limited and manageable size; their shared experience both among themselves and with the preacher created a kind of intimacy. These conditions may be assumed for essential, basic forms of medieval preaching—the sermon in the monastery or the university, of course, but mainly the parish sermon given by the bishop or a priest he had commissioned. That said, Christian sermons in the Middle Ages were naturally arranged along an extremely diverse spectrum, and the border between group and mass communication seems to have been porous. We can probably speak of mass communication from the time when church naves could no longer accommodate the crowds pouring into them from a great distance. To have to preach in the graveyard, in the marketplace, or before the town gates was not an unusual practice. Some preachers were personalities whose methods attracted large crowds—the Cistercian Saint Bernhard of Clairvaux in the twelfth century, the Franciscan Berthold of Regensburg in the thirteenth, and the Dominican Saint Vincent Ferrer at the turn of the fourteenth to the fifteenth. Some scholars have tried to calculate the numbers in Saint Vincent Ferrer's audiences during his twenty years of preaching in Spain, the south of France, Italy, and Switzerland.[2] Estimates run to around several million—a considerable number, given the extent of settled areas at the time. Crowds of this size who came to hear sermons cannot be explained away as isolated occurrences related only to the magnetism of a particular charismatic preacher. Rather, the phenomenon of the mass sermon in the later Middle Ages—in other words, the sermon of that time understood as a means of mass communication—was structured by particular circumstances.

Medieval preaching tended toward mass communication wherever there were special preaching campaigns. The sermon preaching a Crusade was a decisive turning point in this regard.[3] It not only addressed a large local audience but reached a like-minded public outside that narrower group. The papal church provided the organizing framework for preaching the Crusades. The pope, either orally or in writing, empowered appropriate individuals or groups from certain ecclesiastical provinces to preach in order to summon people to a Crusade. Preaching a Crusade was tied in with other church concerns, for example, the institution of indulgences, and it was organized on a larger scale as preaching campaigns, which can be regarded as an early form of public relations.[4] These forms of mass communication took for granted the papal church's infrastructure, in particular, the Dominican and Franciscan Orders, who specialized in preaching and knew no equal anywhere in the world.[5] In this way, mass communication based on *orality* was uniquely organized in Europe as early as the Middle Ages.

Mass communication based on *literacy* emerged from the replication of written texts. Reproduction using printing techniques, as opposed to copying manuscripts, heralded a revolutionary innovation. China invented printing long before Europe did, and it spread from there to other East Asian countries.[6] We will examine more closely China's priority over Europe with regard to the introduction of printing, and, given the general framework of this innovation, we will investigate printing's very different effects in several places. In any case, Johannes (or Johann) Gutenberg's invention of printing with a letterpress and moveable type around the mid-fifteenth century seems to have been decisive for the progress of Europe's special path. Without wishing to question the significance of this fact, we will also address other processes of reproduction using new technologies, especially the woodcut, which provided mass communication via images.[7] Woodcuts were used for mass communication in Europe before written texts were. The woodcut combined image and text, as did other reproductive techniques, thereby correlating the two media. We will pursue in more general terms the links connecting the image to written media. The woodcut was originally printed on a single sheet. Mass communication through works printed using Gutenberg's technology were also single-sheet flyers or a few sheets long, a form that played a substantial, enduring role—indeed, one larger than the book, to which the process owed the term "book" printing (*Buchdruck*)[8]—although without a doubt the printed book occupied a prominent place among early European forms of mass communication based on literacy.

Literacy and orality did not form a dichotomy among the early forms of mass communication in medieval Europe but were interrelated and combined with each other in many different ways.[9] People in the congregation would transcribe and publish a famous preacher's sermon as it had been delivered from the pulpit. Conversely, collections of sermons represented a popular genre that was meant to encourage emulation.[10] University lectures were centered on written texts—a strong stimulus for the growth of late medieval literature.[11] Papal bulls underpinned in writing subsequent spoken communications based on them, from sermons preaching a Crusade to sermons on indulgences. Contemporaries understood religious instruction to be a *praedicatio*, or sermon, whether it was in writing or images.[12] And so the visual medium came to be counted with orality and literacy as a means of mass communication.[13] These forms reinforced one another during the waning Middle Ages, a process that bore consequences for the new print technologies of the fifteenth-century that paved the special path to the media society of modern Europe.

The medium of preaching as an essential origin of modern mass communication obviously indicates a religious context. The sermon is a solemn religious proclamation in all religions with sacred writings. It is also a specific characteristic of religions of the book, in contrast to its opposite ideal type: cult religion.[14] Religions of the book depend upon literacy, which supplies them with the prerequisite audience for mass communication in written form. Holy books are the foundation of religious communities and provide the rudiments for a specific culture of the book. Religious interests are able to stimulate book reproduction en masse. So the rise and dissemination of printing involves religious factors. But because of the sacrosanct nature of fundamental scriptures to a given religious community, religions of the book opposed adopting technical means of reproduction especially strongly. Resistance of this kind—based on religious writings—could also apply to secular literature. Comparing the parameters of different religions of the book for the evolution of mass communication may well give us a preliminary understanding of Europe's unique path toward a media society.

———

Great religions of the book fall into two basic categories. Judaism and the religious communities emanating from that tradition—the various Christian churches, Islam, and we must remember Manichaeism—view their holy scriptures as revelations of God. In contrast, this mode of thought is absent in religions based on scripture in South and East Asia—Buddhism, Confucianism, Taoism. If holy scriptures are *not* regarded as God's word, this tends to make them freer and easier to deal with. This flexibility applies both to the graphic form of how they are written and to their translation into other languages. Since religions of the book have, as a general rule, the character of a universal religion, the problem of translation crops up for them in missionary work. Buddhist missionary monks in East Asia brought with them an enormous number of holy texts from India and translated them into Chinese. The sacredness of the original languages apparently did not stand in their way during what was probably the greatest missionary undertaking of its time.[15] On the other hand, wherever holy scripture is considered to be the word of God, we have less leeway.

This view appears to be most binding for Islam—with particularly long-term consequences for the development of mass communication media. The very text of the Qur'an calls itself an "Arabic Qur'an," thus singling out the one permissible language for its use.[16] Translations are out of the question. And so the spread of Islam made Arabic—the language of the holy book—the holy language of Muslims. But the script itself was invariably fixed too. The Qur'an had to be handed down in the symbols of the sacred script just the way it was passed on in the holy language.[17] Declaring the script holy led to the evolution of Islamic calligraphy, which has almost no equivalent in any other religious culture making use of writing.[18] This holy script was coupled with writing by hand. Even the instrument to be used in writing was determined by religion. The Qur'an expressly names the reed pen as the means of divine revelation. Sura 96 reads in part: "In the Name of God, the Merciful, the Compassionate: Recite: In the Name of the Lord who created, created Man of a blood-clot. Recite: And thy Lord is the Most Generous, who taught by the [Reed] Pen, taught Man that he knew not." These first five verses of sura 96 deal with reading and writing and are traditionally a part of the introductory lesson for children in a Qur'an school.[19] Against this background of the sacralization of handwriting and writing instruments, we can understand why the world of Islam resisted the adoption of printing for so long and so tenaciously. There was not a single printing press anywhere in Islamic lands until the eighteenth century, if we leave aside some printing activity by religious minorities.[20] Printing did not get established until the nineteenth century. Islam had been aware of the print technologies of its eastern and western neighbors for many centuries[21]; they were deliberately not adopted, primarily for religious reasons.[22] This can still be seen in the debates over admitting Muslim printing shops.[23] One of the crucial religious reasons for the hostility to print was the holy character of Arab script as the graphic representation of Allah's word.[24] This blocked the dissemination of printing in an area controlled by a classic religion of the book for the very reason that made the revealed book especially holy. This proved significant for the particular development of the Islamic realm quite apart from the shaping of its communicative structures.

The world's oldest surviving printed book is a single copy of the Diamond Sutra (*Vajra Prajñā Pāramitā Sūtra*) dating from 868.[25] And although canonical writings of religious communities were not paramount when block printing started in China, it was not long before the entire canon of Buddhism, Confucianism, and Taoism was published using this technique.[26] The oldest book printed in Europe with moveable type was Johannes Gutenberg's famous forty-two-line Latin Bible from around 1455.[27] Regarding religions of the book that printed their holy scriptures very quickly, we must proceed on the assumption that the sacredness of these writings was not tied to their transmission by manuscript nor, on the whole, to certain forms of script. This was a decisive factor for the spread of printing in cultures making use of writing. We will see later whether or not this point is related to the rise of printing itself.

Throughout their history, the great religions of the book have shown considerable variation in their attitudes toward the connection between holy scripture and sacred languages. Islam's position is anomalous in this regard because it dictates a sole sacred language. The various Christian churches never adopted a unified position. Translating the Bible does not appear to have been problematic in early Christian times.[28] From the second century on, translations appeared in Syrian, Latin, Coptic, Armenian, Georgian, and Gothic. The Latin version was by far the most successful. If translating from Latin into the different vernaculars was prohibited in the Western Church from the High Middle Ages, it was not because there was a cultural pattern linked to the holy book from the very beginning. Any reference limiting permitted languages to the three inscribed on the cross simply exemplifies an ideology of legitimization. The heart of the matter was the monopoly of the Latin-speaking clergy on the interpretation of holy scripture. Having the Bible in a layman's hands would have jeopardized this monopoly and thus the unity of the community of the faithful. From the thirteenth century on, access to the Bible in the vernacular was the issue again and again for reform movements critical of the church and for heterodox factions—a goal the Reformation was largely able to implement.[29] The papal church's clinging to the Latin Bible created special problems of mediation. For centuries the laity had no access to the message of revelation in written form. It could only be acquired in writing through Bible stories and similar adaptations.[30] Oral forms of transmission were therefore all the more prominent. The enormous significance of preaching in the Western Church during the later Middle Ages came from tying the Bible to the sacred language of Latin—a secondary phenomenon in the evolution of Christianity as a religion of the book that was nevertheless of extraordinary consequence. We have to view the parish sermon and the mass sermon in medieval Western Christendom against the necessity of assimilating the vernacular.

As an instrument of religious instruction, preaching seems to exist in virtually all religions of the book.[31] Buddhism, for example, offers a particularly distinctive form of the sermon in this extended sense of the word, by which the adepts in a group of ascetics, and even lay followers, received instruction—a central and ongoing activity in the community.[32] Buddha's sermons were so emblematic of his mission that his first enlightened address marks the start of the community's formation and is considered one of the four main events of his life, together with his birth, going forth, and death.[33] The role of preacher has for no other great religious founder so defined a life and tradition. However, Buddhism did not employ the sermon in the narrower sense of the word, that is, as part of a liturgy of the word (*Wortgottesdienst*). Nor did Hinduism, which—if we contrast religions of the book and cult religions as ideal types—can also be counted as a cult religion. Hinduism has sacred scriptures in which a distinction is drawn between "holy revelation" and "holy remembrance," but these writings do not function as a basis for a liturgy of the word, where a sermon follows a reading of scripture.[34] This distinction was peculiar to Western Asian religions of the book and the communities derived from them.

For early origins of the sermon as part of a liturgy of the word, we might well think of looking to Zoroastrianism, clearly a prophesying religion. From the perspective of the sociology of religion, preaching is closely connected with the prophet's function.[35] Zoroaster proclaimed, in sermons in verse, the divine revelation visited upon him. Reciting sermons appears to have been central to the divine service at an early time, in any case long before they were written down.[36] The language was extremely difficult, which might well have made interpretation necessary. In the third century AD, in areas where Zoroastrianism was prevalent, Manichaeism syncretized old Iranian, Jewish, Christian, Gnostic, and Buddhist elements in a system in which preaching played a fundamental part in both missionary work and the liturgy of the word.[37] Mani, who came from the Judeo-Christian Baptist community of the Elchasaites, might have borrowed the emphasis on preaching from the Judeo-Christian tradition. It is certain that the liturgy of the word, with the sermon at its heart, was first documented in the special circumstances in which exile and postexile Jews found themselves.[38] Preaching's origin as a proclamation and explication of the holy word can be found in contemporary speeches given to the Jewish community during a liturgy of the word. This is the form of the sermon that Christianity and Islam adopted.

The liturgy of the word, based on holy scripture, features much more in Judaism and Islam than in Christianity. The Christian celebration of the Eucharist is at one and the same time a liturgy of the word and of sacrifice. For this reason, as we have seen, Christianity cannot be considered a religion of the book pure and simple. From the early Middle Ages especially, a period when rates of literacy were low, it developed strong elements of a cult religion, appearing in Europe mainly in places where only cult religions had existed until the arrival of Christian missionaries, who had already claimed the rising northwestern part of the continent. European Christendom was therefore a religion of the book in very different ways, depending on the stage and region in which it was found. As a result, the Christian sermon was folded into the liturgy of the word but occurred in many different forms besides. The spectrum ranged from the total absence of the parish sermon to sermons for the masses, as well as to preaching campaigns conducted over substantial areas. If the Byzantine East initially developed the culture of preaching more elaborately than did the Latin West, the situation was reversed during the course of the Middle Ages.[39] Not only the forms of preaching but the related phenomena of educational institutions and lay piety were to distinguish the Eastern and Western Churches from each other in important and persistent ways. Profound changes in preaching in Western Christendom throughout the Middle Ages also brought about fundamental differences with Islam, despite some degree of earlier conformity based on a common use of the community sermon in the liturgy of the word. These distinctions must be interpreted before we can understand the specific route that led Europe from its medieval foundations toward modern mass communication. The transformation in preaching addressed communication primarily on the level of orality and secondarily, though indirectly—for qualitative and quantitative changes in the religious culture of the ear also altered the culture of reading—on the level of literacy.

———

We have already reviewed two essential preconditions for preaching's particular evolution during the European Middle Ages: the exceptionally high degree of organization in the Western Church, as shown in a cross-cultural comparison, and the specific development of monasticism within the church's cultural reach. The coordination of preaching on a transregional basis, starting with the preaching of the Crusades in the twelfth century, took a decisive step toward targeted public relations. Preaching a Crusade—let alone carrying through with one—was not even possible until it fell within the purview of the emergent papal church. No other religious community that made use of preaching had a similar chance of initiating such a project, then or afterward—neither Buddhism nor Islam, and most certainly not Judaism in the diaspora. Only in Western Christendom was there a central organizing authority: the pope. And it was only there that entire religious orders existed—thanks to the extraordinary expansion of monasticism—that could be recruited for coordinated preaching. This gave the church leadership a unique instrument for a public program of work. Moreover, the Dominicans and the Franciscans—preaching orders created in the early thirteenth century—were not only commissioned for preaching campaigns; their innovative forms of pastoral care motivated them to carry out preaching duties transregionally within the community of the order. The mendicant friars' preaching set a crucial new course within the development of oral mass communication as a whole.

————

The two features of the Western Church described above were also important for the advancement of mass communication through writing. The high level of organization within the papal church generated a sudden increase in written correspondence. The need for standardized written forms skyrocketed. It was no accident that Gutenberg's first printed works, apart from the Latin Bible, were the *Mainz Indulgences* (1454) and the *Turks' Calendar* (1455). The former involved the offering of indulgences occasioned by the Turkish threat to Cyprus; the latter was a follow-up to the fall of Constantinople and was meant as a warning to all Christendom.[40] The voluminous increase in writing within the church itself was only one factor among many that prompted a search for new forms of reproduction. It deserves mention as one of the preconditions for the invention of printing in Europe.

There were quite different connections between the development of new religious orders and the growing need for new forms of mass communication in writing. The Franciscans and Dominicans created "tertiaries," a novel "Third Order" of religious life for both men and women that lay midway between the monastic and secular worlds.[41] Each member of the Third Order was obligated to lead the ascetic life and to pray according to the canonical hours. All in all, this led to a monasticizing of a broad segment of the laity—particularly in urban areas—under the influence of mendicant friars and other newly formed orders. The piety of laymen enhanced the need for images and devotional texts—in fact, for all objects used in the practice of private worship. This surge of lay piety in the late Middle Ages greatly stimulated the invention of new ways of reproducing religious images and texts.[42]

A fundamental issue regarding religions of the book is their relationship to holy scripture, on the one hand, and to sacred images on the other. The question is also important for the development of forms of communication on a mass scale. Religions of the book tend to reject the veneration of sacred images. The adoration of images is a characteristic of cult religions, and yet many religions of the book have adopted some of its elements. Judaism and Islam are strictly opposed to icons. The ban on graven images is prominently spelled out in the Ten Commandments. Accordingly, Christianity adopted this prohibition from its mother religion. The basic prohibition was gradually modified and relativized in many ways, with the Byzantine Church moving furthest ahead in this direction. A synod at the end of the so-called Iconoclastic Controversy, waged so bitterly in the eighth and ninth centuries, proclaimed the following dogma in 869: "We decree that icons of our Lord shall be venerated and honored in the same way as are the Books of the Gospel."[43] This equating of Christ's image with the books of the Gospel was the most radical stance of any medieval Christian Church toward the veneration of images. The Western Church did not go that far but in general allowed the image to be an object of devotion.

There is an interesting parallel here: Buddhism was initially opposed to icons but then permitted figurative representation—a turn similar to Christendom's shift under Hellenistic influence.[44] Now it was precisely Buddhism and Western Christendom—two religions of the book permitting sacred images—that independently came up with a printing method for reproducing writing and images. Chinese Buddhist monks had developed woodblock printing earlier for reduplicating pictures and texts simultaneously.[45] Woodblock printing corresponds, technically speaking, to the woodcut in Europe, which was mainly used for printing images but also for accompanying texts. Europe would later develop the processes of the copper engraving and the metal cut, both of which preceded printing with moveable type.[46] During the first half of the fifteenth century, there seems to have been a very great need in Europe to reproduce images, perhaps even greater than the need for text reproduction. As to technical solutions to this problem, the printing of images antedated the printing of texts. It is remarkable that the image played such a large part in the development of printing in two cultures that invented it independently. Religions of the book that had a relatively relaxed attitude toward images apparently created religious preconditions propitious for these kinds of technical developments. The special sacredness of images could present obstacles here, just as the special sacredness of books did. The situation in the Eastern Church seems comparable to that of Islamic regions, in that the sacralization of the Qur'an through writing was to block for centuries the acceptance of printing. Similarly, the special sacredness of the icon in the Eastern Church barred any new graphic reduplicating processes for images, such as those that preceded and disseminated printing in the Western Church.

––––––––

Another connecting link between early printing and the sphere of religion is of marginal concern for our pair of contrasting ideal types, that is, religions of the book and cult religions. It has to do with the special religious character of texts, images, and objects that existed immediately before printing or were involved in its earliest stages. The world's oldest printed artifact was long thought to be the *Hyakumantō darani* (The dharani of the one million pagodas), which the Japanese empress Shotoku ordered to be drawn up between 764 and 770.[47] The discovery in a Korean temple of a very similar printed document dating from some time before 751 then took pride of place, and that exemplar clearly shows how the religious, mental, and political environments of the Buddhist printing method functioned. The empress, mindful of the terrible smallpox epidemic in Japan from 735 to 737, retained 116 priests at court to drive out the disease-bearing demons. Prompted by Dokyo, her chief adviser, physician, and the leading Buddhist priest, she tried another course. She ordered the printing of a million charms that were then placed in a million miniature wooden pagodas and circulated throughout the whole empire. How the campaign was carried out is documented in historical records and attested by archeological evidence. The texts in the miniature pagodas described contemporary thinking regarding the charms' efficacy. They included the answer that Buddha gave to his disciples when they asked about the charms' power: "Whoever wishes to gain power from the *dharani* must write seventy-seven copies and place them in a pagoda. This pagoda must then be honored with sacrifice."[48] The sutra containing this and other instructions about the religious benefits of copying sacred texts was put into Chinese in 704 by a Tokharian monk. Similar practices are known from earlier archeological finds in India.[49] The whole concept and how to put it into practice migrated from China to Korea and Japan, where manuscript copies were made en masse even before the adoption of printing. The special religious benefits accruing to copying drove the number of copies even higher. In this way, Buddhism's prioritizing of sacred texts for copying made a crucial contribution to the rise of printing and its implementation in East Asia.[50] We would think today that written matter was meant to support missionary work, or at least that this early form of mass communication would have been intended for human beings. But this was not so. The million printed charms were enclosed in tiny wooden pagodas—were the disease-bearing demons meant to be the recipients of the messages? The conceptual apparatus of modern communication scholarship is probably inadequate for doing justice to Empress Shotoku's unique and comprehensive campaign.

Charms had their place at the beginning of printing in another of China's great religions, Taoism.[51] People believed that Taoist priests possessed the magical ability to ward off evil spirits and danger, a power that could be transmitted to someone else through seals and charms. The charms were carved on wood blocks and consisted of up to 120 characters. The stamped Taoist charm seal appeared in the sixth or seventh century. All the basic principles of later block printing were fully embodied in the magical practice employing charm seals. But the question is, how can these magical practices at the beginning of printing be conceptualized in communication theory?

The connection between early printing and charms ultimately leads to a strand in the development of printing that is completely isolated, difficult to categorize, and short-lived. In the oasis of El-Fayyum in the Libyan Desert in Upper Egypt, some fifty bits of block-printed paper were discovered in 1880.[52] All of the texts were in the Arabic language and script; there was some decoration, but Islam's prohibition against images was strictly observed. The subject matter was religious; many were charms, and many were inscribed with verses from the Qur'an so that they would function as talismans. The magic, protective nature of the collection was evident throughout. The texts were printed between 900 and 1350, at a time when Islam was aware of East Asian printing but refused to adopt it, at least in the higher culture. It is odd that only books in manuscript form have survived from the period when Islamic book culture was in full flower, whereas the few dozen charms from popular religious culture that have come down to us were block-printed. In the everyday practice of magic, apparently, other laws were followed. In this lower social stratum, a print process that the religious community's elite stubbornly continued to scorn was kept alive over a fairly long period. The technique applied in this process indicates a Chinese origin, probably transmitted over the heavily traveled routes through Central Asia. The texts' subject matter reminds us once again that belief in magic and acts of magic could be a powerful motivating force in the development and spread of printing.

Two examples from the early stage of printing in Europe will supply the finishing touches on our description of printing and the belief in charms. The oldest dated European woodcut is a portrait of Saint Christopher from 1423.[53] There was a popular late-medieval belief that if you saw an image of Saint Christopher, you would come to no grief on that day. The sight of the saint's image was generally coupled with the assurance that you would not die "unprepared," that is, in sin.[54] For this reason, giant depictions of Saint Christopher were often found on the outside of church walls and on city towers and gates. The emergence of the woodcut changed that practice in a fundamental way: the magic effect of the public image of Saint Christopher could now be replaced by a private image. An Annunciation painted by the Master of Flémalle shows a colored woodcut of Saint Christopher on a mantelpiece.[55] It appears to have been a normal component of a room's furnishings. Considering the magic effect that popular belief ascribed to the image of Saint Christopher, these woodcuts would probably have found buyers very quickly.

One thing we know about Johannes Gutenberg, the inventor of a printing process with moveable type in the West, is that he worked in his early years on a technique for mechanically mass producing badges for the pilgrimage to Aachen.[56] Pilgrim badges were probably produced by stamping; "forms" and "press" are mentioned in the literature of the time. This surely marks an important first stage in the technical development of printing. But these efforts were touched off by a popular belief in magic and religion that aroused interest in standardized mass production. Pilgrim badges belonged on a pilgrim's clothing, but they were chiefly souvenirs brought back home from a pilgrimage, following the tradition of the "contact relic" (*Kontaktreliquie*), a relic that has touched a holy place or person.[57] In a certain sense they were cult objects, sewn into prayer books, nailed onto an altarlike board, or sometimes placed in graves. In any case, they were believed to possess something of the power of the holy place where they originated or which they portrayed or symbolized. Pilgrim badges were made of lead—as were letters used in printing later—or less commonly of silver. The sale of badges at places of pilgrimage numbered hundreds of thousands annually. In choosing the pilgrimage to the relics at Aachen, Gutenberg picked by far the most important contemporary pilgrimage in central Europe for marketing the standardized souvenirs he manufactured. Once again, we find ideas about magical efficacy accompanying the birth of a technique for the mass production of printing.

The significance of magic practices for the origin of printing in East and West is doubly revealing. First, it would be one-sided and incomplete to regard the preconditions for printing in religions of the book solely from the respective position of each religious community's particular holy book. Charms and talismans strongly argue against this point of view; interest in them can be so intense that they could become an exception even in a religion inimical to printing. This is what makes the Egyptian example of El-Fayyum so impressive. Second, the instances analyzed above show that it makes sense to slot religious communities into their proper place within a broad spectrum, with two ideal types—religions of the book and cult religions—at either extreme. Positions along this spectrum might even reflect practices on a lower level, the level of magic objects. In Buddhist and Taoist China, it is texts rather than images that are mostly found on this level, as they are in Islam. Islamic charms rigorously adhered to the ban on images as well. The situation was different in late medieval Europe, where the two examples of the devotional image and the cult object connected to the relic were placed front and center. This provides an instructive counterpoint to the fact that Western Christendom originated as a religion of the book.

———

It would hardly have occurred to a contemporary observer in the early Middle Ages that the sermons being preached in Western Christendom might offer a particularly forward-looking perspective on how mass communication would develop. The odds would probably have seemed to favor other religions of the book, as well as their methods of religious instruction and promulgating the faith. But the situation at the end of the Middle Ages would have confounded this expectation. Preaching in Western Christendom had become highly developed and extremely varied over vast stretches of the continent. It had distinctive qualities lacking in other preaching cultures, effecting changes to Europe's special path. Preaching in the West underwent definitive, occasionally revolutionary, modifications during the Middle Ages. It was a tripartite process: first came the Carolingian preaching reform, then the conflict over the lay sermon that resulted in the founding of the mendicant orders in the early thirteenth century, and finally, the reform movement of the fifteenth century—a prelude to the Reformation, the process that split religion and preaching alike, dividing Europe into various cultural regions that still bear strongly upon us today. The particular dynamic that gripped preaching in the medieval Western Church prompted the drawing of Europe's outermost cultural borders. These developments proved significant for relations with the Eastern Church and, subsequently, with the Islamic world as well.

———

The first phase of medieval preaching highlighted the monastic rather than the parish sermon.[58] The fundamentally cenobitic form of Western monasticism encouraged the organized promulgation of the faith and indoctrination within the community—practices neither feasible nor customary in other forms of religious asceticism. The sermon was part of European monasticism from its early medieval beginnings as a component of the divine service, which was why the monasteries were interested, as a rule, in scholastic learning, book collecting, and educational institutions. Preaching to monks in a monastery was of course still a long way from monks giving sermons to the laity. Early medieval Irish monks were a notable exception in this regard. The principle of *peregrinatio* led these Irishmen to become itinerant and missionary preachers. Irish monks, in their ascetic fervor, voluntarily accepted exile from their homeland—something the tribal societies of their ancestral families regarded as among the severest of punishments.[59] Throughout all of northwestern Europe, they spread the religious traditions peculiar to Irish Christian asceticism—doing penance, for instance, so closely allied with preaching, or producing books, a foundation stone of sermonizing.[60] A special tradition had grown up in Ireland because the island had been denied access to Rome throughout antiquity, so that it had not been Romanized before its conversion.[61] Its reception of antiquity only began when it came to learning how to understand the Latin Bible. Education in Ireland was a key factor in northwestern European culture—whether directly or mediated by the Anglo-Saxons. It might well have played a significant part in bringing literacy to the area and also greatly influenced Carolingian efforts to reform education.[62]

Charlemagne's church reforms initiated the second phase in the history of Western preaching.[63] These reforms were not particularly innovative as far as preaching went; they tended toward a restoration of the patterns of antiquity or an exportation to newly established mission areas in order to create an orderly preaching network. Charlemagne's *Admonitio generalis* from 789 applied to what was then the Frankish Empire; the reform measures it laid out specifically addressed that region. Church law consolidated the following system: the bishop continued to have authority over preaching, as he did in antiquity. Apart from the bishop, the parish priest could also preach, a task, to be sure, that was both delegated and monitored. The reforms' success ultimately depended on whether the clergy who were obligated to preach were up to the job of carrying out both their pastoral and homiletic functions. Charlemagne entrusted Paul the Deacon with putting together a resource book of model sermons. A new, critical requirement was for the parish sermon to be in the vernacular wherever Latin was no longer understood. The sermon thus performed a key mediating function in promulgating the faith and indoctrinating the laity. Charlemagne ordered every diocese to plan schools for training the clergy. Important cathedral schools were founded as a result, particularly in the heartland of the Carolingian Empire; they were on a higher level than monastic schools. The same link between founding new schools and improving the training of the clergy characterized later phases of preaching reform as well.

The most important period of change in Western preaching likely concluded when the mendicant orders were established in the early thirteenth century. The new orders had come in after the turbulent times marked by prophetic and critical agitation by reformers from both inside and outside the church; by confrontations sparked by new forces such as the Crusades and the poverty movement; by political clashes like the one between the emperor and the pope or conflicts within urban communes. The organization of sermons, their content, and who was allowed to preach assumed new guises during this revolution in the systematic promulgation of the faith from the eleventh century on.[64]

A central controversial issue of the day was the lay sermon. The popes by and large tolerated lay sermonizing during the debates over church reform; after all, it preached against simony and nicolaitism (that is, marriage and concubinage) among the higher clergy. Lay preachers, for example, the (in)famous Peter of Amiens, at times gave welcome support to the crusading movement. The church felt threatened, however, when the demand for the lay sermon was picked up by heretical or borderline groups such as the Cathars and the Waldensians, which called into question the monopoly of official priests on promulgating the faith. Furthermore, the lay sermon proved to be an appropriate resource in the fight against heterodox groups. Thirteenth-century popes sought to solve the problem posed by heterodoxy in various ways. In 1201 Innocent III granted the penitent "Third Order" Humiliati permission to preach—limited to its own circle, of course.[65] Gregory IX issued a categorical ban on the lay sermon in 1228.[66] The two great preaching orders, the Franciscans and the Dominicans, were well established at that point. The new system of preaching exhibited radical innovations, to the most important of which we now turn.

The bishop remained in charge of any and all preaching in his diocese. But besides organized diocesan preaching, there was a supradiocesan organization: the great orders directly under the pope. Two of them—again, the Franciscans and the Dominicans—regarded preaching as their main mission. In a matter of decades these orders were represented in all the larger cities within the purview of the Western Church. The Dominicans quite deliberately chose the *celeberrimae urbes* as the seats of their convents. A map of the mendicant orders' convents in the twelfth and thirteenth centuries would give a rather accurate picture of the physical extent and the inner structure of the Western Church.[67] The orders complemented the pastoral care given by the diocesan clergy in the cities; sometimes they would even be in competition with the clergy. Many burghers would attend the city parish church in the morning and then go to hear a mendicant friar preach in the afternoon. In this way, the sermon broke free from its liturgical context; it was liberated in form and substance from its connection with the liturgy of the word, thus losing its traditional character as a homily, that is, as an exposition of the passage from holy scripture that had just been read. This unlinking presented the possibility for an enormous thematic expansion. Religious boundaries could now be transgressed; a sermon might, for instance, bring in political matters.

The evolution of an independent preaching culture fostered by the mendicant orders also had some fallout in architecture. The hall church became an established building type, derived from its function as a hall for preaching.[68] The place where the preacher stood was moved from the ambo near the choir stalls farther forward into the nave, elevated, if possible, so that he could be better heard. The pulpit now generally gained more significance as part of the program of church construction. Outdoor pulpits were occasionally built onto churches—an indication that the church had outgrown its space for a mass audience. But the mass sermon of the time was in principle no longer restricted by a church's structure. It could be preached wherever there was enough room—in the market square, before the city gates, in an open field. These dislocating spatial trends were a strong indicator of the sermon's emancipation from the liturgy of the word and of its development into a separate form of the divine service, something it had already achieved by the late Middle Ages. The Reformation was to reinforce this separation still more.

In regard to the mendicant friars' sermon as an early form of mass communication, the coordination of preaching on a transregional scale for a particular purpose was more critical than was a huge attendance at any given local preaching event. The purpose might be prescribed by the pope or by the order's own highest authorities. We have already shown how the mendicant orders, and the Cistercians before them, were pressed into service to propagandize for the Crusades, but the papal preaching commissions were not only concerned with the church's political goals. Gregory X charged the Dominican Order in 1274 to preach devotion to "the Most Holy Name of Jesus."[69] A religious movement was born from this very specific commission; it led to a great number of "Confraternities of the Holy Name of Jesus," which frequently had their seat in Dominican churches, often paired with a Holy Name of Jesus altar. Confraternities of the Blessed Virgin Mary were regularly created at Dominican churches in the thirteenth century.[70] Their mandatory prayer was the Psalterium Mariae, that is, one hundred and fifty Ave Marias enumerated by using a string of beads—the precursor of today's rosary, which Dominican preachers disseminated far and wide. The Confraternity of the Holy Rosary that Jakob Sprenger—the author of the *Malleus maleficarum*—founded at the Dominican church in Cologne grew to about one hundred thousand members in six years, including the emperor and the pope, all of whom were obligated to say one rosary a week. The rosary was to become so popular that Reformation images displayed it as an emblem to designate a Catholic—just as the book identified a Protestant.[71] We could expand the number of close analogies from the history of Franciscan preaching—for instance, the propagation of devotion to the passion or to the life of Jesus, for which the great popularity of the manger at Christmas, introduced by Saint Francis, can serve as an example.[72] Both preaching orders, along with others, carried out very intense and effective large-scale public relations work through their labor of preaching. This was not the least reason that lay piety in the Latin Church of the waning Middle Ages had taken on a completely different character during the three centuries since the new system of preaching emerged.

The issue of adequate theological education as a precondition for preaching played a crucial, recurring role in the debate over whether or not to permit lay preaching.[73] The mendicants' solution to the problem was to integrate the appropriate course of study into an order's training program and to try to forge relationships with recently founded universities.[74] Not the least reason for the universities' strong growth was the fact that great numbers of clerics were trying to get the proper scholarly training in order to become preachers. The new schools themselves were a product of stepped-up and modified sermonizing. The professorial *cathedra*—the academic chair—derives from the bishop's *cathedra* from which, in the Christian tradition, all legitimate teaching proceeds. Thanks to papal privileges, the new thirteenth-century universities were able to circumvent this intermediate level of authorization and carry on with their teaching. They received the *licentia docendi ubique terrarum* because they were directly subordinate to the *episcopus universalis*.[75] Any member of a mendicant order was permitted to preach without the local bishop's permission because he was directly subordinated to Rome; a *magister* at a university with a papal privilege could also teach without episcopal authorization. And what was taught was *au fond* a specialized form of the sermon.[76] The European universities of the High Middle Ages and later were part of the all-embracing and many-sided preaching culture then evolving—the broad effect of which proved particularly important for Europe's special path, applying to far more than the development of forms of mass communication.

————

Preaching in the Eastern Christian churches during the Middle Ages did not undergo any differentiation or development comparable to those in the West. The Byzantine Empire continued to cultivate the homily, which had originated with Judaism and was a sermon strictly adhering to the Bible readings prescribed for a particular liturgy of the word.[77] Collections of homilies were produced, including, rather remarkably, one authored by Emperor Leo VI, "the Wise" (886–92). Preaching in Byzantium seems to have corresponded somewhat to the caliph's privilege in Islam, but it had no counterpart in the West. That preaching in the Eastern Church developed on the whole with more continuity and fewer breaks, but also with less innovation, probably was connected with the social conditions where ecclesiastical promulgation of the faith was taking place. Great controversies over church reform and investiture were unknown in the Byzantine Empire—conflicts such as those between the popes and their opponents, in which the former would join up with lay preachers, who were thereby given a degree of legitimation. The East did not have the crusading and poverty movements that contributed so greatly to the mobilizing of preaching in the West, in part on orders from the pope, in part without any authority from above. There were no universal religious orders in the East that would have had preaching as their express mission. At the same time, the evolution of church and state in Byzantine history was anything but conflict free. The great controversy that profoundly shook the Byzantine Empire had occurred earlier than the one in the West and steered it in a different direction. That controversy over the veneration of icons in the eighth and ninth centuries brought about an important change, of course. The use of images, rather than the word, to promulgate the faith was given a very high status. Trends tending toward a religion of the ear moved toward a religion of the eye. There were certainly some attempts in various religious communities to integrate this movement with illustrated sermons, but the icon in the Eastern Church does not belong in this context. It is a cult image, not an illustration, which is why it cannot provide a basis for an equivalent preaching culture. And so the Iconoclastic Controversy probably concluded without preaching gaining a central position in the Eastern Church—which would have had any number of consequences for the further development of the culture of the word and writing.

———

Unlike the Byzantine Empire, Islam did separate the sermon from the liturgy of the word, in ways similar to what happened in the Western Church. Two basic types of sermon evolved that were said to go back to the Prophet's time: the *khutba* and the *wa'z*.[78] The *khutba* was under the strict control of ritual as to time, place, subject matter, preacher, and so on. It was part of the official Friday service in the mosque and was unable to develop in any real way. The form of the *wa'z* was much freer. It could be held on a weekday or at night. This type of sermon was not delivered in a mosque but in a square in the prince's palace, before the city gates, or at the school of a given preacher, who was often a member of the *ulama* that headed the school. The dimensions of the preaching site were important, since the *wa'z* was often a sermon for the masses. Given the size of Islamic cities at that time, the audiences were larger than they were in Europe. It is reported that Ibn al-Gauzi—one of the most brilliant preachers in the capital of the caliphate in the latter half of the twelfth century—attracted around fifty thousand people to his first public speech and three hundred thousand to his most famous one.[79] Even if we take these figures with a grain of salt, there is not the slightest doubt that preaching before a mass audience did take place—which means mass communication in a restricted space, delivered orally, and to an amazingly huge audience. The message of Ibn al-Gauzi's sermon was preprogrammed politically, morally, and eschatologically. The highly political nature of the *wa'z* derived from the system that organized it: caliphs, sultans, viziers, governors, and high officials promoted preaching and paid for it.[80] It was consequently much more susceptible to political crises than was preaching in the West, which was rather shielded by its position within the church. Preaching to the masses had a strong influence on lay piety, at least in the short term. Witness reports that tens of thousands would do public penance during and after a sermon, cutting their hair as a sign of repentance. Large numbers were said to faint from the emotional intensity, some even dying in ecstasy.[81] We hear not a word about whether large-scale preaching to the masses was connected with continuous pastoral care; the latter was more likely in Islam to be given by the Sufi orders, which did not make their presence felt primarily through preaching. Scholarship does provide a striking parallel between preaching in the Western Church and the caliphate: both cultures simultaneously experienced an upturn in preaching culture and scholarly teaching. The great Islamic preachers headed schools, were active in scholarship, and owned books, which they made copies of themselves.[82] The upward thrust of these two comparable cultural phenomena was not, of course, to last. By the fourteenth century there was no longer any distinction between the *wa'z* and the normal *khutba* during the Friday service. Subsequently, the institution of public preaching independent of the mosque went into further decline.[83]

―――――

From its beginnings, Buddhism had very different preaching practices. One in particular deserves more thorough examination because it directs us to the route from preaching to public relations and is eminently suited for a cross-cultural comparison. Buddhist monks in Japan enhanced their preaching by means of images with commentary, starting in the second half of the thirteenth century at the latest.[84] This mode of preaching and the preacher were called *etoki*. As early as the Heian period, high-ranking monks would explicate frescoes or other depictions on screens for an equally high-ranking audience. The transition from screen to scroll painting gave the sermon's basic message some mobility. Scrolls could provide a topic for a sermon either in the houses of the well-born or before a larger audience in the open air. They were also well suited for propaganda purposes, for instance, to advertise a particular shrine, perhaps making a request for money at the same time. As Buddhist sects spread throughout Japan, whole sets of displayed images played an important role during recitations of Buddha's biography.[85] Lay *etoki* first appeared in the waning Middle Ages, expanding this form of mass communication beyond religious communities.[86] Preaching campaigns in Japan that were bolstered by *etoki* had many prerequisites: first, paper as a material basis—certainly for the screen in the temple and above all for scroll painting that would free a preacher from having to stay in one place—and second, on a more religious level, the sacred image as sermon illustration. Comparisons drawn above have shown how differently we have to regard the function of sacred images in early forms of mass communication. An icon from the Eastern Church could never under any circumstances have been a similar instrument in a preaching campaign. And Islam would never even have permitted these modes of public relations because images were forbidden as a matter of principle. The Western Church had no precepts preventing frescoes and panel paintings from assuming an auxiliary role in preaching, but the church never possessed a portable device like Japanese scroll painting.

Evidence from relics, however, reveals resemblances between preaching campaigns in Europe and Japanese sermons based on scroll paintings. The work of the Antonite Order supplies us with a prime example.[87] Alms-begging pilgrimages first came on the scene in France in the middle of the eleventh century, and clergymen making a pilgrimage would bring relics with them. The Antonites were the first to use mendicant pilgrimages for charitable purposes, specifically for establishing hospitals for those stricken with "Saint Anthony's fire." These group journeys proceeded systematically through chosen areas. The focus of the preaching was always on the life of Saint Anthony and the miracles he wrought, as well as on the order's hospital work.[88] The efficacy of the relics that were carried along—perhaps together with some particularly beneficial, and marketable, objects—would be considered rewards for a public happy to make donations. Antonite preaching and money collecting highlighted how late medieval preaching campaigns could cover so much territory and be so well organized, down to the last detail. Because of their dubious methods, the Antonites drew a great deal of criticism from preachers during the Reformation. The order has been able to survive public antipathy and criticism in just a few regions.[89]

––––––

Organized preaching gave a big boost to public relations in Europe during the Reformation. At the same time, print forms that were still novelties, such as the flyer, pamphlet, and book, became fully utilized media of mass communication. There is no contradiction here. Oral and written media are frequently interrelated, often building upon or complementing each other. All the great reformers thought of themselves primarily as preachers and anything but authors of religious texts.[90] Luther once said that, in view of the growing number of printed works the Reformation had spawned, he would rather have witnessed an increase in the number of "living books," that is, preachers. But this kind of evidence did not mean that printed works were devalued. Luther himself resorted to the new media on all levels and was absolutely convinced that even pamphlets were "sermons"—which is how they were frequently understood and received whenever they were read out in public.[91] Wittenberg was not only the city where Luther preached but a place he turned into a prominent printing center. Calvin's Geneva likewise developed into a significant hub of printing in Europe.[92]

The traditional view of the schism of faith in early modern Europe is that it led to a dichotomy in which Protestantism as a religion of the written word—based on a personal reading of the Bible—stood against Catholicism as a religion of speaking and listening dependent upon clerical mediation. This comparison is no longer tenable in light of recent research.[93] It appears correct instead—considering the issue of access to the Bible as the Christian holy book—to place Lutheranism and Catholicism on the same side, opposite Calvinism and Pietism. Lutheranism was not one whit more a personal Bible-reading religion than Roman Catholicism was. The Bible in Lutheran Germany and north European countries had the character of a parish book. It was a book for pastors, not for the hands of people who might arrive at heterodox opinions by their own personal reading of it. This explains the essential role that accrued to the pastor's or parish priest's sermon in Lutheran and Catholic regions. Personal and family Bible reading, on the other hand, seems to have been distinctive of Calvinist, Puritan, and Pietistic countries, where individual interpretations, rather than the opinions of clerical officeholders, were foremost. Reformation Europe split into large areas by religious orientation, where preaching and religious literature were to develop along different routes, as would the religious image, music, and many other cultural phenomena.

———————

Whereas preaching was by its very nature a form of communication with an explicitly religious origin, this was not equally true of printing as a means of mass communication. Our earlier comparisons of great religions of the book discovered both favorable and obstructive religious conditions, but they were not the whole story by a long shot, as becomes clear when we follow up on the material and nonmaterial prerequisites for the rise and spread of printing. The fact that China had invented printing several centuries before Gutenberg did in Europe calls for a comparison. Were the preconditions the same in both places? What were the factors determining continuous development in these so different cultures? When and where did the spread of this innovation from these two centers reach its limits and, above all, why? The fact that the European variant of printing was restricted to certain regions of the continent for such a long time tells us a great deal about the sociocultural context it grew out of. Printing thus proved to be an important aspect of Europe's unique path. As a means of communication that extended beyond Europe itself, it appears at the same time to be a decisive factor in globalization.

Among the material prerequisites for the emergence of printing in Europe, the mass manufacture of paper is surely crucial.[94] This is easily demonstrated by the timing of the important stages in the technical development of printing. Ulman Stromer founded the first paper mill in central Europe in 1395.[95] This was where the first innovative printed images surfaced at the end of the fourteenth century: first, the woodcut, then the copper etching, and finally, around 1450, the metal engraving.[96] Paper was fundamental to all these printing techniques. Printing with moveable type emerged at about the same time as metal engraving.[97] Johannes Gutenberg used parchment to print his forty-two-line Bible—given the traditional tie between Christianity's holy book and the parchment codex, probably nothing else would have done at the time.[98] But flyers, pamphlets, and books became instruments of mass communication thanks to paper, a far cheaper printing material.

When paper was first used for printing in Christian Europe at the end of the fourteenth or the beginning of the fifteenth century, it already had a rather long history. Islamic preceded Christian papermakers all over the Mediterranean basin wherever the new material turned

255

up in the twelfth and thirteenth centuries, whether in Sicily or Valencia. Critical technical innovations were created when the Arabs adopted paper production in the Mediterranean area.[99] The most important of these was surely the harnessing of waterpower to the manufacture of paper, which probably began before 1283 in Fabriano, near Ancona in the Marches. This innovation was then linked with European technological developments, and at the same time the utilization of waterpower expanded from a family operation into something approaching the dimensions of an industrial enterprise. The paper mill spread first to Upper Italy, where the water supply was excellent, then increasingly into fourteenth-century France and Germany.[100] The new paper mill stepped up production enormously. Paper became a cheaper writing material competing with parchment.[101] The foundation for greater literacy was now laid, above all in law, commerce, and administration. Many sectors implicated in the new literacy rushed into mass production, the feasibility of which was demonstrated by the success of mass-produced images, many appearing along with brief texts in woodcuts. The step from printing images to printing texts was in the air, so to speak, when Johannes Gutenberg's new process made it possible.

The combination of paper and printed text that first appeared in Europe in the fifteenth century had been in existence since the early Middle Ages in the East Asian country where paper originated, China. Given the diffusion of paper from the Far East to the extreme West of Eurasia, the fact that a suitable method of printing was not transmitted at the same time fairly cries out for an explanation. The Chinese were said to have begun to manufacture paper when they were serving under the Arabs who had defeated them in 751.[102] But Islam had showed great interest in paper from China even before then. Samarkand, a center of Islamic culture, imported paper from China as early as the seventh century. Arabs began making paper themselves in Baghdad at the end of the eighth century, in Damascus in the ninth, in Egypt and Andalusia in the tenth. If we set aside the charms found in El-Fayyum in Egypt, which were ultimately ephemeral phenomena, then the rapid spread of paper manufacturing in Islam was at no point linked with traditional or new print processes.[103] Islam enthusiastically adopted paper as a writing material, but it categorically rejected the printed form of writing that paper made possible. And so the wide-ranging barrier between East Asia and Europe that affected print culture up to the eighteenth and nineteenth centuries had its origins in the early seventh and eighth centuries. The stipulation that copies of the Qur'an were to be handwritten would have been a particularly prominent reason for the rejection of printing at that very early date. Minor reasons have been put forth in modern-day discussions.

If such a tightly-knit cultural pattern of language, handwriting, and even the writing utensil was connected with Islam's holy book, then the question arises how a foreign writing material like paper could conquer the caliphate so rapidly. The answer probably lies in the genesis of the Qur'an itself. We read of Zayd ibn Thabit, whom the first caliph, Abu Bekr, commissioned to assemble the various fragments that were to become the Qur'an: "And he sought for the Qur'an and he gathered it together from the fronds of the date palm and from white stones and from the hearts of men who remembered him."[104] The materials on which the Qur'an verses could be found were "slips of paper, stones, palm fronds, silk cloths, pieces of wood, leather, dried shoulder blades."[105] So there was no sanctified writing material during the religious community's first phase. There were weighty arguments against paper and for parchment, which was especially durable, smooth, neither brittle nor easily torn, and both sides could be written on.[106] But paper had the advantage of being far less costly to manufacture. Paper prevailed over parchment in Islam roughly from the mid-tenth century in the eastern Mediterranean and from the middle of the eleventh in the Maghreb.[107] It took much longer for paper to outstrip parchment in Europe. Parchment had been chosen for Christian books centuries earlier, as well for composing imperial administrative documents. Moreover, it was made of local raw materials, in Islam as well as Europe— from the hides of goats, sheep, and calves. (This material was hard to find in China because of its particular tradition of animal husbandry, and hides could not have been used anyway during the Buddhist period. The writing material that worked for China was made of vegetable matter.) But eventually paper, originally a foreign material, won out in Islam and Europe. The acceptance of this alien material was highly significant for cultural history. It facilitated an enormous rise in literacy and then the reproduction of written material through printing— which was of course long limited to the regions where Western Christendom was dominant.

In China, Ts'ai Lun, a government official, is considered the inventor of paper. He is said to have delivered a report to the court in 105 AD on the process of making paper out of tree bark, hemp, rags, and fish net.[108] But this novel writing material probably had a longer history. Fragments of a prototype of paper have been discovered in a grave dating from the second to the first century BC.[109] Paper quickly beat back the competition—wood, bamboo, and the more expensive silk.[110]

Paper could be used for both writing and painting; thus a common material basis for writing and images existed early on; writing with a brush further connected the two.[111] The traditional close relationship between script and image had a subsequent effect on the early stages of printing: a reduplicating process common to both script and image had to be found, which, as it turned out, was woodblock printing.[112] In Europe things happened very differently. Written texts were set down with pen and ink on parchment, later on paper; images were mainly painted on wood panels with brush and oils. Book illumination did of course provide a link between writing and the image, but it played no role in the rise of printing. It was principally the woodcut, along with other new fifteenth-century graphic techniques, that followed on from panel painting.[113] The European woodcut was created mainly in order to reduplicate images, with the occasional incorporation of textual passages. A technique for replicating written texts alone and for moving beyond the woodcut had yet to be discovered—this was to be Johannes Gutenberg's achievement. Chinese block printing did both jobs at once: texts and images were printed by the same process. Technically speaking, Chinese woodblock printing paralleled the European woodcut.[114] That this process also seems to have offered a practical basis for printing written matter has to do with the peculiar nature of Chinese writing.

The invention of typography—composing with moveable type—is regarded in Europe as the moment when printing was invented. The woodcut and woodblock printing were considered to be comparatively unimportant preliminary stages. But in the Far East, the invention of woodblock printing is regarded as the turning point in the history of printing, moveable type, a later, rather minor addendum.[115] These divergent opinions result from variations in the culture of the written word, where different viewpoints have led to different evaluations. The scripts of European languages are based on an alphabet of two to three dozen letters, which are phonetic symbols. In this context, the invention of typography was decisive. Ideographic writing in the Far East, on the other hand, is based on a huge number of symbols—unlike alphabetic writing—with the Chinese having some forty thousand symbols. Until the arrival of twentieth-century typesetting, printing with moveable type was neither profitable nor technically practical. In spite of all attempts throughout East Asian history to introduce moveable type, mainstream printing was of necessity dictated by block printing until modern times because of the demands of ideographic writing. The dominant role of block printing in East Asia meant that its social and cultural effects were not the same as in the European countries that adopted typography. The way Europe's unique path developed was heavily involved with something specifically European: printing.

Just like the European woodcut, whose inventor is unknown, and unlike Gutenberg's later invention, Chinese woodblock printing was technically unremarkable. The woodcut probably evolved from a long practice of printing with wooden models on textiles; the appearance of paper gave it new opportunities to expand.[116] Playing cards might have been connecting links.[117] The most relevant early form of Chinese woodblock printing was the seal used to stamp impressions, a tradition that went very far back.[118] The transition to printing with moveable type was technically far more demanding. It was attempted in East Asia with frequent success.[119] About the middle of the eleventh century Pi Sheng tried it with type made from baked clay, and Wang Cheng with wooden type in the first half of the fourteenth century.

Fifteenth-century Korea had much greater success with moveable metal type.[120] The political and cultural contexts of this innovation were particularly interesting here. Ruling heads of the empire were struggling fiercely to stem the tide of Chinese influence, in printing and writing especially. King Sejong (r. 1418–50) established a separate printing office that used metal type; its first publication appeared in 1409 at the latest. Most of the books published subsequently using this new technique were authorized by the king. A royal initiative then led to a second, absolutely fundamental innovation. The Korean language was difficult to reproduce in Chinese script. The king appointed a committee of scholars, the Hall of Worthies, to generate a new, alphabetic writing system.[121] The system, developed from 1443 to 1446, came to be called "Hangeul" or "Hangul." This was a remarkable phenomenon: the creation of a brand-new alphabetic script in the midst of ideographic languages. It was admirably suited for and thus promoted the dissemination of a form of printing with metal type. Writing and printing were mutually supportive. Nonetheless, success did not last for long; Korea's social elite still employed Chinese characters.

Japan, too, under the influence of Korea and of some stimulus from printing by sixteenth-century Portuguese missionaries, took some steps in the direction of metal type.[122] But it soon turned away from printing with type and reverted to woodblock printing, the only technique that made sense economically for Japan's complicated hybrid script. Again and again in East Asia, the ideographic form of writing, and the culture it was part of, ultimately blocked the transition to typography until well into modern times—with all that this implied for advances in communications.

The emergence of printing in China in the ninth and tenth centuries did not signal a revolutionary upheaval like the one in fifteenth-century Europe.[123] The copying of religious texts in Buddhist monasteries was already flourishing, but now the technical improvements increased its effectiveness. It took some time for the state to join in, which it did by commissioning the printing of religious books: the canon of Confucian texts in 932, Buddhist texts in 971–83, and Taoist texts in 1019.[124] State printing and the conservation of printed works in state libraries were generally typical of the East Asian countries.[125] In China, printed works fell under bureaucratic oversight at both the provincial and local levels. Authorized copies of canonical texts had to be made accessible everywhere so that people could prepare for the examinations for state officials. The state also required printed matter for its administration and its information policy. In a step taken somewhat hesitantly during the Song dynasty (960–1279), private entrepreneurs were able to set up shop in the printing and book trades, joining the monasteries and state institutions.[126] In Japan, Buddhist monasteries and temples were to dominate printing for eight hundred years before a commercial publishing industry emerged after 1600.[127]

In contrast to the patterns of East Asia, book production in Europe quickly forged ahead by leaps and bounds thanks to the invention of printing with moveable type. This development is encapsulated by the following striking example: a man born in 1453, the year Constantinople fell, could at age fifty look back on a lifetime in which roughly eight million books had been printed, possibly more than all the scribes of Europe had produced since Constantine founded the city in 330.[128] New communication structures—a huge number of broadsides and pamphlets—wrought even greater changes in the public sphere than the flood of printed books did.[129] A tight network of printing shops grew up across Europe in the few decades before 1500, from Santiago to Marienburg and from Granada to Stockholm.[130] Book manufacture was concentrated in Upper Italy, northern Germany, the Rhineland, and the Netherlands. The former heartland of the Carolingian Empire underwent a particularly dynamic development. But the network embraced the entire region occupied by the Western Church. The area of diffusion was more or less congruent with the one that the mendicant orders opened up with their monasteries two hundred years before. At no point did printing spread beyond the limits of the Western Church—not into the territory of the Orthodox Church and decidedly not into lands where Islam held sway. The rapid rise of printing was a phenomenon typical of the Latin Church. This is not to say that the church might have cultivated printing or otherwise directed its course. Unlike the way printing emerged in East Asian lands, European monasteries and European bureaucrats were not the driving force behind the innovation of printing; the private sector had already organized printing earlier and so it was dependent on the marketplace. The so-called printing revolution in Europe can therefore only be accounted for in light of the enormous continental demand for printed material. The demand went beyond material and technical factors to include nonmaterial preconditions for the invention of printing in the waning Middle Ages. The specific nature of this strong demand can be elucidated by taking three public sectors as examples.

———

First, since the close of the fourteenth century, there had been a rather large rural audience for cheap printed materials such as broadsides and pamphlets.[131] An analysis of the techniques by which they were produced suggests that woodblock printing had first been used, followed by type or a combination of the two.[132] This category of printed matter typically paired image and text. The early, single-sheet prints were a rich, motley collection: papal letters and bulls, indulgences, mandates, declarations of feuds, promulgations, book announcements, theses to be posted, holy cards, indulgence images, plague notices, instructional and monitory images, sheets for amusement, sensational news bulletins, reports of miracles, satires, polemical writings, and polemics, theological or otherwise.[133] Some claim there are three major subject areas here: sensations and miracles, because of their entertainment function; devotional images for instruction in the catechism; and news of political and military events.[134] It seems important that much in these printed works was already familiar. Jean Delumeau has shown this to be the case when sermons that played on eschatological fears lived on in print.[135] The broadside was a commodity that met preexisting needs. And it swiftly opened up an eager buying public for itself in broad swaths across Europe, even among the rural populace.

_____

The universities formed the second public sector. They made distinct and substantial contributions to the growing demand for mass copies of texts during the late Middle Ages. The prevailing mode of lecturing assumed that students had copies of texts for lectures,[136] and they were expected to bring them to class. Poor students could borrow library copies or else had to pay copyists or copy the texts themselves. Some universities, particularly Paris and Bologna, institutionalized the so-called *pecia* system during the thirteenth and fourteenth centuries.[137] This meant that an unbound copy of all texts the university needed for teaching had to be delivered to a *stationarius*, a stationer; the pages were then divided up and distributed in parts to several copyists simultaneously. The *stationarius* was a sworn member of the university whose office it was to supply students with books necessary for their instruction. The *pecia* system illustrates the pressure placed on the replication of texts by hand. The urgent demand did not necessarily lead to a new technical solution, but given the extent of the need, the contribution of this public sector should not be underestimated. It was no accident that the first printing shops enjoyed a particularly close relationship to the universities.

_____

A new, fast-growing lay piety was the third and most important factor in the rising, late medieval demand for reduplicated texts and images. Monastic religious practices were being adopted and refined outside the monastery walls. The important point of origin here was the milieu of the mendicant friars and their Third Order. It was typical of the new lay piety that it was practiced by individuals and in private, not communally and in public. This generated a great need for personal books, images, and objects as devotional aids. The connection between a monk's or a clergyman's act of prayer and the practices of the pious laity became most obvious after the introduction of books of hours in the thirteenth century, and their flowering from the late fourteenth century on.[138] The book of hours followed on from the breviary by dividing obligatory prayers according to the hours of the day but varied the prayers' rhythmic sequence in a form the layman could manage in a secular context. Fifty thousand represents one educated guess of the number of books of hours in lay hands in England on the eve of the Reformation.[139] The late Middle Ages witnessed a widespread increase in the number of layman's prayer books. Lay Bible readings, particularly in the vernacular, met with official church resistance but were ultimately unstoppable. Eighteen complete Bibles in German came out before Luther's translation, and they enjoyed extraordinary success.[140] A special expression of personal lay piety was the genre of devotional books, of which Thomas à Kempis's *The Imitation of Christ* (1427) is a good case in point. It was imbued with the spirit of the Dutch-German school of mysticism and was really intended for monks and hermits, yet the religious laity received it with great interest. Numerous copies were circulated in manuscript; a printed version first appeared in 1473. Since then, thousands of editions and translations into fifty languages have appeared—only the Bible itself has beaten this record.[141]

We can regard the spread of silent reading as a parallel phenomenon to personalized lay piety and its interest in new kinds of religious literature.[142] Here again we meet with a monastic origin. Besides reading aloud in church, the refectory, or the convent school, other ways of speaking softly while reading began to surface—in the scriptorium and the library, or during solitary study in one's cell. Again, it was the mendicant orders that made the significant difference in revolutionizing customary reading practices. Reading in private opened up new access to the religious book for those lay circles that retained their old reading habits. Reading aloud *softly* usually promoted mystical forms of piety. The trend toward private ownership of religious books escalated the demand for printing and stimulated its further development.

Many kinds of images were in print even before the printing press arrived. There can be no doubt that the growth of printed graphics was driven by the private devotional picture.[143] Art historians speak of an "era of the private picture" that led to "quantitative expansion" and "qualitative change."[144] "Qualitative change" created forms of personal piety for the layman who seized and expanded upon clerical religious practices; to implement them created a need for concrete objects. The private devotional image—as an object of meditation—became a necessary instrument for the laity's new piety, as did material objects like the prayer bench and rosary, or reading matter such as the book of hours and the breviary. Although technology produced the devotional image before religious texts, this says nothing about their relative importance. Text and image were integrative components of private religiosity, which, as opposed to public devoutness, required a substantial number of objects. The resulting "quantitative expansion" is therefore related causally to "qualitative change." An increase in religious books and images represented a pressing need in an era of burgeoning, privatized lay piety during the late Middle Ages. Making copies by hand could not adequately cover the rising demand, which identified the necessity of finding new technologies of mass reduplication.

———

The three public sectors just discussed—the rural population, the academic audience, and the pious laity—represent but a sampling of the population groups that found literacy of growing importance in the late Middle Ages and who had a serious need for reduplicated texts. We might include many other groups, for instance, ecclesiastical and secular central administrations that had to draw up papal bulls, circulars, mandates, and the like in a standardized form suitable for distribution over a large number of regions. This would have been a labor-intensive affair if copies still had to be made by hand.[145] The printing press afforded a genuine easing of the burden. Mass production of written forms was necessary to standardize church indulgences; letters of indulgence were one of the earliest products to come off the press.[146] Uniformity of multiple texts was also fundamental to the workings of the law. That is why the *Institutes of Roman Law* was among the first works printed in Gutenberg's workshop in Mainz.[147] There was a demand in the fifteenth century for large numbers of copies in many walks of life. The demand factor seems to have been decisive for the very rapid advance in methods of reduplication and their dissemination in Western culture, once paper had provided the material for a solid footing.

———

The swift spread of printing in the regions occupied by the Western Church couldn't have been more different than its gradual adoption by the church's eastern, southeastern, and southern neighbors. The situation in the Eastern Church may be taken as typical. Some liturgical books and the Bible had already been published in Cracow in 1491 for the Greek Orthodox Church.[148] But the first East Slavic printed book came out in Prague between 1517 and 1519 as the "Russian Bible," and the Bible was not printed in Moscow until 1663. The Moscow printing office was able to carry out its work because it enjoyed the patriarchate's support. In the seventeenth century, the initiative lay with the higher church authorities; it passed to the czars under Peter the Great (1682–1725), when some growth in printing finally took place; the cru-

cial motivator here was the emperor's reform policy, not a stronger demand in the marketplace.[149]

In the Ottoman Empire, an Orthodox majority of the population in
southwestern Europe lived under Muslim authority, which obviously
made it difficult to introduce printing, a Christian innovation from the
West. Even so, that was not reason enough to dismiss it out of hand.
If necessary, believers in other religions based on scripture could do
things in a Muslim country that were prohibited to its own Muslim
subjects. There were some attempts in the sixteenth and seventeenth
centuries to set up Christian printing shops—the only ones extant
were in the Danubian principalities of Moldavia and Walachia, where
an exceptional political situation had made certain things possible.[150]
This was not to be the case in the Byzantine capital for a very long
time, until 1627 in fact, when Cyril I Lucaris, a reforming patriarch,
established a printing house—but here again the initiative came from
above.[151] Cyril came to grief because of intrigues against him and not
because of fundamental problems with his project. Consequently, he
had his books printed in Geneva. The first was a translation of the New
Testament into modern Greek, which provoked protests from his own
community. The patriarch's opponents in the church feared that printing holy scripture would introduce unwelcome changes, which was
much the way Muslims felt about the Qur'an. Compared to the West,
the Eastern Church on the whole had more reservations about printing
religious texts and less inclination toward it. Most important, there was
no broad movement toward the private lay piety that monasticism had
generated in the West during the late Middle Ages and that had created
an early and strong demand for printing. Late medieval monasticism
in the East developed along completely different lines. The hesychastic
monk did not require a breviary to have a religious experience.

The situation of Judaism showed that it was not primarily the Muslim authorities who long delayed access to printing for Orthodox Christians in the Ottoman Empire. The Jews in Salonika and Constantinople
established the first printing houses in the Ottoman Empire.[152] A printing press in the capital was operating in 1494, and an eminent printing
house moved from Lisbon to Salonika, to be joined by others at the end
of the sixteenth century. The Jews responded to printing with great
enthusiasm from the moment it was invented. A considerable number of cities in Upper Italy had Jewish printing shops even before the
end of the fifteenth century—significantly, it was often doctors who
founded them.[153] The first printed book in Faro, Portugal, was a 1487

Pentateuch.[154] Like the Christians around them, Jewish communities in the waning Middle Ages and the early modern period had no taboo against publishing a printed version of holy scripture. This marked a fundamental difference from the Islamic world. Since the Jews were a highly literate religious community, they had an enormous need for reduplicating their holy writings.[155] It comes as somewhat of a surprise that the new technology was quickly held in such high esteem that it was regarded as a work of devotion to establish a printing shop.[156] Here, too, the contrast with Islam could not have been greater, which regarded the making of copies *by hand* as an especially meritorious religious act.[157]

The first printing house in Istanbul to work with Arabic letters was opened in 1726—following a decision by the Sheik ul Islam, who was the Grand Mufti, with the proviso that books of the Islamic faith were not to be published.[158] The press was shut down from 1730 to 1780 and again in 1800. Only sixty-three titles appeared between 1726 and 1815—a sure indicator of extremely weak demand.[159] The founding of the printing house was the subject of long discussion beforehand. As early as 1588, Sultan Murad III had permitted the sale of books written in Arabic within the empire provided that they had no religious content—thus contradicting the universal bans of Bayezid II in 1485 and Selim in 1515.[160] The heart of the matter was print technology's supposed menacing of the Qur'an as the fundament of the religious community, coupled with printing's threat to Islamic culture as a whole. All these arguments against allowing printing hinged on this central question, either directly or indirectly. It was not simply that many Muslims would have viewed as sacrilege the replacement of hand copying of religious books—a religiously meritorious act—by some kind of technology, let alone one associated with a culture hostile to the Muslim religion.[161] There were financial as well as religious issues at play in the debate over allowing printing shops. Many thousands in Istanbul earned their living from copying by hand.[162] To take away their jobs would have created a serious social problem, so they understandably mobilized politically in order to oppose the innovation. Copyists were the exponents of the traditional art of calligraphy.[163] For centuries in Islam, calligraphy had been rigorously labored over so that it might do justice to the word of Allah through an appropriate graphic representation. The sacred nature of the script was now being threatened by printing. Some people were of the opinion that the Arabic script was altogether incapable of being adapted to moveable type.[164] Gutenberg's invention was based on separate, isolated letters, each of which remained the same in all letter combinations. In the cursive Arabic script, the ligatures were determined by the juxtaposition of letters, a major problem for typesetting. The solutions that various European print shops came up with for setting Arabic texts were more of a hindrance than a help. This only solidified Muslim opinion that the technology of a foreign culture was unable to express their own; the intellectual legacy of Arabic culture was seen as tied to the tradition of handwriting.[165] For many, the adoption of printing would have meant showing contempt for one's ancestors and a break with a glorious past. It stands to reason that truly fundamental arguments like these would have meant that both the Ottoman imperial government and vast numbers of people would view printing with great skepticism, resisting it for centuries.

The various print technologies developed in fifteenth-century Europe—moveable type above all—initiated a singular evolution in mass communication that initially stood in sharp contrast with neighboring cultures to the east, southeast, and south. The dissimilarities became more accentuated in the centuries that followed. But *parallels* with European media culture were most likely to turn up in East Asia, where woodblock printing had an even older tradition and developed in a more evolutionary fashion. Woodblock printing spread rapidly from China to neighboring cultures, primarily Korea and Japan, thanks to Buddhism, which may be regarded as its most important exponent in its early phase. There were some especially idiosyncratic developments in the various East Asian countries, such as Korea's unique attempt to shift from a traditional, ideographic script to an alphabetic one in the hope of exploiting its particular features for printing.[166] Printing in Japan, from the eighth all the way to the seventeenth century, has been labeled a "dormant technology," but it would later progress quickly toward mass communication.[167] Although the country clung firmly to traditional techniques for manufacturing block-printed books, a heavily commercialized printing business grew up in the early Tokugawa period that has been rightly called a publishing industry.[168] A high-level printing and publishing culture took root, covering a diversified array of subjects.[169] An autonomous Japanese newspaper industry evolved from *kawaraban* (literally, broadsheets printed with tile blocks).[170] Clear traces of a unique information society were visible in Japan long before it was modernized along Western lines in the latter half of the nineteenth century.[171]

China, the birthplace of East Asian woodblock printing, had swung much earlier than Japan from a monastic or state printing policy of preserving canonical scriptures to an open book market that operated jointly with private publishers.[172].This early flowering did not come to full fruition and had a limited revival in the sixteenth century.[173] The peculiar nature of the Chinese writing system proved an obstacle to the furthering of mass communication by means of printed texts. The huge number of ideographic characters made it difficult not only to abandon block printing, but even to learn to read and write in the first place. As a result, literacy would remain a rather elite affair. European alphabetic writing, on the other hand, smoothed the way to literacy. The expansion of elementary education created conditions—mainly by introducing compulsory attendance for everyone—that permitted print media to lay the foundation for concentrated and comprehensive mass communication.

Mass communication in essence gave rise to commonalities in con-sciousness, attitudes, viewpoints, values, sentiments, hopes, and fears that went beyond primary groups, or cliques, in the social-psychological sense. This was true on the level of orality but even more on the level of literacy, which experienced a boom in Europe because of print-ing and the media based on it. This generated intensified processes of exchange and permeation in modern Europe that had never existed before and were not found in other contemporary cultures. The "con-fessionalizing" that took place in the age of religious schism showed how effective the processes of integration and penetration could be on the stage opened up by mass communication. Nation building and the formation of political camps followed. This was in striking contrast to what was happening in adjacent countries. The Ottoman Empire, for instance, or Russia, where the media of mass communication did not function in a comparable way, preserved a greater variety of ethnic, linguistic, religious, and cultural groupings for a much longer time. In Europe, on the other hand, the processes discussed above were able to nip cultural particularism in the bud.

Different types of mass communication created favorable conditions for new kinds of religious, social, and political movements based on su-praregional commonalities of consciousness. By the High Middle Ages, preaching to a mass audience, together with preaching campaigns, had already facilitated the mendicant movement and the crusading move-ment. The image-and-text propaganda using early printing methods played an essential part in the Peasant Wars. Printed theses, polem-ics, exhortations, and teachings were all there at the start of the Reformation. The reformers themselves realized that the success of their efforts would have been impossible without Gutenberg's invention. The inventor of the printing press was accordingly revered as a kind of precursor of Luther. In the High Middle Ages, any teachings deviating from orthodoxy could still be rooted out by burning heretics along with their books. By the dawn of the modern era, the rapid spread of mass literature had shown the futility of such measures. Indeed, it was precisely the nonconformist and heterodox movements that gained strength from the new resources of mass communication. With the invention of printing, Europe as a whole entered into an age of societal movements without which the dynamics of its political, social, and cultural transformation cannot be understood. To look beyond these movements in the age of religious wars: the transformative force of the Enlightenment would have been utterly impossible without the successes of publishing and printing. These were salient factors in Europe's unique path. Their absence in neighboring cultures produced palpable differences that continue to this day.

New forms of public life emerged because of the publishing activity that printing made possible in a way that had never existed until then. Written discourse grew in importance by leaps and bounds. An opinion stated in writing would have greater longevity than one spoken; it would always be readily at hand, and libraries would make copies available for future generations. The diversity of opposed points of view would increase; the spectrum of choices among them would keep growing wider. The new forms of the public sphere based on writing would offer society the chance to become pluralistic, which meant that the individual could find many possibilities for guidance. And wherever that guidance would grow larger, the odds of individualization would be greater. The trend toward stronger individualism is a characteristic of Europe's exceptional path. The consequences of printing and the overall advance of mass communication are of fundamental significance for this specifically European phenomenon.

For one sector of the public—the scholarly world—the tension-filled coexistence of many points of view that the new forms of book publishing made possible seems to have been particularly fruitful. The invention of printing gave many strong, positive impulses to European scholarship.[174] The natural sciences in particular experienced exceptionally dynamic growth in the early modern period. As a result, their mark was felt in many different ways concerning the mastery of nature—in the technical and industrial sectors and medicine, but also in providing a platform for European expansionism. The growth spurt

269

in the natural sciences that printing initiated created all kinds of illuminating approaches that laid the course of Europe's exceptional path.

We have already shown that education had relied to a great extent on the reduplication of essential teaching texts long before Gutenberg. The invention of printing facilitated a quantitative leap in this regard. The book became the pupil's and the university student's constant companion, from elementary school to the university lecture hall. Modern-day state school systems, as they developed in the course of time, routinely recognized that knowledge is to be transmitted orally by the teacher and in writing by the school textbook—and these pedagogies are frequently coordinated. The latter more reliably guarantees that the elementary- or high-school student will be induced to acquire the desired way of thinking. The classroom was not the least of reasons that citizens of a *Staatsnation* (a political or civic nation) could be of like mind.

Printing grew in importance along many avenues as an aid in constructing the centralized, bureaucratic state. This meant more than a simple transition from oral to written administrative records. The key was the ability to reproduce something, anything. It would have cost untold effort to copy out, one by one, every order that the central administration would send out to a large number of regional authorities. Printing made standardized information, instructions, and so on, possible, thus making administrative work much simpler. The rule of law grew increasingly reliable because laws could be printed on a huge scale. The mass distribution of census forms could generate the statistics upon which state administrations came to rely more and more. The printing press also made mass communication in the administrative sphere feasible, which created new forms of the state (*Staatlichkeit*). It is self-evident in this context that mass communication led to increased penetration on the part of the authorities and to more intensive integration of the general public into the state organization.

The great range of linguistic variation prior to the invention of printing gave way to a more or less standard language. This was similar to the development of script: printing brought about processes of standardization as well. Significantly, the vernacular into which the Bible was translated became the established linguistic variant in many regions. This was not a sacralization of language but a persistent, long-term normalization. Besides, the mass communication of religious texts established norms for the broader public sphere. There was an important reevaluation upward of vernaculars vis-à-vis clerical Latin throughout the Reformation. Even Catholic countries shared in this development, where shifts took place in several stages. There was a dual trend, linguistically speaking, in the early period of printing. On the one hand, Latin—the language of the clergy and scholars—was heavily promoted, but on the other hand, so were the various vernaculars. They could not become standard languages (*Hochsprachen*) until after they appeared in printed texts.[175] How the processes of penetration und integration by means of mass communication can affect languages is particularly well illustrated when a vernacular develops into a standard language. Linguistic unification involves similarity of formal signs *and* the unifying of cultural values bound up with them. The innovation of printing, then, created crucial conditions for the formation of linguistically and culturally based nations in modern times. Early nation building and early nationalism seem to be typical features of Europe's development.

But printing had yet another integrating function surpassing nation or its early forms. Virtually the entire region that accepted this technological innovation itself became unified as a result. Printing produced supraregional intercommunication in Europe. The controversies within Christianity, the transmission of classical authors, the mysteries of nature that scholars deciphered—all these stirred up interest everywhere in Europe. Any publications in Latin on these topics would be readily comprehended in the scholarly world. Latin showed that it could be a unifying force even after church unity crumbled during the era of religious schism. But this was not only the privilege of the book printed in Latin: it also belonged to book culture in general, which printing initiated and which was able to inculcate an awareness of unity and belonging in spite of religious schisms and political conflict. The medieval Western Church was able to stay alive in the areas encompassed by Europe and its book culture. What was actually in those books eventually exceeded the scope of church tradition, passing on to secularism as a form of freedom from religion. For all these fundamental transformations, the communicative interconnectedness of Europe's culture of the book created a significant line of continuity stretching from the medieval Western church to our own times.

Conclusion

"Through what concatenation of circumstances . . . ?" Interacting Determinants of Europe's Special Path

Max Weber's preface to his *Collected Essays on the Sociology of Religion*, quoted in the introduction to this book, did not spell out how he expected us to take his first sentence, which questions the causes of "the Occident's" unique development: "Through what concatenation of circumstances was it that precisely, and only, on the soil of the Occident cultural phenomena appeared that nonetheless developed—at least as we like to think—in a direction that is universally significant and valid?" He did not elaborate on his terms "concatenation" (*Verkettung*) or "circumstances" (*Umstände*), so that we have some latitude in our interpretation. We can make an informed attempt at concretizing these abstract terms because of what we have learned in the seven preceding chapters. Our first step will be to probe the internal connections *within* the group of factors found in each chapter title—factors crucial to Europe's special development. The next step will explore the links and interdependencies operating *among* all the groups of factors in the seven main chapters. A third and final stage will describe three additional ways in which Europe's special path was formed. Although connected with some of the above-mentioned factors, they deserve to be included separately because of their intrinsic importance and singular consequences.

We will begin with those phenomena shown to be specific to Europe's development and to have long-term significance. They are crucial nodes, so to speak, in an extensive network. They are "cultural phenomena" (*Kulturerscheinungen*), in Weber's sense of the word, that can be interpreted by a "concatenation of circumstances"; they are also "circumstances" which, in a "concatenation" with other "circumstances," have led to specifically European "cultural phenomena." Conditions shaping the emergence of these key factors have been explored in detail and their effects discussed—although they were delineated only by way of example. We are concerned here with the different basic patterns in the "concatenation of circumstances" that the title to each chapter addresses.

———

The first chapter, "Rye and Oats: The Agrarian Revolution of the Early Middle Ages," proceeded from two introduced crops that were to flourish in Europe's climate and the favorable environment north of the Alps. These natural conditions confined both crops to specific areas; but to investigate this limitation any further here would direct us to factors already determined by physical geography. Furthermore, rye and oats did not always appear at the same time and certainly not in the same place; they were of major importance in the three-field system of farming. Here were two equal, closely allied components that together produced a long-term effect. As agricultural products of the three-field system, they formed part of an extensive agrarian economic system in which the several elements of farming, animal husbandry, pasturing, and forestry were interrelated, along with the coordination of peasant labor. Neither could be separated off without jeopardizing the functioning of the whole system. The metaphor of a "concatenation of circumstances" takes on a special meaning here.

The chapter's subtitle, "The Agrarian Revolution of the Early Middle Ages," situated the model of the three-field system within the larger context of early changes in agrarianism as a whole. Not all aspects of this process were dependent on one another in the same way. For example, the heavy plow seems to have been an essential and necessary addition to the agrarian system described above—a claim that cannot be made for the horse collar in regard to draft animals or the water-driven mill that processed higher grain yields. These aspects were nonetheless part of a broadly typical pattern in the new European agriculture. Other components were connected with this suite of innovations to a greater or lesser degree, but they existed in common, as a rule, and were productive in common. Unlike the more or less contemporary agrarian revolution in the Islamic world, the European revolution encompassed a very broad range of diverse economic activities based on farming, which included transportation and the raising of livestock, but primarily the essential crafts and industries. And so the "agrarian/agricultural revolution" actually meant much more than the term implied. White's "agricultural revolution of the early Middle Ages" was at any rate a crucial factor in the entire economic development of Europe. Its effect moved beyond the primary sector of agriculture into the secondary trade and industrial sectors and even impinged upon the service sector. Many of the economic innovations vital to Europe's special path were linked—usually mediated a number of times—to this key factor. We will turn to some examples of similar "concatenations of circumstances."

The system of agriculture developed in the Frankish Empire was unique worldwide and ran parallel to an equally unique agrarian social system, which the second chapter explored under the title, "Manor and Hide: The Manorial Roots of European Social Structures." As a crucial factor in Europe's exceptional development, that social system appeared to be a relatively homogenous one. The two phenomena treated in the chapter's title overlap to a certain extent: the hide system grew out of the manorial system, so that they were consecutive instead of simultaneous. The older *villicatio* deserves particular emphasis—in spite of the fact that it was relatively short-lived in many places—because it broke the ground for trend-setting elements of the manorial system: the "bipartite manor" with its dues and services and the concept of treating manorial personnel as a *familia*.

The third chapter, unlike the second, proceeded from two separate and contrasting factors. Family and kinship were in many respects independent cultural phenomena, though they developed in a reciprocal relationship. It was a particularly European feature that the two maintained a certain distance from each other and were often shaped by different forces: the family as a household community, for instance, was affected more by changes in the organization of labor; kinship, as a group formed through descent and marriage to one's relatives, was influenced more by religious factors. The principle of descent spilled over into the family, of course. The core idea that Christianity led to more flexible descent relationships applied to family and kinship, as well as to other social groups, as spelled out by the chapter's subtitle, "Social Flexibility through Looser Ties of Descent." In short, a three-sided system of factors ultimately emerged: family, kinship, and the social forms that had taken on family and kinship functions or been modeled on them. The effect of this complex of factors—exemplified by changes in linguistic terms for relatives—proved exceptionally long-lasting among Europe's formative aspects, from early ancient Greece to the present day.

I explored feudalism, another of Europe's special paths, in the fourth chapter, "The Feudal System and the Estates"—the title signaling the chapter's theme: the close link between two largely noncontemporaneous cultural phenomena. I was less concerned here with the many ramifications of the European form of the feudal system than with the particular strand of development that led to parliamentary democracy, to which the Estates system was key. The decisive links in this "concatenation" were rather more separated in time than is the case elsewhere in the present study—a special case among our interpretive models of the separate influences upon Europe's special path.

Chapter 5, "The Papal Church and Universal Religious Orders: Western Christendom as a Highly Organized Religious Community," dealt with the broadest set of factors by far among the cultural phenomena defining Europe's special development. I might have subsumed the evolution of universal religious orders under the rubric "papal church." The orders were, after all, created in the Western Church with the papacy's considerable support during and after the High Middle Ages. But against this argument stand Western asceticism's diverse and independent origins within the development of Europe and its unique contributions to that development; they are not so easily identified as "links" in a "chain" that was forged in Rome. Indeed, the juxtaposition of the papal church and the universal religious orders made us cognizant of some productive tensions that forged Europe's unique path.

Not until chapter 6, "The Crusades and Protocolonialism: The Roots of European Expansionism," did we address the history of political events along Europe's special path, although for our purposes, to be sure, the crusading movement was discussed primarily as a cultural phenomenon, not as a series of separate military and political actions. My juxtaposition of the Crusades and the protocolonialism of Italy's maritime republics yoked together dissimilar political and cultural forces pursuing very dissimilar interests. Their significance to European expansionism—an influence defined in no small part by the tensions they generated—justifies their being treated jointly, even if their interests diverged.

"Preaching and Printing," chapter 7, initially examined the apparently separate parallel developments of two "early forms of mass communication"—orality and literacy. But closer analysis confirmed the intimate relationship between these two factors and the powerful effect they had on each other. Mass communication through images was combined with mass communication via word and script, and the former frequently mediated between the latter. The triad of sermon / woodcut / printed text proved to be a tightly interwoven cluster. Specific tensions among these cultural phenomena were not identified; but their staggered entries on the scene over time were worthy of note. Mass communication via the word long preceded mass communication by means of images, which in turn occurred well ahead of communication through printed texts. The three did not come together as a homogenous complex until the fifteenth century, so that they were a relatively late arrival among the key factors of the Middle Ages we have employed in the interpretation of Europe's special path.

———

Each of the seven chapters above examined medieval cultural phenomena typical of Europe's special path that were causally linked, forming their own "concatenation of circumstances." We can now follow the primary thread that connects all seven in sequence. The first two chapters underscored the causal connection between Frankish agrarianism and the agrarian social system, in which the process of cerealization that began with the early medieval agrarian revolution produced the bipartite manor. Chapter 3 dealt with the emergence, within the context of the manorial system, of the peasant family type, so admirably suited for organizing the labor force that lords and peasants on the manor needed. The manor in turn provided the basis of feudal order into which the imperial church was integrated. The rise of the papal church from the eleventh century on could not have emerged solely from the controversies over the imperial church in central, western, and northwestern Europe; but the so-called Investiture Controversy, or more precisely, the concern in the controversy evidenced by church reform, *did* play an instrumental role. It is obvious that the Crusades were a consequence of the pope's actions—an unambiguous, substantive example of a causal connection. A similarly clear line led from the crusading movement to the Crusade sermon as an early form of mass communication. A comparable bridge might be built linking the universal religious orders to early preaching campaigns in the thirteenth and fourteenth centuries.

But this unilinear connection of causes, stretching from the early medieval agrarian revolution to high and late medieval mass communication, does not really provide a satisfactory interpretive model. Our separate analyses showed that each of the cultural phenomena discussed had many roots, quite apart from those illustrated in the preceding chapter. We found numerous examples of reciprocal effects outside those suggested by the sequence of our analysis. To select but a few: the growth of manorial organizing structures had a strong, long-lasting influence on the structure of the great religious orders—for example, in the organization of the congregation of monasteries around Cluny, or in the Cistercian Order. Moreover, the Cistercians encouraged improvements in agriculture, which kept the agrarian revolution moving ahead. Then, too, the high value placed on consensual marriage had been encouraged in the Western Church for a very long time, even more forcefully after the papal church developed its channels of influence; yet the conjugal family also fit very well into the context of manorial patterns of organization—interactions that make it hard to decide which influence was key. A last example: The Estates system was tied to manorial organization because of its origins in the feudal system. But it seems that the Estates, too, were strongly influenced by church assemblies in matters of codetermination. Finally, the principle of representation so crucial for later developments was also a sign of the Estates' urban roots, among other things. Processes in the "concatenation of circumstances" that produced new "cultural phenomena" therefore brought together factors from very different areas, examined separately below, in accordance with our original system.

———

Some major factors in the early medieval agrarian revolution lend themselves particularly well to demonstrating other determinants of Europe's special path that are significant enough to stand on their own, apart from their relation to topics discussed earlier. The mill—to be precise, the water mill powered by a vertical wheel—crops up time and again as a key and continuing influence in the trades and mining. Absent this particular "concatenation of circumstances," the boom in European mining in the late Middle Ages would have been inconceivable.

There were of course other factors involved in the upswing in mining at that time. First and foremost, appropriate ore deposits had to be available, an ecological requirement fulfilled in Europe in rich measure, at least for iron, the most exploited metal.[1] Even so, only a single iron-ore deposit in Europe was continuously worked from antiquity.[2] Opening up new mining areas meant having to solve complicated problems of supply. Mining is anything but a self-supporting form of production.[3] Feeding miners concentrated in mountainous regions presented a problem because growing food was difficult there. The solution was either to provide food from areas where people had the know-how to farm at high elevations or to transport food supplies over great distances. Wood and charcoal, indispensable to mining, were also contingent upon the ecology of the landscape. But the mining industry's most critical need for expansion was continued technological development. And this is where technology derived from the water mill came into its own.[4] It generated a number of processes employed in various branches of mining—for powering the bellows in the smelter, for processing pig iron in the forge,[5] or in the mining of nonferrous and precious metals to deliver energy for crushing ore. But its primary use was for draining groundwater from the deep adits.[6] The foremost silver mine in Schwaz in Tyrol, for instance, had a drainage adit (*Erbstollen*) two hundred meters beneath the valley floor thanks to the invention of the Schwazer Wasserkunst (a waterwheel), which required only two workers to take off the water instead of six hundred.[7] The drive for precious metals constantly pushed the search for ore deposits down to greater and greater depths, creating more and more ingenious and increasingly expensive draining systems. By the late Middle Ages, the great industrial and technological achievements of Europe in this field were unmatched in any other culture.

Demand was a crucial stimulus in the medieval mining boom in Europe—a demand that engendered reciprocal effects among several of the topics explored in preceding chapters. Agriculture and the military led the call for iron production. It was a peculiarity of agriculture in Europe, unlike many regions outside the continent, that it relied so heavily on iron implements for such a long time—plowshares, for example, and harrows, sickles, and scythes for working the fields; axes for clearing trees and forestry; horseshoes for horses that were employed as draft animals and for transportation; and iron axles for grinding grain.[8] Agriculture and iron tools were so closely linked that the blacksmith had become a fixture in every Frankish village by the eighth century.[9] And so the expansion of agricultural forms within the Frankish Empire promoted the expansion of iron mining and smelting, and vice versa. The equipping of armies of armored cavalry was certainly a powerful stimulus. Charlemagne's "iron men," who so impressed the Langobard king at Pavia, were emblematic of an advance in the military that presented the iron industry with an enormous challenge. The growing demand for precious metals came mainly from the circulation of gold and silver coins.[10] But their use in liturgical implements and reliquaries increased the demand even more. This provided a cross-connection between forms of piety toward both relics and the Eucharist, which in their own way were specific to Europe and were concentrated in the newer centers in its Northwest. We will return to this point below. The church also contributed greatly to copper mining. Church bells used to be cast from bronze. Carlo Cipolla has written about the late medieval shift in the demand for copper: "It is indeed one of the ironies of history that a technique developed in the making of such essentially civilized objects eventually fostered the progress of deadly weapons."[11] Cannons cast in bronze had long been cheaper and more efficient than iron ones, and so the advent of heavy artillery set off a copper boom.[12] Copper mining in the fourteenth century was fraught with technical difficulties similar to the ones that silver mining had to contend with earlier. But the decade from about 1460 to 1470 witnessed new solutions to problems that brought about a fresh upturn in European mining.

Determinants of this late medieval boom have been spelled out in the scholarly literature. For example:

[We find] the interplay of engaged mining and smelting workers; merchants from afar interested in technology, and territorial rulers who promoted new forms of organizing labor and capital. In addition, mining shares [Kuxe] were created . . . , along with an elaborate and reliable mining administration that used Arabic numerals and double bookkeeping to increase efficiency and drew up mining regulations that guaranteed indispensable legal security in an economic sector fraught with high risk.[13]

This quotation, apart from its technological premises, offers an interesting catalog of "circumstances" that together facilitated upward trends in the mining sector: qualified and motivated workers; entrepreneurs well versed in production technology, who would cooperate with authorities interested in promoting this particular economy; new ways of organizing labor and capital; a rational management policy, drawn up according to the newest high accounting standards; making laws for the mining industry to stabilize the precarious situation regarding property title; and finally, a mining administration instituted by the lord who owned the rights to natural resources—an administration that would be in a position to offset the interests of private entrepreneurs. Many of these encouraging conditions established a framework for mining in the waning Middle Ages; they were able to apply as well to later phases of European economic development, which would explain some of their success. In any event, Europe's special pathway to industrialization has many beginnings harking back to the Middle Ages.

It is easy to see why mining encouraged the establishment of large industrial enterprises in various parts of Europe by the late Middle Ages. This was especially true with regard to the mining and smelting of precious and nonferrous metals. But it is ultimately difficult to decide what medieval entity was meant by today's term, "mining concern."[14] Do we take it to mean individual mines and the mine operators who paid the miners? Or mining as a whole, as represented by the *Bergmeister*, who was the overseer in charge of mining in the prince's territory, and his subordinates, the *Hutmeister*, who collectively functioned as the real employers? The strongest arguments support this last view. No matter which definition is chosen, it will have to account for very large numbers of workers and a very complicated personnel structure. The workers could be called "wage earners" in the full sense of the word, as in the industrial revolution—with all the problems, risks, and forms of social care that this definition would have entailed.[15] It is perfectly clear that large smelters existed in the late Middle Ages—particularly those that recrystallized copper ore.[16] If we regard the development of large industrial concerns as an essential aspect of Europe's special path, then we must date the rise of industrialization from late medieval mining production and its organization of labor and not, as is so often done, from the much later beginnings of a large-scale textile industry in the second half of the eighteenth century.

The mining industry developed components of late medieval capitalism more conspicuously than other economic sectors did. From the fourteenth century on, independent mine and smelter owners were sometimes no longer in a position to bear the expense of running their operations themselves. The main problem was the extremely technical factory equipment that was mostly waterpowered; it played a crucial role, for example, in draining water from underground tunnels or galleries, and in stamping mills, blast furnaces, and separating mills.[17] The owners now had to rely on a variety of sources of foreign capital. Territorial princes participated to some degree, although they would often be involved in mining anyway as *Regalherren*, that is, owners of natural resources on their own land. But trading capital from urban metal merchants and other foreign shareholders was more important. Companies were established to profit individual capitalists according to the amount they invested. The term *Kuxe* for mining shares first appeared in 1477.

An outstanding example of an early capitalist mining organization was the Fugger-Thurzo Company, which has been called the "best organized industrial enterprise" of its time.[18] Johann Thurzo was a most gifted mining engineer in the late fifteenth century. In 1475, he succeeded in draining the flooded mines in Kremnica (in Upper Hungary, today's Slovak Republic) by constructing a powerful reversible wheel. His good relations with the heavily indebted Hungarian king enabled him to take over some of the bankrupt mine in Neusohl (now Banská Bystrica in the Slovak Republic). He was unable to expand his mining empire until he allied himself with the merchant-banking house of the Fuggers in Augsburg, which gave him access to mining areas in the eastern Alps and the Thuringian Forest—but most important, it provided him with substantial capital investment. These mining regions were networked by the construction of three great separating mills: in Moschnitz bei Neusohl, Fuggerau bei Villach in Carinthia, and Georgenthal in the Thuringian Forest; all three coordinated their production. The trading company's network extended even farther, over Buda, Trieste, Venice, Frankfurt, Cologne, Posnan, Thoruń, and Gdańsk, all the way to Antwerp. At the dawn of the modern age there was scarcely a capitalist enterprise anywhere of this magnitude, of this economic power, or above all possessing this degree of coordination, molding different branches of production to create a synergy. If capitalism is viewed as a central characteristic of Europe's special path, then we will have to ask what "concatenation of circumstances" might have been conducive to this type of enterprise.

There are no serious doubts today that Europe was already leading the world in energy use by early modern times.[19] Once again, it was energy from mining that was especially widespread, and it could be employed in numerous ways. This sector therefore provided important links in the chain leading to high energy consumption in Europe and the cultures it was to spawn in modern times. Medieval mining used mainly water and wood, or charcoal—and even then there were some difficult consequences for the environment. But Europe was a continent unusually rich in natural resources. One region particularly short of wood experimented quite early with coal as a replacement: England in the thirteenth century.[20] Its bituminous coal deposits were easily worked, and shipping by sea was relatively inexpensive. Coal was used as a substitute for wood in numerous industries during the early modern period, and in the eighteenth century it represented a critical breakthrough in iron production as well.[21] Coal had by then become a particularly desirable product in the mining industry, but its excavation ran into the same problem found in the Middle Ages: drainage of mine shafts. Solving this problem led to the creation of a revolutionary new energy source. The steam pump employed in coal mines eventually became the steam engine.[22] This technology led to the exploitation of fossil energy sources on a grand scale—a transition in mankind's use of energy that would be of centuries-long significance. England was the home of coal technology, which gave it a head start in the industrialization process.[23] Industrial areas reliant on waterpower and wood fell behind. That said, we must not forget that early industrializing processes dependent on these energy sources had a lasting effect, bearing in mind these early stages when we consider how Europe's special path was conditioned by both the potential and use of its energy.

Mining in Europe was of course based on the physical realities of nature, but iron-ore deposits were not the only reason for its extraordinary importance in European history. There were many "concatenations of circumstances" that enabled ore deposits to be worked so efficiently and with such far-reaching social consequences. Some of these "circumstances" take us quite far back—they are the locus of what is specifically European. To list some of the most significant: a well-developed milling technology based on the particulars of an agrarian economy; laws governing mining rights that regulated in detail both an owner's rights and a justice system analogous to manorial structures; a labor system influenced from its beginnings by monastic discipline, particularly by the Cistercians; a lack of religious scruples underpinned by animist ideas against the exploitation of natural resources;[24] and scientifically based mining technologies that were easily disseminated throughout the continent after the invention of the printing press. These advantages spurred progress in mining that made significant forward-looking contributions to European history—industrialization, the growth of capitalism, energy use, and of course military weaponry of extraordinary destructive power. Natural resources alone cannot account for all these developments. And yet the natural world does impinge upon Weber's question. No counterpart to Europe's special path could exist without those very resources, even if another region had been able—with haste and imitation—to catch up after Europe's economic head start. This ecological deficit applies even to regions in close proximity to the European continent.

———

Communalism is a second factor that helped fashion Europe's special path. Although it is linked to factors examined in the preceding seven chapters, it deserves a brief independent outline because of its intrinsic importance and particular consequences. Peter Blickle, the leading scholar in the field, has offered the following definition: "Communalism includes urban municipalities and rural communities that are constructed, in principle, as analogous groups—both functionally and institutionally. They are shaped by the competence of a community's statutes or its representative organs, by an administration operating within the competence covered by its statutes, and by a jurisdiction limited by statutory laws."[25] Wolfgang Reinhard, who has situated communalism in its proper place in his thorough history of European state power, expanded on this view:

[T]he dividing line between rural and urban communities [was] often not clear-cut. Even a conceptual differentiation presents difficulties, because Max Weber's characteristics of the "city" ideal type—with its (1) fortifications, (2) marketplace, (3) judicial court, (4) group character, and (5) autonomy—are not found in every city but might certainly be present in rural communities. . . . The categories of rural and urban communities do not discriminate clearly, but this simply reflects their common origin and political role in the premodern period because the European village, as the predominant form of rural settlement, is no different from most cities in that it dates from the high and late Middle Ages.[26]

Classifying the "autonomous city" under the rubric "communalism" affords a different basis, and probably a better one, for a discussion of this issue, which marks an extraordinary position in Weber's view of the "Occident's" unique development that continues to provoke debate.[27]

Whether or not the autonomous urban community was distinctively European is a matter for cross-cultural dialogue, where much depends on the idea of autonomy you start with. Those who are aware of the very concrete fact that the city hall as a historical building type is limited to Europe—and even then only to certain regions—will probably tend to accept the idea that the autonomous city community is a specific phenomenon of Europe's special path.[28] This was undoubtedly the case with a variety of phenomena relating to communalism. It was, for example, a particularly European affair when representatives to territorial and imperial diets, delegated by municipal, market, or rural communities, sat across from the prince as politically entitled representatives.[29] This was equally true when urban and rural jurisdictions merged into a "confederation" (*Eidgenossenschaft*) that could finally exercise sovereign state rights.[30] Communes of communes are a long-standing tradition in Europe going back to the *Lega lombarda*, which banded together against Frederick Barbarossa in 1167.[31] They are a powerfully persuasive expression of what contemporary scholarship refers to as "communalism."

In spite of all the municipal forms that communalism spanned, its origins unquestionably lay in the growing movement initiated by the citizenry in the towns of Europe's core between Flanders and Lombardy during the eleventh and twelfth centuries.[32] If we consider the constitutional situation from a certain angle, the communal movement could be largely explained against the realities of the imperial church; the chapter on the feudal system and the estates would then represent a countermovement against episcopal town lords. But we cannot understand it simply as a movement that overthrew a system. Many elements of the urban communal system developed seamlessly and continuously from feudal patterns.[33] Urban, market, and rural communities were apparently fully integrated into the territorial and imperial Estates systems.

The chapter on family and kinship contains much material on trends toward "horizontal societies" that can add to our understanding of the rise of the communes in medieval Europe. The loosening of ties of descent promoted the building of corporate social forms. "Confraternities" and similar unions based on equality helped shape the communes' internal structure. And the *coniuratio* of a citizen can be counted as a quasi-kinship social relationship created by oaths.[34] The citizens' relationship to the *patronus* of their bishop's church—a powerful element in their sense of connectedness—brought special developments within Europe into play that were treated in the chapter on kinship.[35] Cases in point are the relationship to Saint Mark in Venice, Saint Ambrose in Milan, Saints Felix and Regula in Zurich, and Saint Sebald in Nurnberg. As pointed out in the opening chapter, the particularities of the European agrarian economy promoted the development of smaller and medium-sized centers for the industrial trades, one of the consequences of the early medieval agrarian revolution. The manorial system described in the second chapter had a similar effect on the formation of central settlements. The blurring of the boundaries between town, market, and rural communities that was typical of European communalism was probably based on the idiosyncrasy of agrarian and lordship structures.

The chapter on the Crusades and protocolonialism takes up a very different strand of development that also points toward communalism. The maritime republics attained the utmost degree of communal autonomy because they were wealthy trading powers and a principal military force during and after the High Middle Ages, thereby serving as a model for other communes. They exhibited no direct continuity with antiquity, but there might have been older structural congruencies that encouraged the later formation of autonomous Mediterranean city republics. This would have stood in contrast to the social factors shaping the rise of European communalism that were anchored in the conditions of medieval society.

Peter Blickle has called communalism "the political bedrock of Europe": "Communalism is a phenomenon that has shaped the history of Europe to a very great extent and over a long period of time—not just haphazardly but definitively as a form of political organization capable of determining the quality of people's lives."[36] Wolfgang Reinhard has pointed out the close affinity of this kind of political life with the republican form of the commonwealth: "The higher the development of communalism, and the stronger its latent republicanism, the more likely a republic will emerge: a free state, the full members of which would be free to practice self-determination but, most importantly, they would be free from having their lives determined by others, by monarchs."[37] Sovereign republics with an overlord seem to have evolved on the margins of Europe until into the sixteenth century, especially in mountain and coastal regions. In the seventeenth century, they emerged in the heartlands through clashes with growing state powers, principally in the Netherlands and England.[38] The pathway to the modern age in Europe is typified by the universal establishment of the republican principle, even if a monarch was retained as the nominal head of state. Communalism—the basis of the republican state—was an especially significant and powerful factor in Europe's special path. Its considerable influence was by no means limited to state or political organizations; there are clear connections with Reformation churches as well. The radical position of some scholars—that the goal of the "common man" in the early Reformation was the "comprehensive and total communalizing of the church"—has met with the objection that urban corporate traditions continued to have an effect, but this extreme position has otherwise gone unchallenged.[39] The synodal form of church government continues the legacy of communalism within a framework of religion in a perfectly obvious manner, linking it with specific ideas about civil and human rights from the religious sphere that reflect back on the secular realm.[40]

––––––

A third key factor in Europe's development to be briefly outlined comes from the religious quarter. Religious factors are generally rather underplayed in the discussion about special paths. This is particularly true if the effects of religion do not have a strong influence upon economics or politics. Devotion to the Eucharist, which emerged in the Western Church in the High Middle Ages, is one such instance. It peaked throughout the area of the pope's jurisdiction after the introduction of the Feast of Corpus Christi. As has been indicated above, this feast marked the real climax in the development of Western Christendom toward a cult religion—a crucial cultic form not found in other Christian churches.[41] There are virtually no cultic practices in non-Christian religious communities that are remotely comparable.

From the perspective of the history of theology, the "concatenation of circumstances" that introduced the doctrine of transubstantiation and the resultant cult of the Eucharist is firmly linked to scholars whose interpretations and controversies ultimately led to the doctrine that was declared obligatory at the Fourth Lateran Council in 1215. The First Eucharistic Controversy was initiated by a dispute between Saint Paschasius Radbertus and his pupil Ratramnus at the monastery of Corbie around the middle of the ninth century—the former powerfully presenting the new view that the priest's repetition of Christ's words at the Last Supper transformed the bread and wine into Christ's flesh and blood, the latter clinging to the traditional platonic and patristic scheme of idea (*Urbild*) and form (*Abbild*). Also worthy of note was the Second Eucharistic Controversy that Berengar of Tours stirred up in 1040, although his spiritualistic position ultimately lost out.[42] These kinds of "concatenations" in intellectual history can be extended backward and forward in time, but they open up just one aspect of the phenomenon. If we wish to understand the enormous significance and huge success of the eucharistic cult in the Western Church, then we will also have to delve into the broader history of cults. An important thread leads to the Western cult of relics, and probably to pre-Christian forms beyond that.

Peter Dinzelbacher has addressed an essential connection between the older cult of holy relics and the later cult of the Eucharist in his article "The 'Real Presence' of Saints in Their Reliquaries and Graves according to Medieval Sources."[43] The concept of a "real presence" derives from the Eucharist debate. Just as Jesus was thought to be in the bread and wine after the words were spoken at the transubstantiation, the saint was thought to be fully present and efficacious in the saint's corpse or its parts. "Corpus Christi" (in German, *Fronleichnam*) literally means "the body of the Lord," making the analogy clear. Parallels between saints' relics and the Host were many and varied: people believed that both could work miracles. Miracles of the Host—a novelty in Christian history—began to turn up sporadically in the eighth century and peaked in the fourteenth and fifteenth centuries.[44] In liturgical practice, some aspects of the way the Host was treated were taken over from the cult of relics; one adoption was the Elevation of the Host after the transubstantiation. Gazing at the Holy now came to the fore.[45] One expected to receive grace from viewing the Host, as from viewing a holy relic. Communion was no longer the focal point. To make beneficial objects more visible, the Blessed Sacrament of the Altar was carried around in solemn procession, just as saints' relics used to be.[46] This was how the Corpus Christi procession originated, by harking back to processions with holy relics. The transubstantiated bread—but not the wine—was displayed in a monstrance, a magnificently wrought vessel that had evolved from earlier ostensoria for holding relics.[47] As the veneration of the Blessed Sacrament of the Altar appeared on the scene, it made full use of the forms and practices of the more ancient veneration of relics. The Western Church, unlike the rest of the Christian churches, decided to interpret the mystery of the Eucharist materialistically, as spelled out in a doctrine of transubstantiation. Not the least reason for this understanding was the conference upon the cult of the Host of the significance that from the early Middle Ages had attached to the cult of holy relics.

To understand why during the early Middle Ages the demand for saints and their relics was so strong in northwest Europe, and nowhere else, we have to factor in the state of the region's agrarian economy. A persuasive quotation from Arnold Angenendt calls to mind contexts and topics from our first chapter:

A further problem with the cult of saints, especially in its medieval form, is that Christianity actually did not offer enough "religion." This may have been less important in the early stages, when the new faith was expanding almost exclusively within cities and presenting itself as a religion of the book with high ethical values. But in that almost totally agrarian society, at least as it existed in the first half of the Middle Ages, there were no fundamental rites that would prevail over all those cosmic forces that people were subjected to every day. Christian doctrine officially denied the existence of any independent natural forces, of course, maintaining instead that everything came directly from God who created and guided it all—if not, then everything was beset and possessed by demons. What was left, from the Christian point of view, was simply a plea to God for revitalization and purification; there was no entreating of natural forces. Here was a profound difference. The agricultural, nature-bound society yearned for direct intervention against all the forces they saw as part of their lives: weather and thunderstorms, fruitfulness and harvest, disease and plague, life and death. The official church sought to remedy this with an array of blessings and exorcisms. Saints were even more important, with their designated responsibilities for the weather and animals, for fruit and field, their protection against fire and lightening, their healing power in pain and suffering, and not least for their vanquishing of demons and the devil. There was a saint standing over and above every natural and calamitous power for people to summon to their immediate aid through his blessing. Indeed, the saint's blessing rendered cosmic forces powerless. For no matter how violently the Christian struggle was fought against superstitious beliefs about sacred springs, stones, and trees, or the choice of a certain day, or casting lots—everything was justified the moment a saint gave his blessing.[48]

This accurately portrays the conditions that transformed early medieval Christianity in the new, central, agrarian regions of northwest Europe. We may take the line leading from the cult of holy relics to the religiosity of the Feast of Corpus Christi as being essential to this transformation.

The Western Church's own particular conception of the Eucharist turned out to be a key feature of new developments in many areas. Communion with the chalice now became an obligatory part of the Eucharist only for the celebrant, whereas the laity were simply given the consecrated Host. The gulf between clergy and laity was now widened by the very mode of expression fundamental to the religious community. To give the chalice to the layman became a major demand of heterodox groups like the Wycliffites and the Hussites; in the latter case, the symbol created both unity and groupings within the various religious currents.[49] The Hussite Wars witnessed the bloody politicizing of this religious demand. Both types of communion would be persistent controversial issues during the Reformation as well.

Establishing the doctrine of transubstantiation in the Western Church went hand in hand with miracles of the Host. The many variants of miracle tales always served the same purpose: to narrate persuasive miraculous events in order to dispel doubts about the reality of the transformation process.[50] But what accompanied this process is remarkable: tales of desecration, charges of sacrilege committed against the Host aimed primarily at Jews, who were accused of stealing the Host, cutting, shredding, and burning it.[51] The first such indictments were brought in Paris in 1290, following by a few years the introduction of the Feast of Corpus Christi. Accusations of Jewish desecrations of the Host originated in, and emanated from, the northwest of the continent, not Rome. The same was true of earlier accusations of ritual murder, made initially in Norwich in 1144. Jews were accused of ritually murdering a Christian child at Easter as a mockery of Christ's passion. At first glance, the anti-Jewish campaign seems irrelevant for the emergence of the doctrine of transubstantiation, but the context illuminates some connections very quickly and clearly. Again and again the miracle stories would tell how the baby Jesus appeared in the Host to skeptical priests during Mass as proof that transubstantiation brought about the real presence of Christ. The baby Jesus and the Host would be collapsed into one. The motive underpinning the legends of ritual murder of children was related to the baby Jesus just as it was to the desecration of the Host. Significantly, drawing blood for ritual purposes was one of the charges at trials for ritual murder when the doctrine of transubstantiation was formulated at the Fourth Lateran Council.[52] The connection between the simultaneous emergence of the idea of transubstantiation and a campaign against Judaism involved more than the two concrete, accusatory syndromes; it also existed on a more general level. If it is believed that the Mass actually—and not only allegorically or spiritually—reenacts Christ's sacrifice on the cross, then time telescopes: "God's murderers" are, according to this view, all Jews of all times, those living now as well as in the far distant past. This principle of the "contemporaneity of the noncontemporaneous" led to horrifying consequences in the persecution of medieval Jews. Moreover, in the thirteenth century the doctrine of transubstantiation enshrined as dogma this overlapping of time horizons, which was by then palpably present in other areas of life, especially as expressed in art.[53]

The history of European theater includes the liturgical dramas of the Middle Ages, and the Feast of Corpus Christi ranks high in their development.[54] Many of the early mystery and miracle plays were performed at precisely the time of this feast. The timing might have been practical, since the Corpus Christi procession began in the church and emerged from it, thus presenting liturgical subjects in a freer form and a public space. But even the mystery of the feast was particularly calculated to bring the story of salvation to life through dramatic performance. This made the salvation story seem part of the present time and appeared to mark a crucial intersection between liturgy and theater.[55] The doctrine that Christ's act of redemption was repeated through transubstantiation had consequences beyónd the act of transformation. Acts of salvation proved to be repeatable, and replaying them in dramatizations was one avenue for that process. Stories recorded in the Bible were thereby connected with the age in which they were performed in a new guise—a process that had begun even before the Corpus Christi plays.

Liturgical drama frequently embellished biblical narrative motifs with features from the contemporary real world, Herod swearing by Mohammed, say, or the high priests appearing as Christian bishops, or Mary Magdalene expressly ordering her maid to do her fine-looking hair in the latest style.[56] Very similar juxtapositions could be found in painting: the so-called Master of the Vienna Schottenstift placed contemporary Vienna in the background of his *Flight into Egypt*. These examples from two of the arts illustrate the principle of the "contemporaneity of the noncontemporaneous." Both might have been contingent upon the doctrine of transubstantiation, which we would then have to consider a key factor in the turn toward realism—a crucial shift in medieval European painting.

The belief in transubstantiation, and its concomitant forms of religiosity, uniquely transformed the concrete setting of the mystery of the Eucharist—the area around the church's altar and the objects appropriate to it. If we compare the function of gold in the Eastern and Western Churches, then we may say that the former used gold in its mosaics as the most worthy material for decorating the cupola—in keeping with the idea that a heavenly act was to be incorporated into the Eucharistic act. On the other hand, a Western goldsmith's highest achievement for the church was to provide settings, in the most dignified forms possible, for the sacrificial offerings whose substance had been transformed: chalices and patens, but mainly monstrances, were the most important utensils for the new cult of the visual.[57] As has been pointed out, the monstrance was a direct descendant of the container for displaying holy relics, and there were many such parallels. The table altar became a box altar (*Kastenaltar*), serving as a repository for relics and fulfilling other needs in the veneration of the Eucharist.[58] The tabernacle altar became prominent—it was connected to the main altar or built into its retable, in imitation of repositories for relics found on the altar itself.[59] The altar cross became a liturgical object during the controversy over the real presence of Christ in the tenth century.[60] Compared with older, more symbolic forms of expression, the crucifix was a new figurative form signifying the real presence of Christ. It seems significant that the oldest crucifix, the Gero Cross from 968 in the Cologne Cathedral, has a repository for the Eucharist in the back of Christ's head, indicating its function as a tabernacle—a combination of forms that did not of course last for long.[61] The "altar cross" that signaled the real presence of Christ was always placed above the "altar of the cross," one of the numerous altars in Western churches reserved for parishioners at Mass. Figures from the passion story were placed around the cross on the altar. They marked the beginning of figurative decoration for the altar, along with reliquaries and images of reliquary and titular saints.[62] Figurative elaboration was meant to be more than just illustration: it was the reference point for a growing cult around the "sacrament of the altar." The sacrament's religious significance was modified by the doctrine of transubstantiation. As opposed to receiving the sacrament, gazing upon the Host was increasingly believed to mediate some religious benefit.[63] The cult of the gaze promoted the importance of decorating the altar with sculpture and painting. The Gothic triptych altar lent movement to the programmatic figures, arguably as a parallel to the liturgical drama, which was evolving at the same time and influenced, in turn, the configuration of the church's interior space. Important elements of church design resulting from the doctrine of transubstantiation were to survive subsequent fluctuations in period styles, at least in Catholic Europe.

———

We could add substantially to the string of further factors that helped to shape Europe's special path, quite apart from those examined above in regard to mining, communalism, and the Feast of Corpus Christi. For example, of the three inventions that Francis Bacon claimed in the early seventeenth century to be the greatest ever known to man—the compass, gunpowder, and printing—we have treated only the last-named. China had all three before Europe did. So the question arises: what "concatenation of circumstances" made these inventions so successful in Europe?[64] Carlo M. Cipolla's fascinating study *Guns, Sails and Empires: Technological Innovation and the Early Phases of European Expansion, 1400–1700* traces some particularly long-term influences.[65] It concludes with a quotation from a Chinese author:

Since cannon balls rendered us *hors de combat*, we naturally took an interest in them because, if we could reproduce them, we hoped to be able to respond to the attack. . . . Yet history seems to go in very different, tortuous paths. While studying cannon balls we hit upon the innovations of mechanics, which in turn led us to political reforms. The political reforms were based on political theories, which in turn were based on western philosophy. Mechanics, on the other hand, got us thinking along the lines of western natural science. We seemed to be distancing ourselves, step by step, from cannon balls but kept getting nearer and nearer to them in the process.

Here was a "concatenation of circumstances" in Europe's special path that was replicated outside the continent.

Some of Europe's defining influences created rather static conditions; the effect of others readily triggered more dynamic ones. A cross-cultural comparison demonstrates the importance of the latter improvements for the continent. Jenö Szücs, in his study "The Three Historical Regions of Europe," sees the vibrancy of Europe's development as the result of processes he calls "productive separations," or "productive divisions," the roots of which, he claims, already existed in the early Middle Ages.[66] Following from the two-power doctrine of Pope Gelasius I (492–96), he writes: "This division into spiritual and secular spheres—into ideological and political ones—is one of those productive separations in the West without which we could not conceive of either future 'freedoms' and the fundamental emancipation of 'society' or later nation states, the Renaissance or the Reformation."[67] To give a first example: the present study argues that the coexistence of a highly organized papal church and a variously organized secular lordship is peculiar to Europe, as is the fact that church and lordship together facilitated productive developments for the future—although this view is not based on a political theory of the papacy but on its much later realization. Sacred organizations are inherently long-lived. Wherever they are connected with organizations of lordship, there is less potential for development; whenever this combination is weak or severed, a more powerful dynamic is possible. A second very similar, if lower-level, example can be observed in investigating the family. Christianity is a communal religion; the family is not imbued with holy significance the way it is, say, in religions involving ancestor worship. The family can as a result develop with a greater degree of flexibility, up to and including trends toward individualization that we find in the more recent past and at the present time. A third example: David Landes characterizes the path to "European exceptionalism" under the heading,

292

"The Invention of Invention."[68] Among the reasons for this "culture of discovery," he lists the "Judeo-Christian subordination of nature to man. This is a sharp departure from widespread animistic beliefs and practices that saw something of the divine in every tree and stream."[69] God and nature—here, too, we find a "productive division" proceeding from a religious concept. These examples could be multiplied to embrace, say, sacred language and national language, canon law and secular law, theology and philosophy, or religion and the sciences. The spectrum of these tension-creating elements may be further enlarged by including antiquity—for instance, the reception of Roman law or the different renaissances in art. The concept of "productive divisions" appears to be a profitable approach for interpreting the specific dynamics of Europe's special path.

The present volume has attempted to interpret, via a "concatenation of circumstances," cultural phenomena that occurred only in Europe and characterized its development. We viewed phenomena in their reciprocal effects and explored their consequences, giving particular emphasis to conditions obtaining in medieval times. We discovered no continuous congruency in the regions of Europe where these factors or clusters of factors constituted a formative force. The early medieval agrarian revolution shifted the center of dynamic development to the Northwest—but it very quickly hit ecological limitations in the Mediterranean basin and the East. The structure of the manorial system based on that revolution continued to grow but could only gain a partial foothold in the Mediterranean South. The same was true of the feudal system. The papal church's purview in the High Middle Ages was much greater. It left untouched the East and the Southeast, to define these areas of the continent as has been the custom since the eighteenth century. Protocolonialism was confined to a few Italian maritime republics until the waning Middle Ages. In this concluding chapter, we have dealt with mining, which had many centers, the most important being in east-central Europe. Communalism experienced its most intensive flowering in the region between Upper Italy and the Netherlands. The cult of Corpus Christi spread rather slowly throughout the area of the Western Church, ultimately becoming a feature of Catholic Europe. At first blush, then, there is much spatial variance among the phenomena discussed. In the light of these findings, can we speak of a special path that can be understood as occupying a defined space?

In the studies above, the "concatenation of circumstances" has been understood synchronically as well as diachronically. If a milling industry were to grow out of a certain agrarian system, and milling technology were to produce a high-level mining industry creating early forms of capitalism and manufacturing highly efficient weaponry, then these derivative phenomena would not be confined to certain regions as the agrarian system had been. Similarly, we could trace a line of development from communalism—initially restricted to one area—to Europewide republicanism, or a line from Italy's homegrown protocolonialism to an expansionism in which most European nations have shared in more recent times. The cultural phenomena analyzed in this book, and their derivatives, spread throughout the continent of Europe within a relatively homogenous cultural region. The intensity of this dissemination was varied—in the way industrial centers were dispersed, or universities, or Gothic churches. We have ascertained above all some differences between core and peripheral areas, with the former frequently identified with central areas of the early medieval Frankish Empire benefiting from the agrarian revolution. But most of the cultural phenomena that kept spreading right up to the end of the Middle Ages did so within a clearly defined framework—the territory occupied by Western Christendom. Outside this area these cultural forces either did not exist or else evolved into clearly divergent forms.

The state of affairs changed with the advent of the early modern era.[70] The expanding European powers brought European cultural phenomena to colonies on other continents, as probably best exemplified by the New England states. But processes of diffusion also took place in colonies with a different structure and on the whole in regions that were to become dependent colonies. Neighboring cultures such as Russia sought Europeanization on their own, without becoming dependent colonies. Recent globalization processes have added to the spread of European cultural phenomena. Whatever goes by the name of "European" can no longer be confined to one culture in one clearly delineated region. Nevertheless, these traditions persist, particularly in the regions where they originated. And old structural borders inside Europe itself have proven to have long aftereffects, such as the dividing line between the Eastern and Western Church, the Hajnal Line, or the border between Frankish and Byzantine spheres of influence in Italy.

"Europe's special path" delineates a cultural development that has wound its way though areas of very different dimensions. Anyone today who tries to see it as an avenue to regions with clearly definable borders confronts a hopeless task. The continent that geography conventionally defines as "Europe" does not have a homogenous cultural tradition that might be construed as a special path through a "concatenation of circumstances" in Weber's sense of the term. Nor can the European

Union be comprehended, spatially, as a consequence of this path, either as its borders now stand or if and when it accepts new candidate countries. Debates over expansion that operate under these premises will necessarily end up talking about ideologies of legitimization.[71]

To follow the origins of Europe's special path in Weber's sense does not imply that we should now begin to delimit and exclude as a result of historical analyses. The point is not to "de-fine" Europe by staking out a precise space. It is a matter instead of making specifically European cultural phenomena intelligible through their historical development—and not just those phenomena that public discourse might view in a positive light. The reason we ride roughshod over nature must be given its due every bit as much as should the origins of broad political participation in parliamentary democracy, or the roots of colonialism every bit as much as modern mass communication. These phenomena, the results of specifically European developments, can be better interpreted by examining the quite specific factors that determined their origins. But an interpretation in the larger context of a "concatenation of circumstances" belonging to Europe's special path will likely yield even more: fresh insights into the causal connections among some of Europe's cultural phenomena, past and present. And so it makes good sense to carry on the debate about special paths on the broadest front possible.

The discussion about Europe's special path as a complex phenomenon nevertheless ought to proceed with another goal in mind. The present study is a provisional response, using comparative methods, to the question of the medieval foundations of this path. The cultures to which we compared Europe have only received partial treatment—an asymmetry that is, to be sure, a shortfall of the present study. We should aim for comparisons of aspects, and possibly for full, balanced comparisons as well. This is the kind of equilibration that research in social history and historical anthropology must work toward, in an effort to respond fully to the need for understanding in a global society that is growing ever more closely together.

Notes

In citing works in the notes, short titles are generally used. Frequently cited works are identified by the following abbreviations:

DI   Thomas Patrick Hughes, *A Dictionary of Islam* (Clifton, NJ, 1965)

ER   Mircea Eliade, ed., *The Encyclopedia of Religion*, 16 vols. (New York, 1987)

IL   Adel Theodor Khoury, Ludwig Hagemann, and Peter Heine, *Islam-Lexikon: Geschichte—Ideen—Gestalten*, 3 vols. (Freiburg im Briesgau, 1991)

LAO   Helmut Freydank, Walter F. Reineke, Maria Schetelich, and Thomas Thilo, *Lexikon Alter Orient: Ägypten, Indien, China, Vorderasien* (Wiesbaden, 1997)

RLAC *Das Reallexikon für Antike und Christentum*, 16 vols. (Stuttgart, 1994)

RLGA *Reallexikon der germanischen Altertumskunde*, 2nd ed., 35 vols. (Berlin, 1968–2007)

TRE   *Theologische Realenzyklopädie*, 38 vols., including indices (Berlin, 1977–2007)

INTRODUCTION

1. "Welche Verkettung von Umständen hat dazu geführt, daß gerade auf dem Boden des Okzidents, und nur hier, Kulturerscheinungen auftraten, welche doch—wie wenigstens wir uns gern vorstellen—in einer Entwicklungsrichtung von universeller Bedeutung und Gültigkeit lagen?" Max Weber, *Gesammelte Aufsätze zur Religionssoziologie* (1920; Tübingen, 1988), 1:1.

2. See William McNeill, *The Rise of the West: A History of the Human Community* (Chicago, 1963), or John A. Hall, *Powers and Liberties: The Causes and Consequences of the Rise of the West* (Oxford, 1985); Douglas C. North and Robert Paul Thomas, *The Rise of the Western World: A New Economic History* (Cambridge, 1973); Eric L. Jones, *The European Miracle: Environments, Economies and Geopolitics in the History of Europe and Asia*, 2nd ed. (Cambridge, 1987); Rolf Peter Sieferle, "Der europäische Sonderweg: Ursachen und Faktoren," in *Der europäische Sonderweg*, vol. 1 (Stuttgart, 2000). I chose the same concept for a preliminary study to the present volume, Michael Mitterauer, *Die Entwicklung Europas—ein Sonderweg? Legitimationsideologien und die Diskussion der Wissenschaft* [The development of Europe—a special path? Ideologies of legitimization and scholarly discourse] (Vienna, 1999).
3. Jürgen Osterhammel, "Sozialgeschichte im Zivilisationsvergleich: Zu künftigen Möglichkeiten komparativer Geschichtswissenschaft," *Geschichte und Gesellschaft* 22 (1996): 156.
4. Jacques Le Goff, "The Making of Europe (*Faire l'Europe/Europa bauen*)," introductions to various volumes of the series with the same name(s) (Munich, 1993ff.). For a detailed critique of this program see Mitterauer, *Die Entwicklung Europas*, 22ff.
5. For the current state of research see Sieferle, "Der europäische Sonderweg," 2ff.
6. Satish Saberwal, "On the Making of Europe: Reflections from Delhi," *History Workshop* 33 (1992): 146.
7. Michael Mitterauer, "Grundlagen politischer Berechtigung im mittelalterlichen Ständewesen," in *Der moderne Parlamentarismus und seine Grundlagen in der ständischen Repräsentation*, ed. Karl Bosl and Karl Möckl (Berlin, 1977), 11–42.
8. Most recently summarized in the section on the Middle Ages in the handbook by Andreas Gestrich et al., *Geschichte der Familie*, vol. 1 of *Europäische Kulturgeschichte* (Stuttgart, 2003), 60–363.
9. Jared Diamond, *Guns, Germs, and Steel: The Fates of Human Societies* (New York, 2003).
10. Michael Mitterauer, "Die Landwirtschaft und der 'Aufstieg Europas': Jared Diamonds Thesen als Forschungsimpuls," *Historische Anthropolgie* 8 (2000): 423–31.
11. Michael Mitterauer, "Roggen, Reis und Zuckerrohr: Drei Agrarrevolutionen des Mittelalters im Vergleich," *Saeculum* 52 (2001): 245–65.
12. Michael Mitterauer, "Der Krieg des Papstes," "Kreuzzüge," *Beiträge zur historischen Sozialkunde* 26, no. 3 (1996): 116–28, and "Predigt—Holzschnitt—Buchdruck," "Geschichte und Kommunikation," *Beiträge zur historischen Sozialkunde* 28, no. 2 (1998): 69–78.
13. Michael Mitterauer, "Religionen," in *Historische Anthropologie im südöstlichen Europa: Eine Einführung*, ed. Karl Kaser et al. (Vienna, 2003), 345–75.

14. Samuel Huntington argues along these lines in his *The Clash of Civilizations and the Remaking of World Order* (New York, 1996).
15. The problematics here have been discussed by Gerald Stourzh in his article "Statt eines Vorworts: Europa, aber wo liegt es?" in *Annäherungen an eine europäische Geschichtsschreibung*, ed. Gerald Stourzh (Vienna, 2002), ix–xx.
16. Michael Mitterauer, ed., "Ein europäischer Sonderweg? Mittelalterliche Grundlagen der Gesellschaftsentwicklung," special issue, *Beiträge zur historischen Sozialkunde* 27, no. 1 (1997).
17. Mitterauer, *Die Entwicklung Europas?* See note 2 above.
18. Weber, *Aufsätze zur Religionssoziologie*, 1:1ff.
19. Osterhammel, "Sozialgeschichte," 155ff.

CHAPTER ONE

1. Diamond, *Guns, Germs, and Steel*, esp. 110–11.
2. Lynn White Jr., *Medieval Technology and Social Change* (Oxford, 1962), 76–78.
3. Ibid., 39–78.
4. William N. Parker, "Agrarian and Industrial Revolutions," in *Revolution in History*, ed. Roy Porter and Mikuláš Teich (Cambridge, 1986): 167–85.
5. Andrew M. Watson, "The Arab Agricultural Revolution and Its Diffusion, 700–1100," *Journal of Economic History* 34, no. 1 (1974): 8–35; Dieter Kuhn, *Die Song-Dynastie (960–1279)* (Weinheim, 1987), 440.
6. Mitterauer, "Roggen, Reis und Zuckerrohr."
7. White, *Medieval Technology*, 39–78.
8. Mitterauer, "Roggen, Reis und Zuckerrohr," 248ff.
9. Alain Guerreau, "L'étude de l'économie médiévale: Genèse et problèmes actuels," in *Le Moyen Âge aujourdhui*, Cahiers du Léopard d'Or 7 (Paris, 1998), 46–47; Jean-Pierre Devroey, "La céréaliculture dans le monde franc," *Settimane di studio del Centro Italiano di Studi sull'Alto Medioevo* 37 (1990): 221–53; Jean-Pierre Devroey et al., eds. *Le seigle: Histoire et ethnologie* (Treignes, 1995); Georges Comet, "Technology and Agricultural Expansion in the Middle Ages: The Example of France North of the Loire," in *Medieval Farming and Technology: The Impact of Agricultural Change in Northwest Europe*, ed. Grenville Astill and John Langdon (Leiden, 1997), 16ff.; Alain Guerreau, *L'avenir d'un passé incertain* (Paris, 2001), 150ff.; "Getreide," *RLGA*, 12:8. Only in Europe did rye become the dominant grain crop; see Devroey, "Avant-propos," in Devroey et al., *Le seigle*, 6.
10. Udelgard Körber-Grohne, *Nutzpflanzen in Deutschland: Kulturgeschichte und Biologie* (Stuttgart, 1988), 41ff., 57ff.; Hansjörg Küster, "Rye," in *The Cambridge World History of Food*, ed. Kenneth F. Kiple and Kriemhild Coneè Ornelas (Cambridge, 2000), 1:151.

11. Guerreau, "L'étude," 47; Devroey, "Avant-propos," in Devroey et al., *Le seigle*, 5ff.

12. Devroey, "La céréaliculture," 240–41; Guerreau, "L'étude," 45ff; Jean-Pierre Devroey, "Entre Loire et Rhin: Les fluctuations du terroir de l'épeautre au moyen âge," in *L'épeautre* (Triticum spelta)*: Histoire et ethnologie*, ed. Jean-Pierre Devroey and J.-J. Van Mol (Brussels, 1989), 89–105; Körber-Grohne, *Nutzpflanzen*, 72ff.; "Getreide," *RLGA*, 12:8.

13. Körber-Grohne, *Nutzpflanzen*, 41, 60–61.

14. Hermann Aubin, "Die Römerzeit in Deutschland und ihr Fortwirken," in *Handbuch der deutschen Wirtschafts- und Sozialgeschichte*, ed. Hermann Aubin and Wolfgang Zorn (Stuttgart, 1971), 1:42; Devroey, "La céréaliculture," 231–32.

15. Guerreau, "L'étude," 46; Devroey, "Avant-propos," in Devroey et al., *Le seigle*, 6.

16. "Getreide," *RLGA*, 12:9.

17. Erich Zöllner, *Geschichte der Franken bis zur Mitte des sechsten Jahrhunderts* (Munich, 1970), 223.

18. François Sigaut, "De l'écobuage au pain d'épice: Quelques questions sur l'histoire du seigle," in Devroey et al., *Le seigle*, 215; Hélène Franconie, "Le seigle à travers les atlas linguistiques et ethnographiques romans," in ibid., 64–65.

19. Wilhelm Abel, "Landwirtschaft, 500–900," in Aubin and Zorn, *Handbuch*, 1:95–96.

20. "Bodennutzungssysteme," *RLGA*, 3:123

21. Abel, "Landwirtschaft," 96.

22. Norbert Benecke, *Der Mensch und seine Haustiere* (Stuttgart, 1994), 162–63.

23. White, *Medieval Technology*, 41–44; Dieter Hägermann, "Technik im frühen Mittelalter zwischen 500 und 1000," in *Landbau und Handwerk: 750 v. Chr. bis 1000 n. Chr.*, ed. Dieter Hägermann and Helmuth Schneider, Propyläen Technikgeschichte 1 (Berlin, 1991), 380ff.

24. Graeme Barker, *Prehistoric Farming in Europe* (Cambridge, 1985), 157.

25. Georges Raepsaet, "The Development of Farming Implements between the Seine and the Rhine from the Second to the Twelfth Centuries," in Astill and Langdon, *Medieval Farming*, 44.

26. Torsten Capelle, "Die Frühgeschichte (1.–9. Jahrhundert ohne römische Provinzen)," in *Deutsche Agrargeschichte: Vor und Frühgeschichte*, ed. Jens Lüning et al. (Stuttgart, 1997), 417; Werner Rösener, *Peasants in the Middle Ages*, trans. Alexander Stützer (Urbana, 1992), 107–8.

27. Helmut Birkhan, *Kelten: Versuch einer Gesamtdarstellung ihrer Kultur* (Vienna, 1997), 1102.

28. White, *Medieval Technology*, 49.

29. Ibid., 59–61; for a differentiating view cf. Hägermann, "Technik im frühen Mittelalter," 400; further to this point see Ann Hyland, *The Horse in the Middle Ages* (Stroud, 1999), 42, 44.

30. Marc Bloch, "The Advent and Triumph of the Watermill," in *Land and Work in Medieval Europe: Selected Papers by Marc Bloch*, trans. J. E. Anderson (London, 1967), 136–68; White, *Medieval Technology*, 79–81; Terry S. Reynolds, *Stronger than a Hundred Men: A History of the Vertical Water Wheel* (Baltimore, 1983), 9–26; Dietrich Lohrmann, "Bedarf und Angebot von Wasserkraft in frühen Siedlungen und Städten," *Saeculum* 42 (1991): 262–65; "Innovationen, technische," *LMA*, 5, col. 430; "Mühle, Müller," *LMA*, 6, cols. 885.

31. Reynolds, *Stronger than a Hundred Men*, 34, 44–45; Helmut Schneider, "Die Gaben des Prometheus: Technik im antiken Mittelmeerraum zwischen 750 v. Chr und 500 n. Chr.," in Hägermann and Schneider, *Landbau und Handwerk*, 309. For Italy as a region where the dry mill came to be dominant, see Karl-Heinz Ludwig, "Technik im hohen Mittelalter zwischen 1000 und 1350/1400," in *Metalle und Macht: 1000 bis 1600*, ed. Karl-Heinz Ludwig and Volker Schmidtchen, Propyläen Technikgeschichte 2 (Berlin, 1992), 105. But the landscape of Lombardy was heavily dotted with water mills by the eighth century; see Hägermann, "Technik im frühen Mittelalter," 366. The importance of various economic and ecological conditions for the distribution of the horizontal and vertical mills was emphasized by Paolo Squatriti in his *Water and Society in Early Medieval Italy, AD 400–1000* (Cambridge, 1998), 136, 139.

32. "Mühle, Müller," *LMA*, 6, col. 886. See also Roberta Magnusson and Paolo Squatriti, "The Technologies of Water in Medieval Italy," in *Working with Water in Medieval Europe: Technology and Resource-Use*, ed. Paolo Squatriti (Leiden, 2000), 262. On the vertical mill's supremacy in northern France, see Paul Benoit and Joséphine Rouillard, "Medieval Hydraulics in France," in ibid., 204.

33. Sigaut, "De l'écobuage," 216.

34. Devroey, "La céréaliculture," 242; Dietrich Lohrmann, "Antrieb von Getreidemühlen," in *Europäische Technik im Mittelalter, 800–1400: Tradition und Innovation, ein Handbuch*, ed. Uta Lindgren, 3rd ed. (Berlin, 1998), 221–32.

35. Zöllner, *Geschichte der Franken*, 223–24.

36. Jean Gimpel, *The Medieval Machine: The Industrial Revolution of the Middle Ages*, 2nd ed. (Aldershot, 1988), 10–12; Reynolds, *Stronger than a Hundred Men*, 49–51, particularly the map on page 50; Hägermann, "Technik im frühen Mittelalter," 347; Dietrich Lohrmann, "Le moulin à eau dans le cadre de l'économie rurale de la Neustrie," in *La Neustrie: Les pays au nord de la Loire de 650 à 850*, ed. Hartmut Atsma (Sigmaringen, 1989), 370ff.

37. White, *Medieval Technology*, 84.

38. Massimo Montanari, *The Culture of Food*, trans. Carl Ipsen (Oxford, 1993), 30–33.

39. Abel, "Landwirtschaft," 97ff.; Reynolds, *Stronger than a Hundred Men*, 107; Hägermann, "Technik im frühen Mittelalter," 358; Lohrmann, "Antrieb

von Getreidemühlen," 226. For other social conditions relating to the water mill in early medieval Italy see Squatriti, *Water and Society*, 136.

40. Guerreau, "L'étude," 48, following Sigaut, "De l'écobuage," 222.

41. Quoted from Hägermann, "Technik im frühen Mittelalter," 394.

42. Werner Rösener, *Einführung in die Agrargeschichte* (Darmstadt, 1997), 91. [*Plaggendüngung*, plaggen manuring, fertilizing with slurry-soaked peat—Trans.]

43. Karl Kaser, *Macht und Erbe: Männerherrschaft, Besitz und Familie im östlichen Europa (1500–1900)* (Vienna, 2000), 244ff.; Colin White, *Russia and America: The Roots of Economic Divergence* (London, 1987), 58–60; "Bauer, Bauerntum," *LMA*, 1, cols. 1592, 1597.

44. White, *Medieval Technology*, 69–70.

45. Albert Jockenhövel, "Agrargeschichte der Bronzezeit und vorrömischen Eisenzeit," in Lüning et al., *Deutsche Agrargeschichte*, 208.

46. Ivan Balassa, "Einleitung," in *Getreidebau in Mittel- und Osteuropa*, ed. Ivan Balassa (Budapest, 1972), 12, also 127, 136, 139.

47. Ibid., 15; Carsten Goehrke, *Frühzeit des Ostslaventums* (Darmstadt, 1992), 111ff.

48. Joachim Herrmann, "Die Slaven der Völkerwanderungszeit," in *Welt der Slaven: Geschichte, Gesellschaft, Kultur*, ed. Joachim Herrmann (Munich, 1986), 33ff.

49. Robert Bartlett, *The Making of Europe: Conquest, Colonization, and Cultural Change, 950–1350* (Princeton, 1993), 149–52.

50. Küster, "Rye," 1:149; E. J. T. Collins, "Rye in Britain," in Devroey et al., *Le seigle*, 119. In the laws of Wihtraed, king of Kent (690–725), the month of August is called "ragun," that is, "Roggenmonat," "rye-month," in ibid., 120.

51. Bruce M. S. Campbell, "Ecology versus Economics in Late Thirteenth- and Early Fourteenth-Century English Agriculture," in *Agriculture in the Middle Ages: Technology, Practice, and Representation*, ed. Del Sweeney (Philadelphia, 1995), 82–83.

52. Nerys Thomas Patterson, *Cattle-Lords and Clansmen: The Social Structure of Early Ireland*, 2nd ed. (Notre Dame, 1994), 63–82.

53. Ibid., 67.

54. "Getreide," *LMA*, 4, cols. 1414ff.

55. Montanari, *Culture of Food*, 30–31.

56. "Getreide," *LMA*, 4, col. 1415.

57. White, *Medieval Technology*, 42–43; Sigaut, "De l'écobuage," 216.

58. Körber-Grohne, *Nutzpflanzen*, 454.

59. "Garten," *LMA*, 4, col. 1123.

60. Diamond, *Guns, Germs, and Steel*, 133–34; Barker, *Prehistoric Farming*, 60.

61. For the potential limits to planting see the map in Barker, *Prehistoric Farming*, 45.

62. Montanari, *Culture of Food*, 15–20.

63. "Ernährung," *LMA*, 3, col. 2162.

64. Guerreau, "L'étude," 49.

65. Montanari, *Culture of Food*, 47–51.

66. Michel Kaplan, *Les hommes et la terre à Byzance du VIe au XIe siècle: Propriété et exploitation du sol* (Paris, 1992), 69ff.

67. Ibid., 465, 29–30.

68. Ibid., 86–87.

69. Ibid., 86, 576.

70. Ibid., 87, 581.

71. Watson, "Arab Agricultural Revolution," 8–35.

72. K. N. Chaudhuri, "The Economy in Muslim Societies," in *The Cambridge Illustrated History of the Islamic World*, ed. Francis Robinson (Cambridge, 1996), 151–52.

73. Kaplan, *Les hommes*, 69.

74. For earlier Byzantine Sicily during Islamic times, see Bernd Rill, *Sizilien im Mittelalter: Das Reich der Araber, Normannen und Staufer* (Darmstadt, 1995), 84–85. For this kind of favorable taxation in general, see Andrew S. Ehrenkreutz, "The Silent Force behind the Rise of Medieval Islamic Civilization," in *The Islamic World from Classical to Modern Times: Essays in Honor of Bernard Lewis*, ed. C. E. Bosworth et al. (Princeton, 1989), 123.

75. Andrew M. Watson, *Agricultural Innovation in the Early Islamic World: The Diffusion of Crops and Farming Techniques, 700–1100* (Cambridge, 1983), 87–98.

76. See the map in ibid., 79.

77. See Mitterauer, "Roggen, Reis und Zuckerrohr," 248–49, following Watson's "Arab Agricultural Revolution" and his *Agricultural Innovation*.

78. Thomas F. Glick and Helena Kirchner, "Hydraulic Systems and Technologies of Islamic Spain: History and Archeology," in Squatriti, *Working with Water*, 267, 276, 281–92, 313.

79. Richard J. Bulliet, *The Camel and the Wheel* (Cambridge, MA, 1973).

80. Maurice Lombard, *L'Islam dans sa première grandeur (VIIIe–XIe siècle)* (Paris, 1971), translated by Joan Spencer as *The Golden Age of Islam* (Princeton, 2005). On the reasons for the decline in general, see Jean-Claude Garcin, "The Mamlūk Military System and the Blocking of Medieval Moslem Society," in *Europe and the Rise of Capitalism*, ed. Jean Baechler et al. (Oxford, 1988), 128.

81. See also Mitterauer, "Roggen, Reis und Zuckerrohr," 246ff.

82. Johannes Müller, *Kulturlandschaft China: Anthropogene Gestaltung der Landschaft durch Landnutzung und Siedlung* (Gotha, 1997), 63–64; Joel Mokyr, *The Lever of Riches: Technological Creativity and Economic Progress* (Oxford, 1990), 209–10, 222.

83. Francesca Bray, *The Rice Economies: Technology and Development in Asian Societies* (Berkeley, 1986), 203; Angela Schottenhammer, "China und Ostasien im Jahre 1000," *Periplus: Jahrbuch für außereuropäische Geschichte* 10

(2000): 31–32; Mark Elvin, *The Pattern of the Chinese Past* (Stanford, 1973), 113–24; Herbert Franke and Rolf Trauzettel, *Das Chinesische Kaiserreich*, Fischer Weltgeschichte 19 (Frankfurt am Main, 1968), 151, 248; Kuhn, *Song-Dynastie*, 152; Müller, *Kulturlandschaft China*, 62ff.

84. Mitterauer, "Roggen, Reis und Zuckerrohr," 252ff.
85. Bray, *Rice Economies*, 46–48.
86. Müller, *Kulturlandschaft China*, 47ff.; Elvin, *Chinese Past*, 118.
87. Benecke, *Der Mensch und seine Haustiere*, 287.
88. White, *Medieval Technology*, 81–82
89. Franke and Trauzettel, *Das Chinesische Kaiserreich*, 162; Hans Steininger, "Der Buddhismus in der chinesischen Geschichte des Mittelalters," *Saeculum* 13 (1962): 150. Steininger also treats the beginnings of early Chinese capitalism with respect to mills and other industrial and mercantile facilities in Buddhist monasteries.
90. Reynolds, *Stronger than a Hundred Men*, 116–17.
91. Müller, *Kulturlandschaft China*, 26ff.
92. Kuhn, *Song-Dynastie*, 143ff.; Schottenhammer, "China und Ostasien," 31ff.; Elvin, *Chinese Past*, 121–24.
93. Müller, *Kulturlandschaft China*, 64ff.
94. Ibid., 64; E[ric] L. Jones, *Growth Recurring: Economic Change in World History* (Oxford,1988), 33; Jones, *European Miracle*, 232.
95. Watson, *Agricultural Innovation*, 129–34; Jerry L. Bentley, "Hemispheric Integration, 500–1500 C.E.," *Journal of World History* 9 (1998): 248.
96. J. C. Russell, "Die Bevölkerung Europas, 500–1500," in *Europäische Wirtschaftsgeschichte*, ed. Carlo M. Cipolla and Knut Borchardt (Stuttgart, 1985), 1:21. See also Christopher Dyer, "Medieval Farming and Technology: Conclusion," in Astill and Langdon, *Medieval Farming*, 302.
97. Jones, *European Miracle*, 4.
98. Montanari, *Culture of Food*, 29–30.
99. Abel, "Landwirtschaft," 100; Lohrmann, "Antrieb von Getreidemühlen," 221.
100. Abel, "Landwirtschaft," 105.
101. Reynolds, *Stronger than a Hundred Men*, 119–20.
102. "Mühle, Müller," *LMA*, 6, col. 890, differing from Glick and Kirchner, "Hydraulic Systems," 311–12.
103. "Nockenwelle," *LMA*, 6, col. 1213; Benoit and Rouillard, "Medieval Hydraulics," 204; Lohrmann, "Antrieb von Getreidemühlen," 226.
104. Gimpel, *The Medieval Machine*, 13–16; Johannes Mager et al., *Die Kulturgeschichte der Mühlen* (Tübingen, 1989), 18ff.; Reynolds, *Stronger than a Hundred Men*, 69–79, 94; Ludwig, "Technik im hohen Mittelalter," 82ff.; "Innovationen, technische," *LMA*, 5, col. 430.
105. Lukas Clemens and Michael Matheus, "Die Walkmühle," in Lindgren, *Europäische Technik*, 233.

106. Gimpel, *The Medieval Machine*, 42ff.; Mager et al., *Die Kulturgeschichte der Mühlen*, 44; Christoph Bartels, "Der Bergbau—im Zentrum das Silber," in Lindgren, *Europäische Technik*, 235ff.; Ludwig, "Technik im hohen Mittelalter," 70.

107. Glick and Kirchner, "Hydraulic Systems," 267, 276, 281–92, 313.

108. Ibid., 311–13.

109. "Mühle, Müller," *LMA*, 6, col. 886; Gimpel *The Medieval Machine*, 23–24; Ludwig, "Technik im hohen Mittelalter," 98ff.

110. Watson, "Arab Agricultural Revolution," 23–26; Watson, *Agricultural Innovation*, 99–102.

111. Müller, *Kulturlandschaft China*, 64; Kuhn, *Song-Dynastie*, 148; Elvin, *Chinese Past*, 114–24.

112. Bulliet, *The Camel and the Wheel*.

113. Franco Cardini, *Alle radici della cavalleria medievale* (Florence, 1997), 260ff., esp. 267. Detailed data for the consumption of oats per horse during mobilizations in medieval England can be found in Michael Prestwich, *Armies and Warfare in the Middle Ages: The English Experience* (New Haven, 1996), 247–48.

114. Werner Rösener, *The Peasantry of Europe*, trans. Thomas M. Barker (Oxford, 1994), 42–44.

CHAPTER TWO

1. "Villikation," *LMA*, 8, col. 1694; "Grundherrschaft II," *LMA*, 4, col. 1742.

2. "Hufe," *LMA*, 5, cols. 154ff.

3. "Grundherrschaft III, c," *LMA*, 4, cols. 1746–47.

4. "Grundeigentum," *RLGA*, 13:104.

5. Karl Bosl, "Die 'Familia' als Grundstruktur der mittelalterlichen Gesellschaft," *Zeitschrift für bayerische Landesgeschichte* 38 (1975): 403–24; "familia," *LMA*, 4, cols. 254–55.

6. Adriaan Verhulst, "La genèse du régime domanial classique en France au haut moyen âge," *Settimane di studio del Centro Italiano di Studi sull'Alto Medioevo* 13 (1966): 135–60.

7. Devroey, "La céréaliculture," 249.

8. Birkhan, *Kelten*, 1100.

9. "Grundherrschaft II," *LMA*, 4, col. 1741; Ernst Pitz, *Die griechisch-römische Ökumene und die drei Kulturen des Mittelalters: Geschichte des mediterranen Weltteils zwischen Atlantik und dem Indischen Ozean, 270–812* (Berlin, 2001), 362–63.

10. Jochen Martin, *Spätantike und Völkerwanderung* (Munich, 1987), 61ff., 173ff.

11. Ibid., 61.

12. "Kolone," *LMA*, 4, col. 1271.

13. "Gynäceum," *LMA*, 4, col. 1811.

14. Karl Brunner, "Continuity and Discontinuity of Roman Agricultural Knowledge in the Early Middle Ages," in Sweeney, *Agriculture*, 25.

15. Abel, "Landwirtschaft," 106.

16. Helmut Bender, "Agrargeschichte Deutschlands in der römischen Kaiserzeit innerhalb der Grenzen des Imperium Romanum," in Lüning et al., *Deutsche Agrargeschichte*, 283.

17. Hans Jürgen Nitz, "Siedlungsstrukturen der königlichen und adeligen Grundherrschaft der Karolingerzeit—der Beitrag der historisch-genetischen Siedlungsgeographie," in *Strukturen der Grundherrschaft im frühen Mittelalter*, ed. Werner Rösener (Göttingen, 1989), 439ff.; Johann-Bernhard Haversath, "Ländliche Siedlungen in hessischen Altsiedelräumen," in *Siedlungsforschung: Archäologie—Geschichte—Geographie* 17 (1999): 36ff.

18. Abel, "Landwirtschaft," 105; Hyland, *The Horse*, 12.

19. "Getreidespeicherung," *RLGA*, 12:24.

20. Harald von Petrikovits, "L'économie rurale à l'époque romaine en Germanie inférieure et dans la région de Trèves," "Villa—Curtis—Grangia," *Beihefte der Francia* 11 (1983): 9.

21. Martin, *Spätantike und Völkerwanderung*, 5.

22. "Grundeigentum," *RLGA*, 13:104; "Grundherrschaft," ibid., 3ff.; Heinrich Dannenbauer, "Adel, Burg und Herrschaft bei den Germanen," *Historisches Jahrbuch* 61 (1941): 16–17.

23. Bender, "Agrargeschichte Deutschlands," 305–6.

24. Herwig Wolfram, *Die Germanen* (Munich, 1995), 109; Erich Zöllner, *Die Franken* (Munich, 1970), 190ff.

25. Martin, *Spätantike und Völkerwanderung*, 5.

26. Wolfgang Metz, *Das karolingische Reichsgut* (Berlin, 1960), 101.

27. Joris Peters, *Römische Tierhaltung und Tierzucht* (Rahden, Westphalia, 1998), 325ff.

28. Martin, *Spätantike und Völkerwanderung*, 67.

29. Abel, "Landwirtschaft," 105–6; Metz, *Reichsgut*, 84ff.

30. Georges Comet, *Le paysan et son outil* (Rome, 1992), 416ff.; Lohrmann, "Antrieb von Getreidemühlen," 225.

31. "Bier- und Brauwesen," *LMA*, 2, cols. 135ff.

32. Benoit and Rouillard, "Medieval Hydraulics," 170.

33. Metz, *Reichsgut*.

34. "Pfalz, Palast," *LMA*, 6, cols. 1993ff.

35. Hans Jürgen Nitz, "Zur Erforschung der frühmittelalterlichen Besiedlung im Raum zwischen Ostharz und jenseits der Saale, mit einem Ausblick auf Thüringen," *Siedlungsforschung: Archäologie—Geschichte—Geographie* 15 (1997): 290–91.

36. Metz, *Reichsgut*, 223.

37. Arnold Angenendt, *Geschichte der Religiosität im Mittelalter* (Darmstadt, 1997), 678; Karl Suso Frank, *Geschichte des christlichen Mönchtums* (Darmstadt, 1993), 56.

38. "Memoria," *LMA*, 6, col. 512.

39. Arnold Angenendt, *Das Frühmittelalter* (Stuttgart, 1990), 413.

40. Frank, *Geschichte des christlichen Mönchtums*, 59.

41. "Grundherrschaft," *LMA*, 6, cols. 1743ff.

42. Ibid., 1745; Rösener, *Peasants*, 19.

43. See also chapter 4.

44. Rösener, *Peasants*, 225.

45. Werner Rösener, "Strukturen und Wandlungen des Dorfes in Altsiedellandschaften," *Siedlungsforschung: Archäologie—Geschichte—Geographie* 17 (1999): 17; Erich Schrader, *Das Befestigungsrecht in Deutschland von den Anfängen bis zum Beginn des 14. Jahrhunderts* (Göttingen, 1909).

46. Marc Bloch, "The Rise of Dependent Cultivation and Seignorial Institutions," in *The Cambridge Economic History of Europe*, 2nd ed. (Cambridge, 1966), 1:239; Wilhelm Ebel, "Zur Rechtsgeschichte der Gemeinde in Ostfriesland," in *Die Anfänge der Landgemeinde und ihr Wesen*, ed. Konstanzer Arbeitskreis für mittelalterliche Geschichte, Vorträge und Forschungen 7-8 (Sigmaringen, 1986), 1:306-7; Heinz Stoob, "Landesbau und Gemeindebildung an der Nordseeküste im Mittelalter," in ibid., 1:368ff., 416; Adriaan Verhulst, "Die Binnenkolonisation und die Anfänge der Landgemeinde in Seeflandern," in ibid., 1:447ff.

47. "Friesen, Friesland," *LMA*, 4, col. 971.

48. Patterson, *Cattle-Lords*, 150-80.

49. Ibid., 162.

50. Ibid., 161-73.

51. Ibid., 155-61.

52. Ibid., 199, 63.

53. Bartlett, *Making of Europe*, 21.

54. Rosamond Faith, *The English Peasantry and the Growth of Lordship* (London, 1997), 76-77.

55. Ibid., 113.

56. "Manor," *LMA*, 6, cols. 197-98.

57. "Hufe," *RLGA*, 15:191.

58. T. M. Charles-Edwards, "Kinship, Status and the Origins of the Hide," *Past and Present* 56, no. 1 (1972): 3-7.

59. Faith, *English Peasantry*, 95-99.

60. Hans Jürgen Nitz, "Introduction from Above: Intentional Spread of Common-Field Systems by Feudal Authorities through Colonization and Reorganization," in *Allgemeine und vergleichende Siedlungsgeographie* (Berlin, 1998), 304-6.

61. Faith, *English Peasantry*, 18.

62. "Ostsiedlung, deutsche," *LMA*, 6, cols. 1545–46.

63. Martin Born, *Die Entwicklung der deutschen Agrarlandschaft* (Darmstadt, 1974), 32; Haversath, "Ländliche Siedlungen," 35.

64. Nitz, "Introduction from Above," 290ff.; Nitz, "Zur Erforschung," 249ff.

65. "Landesausbau und Kolonisation," *LMA*, 5, cols. 1649–50.

66. Michael Mitterauer, "Ostkolonisation und Familienverfassung," in *Vilfanov zbornik: Pravo–zgodovina–narod*, ed. Vincenc Rajšp and Ernst Bruckmüller (Ljubljana, 1999), 203–22.; Kaser, *Macht und Erbe*, 60ff.; "Landesausbau und Kolonisation," *LMA*, 5, cols. 1649–50.

67. Werner Conze, *Agrarverfassung und Bevölkerung in Litauen und Weißrussland* (Leipzig, 1950); Nitz, "Introduction from Above," 292.

68. Bartlett, *Making of Europe*, 152.

69. Ibid., 152–56.

70. "Landesausbau und Kolonisation," *LMA*, 5, cols. 1650–51.

71. Paul Johansen, "Einige Funktionen und Formen mittelalterlicher Landgemeinden in Estland und Finnland," in *Die Anfänge der Landgemeinde*, 2:289ff.

72. "Pelzgeld," *LMA*, 6, col. 1668; "Tribut," *LMA*, 8, col. 987.

73. Manfred Hellmann, "Zum Problem der ostslawischen Landgemeinde," in *Die Anfänge der Landgemeinde*, 2:269ff.; Johansen, "Einige Funktionen," 300.

74. Birkhan, *Kelten*, 1019; "Gastung," *LMA*, 4, cols. 1137–38; "Fodrum," *LMA*, 4, cols. 601–2.

75. "Dienstsiedlungen," *LMA*, 3, cols. 1006–7.

76. Goehrke, *Frühzeit des Ostslaventums*, 112.

77. Ibid.

78. "Bobbio," *LMA*, 2, cols. 295–96.

79. "Nonantola," *LMA*, 6, col. 1232.

80. Vito Fumagalli, *Mensch und Umwelt im Mittelalter* (Berlin, 1992), 61.

81. Eduard Hlawitschka, *Franken, Alemannen, Bayern und Burgunder in Oberitalien (774–962)* (Freiburg, 1960), 30–31.

82. Fumagalli, *Mensch und Umwelt*, 67–68.

83. "Grundherrschaft," *LMA*, 4, col. 1748.

84. "Bauer, Bauerntum," *LMA*, 1, col. 1599.

85. "Sklave," *LMA*, 7, col. 1983; Kaplan, *Les hommes*, 159.

86. Martin, *Spätantike und Völkerwanderung*, 61; "Adscriptio glebae," *LMA*, 1, cols. 168–69.

87. Kaplan, *Les hommes*, 114, 158, 238.

88. Georg Ostrogorsky, *Byzantinische Geschichte 324–1453* (Munich, 1963), 15.

89. "Großgrundbesitz," *LMA*, 4, cols. 1730ff.; "Feudalismus," *LMA*, 4, cols. 415ff.; "Bauer," *LMA*, 1, col. 1601; Ostrogorsky, *Byzantinische Geschichte*, 275ff.

90. Chris Wickham, "The Uniqueness of the East," in Baechler et al., *Europe and the Rise of Capitalism*, 81–82.

91. "Pronoia," *LMA*, 7, col. 249; Peter Feldbauer, *Die islamische Welt, 600–1250* (Vienna, 1995), 452.

92. Feldbauer, *Die islamische Welt*, 75.

93. On the social foundations of the agrarian revolution in Islamic Spain, see Glick and Kirchner, "Hydraulic Systems," 267–329.

94. Wickham, "Uniqueness of the East," 79–82.

95. Ibid., 70.

96. Elvin, *Chinese Past*, 69–83.

97. Ibid., 83; Kuhn, *Song-Dynastie*, 200.

98. Weber, *Religionssoziologie*, 1:352.

99. Kuhn, *Song-Dynastie*, 201.

100. Bray, *Rice Economies*, 55; Franke and Trauzettel, *Das Chinesische Kaiserreich*, 183, 142.

101. Gudula Linck, *Frau und Familie in China* (Munich, 1988), 84.

102. Ibid.

103. "Sklave," *LMA*, 7, col. 1977.

104. Otto Hintze, "Wesen und Verbreitung des Feudalismus," *Staat und Verfassung: Gesammelte Abhandlungen zur allgemeinen Verfassungsgeschichte* (Göttingen, 1970), 84ff.

105. Rösener, *Peasantry of Europe*, 42; Tilman Struve, "Die mittelalterlichen Grundlagen des modernen Europa," *Saeculum* 41 (1990): 106.

106. For the significance of this concept for research, see Janet Carsten and Stephen Hugh-Jones, introduction to *About the House: Lévi-Strauss and Beyond*, ed. Janet Carsten and Stephen Hugh-Jones (Cambridge, 1995), esp. 6–21.

CHAPTER THREE

1. David Herlihy, *Medieval Households*, Studies in Cultural History (Cambridge, MA, 1985), 68–72.

2. Ludolf Kuchenbuch, *Bäuerliche Gesellschaft und Klosterherrschaft im 9. Jahrhundert* (Wiesbaden, 1978), 78–79; Carl I. Hammer, "Family and *familia* in Early-Medieval Bavaria," in *Family Forms in Historic Europe*, ed. Richard Wall et al. (Cambridge, 1983), 217–48, esp. 244.

3. Pierre Guichard and Jean-Pierre Cuvillier, "Barbarian Europe," in *Distant Worlds, Ancient Worlds*, vol. 1 of *A History of the Family*, ed. André Burguière et al., trans. Sarah Hanbury Tenison et al. (Cambridge, MA, 1996), 75.

4. Herlihy, *Medieval Households*, 72.

5. Kaser, *Macht und Erbe*, 60ff.

6. John Hajnal, "European Marriage Patterns in Perspective," in *Population in History: Essays in Historical Demography*, ed. D. V. Glass and D. E. C. Eversley (London, 1965), 101–43.

7. Further to this concept see, for example, Maria Todorova, "Zum erkenntnistheoretischen Wert von Familienmodellen: Der Balkan und die

'europäische Familie,'" in *Historische Familienforschung: Ergebnisse und Kontroversen*, ed. Josef Ehmer et al. (Frankfurt am Main, 1997), 283–300.

8. Jack Goody, *The European Family: An Historico-Anthropological Essay* (Oxford, 2000), 64–66.

9. Massimo Livi Bacci, *The Population of Europe: A History*, trans. Cynthia De Nardi Ipsen and Carl Ipsen (Oxford, 1999), 102–3.

10. Beatrice Moring, "Marriage and Social Change in South-Western Finland, 1700–1870," *Continuity and Change* 11 (1996): 91–113.

11. Herlihy, *Medieval Households*, 72.

12. John Hajnal, "Two Kinds of Pre-industrial Household Formation System," in Wall et al., *Family Forms*, 65–104; Peter Laslett, "Family and Household as Work Group and Kin Group: Areas of Traditional Europe Compared," in ibid., 513–63.

13. Hajnal, "Two Kinds of Pre-industrial Household," 66.

14. Laslett, "Family and Household," 525–28, and "Characteristics of the Western Family Considered over Time," in *Family Life and Illicit Love in Earlier Generations: Essays in Historical Sociology* (Cambridge, 1977), 12–49.

15. Laslett, "Characteristics of the Western Family," 13.

16. Hammer, "Family and *familia*," 245.

17. Examples in Michael Mitterauer, "Sozialgeschichte der Familie als landesgeschichtlicher Forschungsgegenstand," in *Historisch-anthropologische Familienforschung* (Vienna, 1990), 191ff., esp. the plates.

18. Herlihy, *Medieval Households*, 76–77.

19. Ibid., 78.

20. Solvi Sogner and Jacques Dupâquier, introduction to *Marriage and Remarriage in Populations of the Past*, ed. Jacques Dupâquier et al. (London, 1981), 3–10 et passim; Michael Mitterauer, "Formen der ländlichen Familienwirtschaft im österreichischen Raum," in *Familienstruktur und Arbeitsorganisation in ländlichen Gesellschaften*, ed. Josef Ehmer and Michael Mitterauer (Vienna, 1986), 315.

21. Laslett, "Family and Household," 527.

22. Herlihy, *Medieval Households*, 69; Hammer, "Family and *familia*," 246; Kuchenbuch, *Bäuerliche Gesellschaft*, 78–79.

23. Michael Mitterauer, "Gesindedienst und Jugendphase im europäischen Vergleich," *Geschichte und Gesellschaft* 11 (1985), 197–98.

24. David Gaunt, "The Property and Kin Relationships of Retired Farmers in Northern and Central Europe," in Wall et al., *Family Forms*, 249–79.

25. Hammer, "Family and *familia*," 246. On these "other-directed" forms of passing on property and its effects on forms of lending, right of inheritance, and population development, see Wilhelm Brauneder, "Typen mittelalterlichen Erbrechts in ihrer Bedeutung für die Bevölkerungsentwicklung," *Saeculum* 39 (1988): 155.

26. Kaser, *Macht und Erbe*, 68–69.

27. Ibid., 48ff.
28. Rösener, *Peasants*, 191–93.
29. Kaser, *Macht und Erbe*, 55.
30. Ibid., 76ff.
31. Peter Laslett, introduction to *Household and Family in Past Time*, ed. Peter Laslett and Richard Wall (Cambridge, 1972), 23.
32. Michael Mitterauer, "Zur Familienstruktur in ländlichen Gebieten Österreichs im 17. Jahrhundert," in *Familie und Arbeitsteilung: Historisch vergleichende Studien* (Vienna, 1992), 154ff.
33. Konrad Kunze, *dtv-Atlas Namenkunde: Vor- und Familiennamen im deutschen Sprachgebiet* (Munich, 1998), 59ff.
34. Robert T. Anderson, "Changing Kinship in Europe," *Kroeber Anthropological Society* 28, no. 1 (1963): 1–47; Jack Goody, *The Development of the Family and Marriage in Europe* (Cambridge, 1983); Michael Mitterauer, "Die Terminologie der Verwandtschaft: Zu mittelalterlichen Grundlagen von Wandel und Beharrung im europäischen Vergleich," *Ethnologia Balkanica* 4 (2000): 11–43.
35. Anderson, "Changing Kinship," 10; Goody, *The Development of the Family*, 264.
36. Anderson, "Changing Kinship," 10; Goody, *The Development of the Family*, 263.
37. Anderson, "Changing Kinship," 19–20; Goody, *The Development of the Family*, 264.
38. Germán Ruipérez, *Die strukturelle Umschichtung der Verwandtschaftsbezeichnungen im Deutschen* (Marburg, 1984), 83, 43ff.
39. Goody, *The Development of the Family*, 272; Kirsten Hastrup, *Island of Anthropology: Studies in Past and Present Iceland*, Studies in Northern Civilization 5 (Odense, 1990), 47.
40. Anderson, "Changing Kinship," 12–15; Paul Friedrich, "An Evolutionary Sketch of Russian Kinship," *Proceedings of the Annual Spring Meeting of the American Sociological Society* (n.p., 1963), 1–26.
41. Karl Kaser, *Familie und Verwandtschaft auf dem Balkan* (Vienna, 1995), 170ff.
42. Goody, *The Development of the Family*, 270; Giorgio Raimondo Cardona, "I nomi della parentela," in *La famiglia italiana dall'Ottocento a oggi*, ed. Piero Melograni (Rome, 1988), 287–325.
43. Anderson, "Changing Kinship," 29.
44. Joseph H. Lynch, *Godparents and Kinship in Early Medieval Europe* (Princeton, 1986), 333; Agnès Fine, *Parrains, marraines: La parenté spirituelle en Europe* (Paris, 1994); Goody, *The Development of the Family*, 194–206.
45. Bernhard Jussen, *Patenschaft und Adoption im frühen Mittelalter* (Göttingen, 1991), 136.
46. Fine, *Parrains*, 67.

47. Anderson, "Changing Kinship," 29.

48. Michael Mitterauer, "Christentum und Endogamie," in Mitterauer, *Historisch-anthropologische Familienforschung*, 41–86.

49. Angenendt, *Geschichte der Religiosität*, 269–70.

50. Ibid., 299.

51. Michael Mitterauer, "'Und sie ließen ihren Vater zurück . . .': Die Schwäche der Ahnenbindung im Christentum als Voraussetzung des europäischen Sonderwegs der Familien- und Gesellschaftsentwicklung," in Michael Mitterauer, *Dimensionen des Heiligen: Annäherungen eines Historikers* (Vienna, 2000), 214–27.

52. Günter Kehrer, *Einführung in die Religionssoziologie* (Darmstadt, 1988), 139.

53. Angenendt, *Geschichte der Religiosität*, 298–99; "Haus," *RLAC*, 13:856, 878.

54. Cardona, "I nomi della parentela," 298–99.

55. "Bruder," *RLAC*, 2:631ff.

56. For greater detail, see Michael Mitterauer, "Entwicklungstendenzen von Verwandtschaft und Familie im Mittelalter," in *Geschichte der Familie*, ed. Andreas Gestrich, Jens-Uwe Krause, and Michael Mitterauer, *Europäische Kulturgeschichte* 1 (Stuttgart, 2003), 160–263.

57. Kaser, *Macht und Erbe*, and *Familie und Verwandtschaft*, passim.

58. Paul Frauenstädt, *Blutrache und Totschlagsühne im deutschen Mittelalter* (Leipzig, 1881).

59. Julius Bardach, "L'indivision familiale dans les pays du Centre-Est européen," in *Famille et parenté dans l'Occident médiéval*, ed. Georges Duby and Jacques Le Goff (Rome, 1977), 335–53; Kaser, *Macht und Erbe*, 114–15; Reinhard Wenskus, *Stammesbildung und Verfassung: Das Werden der frühmittelalterlichen gentes*, 2nd ed. (Cologne, 1977), 325, and "Kleinverbände und Kleinräume bei den Prußen des Samlandes," in *Die Anfänge der Landgemeinde*, 2:242ff., 251; Matthias Hardt, "Das 'slawische Dorf' und seine kolonisationszeitliche Umformung nach schriftlichen und historisch-geographischen Quellen," *Siedlungsforschung: Archäologie— Geschichte—Geographie* 17 (1999): 269–91. A particularly detailed example of a church parish replacing a descent group's cemetery with its own is in Andrej Pleterski, "Die Methode der Verknüpfung der retrogressiven Katasteranalyse mit schriftlichen und archäologischen Quellen," *Siedlungsforschung: Archäologie—Geschichte—Geographie* 13 (1995): 271ff. On differences and changes in burial practices in general, see "Grab, -formen, -mal," *LMA*, 4, cols. 1621–22.

60. Eve Levin, *Sex and Society in the World of the Orthodox Slavs, 900–1700* (Ithaca, 1989), 136–59.

61. Kaser, *Macht und Erbe*, 244ff., 250ff.

62. Kaser, *Familie und Verwandtschaft*, 233ff.

63. Ibid., 227ff.

64. Ibid., 197ff.

65. Ibid., 211ff.

66. Goehrke, *Frühzeit des Ostslaventums*, 146–47.
67. Felix Haase, *Volksglaube und Brauchtum der Ostslaven* (Wrocław, 1939), esp. 16, 23, 124ff., 130, 253.
68. Ludwig Steindorf, *Memoria in Altrussland: Untersuchungen zu den Formen christlicher Totensorge* (Stuttgart, 1994), 54–55.
69. Uno Harva, "Der Bau des Verwandtschaftssystems und der Verwandtschaftsverhältnisse bei den Fenno-Ugriern," *Finnisch-Ugrische Studien* 26 (1939): 119.
70. Yvonne Luven, *Der Kult der Hausschlange: Eine Studie zur Religionsgeschichte der Letten und Litauer* (Cologne, 2001), esp. 246, 293ff., 313–14, 323–24.
71. Patricia Buckley Ebrey, *Confucianism and Family Rituals in Imperial China: A Social History of Writing about Rites* (Princeton, 1991), 3. See also the articles in *Religion and Family in East Asia*, ed. George De Vos and Takao Sofue, Senri Ethnological Studies 11 (Osaka, 1984), esp. 155–213.
72. Ebrey, *Confucianism*, 15.
73. Monika Tworuschka and Udo Tworuschka, eds., *Religionen der Welt: Grundlagen, Entwicklung und Bedeutung in der Gegenwart* (Munich, 1996), 353ff.
74. Ibid., 357ff., 322ff.
75. Franke and Trauzettel, *Das Chinesische Kaiserreich*, 142.
76. Frank R. Hamm, "Buddhismus und Jinismus: Zwei Typen indischer Religiosität und ihr Weg in die Geschichte," *Saeculum* 15 (1964): 44.
77. Ebrey, *Confucianism*, 78–79; Steininger, "Der Buddhismus," 141.
78. George De Vos, "Religion and Family: Structural and Motivational Relationship," in De Vos and Sofue, *Religion and Family*, 25; Lewis Lancaster, "Buddhism and Family in East Asia," in ibid., 139; Steininger, "Der Buddhismus," 141.
79. De Vos, "Religion and Family," 25; Masaharu Ozaki, "The Taoist Priesthood: From Tsai-chia to Ch'u-chia," in De Vos and Sofue, *Religion and Family*, 108; Lancaster, "Buddhism," 143.
80. Lancaster, "Buddhism," 143.
81. Franke and Trauzettel, *Das Chinesische Kaiserreich*, 181; Jerry H. Bentley, *Old World Encounters* (New York, 1993), 83; Helwig Schmidt-Glintzer, "Der Buddhismus im frühen chinesischen Mittelalter und der Wandel der Lebensführung bei der Gentry im Süden," *Saeculum* 23 (1972): 293.
82. Bentley, *Old World Encounters*, 83.
83. Ebrey, *Confucianism*, 6 et passim.
84. Lancaster, "Buddhism," 140–45. Regarding the cult of ancestors, the same holds for Japanese Buddhism as opposed to Shintoism and Confucianism. See Susanne Formanek, *Denn dem Alter kann keiner entfliehen: Altern und Alten im Japan der Nara- und Heian-Zeit*, Beiträge zur Kultur- und Geistesgeschichte Asiens 13 (Vienna, 1994), 3.
85. Claude Lévi-Strauss, *The Elementary Structures of Kinship*, trans. James Harle Bell et al. (Boston, 1969), 328.

86. Michel Cartier, "China: The Family as a Relay of Government," in Bur-
    guière et al., *Distant Worlds*, 492.
87. Lévi-Strauss, *Elementary Structures*, 393–99, 374.
88. Cartier, "China," 491–522.
89. John C. Pelzel, "Japanese Kinship: A Comparison," in *Family and Kin-
    ship in Chinese Society*, ed. Maurice Freedman (Stanford, 1970), 227;
    Lawrence Krader, "Principles and Structures in the Organization of the
    Asiatic Steppe-Pastoralists," *Southwestern Journal of Anthropology* 11, no. 2
    (1955): 74, 84–90; Kh. A. Argynbaev, "The Kinship System and Customs
    Connected with the Ban on Pronouncing the Personal Names of Elder
    Relatives among the Kazakhs," in *Kinship and Marriage in the Soviet Union:
    Field Studies*, ed. Tamara Dragadze (London, 1984), 45–53; Harva, "Bau des
    Verwandtschaftssystems," 98ff.
90. Mitterauer, "Terminologie der Verwandtschaft," 37ff.
91. Krader, "Organization of the Steppe-Pastoralists," 78.
92. Lévi-Strauss, *Elementary Structures*, 316, 329; Cartier, "China," 492–94;
    Ebrey, *Confucianism*, 75, 118.
93. Shuzo Shiga, "Family Property and the Law of Inheritance in Traditional
    China," in *Chinese Family Law and Social Change in Historical and Compara-
    tive Perspective*, ed. David C. Buxbaum (Seattle, 1978), 124.
94. Lévi-Strauss, *Elementary Structures*, 388–89.
95. Goody, *The Development of the Family*, 31–33.
96. Lévi-Strauss, *Elementary Structures*, 333–34.
97. Ibid., 371–76.
98. Ebrey, *Confucianism*, 182.
99. Michael Mitterauer, "Die Witwe des Bruders: Leviratsehe und Familienver-
    fassung," *Otium* 3 (1995): 53–70.
100. Ebrey, *Confucianism*, 210; Jack Goody, *The Oriental, the Ancient and the
    Primitive: Systems of Marriage and the Family in the Pre-Industrial Societies of
    Eurasia* (Cambridge, 1990), 473.
101. Mitterauer, "Witwe des Bruders," 63.
102. Ann Waltner, *Getting an Heir: Adoption and the Construction of Kinship in
    Late Imperial China* (Honolulu, 1990).
103. Lloyd E. Eastman, *Family, Fields and Ancestors: Constancy and Change in
    China's Social and Economic History, 1550–1949* (New York, 1988), 47.
104. Waltner, *Getting an Heir*, 2, 93; Ebrey, *Confucianism*, 210.
105. Waltner, *Getting an Heir*, 23.
106. Ibid., 4, 12, 59.
107. Ibid., 100–103.
108. "Adoption," *RLAC*, 1:99–100; Goody, *The Development of the Family*,
    71–75.
109. Ebrey, *Confucianism*, 164.
110. Arland Thornton and Hui-Sheng Lin, *Social Change and the Family in Tai-
    wan* (Chicago, 1994), 27.

111. Jack M. Potter, "Land and Lineage in Traditional China," in Freedman, *Family and Kinship*, 121–38; Maurice Freedman, "Ritual Aspects of Chinese Kinship and Marriage," in ibid., 167–69; Michio Suenari, "The 'Religious Family' among the Chinese of Central Taiwan," in De Vos and Sofue, *Religion and Family*, 169–84.

112. Eastman, *Family, Fields and Ancestors*, 56.

113. Linck, *Frau und Familie*, 84.

114. Lévi-Strauss, *Elementary Structures*, 346; Potter, "Land and Lineage," 130; Thornton and Lin, *Social Change and the Family*, 28; Müller, *Kulturlandschaft China*, 75.

115. Ebrey, *Confucianism*, 195; Tatsuo Chikusa, "Succession to Ancestral Sacrifices and Adoption of Heirs to the Sacrifices: As Seen from an Inquiry into Customary Institutions in Manchuria," in Buxbaum, *Chinese Family Law*, 153–56; Linck, *Frau und Familie*, 83.

116. Kaser, *Familie und Verwandtschaft*, 236–37, and *Macht und Erbe*, 105; Gabriele Schwarz, *Allgemeine Siedlungsgeographie* (Berlin, 1966), 147.

117. Annegret Nippa, *Haus und Familie in arabischen Ländern: Vom Mittelalter bis zur Gegenwart* (Munich, 1991), 126ff.; Anderson, "Changing Kinship," 8, 13, 15–16; Peter Heine, *Ethnologie des Nahen und Mittleren Ostens: Eine Einführung* (Berlin, 1989), 72.

118. Walter Dostal, "Mecca before the Time of the Prophet—an Attempt of an Anthropological Interpretation," *Der Islam* 68 (1991): 200.

119. Gerhard Endress, *Islam: An Historical Introduction*, 2nd ed., trans. Carole Hillenbrand (New York, 2002), 142–46; Thierry Bianquis, "The Family in Arab Islam," in Burguière et al., *Distant Worlds*, 631–33; Michael Mitterauer, *Ahnen und Heilige: Namengebung in der europäischen Geschichte* (Munich, 1993), 189ff.

120. Harald Motzki, "Das Kind und seine Sozialisation in der islamischen Familie des Mittelalters," in *Zur Soziologie der Kindheit*, ed. Jochen Martin and August Nitschke (Freiburg, 1986), 414.

121. S. D. Goitein, *A Mediterranean Society: The Jewish Communities of the Arab World as Portrayed in the Documents of the Cairo Ganiza* (Berkeley, 1978), 3:8.

122. Ebrey, *Confucianism*, 38; Thomas Emmrich, *Tabu und Meidung im antiken China: Aspekte des Verpönten* (Bad Honnef, 1992), 141ff.

123. Mitterauer, *Ahnen und Heilige*, esp. 386ff.

124. Bianquis, "The Family," 631–32.

125. Goody, *The Oriental*, 276, 370, 379; Harald Motzki, "Geschlechtsreife und Legitimation zur Zeugung im frühen Islam," in *Geschlechtsreife und Legitimation zur Zeugung*, ed. Wilhelm E. Müller (Munich, 1985), 540.

126. Kaser, *Familie und Verwandtschaft*, 140ff.

127. Harald Motzki, "Dann macht er daraus die beiden Geschlechter, das männliche und das weibliche," in *Aufgaben, Rollen und Räume von Frau und Mann*, ed. Jochen Martin and Renate Zoepfel (Munich, 1984), 2:616; Goody, *The Oriental*, 379.

128. Nippa, *Haus und Familie*, 13ff. Goody, *The Oriental*, 380–82; Heine, *Ethnologie*, 75ff.
129. Dostal, "Mecca," 205ff.
130. Lévi-Strauss, *Elementary Structures*, 371–76.
131. Mitterauer, "Christentum und Endogamie," 60ff., 67ff.
132. See, for example, Raphael Patai, "Cousin-Right in the Middle Eastern Marriage," *Southwestern Journal of Anthropology* 11 (1955): 325–50; Fuad Khuri, "Parallel Cousin Marriage Reconsidered: A Middle Eastern Practice that Nullifies the Effects of Marriage on the Intensity of Family Relationships," *Man*, n.s. 5, no. 4 (1970): 597–618.
133. Dostal, "Mecca," 206.
134. See, for example, Joachim Jeremias, *Jerusalem zur Zeit Jesu* (Göttingen, 1958), 83ff., 11, 141; Mitterauer, "Christentum und Endogamie," 41ff.
135. Nippa, *Haus und Familie*, 177; Gabriele von Bruck, "Heiratspolitik der 'Prophetennachfahren,'" *Saeculum* 40 (1989): 272–95.
136. Formanek, *Denn dem Alter kann keiner entfliehen*, 2.

CHAPTER FOUR

1. Otto Hintze, "Weltgeschichtliche Bedingungen der Repräsentativverfassung," in *Staat und Verfassung*, 140; see also "Wesen und Verbreitung des Feudalismus" (84–119) and "Typologie der ständischen Verfassungen des Abendlandes" (120–39). For a basic account of Hintze's approach, see, among others, Helmut G. Koenigsberger, "Dominium regale or dominium politicum et regale? Monarchies and Parliaments in Early Modern Europe," in *Der moderne Parlamentarismus und seine Grundlagen in der ständischen Repräsentation*, ed. Karl Bosl and Karl Möckl (Berlin, 1977), 49ff.; Richard Löwenthal, "Kontinuität und Diskontinuität: Zur Grundproblematik des Symposiums," in ibid., 342–43; Heinz Rausch, "Einleitung," in *Die geschichtlichen Grundlagen der modernen Volksvertretung: Die Entwicklung von den mittelalterlichen Korporationen zu den modernen Parlamenten*, ed. Heinz Rausch (Darmstadt, 1980), 1:1, 11; Peter Blickle, "Communalism, Parliamentarism, Republicanism," *Parliaments, Estates and Representation* 6 (1986): 4–8.
2. Wolfgang Reinhard, *Geschichte der Staatsgewalt* (Munich, 2000), 216ff. Regarding the continuity between the older corporate system and parliamentarianism in Otto Hintze's sense, see also Kersten Krüger, "Die ständischen Verfassungen in Skandinavien in der frühen Neuzeit: Modelle einer europäischen Typologie?" *Zeitschrift für historische Forschung* 10 (1983): 129–48.
3. Struve, "Die mittelalterlichen Grundlagen," 106.
4. "Lehen, Lehenswesen, Lehnrecht," *LMA*, 5, cols. 1807ff.; Heinrich Mitteis, *Lehnrecht und Staatsgewalt*, Untersuchungen zur mittelalterlichen Verfassungsgeschichte 1 (Weimar, 1933), 207ff.

5. For the Carolingian beginnings of vassalage, see Bernard S. Bachrach, *Early Carolingian Warfare: Prelude to Empire* (Philadelphia, 2001), 65–68, 75–85, 163–70.

6. Mitterauer, *Ahnen und Heilige*, 293ff.; Mitterauer, "'Senioris sui nomine': Zur Verbreitung von Fürstennamen durch das Lehenswesen," *Mitteilungen des Instituts für österreichische Geschichtsforschung* 96 (1988): 275–330; Mitterauer, "Une intégration féodale? La dénomination, expression des relations de service et de vassalité," *L'anthroponymie: Document de l'histoire sociale des mondes médiévaux méditerranéens*, ed. Monique Bourin et al. (Rome, 1996), 295–311.

7. Arnold Angenendt, *Kaiserherrschaft und Königstaufe: Kaiser, Könige und Päpste als geistliche Patrone in der abendländischen Missionsgeschichte* (Berlin, 1984); Angenendt, *Das Frühmittelalter*, 430ff.

8. Otto Brunner, *Land und Herrschaft* (Vienna, 1959), 263ff.; Mitteis, *Lehnrecht*, 59ff., 534ff.; "Consilium et auxilium," *LMA*, 3, col. 162.

9. A summary of the debate over Heinrich Brunner's simplifying thesis on Charles Martel's creation of vassalage and benefices in order to provide for mounted troops is in Herwig Wolfram, *Salzburg, Bayern, Österreich: Die Conversio Bagoariorum et Carantanorum und die Quellen ihrer Zeit*, Mitteilungen des Instituts für Österreichische Geschichtsforschung, Ergänzungsband 31 (Vienna, 1995), 126–27.

10. "Bewaffnung," *RLGA*, 2:378; see also 2:456.

11. "Plattenharnisch," *LMA*, 7, cols. 14–15; Richard Barber, *The Knight and Chivalry*, rev. ed. (Woodbridge, UK, 1995), 5–46.

12. François L. Ganshof, "L'armée sous les Carolingiens," *Settimane di studio del Centro Italiano di Studi sull'Alto Medioevo* 15, no.1 (1968): 109ff.

13. Zöllner, *Geschichte der Franken*, 152; Herwig Wolfram, *History of the Goths*, trans. Thomas J. Dunlap (Berkeley, 1988), 190–93.

14. "Maifeld," *LMA*, 6, col. 113; Hyland, *The Horse*, 143; Cardini, *Alle radici*, 270, 294; J. F. Verbruggen, *The Art of Warfare in Western Europe during the Middle Ages: From the Eighth Century to 1340*, 2nd ed., trans. Sumner Willard and S. C. M. Southern (Woodbridge, UK, 1977), 22.

15. Heinrich Brunner, "Der Reiterdienst und die Anfänge des Lehenswesens," *Zeitschrift der Savigny-Stiftung für Rechtsgeschichte*, Germanistische Abteilung 8 (1987): 13.

16. Ibid., 11.

17. Devroey, "La céréaliculture," 241–42. See also chapters 1 and 2 above.

18. Brunner, "Reiterdienst," 10ff.; Ganshof, "L'armée," 125ff.

19. "Bewaffnung," *RLGA*, 2:470.

20. Ganshof, "L'armée," 124; Cardini, *Alle radici*, 282ff.

21. Peter Dinzelbacher, "Mittelalter," in *Mensch und Tier in der Geschichte Europas*, ed. Peter Dinzelbacher (Stuttgart, 2000), 199; Benecke, *Der Mensch und seine Haustiere*, 308; Ann Hyland, *The Warhorse, 1250–1600* (Stroud, UK, 1998); Bachrach, *Carolingian Warfare*, 119.

22. "Bewaffnung," *RLGA*, 2:470; on the *Verreiterung* of the Visigoths, see Wolfram, *History of the Goths*, 173ff.
23. The literature on this term in military history is summarized in Stephen Morillo, "The 'Age of Cavalry' Revisited," in *The Circle of War in the Middle Ages: Essays in Medieval Military and Naval History*, ed. Donald J. Kagay and L. J. Andrew Villalon (Woodbridge, UK, 1999), 45–58.
24. Franz Altheim, *Gesicht von Abend und Morgen: Von der Antike zum Mittelalter* (Frankfurt am Main, 1954), 10; Peter P. Golden, *An Introduction to the History of the Turkic Peoples* (Wiesbaden, 1992), 42ff.; Cardini, *Alle radici*, 9ff.
25. David Christian, "Inner Eurasia as a Unit of World History," *Journal of World History* 5 (1994): 173–211, esp. 180ff.; Nicola Di Cosmo, "Inner Asian Warfare in Historical Perspective," introduction to *Warfare in Inner Asian History (500–1800)*, ed. Nicola Di Cosmo (Leiden, 2002), 2–6.
26. Elvin, *Chinese Past*, 26–27; Altheim, *Gesicht von Abend und Morgen*, 55ff.; Di Cosmo, "Inner Asian Warfare," 11.
27. Altheim, *Gesicht von Abend und Morgen*, 98ff.; Wolfram, *Die Germanen*, 71; Otto J. Maenchen-Helfen, *Die Welt der Hunnen* (Vienna, 1978), 155ff. On the stirrup: White, *Medieval Technology*, 15–23. The controversy that Lynn White provoked over the stirrup's significance for the formation of feudal structures is summarized by Kelly De Vries, *Medieval Military Technology* (New York, 1992).
28. "Kriegswesen," *RLGA*, 17:364; Wolfram, *Die Germanen*, 70ff.; Maenchen-Helfen, *Die Welt der Hunnen*, 155ff.
29. White, *Medieval Technology*, 16–23; Klaus Schippmann, *Grundzüge der Geschichte des sasanidischen Reiches* (Darmstadt, 1990), 105.
30. Christian, "Inner Eurasia," 192, 197.
31. Georg Scheibelreiter, *Tiernamen und Wappenwesen* (Vienna, 1992), 117.
32. Franz Altheim and Ruth Stiehl, *Ein asiatischer Staat: Feudalismus unter den Sasaniden und ihren Nachbarn* (Wiesbaden, 1954); Schippmann, *Grundzüge der Geschichte*, 85; Pitz, *Ökumene*, 35–36, 211–12, 224, 236, 311–12, 402.
33. Altheim, *Gesicht von Abend und Morgen*, 100.
34. Josef Wiesehöfer, *Das antike Persien* (Düsseldorf, 1998), 202.
35. Schippmann, *Grundzüge der Geschichte*, 104.
36. Wiesehöfer, *Das antike Persien*, 263.
37. Schippmann, *Grundzüge der Geschichte*, 104.
38. Wiesehöfer, *Das antike Persien*, 264; Pitz, *Ökumene*, 402.
39. Altheim, *Gesicht von Abend und Morgen*, 86.
40. Wiesehöfer, *Das antike Persien*, 264; Schippmann, *Grundzüge der Geschichte*, 205–6.
41. Ian Blanchard, *Mining, Metallurgy and Minting in the Middle Ages* (Stuttgart, 2001), 1:13, 18, 20–23.
42. Ganshof, "L'armée," 117. On the conventions held by the nobility in the Persian Empire, see Altheim and Stiehl, *Ein asiatischer Staat*, 35ff.

43. Altheim, *Gesicht von Abend und Morgen*, 160; Cardini, *Alle radici*, 16ff., 116ff.

44. Altheim, ibid., 140, 160.

45. Martin, *Spätantike und Völkerwanderung*, 23.

46. "Flotte," *LMA*, 4, col. 579.

47. Altheim, *Gesicht von Abend und Morgen*, 172; Wolfram, *Die Germanen*, 71.

48. Wolfram, *Die Germanen*, 196.

49. Benecke, *Der Mensch und seine Haustiere*, 304; Cardini, *Alle radici*, 12.

50. Fernand Braudel, *The Structures of Everyday Life: The Limits of the Possible*, vol. 1, *Civilization and Capitalism, 15th–18th Century*, rev. trans. Siân Reynolds (New York, 1981), 376–77.

51. Altheim, *Gesicht von Abend und Morgen*, 53, 98.

52. Agostino Pertusi, "Ordinamenti militari, guerre in occidente e teorie di guerra dei Bizantini (secc. VI–X)," *Settimane di studio del Centro Italiano di Studi sull'Alto Medioevo* 15, no. 2 (1968): 683–84.

53. Ostrogorsky, *Byzantinische Geschichte*, 101ff.; "Thema," *LMA*, 8, cols. 615–16; Warren Treadgold, *Byzantium and Its Army, 284–1081* (Stanford, 1995), 21–25, 98–109; John Haldon, *Warfare, State and Society in the Byzantine World, 565–1204* (London, 1999), 71–78.

54. "Flotte," *LMA*, 4, col. 581.

55. Ostrogorsky, *Byzantinische Geschichte*, 154.

56. Ibid., 276.

57. "Lehen, Lehenswesen, Lehnrecht," *LMA*, 5, col. 1807.

58. Paul Schmitthenner, *Krieg und Kriegsführung im Wandel der Weltgeschichte* (Potsdam, 1930), 246, 347.

59. Bachrach, *Carolingian Warfare*, 83, 243.

60. Ursula Koch, "Damaszieren von Waffen," in Lindgren, *Europäische Technik*, 219.

61. Rolf Sprandel, *Das Eisengewerbe im Mittelalter* (Stuttgart, 1968), 42.

62. Angenendt, *Das Frühmittelalter*, 369; Leopold, Auer, "Der Kriegsdienst des Klerus unter den sächsischen Kaisern," *Mitteilungen des Instituts für österreichische Geschichtsforschung* 79 (1971): 379; Friedrich Prinz, "Vasallität und Stiftsvasallität im karolingischen und ottonischen Herrschaftssystem," *Settimane di studio del Centro Italiano di Studi sull'Alto Medioevo* 47 (2000): 851–72.

63. Angenendt, *Das Frühmittelalter*, 369; Bachrach, *Carolingian Warfare*, 57–65.

64. Prinz, "Vasallität und Stiftsvasallität," 861.

65. Angenendt, *Das Frühmittelalter*, 270. For Boniface's equivalent oath of allegiance in 722, see Bachrach, *Carolingian Warfare*, 23.

66. Bartlett, *Making of Europe*, 70–71.

67. Patterson, *Cattle-Lords*, 85–86; Michael Richter, *Irland im Mittelalter* (Stuttgart, 1983), 21; Birkhan, *Kelten*, 829.

68. Benecke, *Der Mensch und seine Haustiere*, 297ff.; "Streitwagen," *LAO*, 415–16; "Heer," *LAO*, 184–85.

69. Richter, *Irland*, 21.

70. Erna Patzelt and Herbert Patzelt, *Schiffe machen Geschichte: Beiträge zur Kulturentwicklung im vorchristlichen Schweden* (Vienna, 1981), esp. 50ff.; "Leidang, Leding, Ledung," *LMA*, 5, cols. 1851–52; "Flotte," *LMA*, 4, cols. 588–89.

71. Michael Mitterauer, "Herrenburg und Burgstadt," in *Bayerische Geschichte als Tradition und Modell*, Festschrift für Karl Bosl, *Zeitschrift für bayerische Landesgeschichte* 36 (1972): 470–521; quoted from rpt. in Mitterauer, *Markt und Stadt*, 192–234. Michael Mitterauer, "Städte als Zentren im mittelalterlichen Europa," in *Die vormoderne Stadt: Asien und Europa im Vergleich*, ed. Peter Feldbauer et al. (Vienna, 2002), 60ff. For the early equating of "baúrgs" and "city" in Ulfilas's Gothic translation of the Bible, see Wolfram, *History of the Goths*, 109–10.

72. Rafael von Uslar outlines an overview of how different types of medieval fortifications developed in *Studien zu frühgeschichtlichen Befestigungsanlagen zwischen Nordsee und Alpen* (Cologne, 1964), 221. For the hill fort (*Wallburg*) and the keep, donjon, or tower house (*Wohnturm*), as the European nobility's two basic types of castle, see Michael Bur, *Le château* (Turnhout, 1999), 25.

73. Bur, *Le château*, 24; "Kastellanei," *LMA*, 5, cols. 1036ff.

74. Elvin, *Chinese Past*, 87; "Befestigungsanlagen," *LAO*, 70–71.

75. Müller, *Kulturlandschaft China*, 330–31.

76. Bur, *Le château*, 27.

77. Uslar, *Studien zu frühgeschichtlichen Befestigungsanlagen*, 8ff.; Birkhan, *Kelten*, 344ff.

78. Michael Mitterauer, "Jahrmärkte in Nachfolge antiker Zentralorte," *Markt und Stadt*, 68ff., and "Von der antiken zur mittelalterlichen Stadt," in ibid., 54ff.

79. "Burg," *LMA*, 2, cols. 994ff.; "Befestigung," *LMA*, 1, cols. 1785ff.

80. "Befestigung," *LMA*, 1, col. 1785.

81. Herman Vetters, "Von der spätantiken zur frühmittelalterlichen Festungsbaukunst," *Settimane di studio del Centro Italiano di Studi sull'Alto Medioevo* 15, no. 2 (1968): 929–60.

82. Fedor Schneider, *Die Entstehung von Burg und Landgemeinde in Italien* (Berlin, 1924), 3ff.

83. Ernst Pitz, *Europäisches Städtewesen und Bürgertum: Von der Spätantike bis zum hohen Mittelalter* (Darmstadt, 1991), 161.

84. See, for example, Schneider, *Die Entstehung*, 21, for the territory of the city of Trent.

85. Pitz, *Europäisches Städtewesen*, 160–61, 260; Schneider, *Die Entstehung*, esp. 259ff. Schneider's term *Kollektivburg*, on pp. 291ff., has rightly not gained acceptance.

86. Schneider, *Die Entstehung.*, 91ff.

87. Kaplan, *Les hommes*, 102, 115ff., 455.

88. "Incastellamento," *LMA*, 5, cols. 397ff.; Heinrich Fichtenau, *Lebensordnungen des 10. Jahrhunderts: Studien über Denkart und Existenz im einstigen Karolingerreich* (Munich, 1984), 461ff.; Bur, *Le château*, 134–35.

89. Martin, *Spätantike und Völkerwanderung*, 69ff.

90. Ibid., 5–6.

91. Kaplan, *Les hommes*, 238, 158.

92. Schneider, *Entstehung von Burg*, 322–23.

93. Erich Schrader, *Das Befestigungsrecht in Deutschland von den Anfängen bis zum Beginn des 14. Jahrhunderts* (Göttingen, 1901), 2ff.; Ernst Mayer, *Deutsche und französische Verfassungsgeschichte vom 9. bis zum 14. Jahrhundert* (Leipzig, 1899), 67ff.

94. *MGH*, Dipl. Kar. I, Nr. 91. See Bachrach, *Carolingian Warfare*, 137, for the significance of bridge building in the early Carolingian military.

95. *MGH*, Cap. 2, 321–22.

96. W. H. Stevenson, "Trinoda necessitas," *English Historical Review* 29 (1914): 689.

97. Wolfgang Fritze, "Probleme der abodritischen Stammes- und Reichsverfassung und ihrer Entwicklung vom Stammesstaat zum Herrschaftsstaat," in *Siedlung und Verfassung der Slawen zwischen Elbe, Saale und Oder*, ed. Herbert Ludat et al. (Gießen, 1960), 194; Otto Peterka, *Rechtsgeschichte der böhmischen Länder* (Reichenberg, 1923), 1:46.

98. Heinrich Felix Schmid, "Die Burgbezirksverfassung bei den slavischen Völkern in ihrer Bedeutung für die Geschichte ihrer Siedlung und ihrer staatlichen Organisation," *Jahrbücher für Kultur und Geschichte der Slaven*, n.s. 2, no. 2 (1926): 93, 104, 110.

99. Uslar, *Studien zu frühgeschichtlichen Befestigungsanlagen*, 65ff.; Bartlett, *Making of Europe*, 65–70.

100. For more detail see Mitterauer, "Herrenburg und Burgstadt," 192–234.

101. Bur, *Le château*, 24, 131–32; "Kastellanei," *LMA*, 5, col. 1036.

102. Bur, *Le château*, 204ff.

103. "Vogt, Vogtei," *LMA*, 8, col. 1813.

104. Hintze, "Typologie."

105. "Seigneurie," *LMA*, 7, col. 1714; Georges Duby, *La société aux XIe et XIIe siècles dans la région mâconnaise* (Paris, 1953), 445; Karl Lechner, "Leistungen und Aufgaben siedlungskundlicher Forschung in den österreichischen Ländern mit besonderer Berücksichtigung von Niederösterreich," in *Ausgewählte Schriften* (Vienna, 1947), 150; Mitterauer, "Herrenburg und Burgstadt," 195, 228.

106. Bartlett, *Making of Europe*, 65–70.

107. Typical of this synthesis was the simultaneous emergence of the lord's castle and the heavy cavalry in England after the Conquest. See R. Allen Brown, "The Norman Conquest and the Genesis of English Castles," in R. Allen Brown, *Castles, Conquest and Charters* (Woodbridge, UK, 1989), 81–84.

108. Mitterauer, "Herrenburg und Burgstadt," 218ff.

109. "Heerschild, Herrenburg," *LMA*, 4, cols. 2007–8.

110. This new type was initially created for the *incastellamento* movement in Italy. See Fichtenau, *Lebensordnungen*, 461.

111. See Bachrach, *Carolingian Warfare*, 163–70, regarding this aspect of Carolingian military organization.

112. Franke and Trauzettel, *Das Chinesische Kaiserreich*, 168, 171ff.

113. Michael R. Drompp, "The Uighur-Chinese Conflict of 840–848," in Di Cosmo, *Warfare in Inner Asian History*, 73.

114. Patricia Crone, *Slaves on Horses: The Evolution of the Islamic Polity* (Cambridge, 1980); Jean-Claude Garcin, "The Mamlūk Military System and the Blocking of Medieval Moslem Society," in Baechler et al., *Europe and the Rise of Capitalism*, 113–30; Feldbauer, *Die islamische Welt*, 291ff.; "Mamluken," *LMA*, 6, cols. 181–82; "Heerwesen," *LMA*, 4, cols. 2005ff. On the differences between Islamic feudalism based on benefices and European feudalism based on fiefs—following Weber's distinction—see Wolfgang Schluchter, *Religion und Lebensführung* (Frankfurt am Main, 1988), 2:338.

115. For later breakthroughs of this principle in Egypt, see Donald S. Richards, "Mamluk Amirs and Their Families and Households," in *The Mamluks in Egyptian Politics and Society*, ed. Thomas Philipp and Ursula Haarmann (Cambridge, 1998), 34.

116. Mitteis, *Lehnrecht*, 16ff.

117. Bachrach, *Carolingian Warfare*, 65–68, 75–76, 163–70.

118. Birkhan, *Kelten*, 665–66, 993, 1040ff.; Wolfram, *Die Germanen*, 65ff.

119. Marc Bloch, *The Growth and Ties of Dependence*, vol. 1 of *Feudal Society*, trans. L. A. Manyon (Chicago, 1961), 182.

120. Bachrach, *Carolingian Warfare*, 119–301, 65–76.

121. Gina Fasoli, "Grundzüge einer Geschichte des Rittertums," in *Das Rittertum im Mittelalter*, ed. Arno Borst (Darmstadt, 1976), 200; Carlo Guido Mor, "Das Rittertum," in ibid., 254ff.

122. Otto Brunner, "Die ritterlich-höfische Kultur," in Borst, *Das Rittertum*, 142ff.; Arno Borst, "Das Rittertum im Hochmittelalter: Idee und Wirklichkeit," in ibid., 222ff.

123. Angenendt, *Das Frühmittelalter*, 368; Hans-Walter Klewitz, "Königtum, Hofkapelle und Domkapitel im 10. und 11. Jahrhundert," *Archiv für Urkundenforschung* 16 (1939): 102–56.

124. Bloch, *Growth and Ties of Dependence*, 225. See also Cardini, *Alle radici*, 93.

125. Arno Borst, *Lebensformen im Mittelalter* (Frankfurt am Main, 1973), 475–76.

126. Bloch, *Growth and Ties of Dependence*, 223. On the weaker form of the *aides féodales* in Germany see Mitteis, *Lehnrecht*, 61.

127. Bloch, *Growth and Ties of Dependence*, 145–46.

128. "Vasall, Vasallität," *LMA*, 8, cols. 1417–18; "Kommendation," *LMA*, 5, col. 1278; Barber, *The Knight*, 9–10.

129. On the mutually obligating oath of allegiance within the retinue, see Wolfram, *History of the Goths*, 108-9.
130. Further to the beginnings of this relationship, see Bachrach, *Carolingian Warfare*, 68, 165.
131. Percy Ernst Schramm, *Der König von Frankreich: Das Wesen der Monarchie vom 9. bis zum 16. Jahrhundert* (Darmstadt, 1960), 1:14ff.
132. Jürgen Hannig, *Consensus fidelium: Frühfeudale Interpretationen des Verhältnisses von Königtum und Adel am Beginn des Frankenreiches*, Monographien zur Geschichte des Mittelalters 27 (Stuttgart, 1982), esp. 292ff.; Fritz Kern, *Gottesgnadentum und Widerstandsrecht im frühen Mittelalter: Zur Entwicklungsgeschichte der Monarchie* (Leipzig, 1914), 129ff.
133. Mitteis, *Lehnrecht*, 83ff.; Gerd Althoff, *Verwandte, Freunde und Getreue: Zum politischen Stellenwert der Gruppenbildungen im frühen Mittelalter* (Darmstadt, 1990), 164.
134. "Consilium et auxilium," *LMA*, 3, col. 162.
135. Mitteis, *Lehnrecht*, 40-41, 623ff., 678-79, 592ff.
136. Ganshof, "L'armée," 116-17.
137. Engelbert Mühlbacher, *Deutsche Geschichte unter den Karolingern* (Stuttgart, 1959), 261; Hannig, *Consensus fidelium*, 168.
138. Mühlbacher, *Deutsche Geschichte*, 262.
139. Hannig, *Consensus fidelium*, 171.
140. Angenendt, *Das Frühmittelalter*, 322.
141. Hannig, *Consensus fidelium*, 170ff.
142. Ibid., 152.
143. Dietrich Claude, *Adel, Kirche und Königtum im Westgotenreich* (Sigmaringen, 1971), 77ff. et passim; "Toledo," *LMA*, 8, col. 847.
144. "Synodos endemusa," *LMA*, 8, col. 378.
145. *MGH*, Cap. I, No. 12, 28-30.
146. Hannig, *Consensus fidelium*, 152ff.
147. "Curia regis," *LMA*, 3, cols. 373ff.; Giancarlo Vallone, "La 'curia regis' tra ammistrazione e giuridizione," in *Contributi alla storia parlamentare Europea (secoli XIII–XX)*, ed. Maria Sofia Corciulo, Atti del 43° Congresso ICHRPI (Camerino, 1996), 100ff.
148. "Rat," *LMA*, 7, cols. 449-50; "Conseil du roi," *LMA*, 3, 145ff.
149. Hagen Schulze, *Staat und Nation in der europäischen Geschichte* (Munich, 1994), 38ff.; Vallone, "La 'curia regis,'" 100ff.
150. Hintze, "Typologie," 127-28; Franz Petri, "Territorienbildung und Territorialstaat des 14. Jahrhunderts im Nordwestraum," *Vorträge und Forschungen* 13 (1970): 389; Jan Dhondt, "Les origines des États de Flandre," *Anciens pays et assemblées d'États* 1 (1950): 16ff.
151. Hintze "Typologie," 130-31. For French *parlements*, the judicial courts that grew out of the Estates system, see Krüger, "Die ständischen Verfassungen," 134.

152. Karól Gorski, "The Origins of the Polish Sejm," *Slavonic and East European Review* 44 (1965–66): 132–33, and "Die Anfänge des Ständewesens in Nord- und Ostmitteleuropa im Mittelalter," *Anciens pays et assemblées d'États* 40 (1966): 50ff.

153. Bartlett, *Making of Europe*, 63–64; Borst, "Rittertum im Hochmittelalter," 244.

154. Mitteis, *Lehnrecht*, 616, and *Der Staat im hohen Mittelalter* (Berlin, 1941), 375.

155. Susan Reynolds, *Kingdoms and Communities in Western Europe, 900–1300* (Oxford, 1984), 305; Reinhard, *Geschichte der Staatsgewalt*, 217–18, 221–22; Thomas Ertman, *Birth of the Leviathan: Building States and Regimes in Medieval and Early Modern Europe* (Cambridge, 1997), 20–22.

156. Willem Pieter Blokmans, "A Typology of Representative Institutions in Late Medieval Europe," *Journal of Medieval History* 4 (1978): 192.

157. Otto Brunner, *Land und Herrschaft* (Vienna, 1959), 413. An example of Brunner's approach is Dietrich Gerhard's article "Assemblies of Estates and the Corporate Order," in Rausch, *Die geschichtlichen Grundlagen*, 1:306ff.

158. Brunner, *Land und Herrschaft*, 404ff. For criteria of *Landstandschaft* as found in the Austrian territories see Peter Feldbauer, *Herren und Ritter*, Herrschaftsstruktur und Ständebildung 1 (Vienna, 1973); Herbert Knittler, *Städte und Märkte*, Herrschaftsstruktur und Ständebildung 2 (Vienna, 1973); Ernst Bruckmüller, "Täler und Gerichte," in *Herrschaftsstruktur und Ständebildung*, ed. Ernst Bruckmüller et al., Herrschaftsstruktur und Ständebildung 3 (Vienna, 1973), 11–51; Helmuth Stradal, "Die Prälaten," in ibid., 53–114.

159. Hintze, *Staat und Verfassung*, 120, 140ff. Michael Mitterauer builds on these views while following in Otto Brunner's footsteps in his "Grundlagen politischer Berechtigung im mittelalterlichen Ständewesen," in Bosl and Möckl, *Der moderne Parlamentarismus*, 11–42. Among the criticisms of Hintze's typology is Karól Gorski's "Institutions représentatives et émancipation de la noblesse: Pour une typologie des assemblées d'États au XVIème siècle," *Études présentées à la CIHAE* 52 (1975), 133–47.

160. Hintze, "Weltgeschichtliche Bedingungen," 143; Günther Stökl, "Das frühneuzeitliche Ständewesen im östlichen Europa," in *Stände und Landesherrschaft in Ostmitteleuropa in der frühen Neuzeit*, ed. Hugo Weczerka (Marburg, 1995), 193–200.

161. Hintze, "Weltgeschichtliche Bedingungen," 142.

162. Hintze, "Typologie," 124. Following on from Hintze's typology, Ertman offers a modified interpretative approach in *Leviathan*, 20–22. On the validity in principle of Hintze's typology, see Krüger, "Die ständischen Verfassungen," 131; Ferdinand Seibt, "Landesherr und Stände in Westmitteleuropa am Ausgang des Mittelalters," in Weczerka, *Stände und Landesherrschaft*, 17.

163. Mitterauer, "Grundlagen politischer Berechtigung," 15ff., 29ff.; Reinhard, *Geschichte der Staatsgewalt*, 223.
164. Knittler *Städte und Märkte*, 160; Bruckmüller, "Täler und Gerichte," 50–51.
165. Brunner, *Land und Herrschaft*, 303ff., 361ff., 374ff.
166. Kazimierz Orzechowski, "Les systèmes des assemblées d'état: Origines, évolution, typologie," *Parliaments, Estates and Representation* 6 (1986): 110. For eastern Europe, see Klaus Zernack, "Staatsmacht und Ständefreiheit: Politik und Gesellschaft in der Geschichte des östlichen Mitteleuropa," in Weczerka, *Stände und Landesherrschaft*, 3.
167. Mitterauer, "Grundlagen politischer Berechtigung," 19ff.
168. Helmut G. Koenigsberger, "Zusammengesetzte Staaten, Repräsentativversammlungen und der amerikanische Bürgerkrieg," *Zeitschrift für historische Forschung* 18 (1991): 399–423.
169. Gaines Post, "Plena Potestas and Consent in Medieval Assemblies: A Study in Romano-Canonical Procedure and the Rise of Representation, 1150–1325," in Rausch, *Die geschichtlichen Grundlagen*, 1:30–114; Yves M.-J. Congar, "Quod omnes tangit, ab omnibus tractari et approbari debet," in ibid., 1:115–82.
170. Vallone, "La 'curia regis,'" 100.
171. Thomas N. Bisson, *Assemblies and Representation in Languedoc in the Thirteenth Century* (Princeton, 1964), 143–46; C. H. McIlwain, "Medieval Estates," in *The Cambridge Medieval History* (Cambridge, 1958), 7:669ff.; Mitterauer, "Grundlagen politischer Berechtigung," 35.
172. Karol Koranyi, "Zum Ursprung des Anteils der Städte an den ständischen Versammlungen und Parlamenten des Mittelalters," in Album Helen Maud Cam 1, *Études présentées à la CIHAE* 23 (1960): 40–41; Thomas N. Bisson, "The Origin of the Corts of Catalonia," *Parliaments, Estates and Representation* 16 (1996): 40–45; Porfirio Sanz, "The Cities in the Aragonese Cortes in the Medieval and Early Modern Periods," *Parliaments, Estates and Representation* 14 (1994): 95–108; Maria Rosa Muñoz and Regina Pinilla, "Les municipalités et leur participation dans les Cortès valenciennes de l'époque forale," *Parliaments, Estates and Representation* 13 (1993): 1–15.
173. Post, "Plena Potestas," 1:51; "Roncaglia, Reichstag von," *LMA*, 7, cols. 1021–22.
174. "Lombardische Liga," *LMA*, 5, col. 2100.
175. Bruckmüller, "Täler und Gerichte," 11ff.; Blickle, "Communalism," 9–12.
176. Koranyi, "Zum Ursprung," 46.
177. Dhondt, "Les origines des États de Flandre."
178. A vivid example for this kind of coexistence, which clearly shows the significance of vasallage for *Landstandschaft*, is the composition of the Estates of Old Livonia before 1561. See Heinz von zur Mühlen, "Autonomie und Selbstbehauptung der baltischen Stände von der Reformation bis zum Nordischen Krieg," in Weczerka, *Stände und Landesherrschaft*, 39.

179. Bloch, *Growth and Ties of Dependence*, 56. See also Jürgen Osterhammel, "Transkulturell vergleichende Geschichtswissenschaft," in *Geschichte und Vergleich: Ansätze und Ergebnisse international vergleichender Geschichtsschreibung*, ed. Heinz-Gerhard Haupt and Jürgen Kocka (Frankfurt am Main, 1996), 271ff.

180. Masahide Bito, "Confucian Thought during the Tokugawa Period," in De Vos and Sofue, *Religion and Family*, 129; Hintze, "Wesen und Verbreitung," 113ff.

181. Gerhard Buchda, "Reichsstände und Landstände im 16. und 17. Jahrhundert," in Rausch, *Die geschichtlichen Grundlagen*, 2:234; Vallone, "La 'curia regis,'" 100ff.

CHAPTER FIVE

1. Sieghart Döhring, "Europäische Musik im interkulturellen Vergleich," in *Europa—aber was ist es? Aspekte einer Identität in interdisziplinärer Sicht*, ed. Jörg A. Schlumberger and Peter Segl (Cologne, 1994), 119.

2. Günter Kehrer, *Einführung in die Religionssoziologie* (Darmstadt, 1988), 83.

3. Isnard Wilhelm Frank, *Kirchengeschichte des Mittelalters* (Düsseldorf, 1984), 76.

4. Hans Küng, *Christianity: Essence, Genius, Nature*, trans. John Bowden (New York, 1995), 391–403.

5. Hans-Joachim Schmidt, *Kirche, Staat, Nation: Raumgliederung der Kirche im mittelalterlichen Europa* (Weimar, 1999), 11, speaks in this context of a "systematized church" (*verfaßte Kirche*), as opposed to Judaism and Islam; Kehrer, *Religionssoziologie*, 80–81, places "organized religions" over against "diffused religions."

6. "Laterankonzil," *LMA*, 5, cols. 1739ff.

7. Peter Dinzelbacher and Hermann Joseph Roth, "Zisterzienser," in *Kulturgeschichte der christlichen Orden in Einzeldarstellungen*, ed. Peter Dinzelbacher and James Lester Hogg (Stuttgart, 1997), 356–57.

8. "Laterankonzil," *LMA*, 5, cols. 1739ff.

9. Bernhard Schimmelpfennig, *Das Papsttum: Von der Antike bis zur Renaissance* (Darmstadt, 1984), 168.

10. "Kurie," *LMA*, 5, cols. 1583ff.

11. Reinhard, *Geschichte der Staatsgewalt*, 210.

12. Schmidt, *Kirche, Staat, Nation*, 251–52.

13. "Legat, päpstlicher," *LMA*, 5, cols. 1795–96.

14. Küng, *Christianity*, 393.

15. Ibid., 401–3.

16. Angenendt, *Geschichte der Religiosität*, 457.

17. Frank, *Geschichte des christlichen Mönchtums*, 66ff.; Schimmelpfennig, *Das Papsttum*, 157–58.

18. Rolf Sprandel, "Zu den Funktionen des Mönchtums," *Saeculum* 25 (1974): 213.

19. For more detail on these responsibilities, see Dinzelbacher and Hogg, *Kulturgeschichte der christlichen Orden.*
20. Paul Volz, *Die biblischen Altertümer*, rpt. (Wiesbaden, 1989), 59–60.
21. Ibid., 56ff.
22. "Ordination," *ER*, 11:97ff.
23. "Genealogie," *RLAC*, 9, cols. 1158, 1177–78; Walter Burkert, *Antike Mysterien* (Munich, 1990), 41.
24. Burkert, *Antike Mysterien*, 37.
25. Johann Maier, *Grundzüge der Geschichte des Judentums im Altertum* (Darmstadt, 1981), 95.
26. Ibid., 111ff.; Günter Stemberger, *Juden und Christen im Heiligen Land* (Munich, 1987), 184ff.
27. Maier, *Grundzüge der Geschichte des Judentums*, 112.
28. Ibid., 97.
29. Ibid., 112.
30. Stemberger, *Juden und Christen*, 190ff.
31. Maier, *Grundzüge der Geschichte des Judentums*, 114.
32. Ibid., 127ff.
33. Ibid., 130.
34. "Juden, Judentum," *LMA*, 5, cols. 787–88.
35. Bernard Lewis, *The Jews of Islam* (Princeton, 1984), 79.
36. Siegfried Morenz, "Entstehung und Wesen der Buchreligionen," *Theologische Literaturzeitung* 75 (1950): 709ff.
37. Bernard G. Weiss and Arnold H. Green, *A Survey of Arab History* (Cairo, 1998), 154; Albrecht Noth, "Von den medinensischen 'Umma' zu einer muslimischen Ökumene," in *Der islamische Orient: Grundzüge seiner Geschichte*, ed. Albrecht Noth and Jürgen Paul (Würzburg, 1998), 124; Lewis, *Jews of Islam*, 79.
38. Albert Hourani, *Die Geschichte der arabischen Völker* (Frankfurt am Main, 1992), 206ff.
39. Heinz Halm, "Die 'Regierung der Rechtsgelehrten': Die Schia an der Macht," in *Die Welten des Islam*, ed. Gernot Rotter (Frankfurt am Main, 1993), 61; Lewis, *Jews of Islam*, 79–80.
40. "Tradition," *DI*, 639.
41. "Ulama," *ER*, 15:115; Harald Motzki, "Die Entstehung des Rechts," in Noth, *Der islamische Orient*, 170; Tilman Nagel, *Staat und Glaubensgemeinschaft im Islam* (Zurich, 1981), 1:298.
42. Johann Christoph Bürgel, *Allmacht und Mächtigkeit: Religion und Welt im Islam* (Munich, 1991), 39.
43. "Ulama," *ER*, 15:116; Dietrich Brandenburg, *Die Madrasa: Ursprung, Entwicklung, Ausbreitung und künstlerische Gestaltung der islamischen Moschee-Hochschule* (Graz, 1978).
44. Bürgel, *Allmacht und Mächtigkeit*, 94, 111; Annemarie Schimmel, *Der Islam* (Stuttgart, 1990), 53.

45. George Makdisi, "Authority in the Islamic Community," *History and Politics in Eleventh-Century Baghdad* (Aldershot, 1990), sect. 8, 120.

46. "Kalif, Kalifat," *LMA*, 5, col. 868.

47. Bassam Tibi, *Der wahre Imam: Der Islam von Mohammed bis zur Gegenwart* (Munich, 1996), 28.

48. Claude Cahen, *Der Islam I*, Fischer Weltgeschichte 14 (Frankfurt am Main, 1968), 75ff.; Feldbauer, *Die islamische Welt*, 285ff.; Nagel, *Staat und Glaubensgemeinschaft*, 1:298, 307; Makdisi, "Authority in the Islamic Community," 120; Noth, "Von den medinensischen 'Umma,'" 124; Basim Musallam, "The Ordering of Muslim Societies," in Robinson, *Islamic World*, 176–81.

49. Hamid Dabashi, *Authority in Islam: From the Rise of Muhammad to the Establishment of the Umayyads* (New Brunswick, 1993), 92–93; Nagel, *Staat und Glaubensgemeinschaft*, 1:304–5.

50. Nagel, *Staat und Glaubensgemeinschaft*, 1:131ff.

51. Tibi, *Der wahre Imam*, 64, 66, 114; Dominique Sourdel, *Medieval Islam* (London, 1985), 112.

52. Cahen, *Der Islam I*, 75.

53. Wilferd Madelung, *The Succession to Muhammad: A Study of the Early Caliphate* (Cambridge, 1997).

54. Gernot Rotter, "Der Islam hat die Demokratie erfunden," in Rotter, *Die Welten des Islam*, 174.

55. C. Detlef Müller, *Geschichte der orientalischen Nationalkirchen* (Göttingen, 1981), 309; "Nestorianische Kirche," *TRE*, 24:264–76.

56. Schimmelpfennig, *Das Papsttum*, 192.

57. Ibid., 223ff.

58. Schmidt, *Kirche, Staat, Nation*, 328.

59. Schimmelpfennig, *Das Papsttum*, 266ff.

60. "Faqir," *DI*, 116; "Celibacy," *DI*, 50; Bertold Spuler, "Die Bedeutung der Derwische im Islam," *Saeculum* 25 (1974): 214.

61. See, for example, Schimmel, *Der Islam*, 91ff.; Nagel, *Staat und Glaubensgemeinschaft*, 1:419.

62. Schimmel, *Der Islam*, 92; Spuler, "Bedeutung der Derwische," 214.

63. Schimmel, *Der Islam*, 100; Spuler, "Bedeutung der Derwische," 214.

64. Hourani, *Geschichte der arabischen Völker*, 201–2.

65. "Mystik," *IL*, 2:579.

66. *ER*, 14:118. See also Ira M Lapidus, "Die Institutionalisierung der frühislamischen Gesellschaften," in *Max Webers Sicht des Islam*, ed. Wolfgang Schluchter (Frankfurt am Main, 1987), 132.

67. Suraya Faroqhi, *Kultur und Alltag im Osmanischen Reich: Vom Mittelalter bis zum Anfang des 20. Jahrhunderts* (Munich, 1995), 210–11; "Orden, mystische," *LMA*, 6, col. 1430; "Mystik, Islam," *LMA*, 6, col. 992; "Zawiya," *LMA*, 9, col. 495; Spuler, "Bedeutung der Derwische," 214.

68. A concrete example is the founder of the Safawiya Order, Safi al-din Ishaq, the favorite disciple who married his sheikh's daughter, but who had to

yield in favor of the sheikh's eldest son when it came to the succession of leadership of the old order, resulting in the founding of a new convention. See Monika Gronke, "Auf dem Weg von der geistlichen zur weltlichen Macht: Schlaglichter zur frühen Safawiya," *Saeculum* 42 (1991): 171.

69. Bürgel, *Allmacht und Mächtigkeit*, 100.
70. Harald Haarmann, *Universalgeschichte der Schrift* (Frankfurt am Main, 1990), 493ff., 319ff.; "Arabische Sprache und Literatur," *LMA*, 1, col. 849.
71. See Kehrer, *Religionssoziologie*, 76.
72. Bürgel, *Allmacht und Mächtigkeit*, 88ff.
73. Müller, *Geschichte der orientalischen Nationalkirchen*, D 294ff.
74. Bayrischer Schulbuch-Verlag, ed., *Großer Historischer Weltatlas*, part 2, *Mittelalter*, 2nd ed. (Munich, 1979), 73.
75. Michael von Brück and Whalen Lai, *Buddhismus und Christentum* (Munich, 2000), 481.
76. Franke and Trauzettel, *Das Chinesische Kaiserreich*, 141. For trends in Chinese Buddhism leading towards a state church, see also Steininger, "Der Buddhismus," 132; Schmidt-Glintzer, "Der Buddhismus," 275.
77. Franke and Trauzettel, *Das Chinesische Kaiserreich*, 183ff.
78. Tworuschka and Tworuschka, *Religionen der Welt*, 361.
79. Martin, *Spätantike und Völkerwanderung*, 126ff.; Schmidt, *Kirche, Staat, Nation*, 40ff.
80. Peter Brown, *The Rise of Western Christendom: Triumph and Diversity, A. D. 200–1000* (Oxford, 1996), 75.
81. Schimmelpfennig, *Das Papsttum*, 87ff.
82. Ibid., 96ff.
83. Angenendt, *Das Frühmittelalter*, 328ff., and "Die religiösen Wurzeln Europas," in *Das gemeinsame Haus Europa: Handbuch zur europäischen Kulturgeschichte*, ed. Museum für Völkerkunde in Hamburg (Munich, 1999), 484.
84. "Bischof, Bischofsamt," *LMA*, 2, col. 230.
85. Martin, *Spätantike und Völkerwanderung*, 131–32.
86. Schimmelpfennig, *Das Papsttum*, 28–29.
87. Ibid., 95.
88. Küng, *Christianity*, 383.
89. Schimmelpfennig, *Das Papsttum*, 85.
90. Angenendt, *Das Frühmittelalter*, 223ff.
91. "Pallium," *LMA*, 6, col. 1643; "Bischof," *LMA*, 2, col. 230.
92. Angenendt, *Das Frühmittelalter*, 225.
93. Ibid., 268ff.
94. Ibid., 276.
95. Müller, *Geschichte der orientalischen Nationalkirchen*, D. 345ff.
96. Ibid., D 351.
97. Ibid., D 346.
98. Ibid., D 363.
99. "Mission," *LMA*, 6, col. 676.

100. "Fronleichnam," *LMA*, 4, cols. 990–91.

101. Peter Dinzelbacher and Daniel Krochmalnik, eds., *Hoch- und Spätmittelalter*, vol. 2 of *Handbuch der Religionsgeschichte im deutschsprachigen Raum* (Paderborn, 2000), 233.

102. Peter Dinzelbacher, "Die 'Realpräsenz' der Heiligen in ihren Reliquiaren und Gräbern nach mittelalterlichen Quellen," in *Heiligenverehrung in Geschichte und Gegenwart*, ed. Peter Dinzelbacher and Dieter R. Bauer (Ostfildern, 1990), 115ff., esp. 124; Arnold Angenendt, *Heilige und Reliquien* (Munich, 1994), 173, 157.

103. Theodor Nikolaou, *Askese, Mönchtum und Mystik in der Orthodoxen Kirche* (St. Ottilien, 1995), 178ff.; "Sakrament, Sakramentalien," *LMA*, 7, cols. 1267ff.

104. See Angenendt, *Heilige und Reliquien*, 186ff.

105. Angenendt, *Geschichte der Religiosität*, 446.

106. "Tonsur," *LMA*, 8, col. 861.

107. Jochen Martin, "Zwei Alte Geschichten: Vergleichende historisch-anthropologische Betrachtungen zu Griechenland und Rom," *Saeculum* 48 (1997): 20.

108. "Cursus honorum," *LMA*, 3, col. 392.

109. Schimmelpfennig, *Das Papsttum*, 8, 22, 25, 30, 33.

110. Angenendt, *Das Frühmittelalter*, 232.

111. "Pallium," *LMA*, 6, col. 1644.

112. Angenendt, *Geschichte der Religiosität*, 630ff.; "Busse," *LMA*, 2, col. 1134.

113. Angenendt, *Geschichte der Religiosität*, 655ff.

114. Steven Runciman, *A History of the Crusades* (Cambridge, 1951–54), 1: 49–50.

115. Carl Erdmann, *The Origin of the Idea of Crusade*, trans. Marshall W. Baldwin and Walter Goffart (Princeton, 1977), 269–72; Borst, "Rittertum im Hochmittelalter," 222ff.

116. Angenendt, *Das Frühmittelalter*, 331ff.

117. Angenendt, *Geschichte der Religiosität*, 706ff.

118. Ibid., 453ff.

119. "Vita communis," *LMA*, 8, col. 1756.

120. Angenendt, *Das Frühmittelalter*, 229–30.

121. Ibid., 289, 367.

122. Alfred Bertholet, *Wörterbuch der Religionen* (Stuttgart, 1985), 442; Kurt Rudolph, *Die Gnosis* (Leipzig, 1977), 363; Hamm, "Buddhismus und Jinismus," 52.

123. Müller, *Geschichte der orientalischen Nationalkirchen*, D 322, D 326, D 348; Berthelot, *Wörterbuch*, 286; Angenendt, *Das Frühmittelalter*, 205ff.

124. Angenendt, *Das Frühmittelalter*, 205, 215.

125. Ibid., 220.

126. Frank, *Geschichte des christlichen Mönchtums*, 23ff.

127. Nikolaou, *Askese, Mönchtum und Mystik*, 103.

128. Angenendt, *Geschichte der Religiosität*, 332.
129. Angenendt, *Das Frühmittelalter*, 221.
130. "Cluny," *LMA*, 2, cols. 2172–73.
131. "Exemtion," *LMA*, 4, cols. 165–66.
132. Angenendt, *Das Frühmittelalter*, 290, and *Geschichte der Religiosität*, 312.
133. Angenendt, *Das Frühmittelalter*, 288.
134. See the map, ibid., 291.
135. Bartlett, *Making of Europe*, 256; Angenendt, *Geschichte der Religiosität*, 712.
136. Steindorf, *Memoria in Altrussland*, esp. 131, 155–56, 250–51.
137. Angenendt, *Das Frühmittelalter*, 366.
138. Ibid., 364; "Benedikt von Aniane," *LMA*, 1, cols. 1864ff.
139. Frank, *Geschichte des christlichen Mönchtums*, 66.
140. "Hirsau," *LMA*, 5, cols. 35–36.
141. "Gorze," *LMA*, 4, cols. 1565ff.
142. "Cluny," *LMA*, 2, cols. 2172ff.
143. Angenendt, *Geschichte der Religiosität*, 333–34.
144. "Benediktiner, -innen," *LMA*, 1, col. 1874.
145. "Cluny," *LMA*, 2, cols. 2175–76.
146. Nikolaou, *Askese, Mönchtum und Mystik*, 119ff.
147. Bayrischer Schulbuch-Verlag, *Großer Historischer Weltatlas*, part 2, 80.
148. "Cluny," *LMA*, 2, col. 2171.
149. "Athos," *LMA*, 1, col. 1168.
150. Nikolaou, *Askese, Mönchtum und Mystik*, 135.
151. Ulrich Meyer, *Soziales Handeln im Zeichen des 'Hauses': Zur Ökonomik in der Spätantike und im frühen Mittelalter* (Göttingen, 1998), 302ff.
152. Georg Stadtmüller, "Bemerkungen zu den Unterschieden des Mönchtums im Osten und im Abendland," *Saeculum* 25 (1974): 209.
153. Hans-Georg Beck, ed. *Lust an der Geschichte: Leben in Byzanz: Ein Lesebuch* (Munich, 1991), 338.
154. "Laura, Lavra," *LMA*, 5, col. 1757.
155. Beck, *Lust an der Geschichte*, 334ff.; Nikolaou, *Askese, Mönchtum und Mystik*, 125.
156. Frank, *Geschichte des christlichen Mönchtums*, 200; "Mönch, Mönchtum," *LMA*, 6, cols. 733ff.
157. Frank, *Geschichte des christlichen Mönchtums*, 198. On the far-reaching consequences of this distinction for technological progress, see Lynn White Jr., "Cultural Climates and Technological Advance in the Middle Ages," in *Medieval Religion and Technology: Collected Essays* (Berkeley, 1978), 241–46; Reynolds, *Stronger than a Hundred Men*, 109–12.
158. Frank, *Geschichte des christlichen Mönchtums*, 202; Nikolaou, *Askese, Mönchtum und Mystik*, 84ff.
159. See the map "Drei der prägenden Strukturgrenzen Europas," in Peter Segl, "Europas Grundlegung im Mittelalter," in Schlumberger and Segl, *Europa—aber was ist es?* 35.

CHAPTER SIX

1. Wolfgang Reinhard, *Geschichte der europäischen Expansion* (Stuttgart, 1983), 1:8.
2. "Expansion, europäische," *LMA*, 4, cols. 174ff.
3. See, for example, Peter Feldbauer et al., eds., *Vom Mittelmeer zum Atlantik: Die mittelalterlichen Anfänge der europäischen Expansion* (Vienna, 2001). Pierre Chaunu makes the basic argument for the need of such an extensive study into the past in *L'Expansion européenne du XIIIe au XVe siècle* (Paris, 1969).
4. Jan Dhondt, *Das frühe Mittelalter*, Fischer Weltgeschichte 10 (Frankfurt am Main, 1968), 279ff.
5. Jacques Le Goff, *Das Hochmittelalter*, Fischer Weltgeschichte 11 (Frankfurt am Main, 1965), 136; Runciman, *The Crusades*, 1:313, 3:355–57.
6. Karl-Heinz Alllmendinger, *Die Beziehungen zwischen der Kommune Pisa und Ägypten im hohen Mittelalter* (Wiesbaden, 1967), 2ff.
7. Runciman, *The Crusades*, 1:32.
8. Bertold Spuler, "Die Ostgrenze des Abendlandes und die orthodoxe Kirche," in *Gesammelte Aufsätze* (Leiden, 1980), 101.
9. Runciman, *The Crusades*, 1:107–110.
10. Erdmann, *The Idea of Crusade*, 136–40.
11. Ibid., 140.
12. Ibid., 293–94.
13. Ibid., 129–36.
14. Ibid., 131.
15. Ibid., 135.
16. Ibid., 133–34.
17. Ibid., 111–12.
18. Angenendt, *Geschichte der Religiosität*, 652.
19. Carl Erdmann, "Die Fortbildung des populären Kreuzzugsgedankens," in Borst, *Das Rittertum*, 53.
20. Erdmann, *The Idea of Crusade*, 4.
21. "Jihad," *DI*, 244.
22. Runciman, *The Crusades*, 1:32; Ostrogorsky, *Byzantinische Geschichte*, 241. On the Islamic, Jewish, and Christian concepts of martyrdom, see Lewis, *Jews of Islam*, 82–84.
23. Maurice Keen, *Chivalry* (New Haven, 1984), 46.
24. Erdmann, *The Idea of Crusade*, 27; Hans Eberhard Mayer, *Geschichte der Kreuzzüge* (Stuttgart, 1965), 22.
25. Lewis, *Jews of Islam*, 80–81.
26. "Krieg, heiliger," *LMA*, 5, col. 1527; Bertold Spuler, "The Arab Expansion and the Crusades," in Spuler, *Gesammelte Aufsätze*, 64; Bassam Tibi, *Kreuzzug und Djihad: Der Islam und die christliche Welt* (Munich, 1999), 51ff.
27. Erdmann, *The Idea of Crusade*, 4; Tibi, *Kreuzzug und Djihad*, 73.

28. "Krieg, heiliger," *LMA*, 5, col. 1527.
29. Runciman, *The Crusades*, 2:47–50.
30. Ibid., 2:48.
31. Ibid., 3:113–24.
32. "Kreuzzüge," *LMA*, 5, 1517.
33. Angenendt, "Die religiösen Wurzeln Europas," 485.
34. Erdmann, *The Idea of Crusade*, 118–20.
35. Ibid., 148–81.
36. "Kreuzzüge," *LMA*, 5, 1516–17.
37. "Ibid., 1511; Michael Mitterauer, "Der Krieg des Papstes," in "Kreuz-züge," special issue, *Beiträge zur historischen Sozialkunde* 26, no. 3 (1996): 116–28.
38. Dinzelbacher and Hogg, *Kulturgeschichte der christlichen Orden*, 329ff.; "Ritterorden," *LMA*, 7, col. 878.
39. "Ribat," *LMA*, 7, col. 804.
40. "Pilger," *LMA*, 6, col. 2148.
41. An exemplary treatment is Alain Demurger, *Vie et mort de l'ordre du Temple, 1120–1314* (Paris, 1985); Peter Dinzelbacher, *Die Templer—ein geheimnisumwitterter Orden* (Freiburg, 2002), 50.
42. Cardini, *Alle radici*, 313–14; Joachim Bumke, "Der adelige Ritter," in Borst, *Das Rittertum*, 283ff.
43. Erdmann, "Fortbildung," 53ff.; Cardini, *Alle radici*, 227ff.
44. "Geraldus von Aurillac," *LMA*, 4, col. 1297.
45. Erdmann, *The Idea of the Crusade*, 53ff.; "Gottesfrieden," *LMA*, 4, cols. 1587ff.
46. Bartlett, *Making of Europe*, 24, 10–15.
47. Ibid., 102.
48. "Kreuzzüge," *LMA*, 5, 1516.
49. "Deutscher Orden," *LMA*, 3, cols. 768ff.
50. Runciman, *The Crusades*, 3:351–52; Mayer, *Geschichte der Kreuzzüge*, 144.
51. Michel Balard, "Communes italiennes, pouvoir et habitants des États Francs de Syrie-Palestine au XIIe siècle," in *Crusades and Muslims in Twelfth-Century Syria*, ed. Maya Schatzmiller, The Medieval Mediterranean 1 (Leiden, 1993), 58.
52. Peter Feldbauer and John Morrissey, "Italiens Kolonialexpansion—östlicher Mittelmeerraum und die Küsten des Schwarzen Meeres," in Feldbauer et al., *Vom Mittelmeer zum Atlantik*, 84ff.; Runciman, *The Crusades*, 3:353.
53. Peter Feldbauer and John Morrissey, *Venedig, 800–1600: Wasservögel als Weltmacht* (Vienna, 2002), 52ff.; Feldbauer and Morrissey, "Italiens Kolonialexpansion," 85ff.; Bartlett, *Making of Europe*, 182–91.
54. "Cruzada," *LMA*, 3, col. 362; "Kreuzzüge," *LMA*, 5, 1515.
55. Horst Gründer, *Welteroberung und Christentum* (Gütersloh, 1992), 73–74.

56. Renate Pieper, "Die Anfänge der europäischen Partizipation am welt-weiten Handel: Die Aktivitäten der Portugiesen und Spanier im 15. und 16. Jahrhundert," in *Die Geschichte des europäischen Welthandels und der wirtschaftliche Globalisierungsprozeß*, ed. Friedrich Edelmayer et al. (Vienna, 2001), 34.

57. "Ceuta," *LMA*, 2, col. 1644; Reinhard, *Geschichte der europäischen Expansion*, 1:39.

58. "Heinrich 'der Seefahrer,'" *LMA*, 4, col. 2061.

59. Reinhard, *Geschichte der europäischen Expansion*, 1:39.

60. "Fraxinetum," *LMA*, 4, col. 882; Xavier de Planhol, *L'Islam et la mer: La mosquée et le matelot, VIIe–XXe siècle* (Paris, 2000), 28, and 39, regarding the lack of wood in Islamic areas.

61. As argued by Ernst Dümmler in *Geschichte des Ostfränkischen Reiches* (1887; Darmstadt, 1960), 3: 317. The term "colony" for the stronghold of Garigliano, which was much like Fraxinetum, is used by Francesco Gabrieli, *Muhammad and the Conquests of Islam*, trans. Virginia Luling and Rosamund Linell (London, 1968), 204.

62. See also Archibald Lewis, "Mediterranean Maritime Commerce, A.D. 300–1100: Shipping and Trade," *Settimane di studio del Centro Italiano di Studi sull'Alto Medioevo* 25, no. 2 (1978): 481–501.

63. "Eisen," *LMA*, 3, col. 1750.

64. Sylvia L. Thrupp, "Das mittelalterliche Gewerbe, 1000–1500," in Cipolla and Borchardt, *Europäische Wirtschaftsgeschichte*, 1:163–64.

65. "Elba," *LMA*, 3, col. 1774.

66. Francesco Surdich, "Le città marinare tra rivoluzione commerciale e crociate fino all'inizio del Duecento," in *La società comunale e il policen-trismo*, ed. Anna Benvenuti et al., Storia della Società Italiana 6 (Milan, 1986), 32.

67. Feldbauer and Morrissey, "Italiens Kolonialexpansion," 86.

68. Blanchard, *Mining*, 2:715, 752, 776.

69. Surdich, "Le città marinare," 35; John Morrissey, "Die italienischen Seere-publiken," in Feldbauer et al., *Vom Mittelmeer zum Atlantik*, 69.

70. John Day, "La Sardegna e suoi dominatori dal secolo XI al secolo XIV," in *La Sardegna medioevale e moderna*, ed. John Day et al., Storia d'Italia 10 (Turin, 1984), 175ff.

71. Ibid., 141, 159.

72. Ibid., 151; Morrissey, "Seerepubliken," 69; Karl-Heinz Allmendinger, *Die Beziehungen zwischen der Kommune Pisa und Ägypten im hohen Mittelalter* (Wiesbaden, 1967), 86ff..

73. Day, "La Sardegna," 151.

74. Morrissey, "Seerepubliken," 69.

75. Rainer Pauli, *Sardinien: Geschichte—Kultur—Landschaft* (Cologne, 1978), 258; Marco Tangheroni explicitly calls Sardinia a Pisan "colony," in *Politica, commercio, agricoltura a Pisa nel Trecento* (Pisa, 1973), 114.

76. "Sardinien," *LMA*, 7, cols. 1378ff.; Alain Ducellier et al., eds., *Byzance et le monde orthodoxe* (Paris, 1986), 92.

77. Erdmann, *The Idea of Crusade*, 112; Allmendinger, *Beziehungen zwischen Pisa und Ägypten*, 19.

78. J. K. Hyde, *Society and Politics in Medieval Italy* (London, 1973), 29–31; "Pisa," *LMA*, 6, col. 2177.

79. "Daimbert," *LMA*, 3, col. 433.

80. "Amalfi," *LMA*, 1, col. 507; "Neapel," *LMA*, 6, col. 1074.

81. "Barcelona," *LMA*, 1, col. 1451.

82. Genua," *LMA*, 4, col. 1253.

83. Hans-Joachim Diesner, *Das Vandalenreich* (Stuttgart, 1966), 125.

84. Edith Ennen, *Die europäische Stadt des Mittelalters* (Göttingen, 1972), 152.

85. "Korsika," *LMA*, 5, col. 1453.

86. Ibid., col. 1454.

87. Surdich, "Le città marinare," 32; Allmendinger, *Beziehungen zwischen Pisa und Ägypten*, 13–14; David Abulafia, *The Two Italies: Economic Relations between the Norman Kingdom of Sicily and the Northern Communes* (Cambridge, 1977), 123–26.

88. "Levantehandel," *LMA*, 5, col. 1922.

89. Allmendinger, *Beziehungen zwischen Pisa und Ägypten*, 45ff.; Morrissey, "Seerepubliken," 72.

90. "Fondaco," *LMA*, 4, cols. 617–18.

91. Allmendinger, *Beziehungen zwischen Pisa und Ägypten*, 86ff.

92. Wolfgang Reinhard's article emphasizes the merchants' involvement in city rule as a precondition of European expansion: "Die Europäisierung der Erde und deren Folgen," in Schlumberger and Segl, *Europa—aber was ist es?* 84.

93. "Flotte," *LMA*, 4, col. 580.

94. "Pisa," *LMA*, 6, col. 2177; Morrissey, "Seerepubliken," 67.

95. Morrissey, "Seerepubliken," 62.

96. Abraham L. Udovitch, "Time, Sea and Society," *Settimane di studio del Centro Italiano di Studi sull'Alto Medioevo* 25, no. 2 (1978): 518ff.

97. "Amalfi," *LMA*, 1, col. 508; Morrissey, "Seerepubliken," 66.

98. Georges Duby, *The Early Growth of the European Economy: Warriors and Peasants from the Seventh to the Twelfth Century*, trans. Howard B. Clarke (London, 1974), 147.

99. Randall Rogers, *Latin Siege Warfare in the Twelfth Century* (Oxford, 1997), 208–12.

100. Ibid., 201–7.

101. Morrissey, "Seerepubliken," 65–66.

102. Allmendinger, *Beziehungen zwischen Pisa und Ägypten*, 13.

103. Pitz, *Europäisches Städtewesen*, 335–36.

104. Peter Burke, "City-States," in *States in History*, ed. John A. Hall (Oxford, 1986), 137–53.

105. Burke refers to these facts of lordship structures in formulating a "'vacuum theory' of the city-state" (ibid., 152).

106. Horst Klengler, *Handel und Händler im alten Orient* (Vienna, 1979), 201ff.

107. Gabriella Airaldi, "Genova e la Liguria nel Medioevo," in *Comuni e signorie nell'Italia settentrionale: Il Piemonte e Liguria*, ed. Ana M. N. Patrone and Gabriella Araldi, Storia d'Italia 5 (Turin, 1986), 403; Surdich, "Le città marinare," 41–42.

108. Reinhard, *Geschichte der europäischen Expansion*, 1:38.

109. "Atlantische Inseln," *LMA*, 1, 1170.

110. Reinhard, *Geschichte der europäischen Expansion*, 1:28ff.

111. Peter Partner, *God of Battles: Holy Wars of Christianity and Islam* (Princeton, 1997), 162–84.

112. Frederic C. Lane, *Venice: A Maritime Republic* (Baltimore, 1973), 369–73.

CHAPTER SEVEN

1. Alphons Silberman, "Massenkommunikation," in *Handbuch der empirischen Sozialforschung*, ed. René König (Stuttgart, 1977), 10:146ff.

2. Jean Delumeau, *La peur en Occident (XIVe–XVIIIe siècles): Une cité assiégée* (Paris, 1978), 208–9.

3. Penny J. Cole, *The Preaching of the Crusades to the Holy Land, 1095–1270* (Cambridge, MA, 1991), ix–xii; Michael Menzel, "Predigt und Predigtorganisation im Mittelalter," *Historisches Jahrbuch* 111 (1991): 382.

4. Michael Kunczik, *Geschichte der Öffentlichkeitsarbeit in Deutschland* (Cologne, 1997), 24.

5. Carsten Winter, *Predigen unter freiem Himmel: Die medienkulturellen Funktionen der Bettelmönche und ihr geschichtlicher Hintergrund* (Bardowick, 1996).

6. Constance R. Miller, *Technical and Cultural Prerequisites for the Invention of Printing in China and the West* (San Francisco, 1983); Thomas Francis Carter, *The Invention of Printing in China and Its Spread Westward* (New York, 1925); Peter Kornicki, *The Book in Japan: A Cultural History from the Beginnings to the Nineteenth Century* (Leiden, 1998).

7. Heinrich Theodor Musper, *Der Holzschnitt in fünf Jahrhunderten* (Stuttgart, 1964); Max J. Friedländer, *Der Holzschnitt* (Berlin, 1970).

8. Werner Faulstich, *Medien zwischen Herrschaft und Revolte: Die Medienkultur der frühen Neuzeit* (Göttingen, 1998), 250ff.

9. "Schriftlichkeit, Schriftkultur," *LMA*, 7, col. 1566.

10. Menzel, "Predigt," 343.

11. Jacqueline Hamesse, "The Scholastic Model of Reading," in *A History of Reading in the West*, ed. Guglielmo Cavallo and Roger Chartier, trans. Lydia G. Cochrane (Oxford, 1999), 111–15.

12. "Bildkatachese," *LMA*, 2, col. 153.

13. See also Horst Wenzel, *Hören und Sehen: Kultur und Gedächtnis im Mittelalter* (Munich, 1995).

14. Cf. Morenz, "Entstehung und Wesen der Buchreligionen," 709ff.
15. Franke and Trauzettel, *Das Chinesische Kaiserreich*, 138–39; Hans Küng and Julia Ching, *Christentum und Weltreligionen: Chinesische Religion* (Munich, 1999), 227ff.; Hamm, "Buddhismus und Jinismus," 45, 54.
16. Raphael Patai, *The Arab Mind* (New York, 1973), 47.
17. Ibid. On artistic scripts as the imitation of God, 170. On the correlation of religion, language, and the system of writing, see Haarmann, *Universalgeschichte der Schrift*, 493.
18. Bürgel, *Allmacht und Mächtigkeit*, 276–77.
19. A. J. Arberry, *The Koran Interpreted: A Translation* (New York, 1955), 563; Fritz Köster, *Religiöse Erziehung in den Weltreligionen: Hinduismus, Buddhismus, Islam* (Darmstadt, 1986), 174–75.
20. Wahid Gdoura, *Le début de l'imprimerie arabe à Istanbul et en Syrie: Évolution de l'environnement culturel (1706–1787)* (Tunis, 1985).
21. Ibid., 13, 76.
22. George N. Atiyeh, "The Book in the Modern Arab World: The Cases of Lebanon and Egypt," in *The Book in the Islamic World*, ed. George N. Atiyeh (New York, 1995), 235.
23. Gdoura, *Début de l'imprimerie arabe*, 71ff.
24. Ibid., 104.
25. Carter, *Invention of Printing*, 39–46.
26. Ibid., 45, 66–69.
27. John Carter and Percy H. Muir, eds., *Printing and the Mind of Man* (London, 1967), 1.
28. "Bibelübersetzungen," *LMA*, 2, cols. 88ff.
29. "Bibel," *LMA*, 2, cols. 69ff.
30. "Bibeldichtung," *LMA*, 2, cols. 75ff.
31. "Predigt I," *TRE*, 27:225ff.
32. Heinrich von Stietencron, "Die Wertmotivation der religiösen Aussonderungen in Indien," in "Versuch einer Historischen Anthropologie," ed. Oskar Köhler, special issue, *Saeculum* 25, nos. 2–3 (1974): 205; Hamm, "Buddhismus und Jinismus," 54ff.
33. "Predigt I," *TRE*, 27:230.
34. Ibid., 229.
35. Max Weber, *Economy and Society: An Outline of Interpretive Sociology*, ed. Guenther Roth and Claus Wittich, trans. Ephraim Fischoff et al. (New York, 1968), 2:439–68.
36. "Predigt I," *TRE*, 27:226–27.
37. Ibid., 227–28.
38. Ibid., 226.
39. "Predigt," *LMA*, 7, cols. 171ff.
40. Michael Giesecke, *Der Buchdruck in der frühen Neuzeit* (Frankfurt am Main, 1998), 256–57.
41. "Tertiarier," *LMA*, 8, cols. 556ff.

42. Hans Belting, *Bild und Kult* (Munich, 1990), 457ff., 474ff.; Giesecke, *Der Buchdruck*, 299ff.

43. Belting, *Bild und Kult*, 172.

44. Jacques Gernet, *A History of Chinese Civilization*, 2nd ed. (Cambridge, 1996), 226; Hermann Müller-Karpe, *Grundzüge antiker Menschheitsreligion: 1. Jahrhundert v. Chr. bis 5. Jahrhundert* (Stuttgart, 2000), 27, 75–76.

45. Carter, *Invention of Printing*, 17–19.

46. "Graphik," *LMA*, 4, col. 1655; "Metallschnitt," *LMA*, 6, col. 569; "Buchdruck," *LMA*, 2, col. 815.

47. Kornicki, *The Book in Japan*, 114–17; Carter, *Invention of Printing*, 35–38; Miller, *Technical and Cultural Prerequisites for Printing*, 51.

48. Carter, *Invention of Printing*, 37.

49. Kornicki, *The Book in Japan*, 115.

50. Miller, *Technical and Cultural Prerequisites for Printing*, 49–54.

51. Ibid., 52–53.

52. Carter, *Invention of Printing*, 133–36.

53. Musper, *Der Holzschnitt*, 15.

54. Hannelore Sachs et al., *Erklärendes Wörterbuch zur christlichen Kunst* (Hanau, 1983), 76ff.

55. Musper, *Der Holzschnitt*, 15.

56. "Gutenberg, Johannes," *LMA*, 4, col. 1801.

57. "Pilgerandenken, Pilgerzeichen," *LMA*, 6, col. 2154.

58. Menzel, "Predigt," 342.

59. Angenendt, *Das Frühmittelalter*, 212–13.

60. Ibid., 208ff.

61. Ibid., 204ff.

62. Ibid., 306–7.

63. "Predigt VI," *TRE*, 27:249; Angenendt, *Das Frühmittelalter*, 320ff., and *Geschichte der Religiosität*, 478–79.

64. Rolf Zerfaß, *Der Streit um die Laienpredigt* (Freiburg, 1974), 121; Winter, *Predigen unter freiem Himmel*, 84ff.

65. Zerfaß, *Der Streit*, 202.

66. Ibid., 254.

67. Winter, *Predigen unter freiem Himmel*, 8, 105. See also the map in Bayrischer Schulbuch-Verlag, *Großer Historischer Weltatlas*, part 2, 83.

68. Meinolf Lohrum, "Dominikaner," in Dinzelbacher and Hogg, *Kulturgeschichte der christlichen Orden*, 134.

69. Ibid., 126–27.

70. Ibid., 127.

71. Elizabeth L. Eisenstein, "The Impact of Printing on European Education," in *Sociology, History and Education*, ed. P. W. Musgrave (London, 1970), 87.

72. Leonhard Lehmann, "Franziskaner und Klarissen," in Dinzelbacher and Hogg, *Kulturgeschichte der christlichen Orden*, 156.

73. Zerfaß, *Der Streit*, 281.

74. Frank, *Kirchengeschichte des Mittelalters*, 136; Winter, *Predigen unter freiem Himmel*, 109ff.

75. Frank, *Kirchengeschichte des Mittelalters*, 135.

76. "Bibel," *LMA*, 2, col. 43.

77. "Predigt," *LMA*, 7, cols. 181ff.; "Predigt V," *TRE*, 27:245.

78. Merlin L. Swartz, "The Rules of the Popular Preaching in Twelfth-Century Bagdad, according to Ibn al-Jawzî," in *Prédication et propagande au Moyen Age: Islam, Byzance, Occident*, ed. George Makdisi et al. (Paris, 1983), 224–27; Angelika Hartmann, "Islamisches Predigtwesen im Mittelalter: Ibn al-Gauzi und sein 'Buch der Schlußreden' (1186 n. Chr.)," *Saeculum* 38 (1978): 336–65; Johannes Pedersen, "The Islamic Preacher: wa' iz, mudhakkir, gass," in *Ignace Goldziher Memorial Volume*, ed. Samuel Löwinger and Joseph Somogyi (Budapest, 1948), 1:226–51.

79. Hartmann, "Islamisches Predigtwesen," 348.

80. Ibid., 341.

81. Ibid., 354; Swartz, "The Rules of Popular Preaching," 233–35.

82. Hartmann, "Islamisches Predigtwesen," 347ff.

83. Pedersen, "Islamic Preacher," 250–51.

84. Susanne Formanek, "Etoki: Mittelalterliche religiöse Welten erklärt in Bildern," in *Buch und Bild als gesellschaftliche Kommunikationsmittel in Japan einst und jetzt*, ed. Susanne Formanek und Sepp Linhart (Vienna, 1995), 11–44.

85. Ibid., 13.

86. Ibid., 14.

87. Wolfram Aichinger, "Das Schwein des heiligen Antonius: Vom mittelalterlichen Spital ins spanische Gebirgsdorf," *Historische Anthropologie* 6 (1998): 3ff.

88. Ibid., 8.

89. Jürgen Sarnowsky, "Hospitalorden," in Dinzelbacher and Hogg, *Kulturgeschichte der christlichen Orden*, 194.

90. Jean-François Gilmont, "Protestant Reformations and Reading," in Cavallo and Chartier, *Reading in the West*, 224.

91. Ibid., 225.

92. Ibid., 216.

93. Cavallo and Chartier, introduction to *Reading in the West*, 31.

94. Miller, *Technical and Cultural Prerequisites for Printing*, 10.

95. "Papier," *LMA*, 6, col. 1665.

96. "Graphik," *LMA*, 4, cols. 1655ff.; "Metallschnitt," *LMA*, 6, col. 669.

97. "Buchdruck," *LMA*, 2, cols. 815ff.

98. Brian Stock, "Schriftgebrauch und Rationalität im Mittelalter," in *Max Webers Sicht des okzidentalen Christentums*, ed. Wolfgang Schluchter (Frankfurt am Main, 1988), 169.

99. Robert L. Burns, "Paper Comes to the West, 800–1400," in Lindgren, *Europäische Technik*, 413–22; Volker Schmidtchen, "Technik im Übergang zur

Neuzeit zwischen 1350 und 1600," in Ludwig and Schmidtchen, *Metalle undMacht*, 575ff.

100. Burns, "Paper Comes to the West," 416–17; "Papier," *LMA*, 6, col. 1665.
101. Braudel, *Structures of Everyday Life*, 397.
102. "Papier," *LMA*, 6, col. 1664; Burns, "Paper Comes to the West," 413.
103. Carter, *Invention of Printing*, 113–38.
104. "Qur'an," *DI*, 483.
105. Ibid., 530.
106. "Pergament," *LMA*, 6, col. 1885.
107. Burns, "Paper Comes to the West," 413.
108. Carter, *Invention of Printing*, 3; Miller, *Technical and Cultural Prerequisites for Printing*, 10–11.
109. "Papier," *LAO*, 333.
110. Miller, *Technical and Cultural Prerequisites for Printing*, 11.
111. Ibid., 44–45.
112. Carter, *Invention of Printing*, 23–27.
113. Belting, *Bild und Kult*, 474ff.
114. Carter, *Invention of Printing*, 23.
115. Ibid.
116. "Graphik," *LMA*, 4, col. 1665; "Zeugdruck," *LMA*, 9, col. 582; Friedländer, *Der Holzschnitt*, 9; Belting, *Bild und Kult*, 474.
117. "Spielkarten," *LMA*, 7, col. 2111; Belting, *Bild und Kult*, 475.
118. Carter, *Invention of Printing*, 7–11; Miller, *Technical and Cultural Prerequisites for Printing*, 15–17.
119. Carter, *Invention of Printing*, 159–68.
120. Ibid., 169–79.
121. Haarmann, *Universalgeschichte der Schrift*, 356.
122. Ekkehard May, "Buch und Buchillustration im vormodernen Japan," in Formanek and Linhart, *Buch und Bild in Japan*, 46.
123. Gernet, *Chinese Civilization*, 332.
124. Kuhn, *Song-Dynastie*, 57.
125. Elvin, *Chinese Past*, 180; see 261 for Korea.
126. Ibid., 181; Carter, *Invention of Printing*, 57.
127. Kornicki, *The Book in Japan*, 5, 124.
128. Elizabeth Eisenstein, *The Printing Revolution in Early Modern Europe* (Cambridge, 1983), 11, 13, 16.
129. Faulstich, *Medien zwischen Herrschaft und Revolte*, 250–51.
130. See the maps in Eisenstein, *The Printing Revolution*, 14–15.
131. Faulstich, *Medien zwischen Herrschaft und Revolte*, 119.
132. "Einblattdrucke," *LMA*, 3, 1732.
133. Ibid.
134. Faulstich,*Medien zwischen Herrschaft und Revolte*, 119.
135. Delumeau, *La peur*, 208–11.

136. Paul Saenger, "Reading in the Later Middle Ages," in Cavallo and Chartier, *Reading in the West*, 133.

137. Elizabeth Eisenstein, *The PrintingPress as an Agent of Change: Communications and Cultural Transformations in Early Modern Europe* (Cambridge, 1979), 1:12–14; "Pecia, petia," *LMA*, 6, col. 1847.

138. Klaus Schreiner, "Laienfrömmigkeit—Frömmigkeit von Eliten oder Frömmigkeit des Volkes? Zur sozialen Verfaßtheit laikaler Frömmigkeitspraxis im späten Mittelalter," in *Laienfrömmigkeit im späten Mittelalter* (Munich, 1992), 31; "Stundenbuch," *LMA*, 8, col. 259.

139. Angenendt, *Geschichte der Religiosität*, 486; Schreiner, "Laienfrömmigkeit," 72ff.

140. Angenendt, *Geschichte der Religiosität*, 180.

141. Carter and Muir, *Printing and the Mind of Man*, 1.

142. Cavallo and Chartrier, introduction to *Reading in the West*, 16–18; Saenger, "Reading in the Later Middle Ages," 133.

143. Belting, *Bild und Kult*, 470ff.

144. Ibid., 457.

145. Eisenstein, *The Printing Press*, 46.

146. Giesecke, *Der Buchdruck*, 230ff.

147. Carter and Muir, *Printing and the Mind of Man*, 3.

148. Hans-Dieter Düpmann, *Die Russische Orthodoxe Kirche in Geschichte und Gegenwart* (Vienna, 1977), 86.

149. Gary Marker, *Publishing, Printing, and the Origins of Intellectual Life in Russia, 1700–1800* (Princeton, 1985), 17.

150. Maximilian Peyfuss, "Die Druckerei von Moschopolis, 1731–1769: Buchdruck und Heiligenverehrung im Erzbistum Achrida," *Habilitations-Schrift* (University of Vienna, 1988), 66ff.

151. Steven Runciman, *The Great Church in Captivity: A Study of the Patriarchate of Constantinople from the Eve of the Turkish Conquest to the Greek War of Independence* (Cambridge, 1968), 271–73; Peyfuss, "Die Druckerei von Moschopolis," 78–79.

152. Gunnar Hering, "Die Juden von Saloniki," *Südostforschungen* 58 (1999): 34.

153. Raphael Patai, *The Jewish Mind* (New York, 1977), 166.

154. Fernand Braudel, *The Mediterranean and the Mediterranean World in the Age of Philip II*, trans. Siân Reynolds (New York, 1975), 2:808.

155. Robert Bonfil, "Reading in the Jewish Communities of Western Europe in the Middle Ages," in Cavallo and Chartier, *Reading in the West*, 166.

156. Braudel, *The Mediterranean*, 2:808.

157. Gdoura, *Début de l'imprimerie arabe*, 104.

158. Ibid., 107.

159. Jones, *European Miracle*, 67.

160. Gdoura, *Début de l'imprimerie arabe*, 85; Toby Huff, *The Rise of Early Modern Science: Islam, China, and the West* (Cambridge, 1993), 225.

161. Gdoura, *Début de l'imprimerie arabe*, 104.
162. Ibid., 115.
163. Ibid., 94ff.
164. Ibid., 102.
165. Ibid., 98.
166. Giesecke, *Der Buchdruck*, 131.
167. Kornicki, *The Book in Japan*, 21.
168. Ibid., 5.
169. Formanek and Linhart, introduction to *Buch und Bild in Japan*, 9.
170. Sepp Linhart, "Kawaraban—die ersten japanischen Zeitungen," in Formanek and Linhart, *Buch und Bild in Japan*, 139–66.
171. Formanek and Linhart, introduction to *Buch und Bild in Japan*, 7.
172. Elvin, *Chinese Past*, 181; Carter, *Invention of Printing*, 55.
173. Kai-wing Chow, "Writing for Success: Printing, Examinations, and Intellectual Change in Late Ming China," in "Publishing and the Print Culture in Late Imperial China," special issue, *Late Imperial China* 17, no. 1 (1996): 123.
174. Giesecke, *Der Buchdruck*, 665ff.; Eisenstein, *The Printing Revolution*, 185–252.
175. On the historical-anthropological effects of this "biculturalism," see Wolfgang Reinhard, "Die lateinische Variante von Religion und ihre Bedeutung für die politische Kultur Europas: Ein Versuch in historischer Anthropologie," *Saeculum* 43 (1992): 237.

CONCLUSION

1. Erich Obst, *Allgemeine Wirtschafts- und Verkehrsgeographie* (Berlin, 1959), 56ff.; Hägermann, "Technik im frühen Mittelalter," 419ff.
2. Sprandel, *Das Eisengewerbe*, 33.
3. Michael Mitterauer, "Produktionsweise, Siedlungsstruktur und Sozialformen im österreichischen Montanwesen des Mittelalters und der Frühen Neuzeit," in *Österreichisches Montanwesen*, ed. Michael Mitterauer (Vienna, 1974), 234–315.
4. Braudel, *Structures of Everyday Life*, 355; Reynolds, *Stronger than a Hundred Men*, 85–88; Ludwig, "Technik im hohen Mittelalter," 51ff., 70ff.
5. Radomir Pleiner, "Vom Rennfeuer zum Hochofen: Die Entwicklung der Eisenverhüttung, 9.–14. Jahrhundert," in Lindgren, *Europäische Technik*, 254–55.
6. Bartels, "Der Bergbau," 236; "Wasserkunst," *LMA*, 8, col. 2076.
7. Roman Sandgruber, *Ökonomie und Politik: Österreichische Wirtschaftsgeschichte vom Mittelalter bis zur Gegenwart* (Vienna, 1995), 70.
8. Konrad Bedal, *Mühlen und Müller in Franken* (Bad Windsheim, 1984), 45; Hägermann, "Technik im frühen Mittelalter," 420ff.
9. "Schmied, Schmiede," *LMA*, 7, col. 1505.
10. Blanchard, *Mining*.

11. Carlo M. Cipolla, *Guns, Sails and Empires: Technological Innovation and the Early Phases of European Expansion, 1400–1700* (New York, 1966), 23.

12. Ibid., 23–24.

13. "Silber," *LMA*, 7, cols. 1899–1900.

14. Mitterauer, "Produktionsweise, Siedlungsstruktur und Sozialformen," 303ff.

15. Ibid., 276ff.

16. Lothar Suhling, "Verhüttung silberhaltiger Kupfererze," in Lindgren, *Europäische Technik*, 269–76; Thomas Sokoll, *Bergbau im Übergang zur Neuzeit* (Idstein, 1994), 54ff.

17. "Frühkapitalismus," *LMA*, 4, col. 1001.

18. Sokoll, *Bergbau im Übergang*, 55–56.

19. Kenneth Pomeranz, *The Great Divergence: China, Europe, and the Making of the Modern World Economy* (Princeton, 2000), 13.

20. Rudolf Sieferle, *Der unterirdische Wald: Energiekrise und Industrielle Revolution* (Munich, 1982), 114.

21. Ibid., 152.

22. Ibid., 166.

23. Ibid., 108.

24. David S. Landes, *The Wealth and Poverty of Nations: Why Some Are So Rich and Some So Poor* (New York, 1999), 58–59.

25. Peter Blickle, *Kommunalismus: Skizzen einer gesellschaftlichen Organisationsform* (Munich, 2000), 2:1.

26. Reinhard, *Geschichte der Staatsgewalt*, 239.

27. Hinnerk Bruhns and Wilfried Nippel, eds. *Max Weber und die Stadt im Kulturvergleich*, Kritische Studien zur Geschichtswissenschaft 140 (Göttingen, 2000), esp. 36ff.; Wolfgang Schwentker, "Die 'vormoderne' Stadt in Europa und Asien: Überlegungen zu einem strukturgeschichtlichen Vergleich," in Feldbauer et al., *Die vormoderne Stadt*, 260–61, along with other articles in this volume passim.

28. Mitterauer, "Städte als Zentren," in Feldbauer, et al., *Die vormoderne Stadt*, 69.

29. Blickle, "Communalism, Parliamentarism, Republicanism," 1; Mitterauer, "Grundlagen," in Bosl and Möckl, *Der moderne Parlamentarismus*, esp. 38ff.

30. Reinhard, *Geschichte der Staatsgewalt*, 251.

31. "Lombardische Liga," *LMA*, 5, col. 2100.

32. Knut Schulz, *"Denn sie lieben die Freiheit so sehr . . .": Kommunale Aufstände und Entstehung des europäischen Bürgertums im Hochmittelalter* (Darmstadt, 1992). See also the chapter "Coniuratio und Kommune," which critically analyzes the relevant literature, in Michael Borgolte, "Sozialgeschichte des Mittelalters: Eine Forschungsbilanz nach der deutschen Einheit," *Historische Zeitschrift*, n.s., supplement 22 (Munich, 1996), 278ff.

33. Pitz, *Europäisches Städtewesen*, 358 et passim.

34. Althoff, *Verwandte, Freunde und Getreue*, 85ff., 119ff.

35. Angenendt, *Heilige und Reliquien*, 127.
36. Blickle, *Kommunalismus*, 2:359.
37. Reinhard, *Geschichte der Staatsgewalt*, 240.
38. Ibid., 248ff.
39. Kaspar von Greyerz, *Religion und Kultur: Europa, 1500–1800* (Göttingen, 2000), 175, 178, 173.
40. Küng, *Christianity*, 582.
41. See chap. 5 above.
42. Angenendt, *Geschichte der Religiosität*, 503; Bernhard Lang, *Heiliges Spiel: Eine Geschichte des christlichen Gottesdienstes* (Munich, 1998), 345; "Abendmahl, Abendmahlstreit," *LMA*, 1, cols. 22ff.
43. Dinzelbacher, "Die 'Realpräsenz,'" in Dinzelbacher and Bauer, *Heiligenverehrung*, 115ff.
44. Angenendt, *Geschichte der Religiosität*, 506.
45. Angenendt, *Heilige und Reliquien*, 158ff.
46. Ibid., 179.
47. "Monstranz," *LMA*, 6, col. 771.
48. Angenendt, *Heilige und Reliquien*, 12.
49. "Kelchkommunion," *LMA*, 5, cols. 1069–70.
50. Angenendt, *Geschichte der Religiosität*, 506ff.
51. R. Po-Chia Hsia, *The Myth of Ritual Murder: Jews and Magic in Reformation Germany* (New Haven, 1988); Michael Mitterauer, "'Heut' ist eine heilige Samstagnacht,'" in Mitterauer, *Dimensionen des Heiligen*, 107ff.
52. "Ritualmordbeschuldigung," *LMA*, 7, col. 879.
53. Wolfram Aichinger, "'Gegenwart der Vergangenheit' und 'Gegenwart der Zukunft' im 'Espill de la vida religiosa': Mittelalterliche Passionsfrömmigkeit als Ausgangspunkt für interdisziplinäre Forschung," *Historische Anthropologie* 9 (2001): 93–102; see also Ferdinand Seibt, *Die Begründung Europas: Ein Zwischenbericht über die letzten tausend Jahre* (Frankfurt am Main, 2002), 91–92.
54. Heinz Kindermann, *Theatergeschichte Europas* (Salzburg, 1957), 1:226ff.; Dinzelbacher and Krochmalnik, *Hoch- und Spätmittelalter*, 124; "Geistliches Spiel," *LMA*, 4, col. 1194.
55. Aichinger, "'Gegenwart der Vergangenheit,'" 95.
56. "Geistliches Spiel," *LMA*, 4, col. 1195.
57. "Goldschmiedekunst," *LMA*, 4, cols. 1548–49.
58. "Altar," *LMA*, 1, col. 463.
59. "Tabernakel," *LMA*, 8, col. 393.
60. "Kreuz, Kruzifix," *LMA*, 5, cols. 1495–96; Wilhelm Ziehr, *Das Kreuz: Symbol—Gestalt—Bedeutung* (Darmstadt, 1997), 96, 112.
61. Dinzelbacher, "Die 'Realpräsenz,'" 139.
62. Belting, *Bild und Kult*, 497.
63. Angenendt, *Geschichte der Religiosität*, 505–6; Dinzelbacher and Krochmalnik, *Hoch- und Spätmittelalter*, 67–68.

64. Jones, *European Miracle*, 58.

65. See note 11 above.

66. Jenö Szücs, *Die drei historischen Regionen Europas* (Frankfurt am Main, 1994), 20, 26 et passim.

67. Ibid., 26. On the productive effect of this dualism on Europe's political culture, see also Reinhard, "Die lateinische Variante," 240ff.

68. Landes, *Wealth and Poverty*, 45–59, 60–78.

69. Ibid., 58.

70. Reinhard, "Die Europäisierung," 119.

71. A classic statement of this line of thought is in Huntington, *Clash of Civilizations*, 158–61.

Bibliography

Abel, Wilhelm. "Landwirtschaft, 500–900." In *Handbuch der deutschen Wirtschafts- und Sozialgeschichte*, edited by Hermann Aubin and Wolfgang Zorn, 1:83–108. Stuttgart, 1971.

Abulafia, David. *The Two Italies: Economic Relations between the Norman Kingdom of Sicily and the Northern Communes*. Cambridge, 1977.

Abu-Lughod, Janet L. *Before European Hegemony: The World System, 1250–1350*. New York, 1989.

Aichinger, Wolfram. "'Gegenwart der Vergangenheit' und 'Gegenwart der Zukunft' im 'Espill de la vida religiosa': Mittelalterliche Passionsfrömmigkeit als Ausgangspunkt für interdisziplinäre Forschung." *Historische Anthropologie* 9 (2001): 93–102.

———. "Das Schwein des heiligen Antonius: Vom mittelalterlichen Spital ins spanische Gebirgsdorf." *Historische Anthropologie* 6 (1998): 1–32.

Airaldi, Gabriella. "Genova e la Liguria nel Medioevo." In *Comuni e signorie nell'Italia settentrionale: Il Piemonte e Liguria*, edited by Ana M. N. Patrone and Gabriella Airaldi, 365–514. Storia d'Italia 5, edited by Giuseppe Galasso. Turin, 1986.

Allmendinger, Karl-Heinz. *Die Beziehungen zwischen der Kommune Pisa und Ägypten im hohen Mittelalter*. Wiesbaden, 1967.

Altheim, Franz. *Gesicht von Abend und Morgen: Von der Antike zum Mittelalter*. Frankfurt am Main, 1954.

Altheim, Franz, and Ruth Stiehl. *Ein asiatischer Staat: Feudalismus unter den Sasaniden und ihren Nachbarn*. Wiesbaden, 1954.

Althoff, Gerd. *Verwandte, Freunde und Getreue: Zum politischen Stellenwert der Gruppenbildungen im frühen Mittelalter*. Darmstadt, 1990.

Anderson, Matthew Smith. *The Origins of the European State System, 1494–1618*. London, 1998.

Anderson, Robert T. "Changing Kinship in Europe." *Kroeber Anthropological Society* 28, no. 1 (1963): 1–47.

Angenendt, Arnold. *Das Frühmittelalter.* Stuttgart, 1990.

———. *Geschichte der Religiosität im Mittelalter.* Darmstadt, 1997.

———. *Heilige und Reliquien.* Munich, 1994.

———. *Kaiserherrschaft und Königstaufe: Kaiser, Könige und Päpste als geistliche Patrone in der abendländischen Missionsgeschichte.* Berlin, 1984.

———. "Die religiösen Wurzeln Europas." In *Das gemeinsame Haus Europa: Handbuch zur europäischen Kulturgeschichte,* edited by the Museum für Völkerkunde in Hamburg, 481–88. Munich, 1999.

Argynbaev, Kh. A. "The Kinship System and Customs Connected with the Ban on Pronouncing the Personal Names of Elder Relatives among the Kazakhs." In *Kinship and Marriage in the Soviet Union,* edited by Tamara Dragadze, 40–59. London, 1984.

Astill, Grenville, and John Langdon, eds. *Medieval Farming and Technology: The Impact of Agricultural Change in Northwest Europe.* Leiden, 1997.

Atiyeh, George N. "The Book in the Modern Arab World: The Cases of Lebanon and Egypt." In *The Book in the Islamic World: The Written Word and Communication in the Middle East,* edited by George N. Atiyeh, 233–54. New York, 1995.

Aubin, Hermann. "Die Römerzeit in Deutschland und ihr Fortwirken." In *Handbuch der deutschen Wirtschafts- und Sozialgeschichte,* edited by Hermann Aubin and Wolfgang Zorn, 1:39–55. Stuttgart, 1971.

Auer, Leopold. "Der Kriegsdienst des Klerus unter den sächsischen Kaisern." *Mitteilungen des Instituts für österreichische Geschichtsforschung* 79 (1971): 316–444, and 80 (1972): 48–70.

Bachrach, Bernard S. *Early Carolingian Warfare: Prelude to Empire.* Philadelphia, 2001.

Baechler, Jean. *The Origins of Capitalism.* Oxford, 1975.

———. "The Origins of Modernity: Caste and Feudality (India, Europe and Japan)." In Baechler et al., *Europe and Capitalism,* 39–65.

Baechler, Jean, John A. Hall, and Michael Mann, eds. *Europe and the Rise of Capitalism.* Oxford, 1988.

Balard, Michel. "Communes italiennes, pouvoir et habitants des États Francs de Syrie-Palestine au XIIᵉ siècle." In *Crusades and Muslims in Twelfth-Century Syria,* edited by Maya Schatzmiller, 43–64. The Medieval Mediterranean 1. Leiden, 1993.

Balassa, Ivan. "Einleitung." In *Getreidebau in Mittel- und Osteuropa,* edited by Ivan Balassa, 7–20. Budapest, 1972.

Barber, Richard. *The Knight and Chivalry.* Woodbridge, UK, 1970.

Bardach, Julius. "L'indivision familiale dans les pays du Centre-Est européen." In *Famille et parenté dans l'Occident médiéval,* edited by Georges Duby and Jacques Le Goff, 335–53. Rome, 1977.

Barker, Graeme. *Prehistoric Farming in Europe.* Cambridge, 1985.

Bartels, Christoph. "Der Bergbau—im Zentrum das Silber." In Lindgren, *Europäische Technik*, 235–48.

Bartlett, Robert. *The Making of Europe: Conquest, Colonization, and Cultural Change, 950–1350.* Princeton, 1993.

Bayrischer Schulbuch-Verlag, ed. *Großer Historischer Weltatlas.* Part 2, *Mittelalter.* 2nd ed. Munich, 1979.

Beck, Hans-Georg, ed. *Lust an der Geschichte: Leben in Byzanz, ein Lesebuch.* Munich, 1991.

Bedal, Konrad. *Mühlen und Müller in Franken.* Bad Windsheim, 1984.

Belting, Hans. *Bild und Kult.* Munich, 1990.

Bender, Helmut. "Agrargeschichte Deutschlands in der römischen Kaiserzeit innerhalb der Grenzen des Imperium Romanum." In Lüning et al., *Deutsche Agrargeschichte*, 263–374.

Benecke, Norbert. *Der Mensch und seine Haustiere.* Stuttgart, 1994.

Benoit, Paul, and Joséphine Rouillard. "Medieval Hydraulics in France." In Squatriti, *Working with Water*, 161–215.

Bentley, Jerry H. "Hemispheric Integration, 500–1500 C.E." *Journal of World History* 9 (1998): 237–54.

———. *Old World Encounters.* New York, 1993.

Berkemer, Georg. "Gedanken zur Geschichte Südasiens um das Jahr 1000." *Periplus: Jahrbuch für außereuropäische Geschichte* 10 (2000): 73–91.

Bertholet, Alfred. *Wörterbuch der Religionen.* Stuttgart, 1985.

Besançon, Alain. "The Russian Case." In Baechler et al., *Europe and Capitalism*, 159–68.

Bianquis, Thierry. "The Family in Arab Islam." In Burguière et al., *Distant Worlds, Ancient Worlds*, 601–47.

Birkhan, Helmut. *Kelten: Versuch einer Gesamtdarstellung ihrer Kultur.* Vienna, 1997.

Bisson, Thomas N. *Assemblies and Representation in Languedoc in the Thirteenth Century.* Princeton, 1964.

———. "The 'Feudal Revolution.'" *Past and Present* 142 (1994): 6–42.

———. "The Origin of the Corts of Catalonia." *Parliaments, Estates and Representation* 16 (1996): 31–45.

Bito, Masahide. "Confucian Thought during the Tokugawa Period." In De Vos and Sofue, *Religion and Family*, 127–38.

Blaine, Bradford B. "The Enigmatic Water-Mill." In *On Pre-Modern Technology and Science: A Volume of Studies in Honor of Lynn White, Jr.*, 163–76. Malibu, 1976.

Blanchard, Ian. *Mining, Metallurgy and Minting in the Middle Ages.* 2 vols. Stuttgart, 2001.

Blickle, Peter. "Communalism, Parliamentarism, Republicanism." *Parliaments, Estates and Representation* 6 (1986): 1–13.

———. "Der Kommunalismus als Gestaltungsprinzip zwischen Mittelalter und Moderne." In *Gesellschaft und Gesellschaften: Festschrift zum 65. Geburtstag von Professor Dr. Ulrich im Hof,* edited by Nicolai Bernard and Quirinus Reichen, 95–113. Bern, 1982.

———. *Kommunalismus: Skizzen einer gesellschaftlichen Organisationsform.* 2 vols. Munich, 2000.

———, ed. *Landgemeinde und Stadtgemeinde in Mitteleuropa: Ein struktureller Vergleich.* Munich, 1991.

Bloch, Marc. "The Advent and Triumph of the Watermill." In *Land and Work in Medieval Europe: Selected Papers by Marc Bloch.* Translated by J. E. Anderson, 136–68. London, 1967. Originally published as "Avènement et conquêtes du moulin à eau," *Annales d'histoire économique et sociale* 7 (1935): 538–63.

———. *The Growth and Ties of Dependence.* Vol. 1 of *Feudal Society.* Translated by L. A. Manyon. Chicago, 1961. Originally published as *La société féodale,* 2 vols. (1939–40; Paris, 1960–62).

———. "Problèmes d'Europe." In *Histoire et historiens,* edited by Étienne Bloch, 133–44. Paris, 1995.

———. "The Rise of Dependent Cultivation and Seignorial Institutions." In *The Cambridge Economic History of Europe,* 2nd ed., 1:235–90. Cambridge, 1966.

Blokmans, Willem Pieter. "A Typology of Representative Institutions in Late Medieval Europe." *Journal of Medieval History* 4 (1978): 189–215.

Bonfil, Robert. "Reading in the Jewish Communities of Western Europe in the Middle Ages." In Cavallo and Chartier, *Reading in the West,* 149–78.

Borgolte, Michael. "'Europa ein christliches Land': Religion als Weltstifterin im Mittelalter." *Zeitschrift für Geschichtswissenschaft* 48 (2000): 1061–74.

———. *Die mittelalterliche Kirche.* Enzyklopädie deutscher Geschichte 17. Munich, 1992.

———. "Sozialgeschichte des Mittelalters: Eine Forschungsbilanz nach der deutschen Einheit." *Historische Zeitschrift,* n.s., supplement 22. Munich, 1996.

Born, Martin. *Die Entwicklung der deutschen Agrarlandschaft.* Darmstadt, 1974.

Borst, Arno. *Lebensformen im Mittelalter.* Frankfurt am Main, 1973.

———. "Das Rittertum im Hochmittelalter: Idee und Wirklichkeit." In Borst, *Das Rittertum,* 212–46.

———, ed. *Das Rittertum im Mittelalter.* Darmstadt, 1976.

Boserup, Ester. *The Conditions of Agricultural Growth: The Economics of Agrarian Change under Population Pressure.* Chicago, 1965.

Bosl, Karl. "Die 'Familia' als Grundstruktur der mittelalterlichen Gesellschaft." *Zeitschrift für bayerische Landesgeschichte* 38 (1975): 403–24.

Bosl, Karl, and Karl Möckl, eds. *Der moderne Parlamentarismus und seine Grundlagen in der ständischen Repräsentation.* Berlin, 1977.

Bosworth, C. E., Charles Issawi, Roger Savory, and A. L. Udovitch, eds. *The Islamic World from Classical to Modern Times: Essays in Honor of Bernard Lewis.* Princeton, 1989.

Bowersock, Glen W. "From Emperor to Bishop: The Self-Conscious Transformation of Political Power in the Fourth Century A.D." *Classical Philology* 81 (1986): 298–307.

Brandenburg, Dietrich. *Die Madrasa: Ursprung, Entwicklung, Ausbreitung und künstlerische Gestaltung der islamischen Moschee-Hochschule.* Graz, 1978.

Braudel, Fernand. *The Structures of Everyday Life: The Limits of the Possible.* Vol. 1 of *Civilization and Capitalism, 15th–18th Century.* Revised translation by Siân Reynolds. New York, 1981.

———. *The Mediterranean and the Mediterranean World in the Age of Philip II.* Translated by Siân Reynolds. 2 vols. New York, 1975.

Brauneder, Wilhelm. "Typen mittelalterlichen Erbrechts in ihrer Bedeutung für die Bevölkerungsentwicklung." *Saeculum* 39 (1988): 154–67.

Bray, Francesca. *The Rice Economies: Technology and Development in Asian Societies.* Berkeley, 1986.

Breuer, Stefan. "Der okzidentale Feudalismus in Max Webers Gesellschaftsgeschichte." In Schluchter, *Max Webers Sicht des okzidentalen Christentums,* 437–75.

Brown, Peter. *The Rise of Western Christendom: Triumph and Diversity, AD 200–1000.* Cambridge, MA, 1996.

Brown, R. Allen. "The Norman Conquest and the Genesis of English Castles." In *Castles, Conquest and Charters,* 75–89. Woodbridge, UK, 1989.

Bruck, Gabriele von. "Heiratspolitik der 'Prophetennachfahren.'" *Saeculum* 40 (1989): 272–95.

Brück, Michael von, and Whalen Lai. *Buddhismus und Christentum.* Munich, 2000.

Bruckmüller, Ernst. "Täler und Gerichte." In Bruckmüller et al., *Herrschaftsstruktur und Ständebildung,* 3:11–51.

Bruckmüller, Ernst, Michael Mitterauer, and Helmuth Stradal, eds. *Herrschaftsstruktur und Ständebildung: Beiträge zur Typologie der österreichischen Länder aus ihren mittelalterlichen Grundlagen.* 3 vols. Vienna, 1973.

Bruhns, Hinnerk, and Wilfried Nippel, eds. *Max Weber und die Stadt im Kulturvergleich.* Kritische Studien zur Geschichtswissenschaft 140. Göttingen, 2000.

Brunner, Heinrich. "Der Reiterdienst und die Anfänge des Lehenswesens." *Zeitschrift der Savigny-Stiftung für Rechtsgeschichte, Germanistische Abteilung* 8 (1987): 1–38.

Brunner, Karl. "Continuity and Discontinuity of Roman Agricultural Knowledge in the Early Middle Ages." In Sweeney, *Agriculture,* 21–40.

Brunner, Otto. *Land und Herrschaft.* Vienna, 1959.

———. "Die ritterlich-höfische Kultur." In Borst, *Das Rittertum,* 142–71.

Buck, David. "Was It Pluck or Luck That Made the West Grow Rich?" *Journal of World History* 10, no. 2 (1999): 413–30.

Bulliet, Richard J. *The Camel and the Wheel.* Cambridge, MA, 1973.

Bumke, Joachim. "Der adelige Ritter." In Borst, *Das Rittertum,* 266–92.

Bur, Michael. *Le château*. Turnhout, 1999.

Bürgel, Johann Christoph. *Allmacht und Mächtigkeit: Religion und Welt im Islam*. Munich, 1991.

Burke, Peter. "City-States." In *States in History*, edited by John A. Hall, 137–53. Oxford, 1986.

———. "Republics of Merchants in Early Modern Europe." In Baechler et al., *Europe and Capitalism*, 220–33.

Burkert, Walter. *Antike Mysterien*. Munich, 1990.

Burns, Robert L. "Paper Comes to the West, 800–1400." In Lindgren, *Europäische Technik*, 413–22.

Buxbaum, David C., ed. *Chinese Family Law and Social Change in Historical and Comparative Perspective*. Seattle, 1978.

Cahen, Claude. *Der Islam*. Vol. 1, *Vom Ursprung bis zu den Anfängen des Osmannenreiches*. Fischer Weltgeschichte 14. Frankfurt am Main, 1968.

Campbell, Bruce M. S. "Ecology versus Economics in Late Thirteenth- and Early Fourteenth-Century English Agriculture." In Sweeney, *Agriculture*, 76–108.

Capelle, Torsten. "Die Frühgeschichte (1.–9. Jahrhundert ohne römische Provinzen)." In Lüning et al., *Deutsche Agrargeschichte*, 375–448.

Cardini, Franco. *Alle radici della cavalleria medievale*. Florence, 1997.

Cardona, Giorgio Raimondo. "I nomi della parentela." In *La famiglia italiana dall'Ottocento a oggi*, edited by Piero Melograni, 287–325. Rome, 1988.

Carsten, Janet, and Stephen Hugh-Jones. Introduction to *About the House: Lévi-Strauss and Beyond*, edited by Janet Carsten and Stephen Hugh-Jones, 6–21. Cambridge, 1995.

Carter, John, and Percy H. Muir, eds. *Printing and the Mind of Man: A Descriptive Catalogue Illustrating the Impact of Print on the Evolution of Western Civilization during Five Centuries*. London, 1967.

Carter, Thomas Francis. *The Invention of Printing in China and Its Spread Westward*. New York, 1925.

Cartier, Michel. "China: The Family as a Relay of Government." In Burguière et al., *Distant Worlds, Ancient Worlds*, 491–522.

Cavallo, Guglielmo, and Roger Chartier, eds. *A History of Reading in the West*. Translated by Lydia G. Cochrane. Oxford, 1999.

Charles-Edwards, T. M. "Kinship, Status and the Origins of the Hide." *Past and Present* 56, no. 1 (1972): 3–33.

Chartier, Roger. "Gutenberg Revisited from the East." Translated by Jill A. Friedman. In "Publishing and the Print Culture in Late Imperial China." Special issue, *Late Imperial China* 17, no. 1 (June 1996): 1–9.

Chaudhuri, K. N. "The Economy in Muslim Societies." In Robinson, *Islamic World*, 124–63.

Chaunu, Pierre. *L'expansion européenne du XIIIᵉ au XVᵉ siècle*. Paris, 1969.

Chikusa, Tatsuo. "Succession to Ancestral Sacrifices and Adoption of Heirs to the Sacrifices: As Seen from an Inquiry into Customary Institutions in Manchuria." In Buxbaum, *Chinese Family Law*, 151–75.

Chow, Kai-wing. "Writing for Success: Printing, Examinations, and Intellectual Change in Late Ming China." In "Publishing and the Print Culture in Late Imperial China." Special issue, *Late Imperial China* 17, no. 1 (June 1996): 120–57.

Christian, David. "Inner Eurasia as a Unit of World History." *Journal of World History* 5 (1994): 173–211.

Cipolla, Carlo M. *Guns, Sails and Empires: Technological Innovation and the Early Phases of European Expansion, 1400–1700.* New York, 1966.

Cipolla, Carlo M., and Knut Borchardt, eds. *Europäische Wirtschaftsgeschichte / The Fontana Economic History of Europe.* 5 vols. Stuttgart and New York, 1983–86.

Claude, Dietrich. *Adel, Kirche und Königtum im Westgotenreich.* Sigmaringen, 1971.

Clemens, Lukas, and Michael Matheus. "Die Walkmühle." In Lindgren, *Europäische Technik*, 233–34.

Cole, Penny J. *The Preaching of the Crusades to the Holy Land, 1095–1270.* Cambridge, MA, 1991.

Collins, E. J. T. "Rye in Britain." In Devroey et al., *Le seigle*, 117–33.

Comet, Georges. *Le paysan et son outil.* Rome, 1992.

———. "Technology and Agricultural Expansion in the Middle Ages: The Example of France North of the Loire." In Astill and Langdon, *Medieval Farming*, 11–39.

Conerman, Stephan. "Türken, Iraner, Araber: Zentralasien und der Vordere Orient zur Zeit des christlichen Jahres 1000." *Periplus: Jahrbuch für außereuropäische Geschichte* 10 (2000): 92–119.

Congar, Yves M.-J. "Quod omnes tangit, ab omnibus tractari et approbari debet." In Rausch, *Die geschichtlichen Grundlagen*, 1:115–82.

Conze, Werner. *Agrarverfassung und Bevölkerung in Litauen und Weißrußland.* Leipzig, 1950.

Crefeld, Martin van. *The Rise and Decline of the State.* Cambridge, 1999.

Crone, Patricia. "Max Weber, das islamische Recht und die Entstehung des Kapitalismus." In Schluchter, *Max Webers Sicht des Islams*, 294–333.

———. *Pre-Industrial Societies: Anatomy of the Pre-Modern World.* 2nd ed. Oxford, 2003.

———. *Slaves on Horses: The Evolution of the Islamic Polity.* Cambridge, 1980.

Crosby, Alfred. *Ecological Imperialism: The Biological Expansion of Europe, 900–1900.* Cambridge, 1986.

Curtin, Philip D. *The World and the West: The European Challenge and the Overseas Response in the Age of Empire.* Cambridge, 2000.

Dabashi, Hamid. *Authority in Islam: From the Rise of Muhammad to the Establishment of the Umayyads.* New Brunswick, 1993.

Dannenbauer, Heinrich. "Adel, Burg und Herrschaft bei den Germanen." *Historisches Jahrbuch* 61 (1941): 1–50.

Day, John. "La Sardegna e suoi dominatori dal secolo XI al secolo XIV." In *La Sardegna medioevale e moderna*, edited by John Day, B. Anatra, and L. Scaraffia. Storia d'Italia 10, edited by Giuseppe Galasso, 1–186. Turin, 1984.

Delumeau, Jean. *La peur en Occident (XIVe–XVIIIe siècles): Une cité assiégée.* Paris, 1978.

Demurger, Alain. *Vie et mort de l'ordre du Temple, 1120–1314.* Paris, 1985.

Deng, Kent G. "A Critical Survey of Recent Research in Chinese Economic History." *Economic History Review* 53, no. 1 (2000): 1–28.

De Vos, Georges. "Religion and Family: Structural and Motivational Relationship." In De Vos and Sofue, *Religion and Family*, 3–34.

De Vos, Georges, and Takao Sofue, eds. *Religion and Family in East Asia.* Senri Ethnological Studies 11. Osaka, 1984.

De Vries, Kelly. *Medieval Military Technology.* New York, 1992.

Devroey, Jean-Pierre. Avant-propos to Devroey et al., *Le seigle*, 5–8.

———. "La céréaliculture dans le monde franc." *Settimane di studio del Centro Italiano di Studi sull'Alto Medioevo* 37 (1990): 221–53.

———. "Entre Loire et Rhin: Les fluctuations du terroir de l'épeautre au moyen âge." In *L'épeautre* (Triticum spelta): *Histoire et ethnologie*, edited by Jean-Pierre Devroey and J.-J. Van Mol, 89–105. Brussels, 1989.

Devroey, Jean-Pierre, J.-J. Van Mol, and C. Billen, eds. *Le seigle: Histoire et ethnologie.* Treignes, 1995.

Dhondt, Jan. *Das frühe Mittelalter.* Fischer Weltgeschichte 10. Frankfurt am Main, 1968.

———. "Les origines des États de Flandre." *Anciens Pays et Assemblées d'États* 1 (1950): 3–52.

Di Cosmo, Nicola. "Introduction: Inner Asian Ways of Warfare in Historical Perspective." In *Warfare in Inner Asian History (500–1800)*, edited by Nicola Di Cosmo, 1–32. Leiden, 2002.

Diamond, Jared. *Guns, Germs, and Steel: The Fates of Human Societies.* New York, 1997.

Diesner, Hans-Joachim. *Das Vandalenreich.* Stuttgart, 1966.

Dinzelbacher, Peter, ed. *Europäische Mentalitätsgeschichte: Hauptthemen in Einzeldarstellungen.* Stuttgart, 1993.

———. *Mensch und Tier in der Geschichte Europas.* Stuttgart, 2001.

———. "Die 'Realpräsenz' der Heiligen in ihren Reliquiaren und Gräbern nach mittelalterlichen Quellen." In *Heiligenverehrung in Geschichte und Gegenwart*, edited by Peter Dinzelbacher and Dieter R. Bauer, 115–74. Ostfildern, 1990.

———. *Die Templer—ein geheimnisumwitterter Orden.* Freiburg, 2002.

Dinzelbacher, Peter, and James Lester Hogg, eds. *Kulturgeschichte der christlichen Orden in Einzeldarstellungen.* Stuttgart, 1997.

Dinzelbacher, Peter, and Daniel Krochmalnik, eds. *Hoch- und Spätmittelalter.* Vol. 2 of *Handbuch der Religionsgeschichte im deutschsprachigen Raum.* Paderborn, 2000.

Dinzelbacher, Peter, and Hermann Joseph Roth. "Zisterzienser." In Dinzelbacher and Hogg, *Kulturgeschichte der christlichen Orden,* 349–79.

Döhring, Sieghart. "Europäische Musik im interkulturellen Vergleich." In Schlumberger and Segl, *Europa—aber was ist es?* 115–25.

Dostal, Walter. "Mecca before the Time of the Prophet—an Attempt of an Anthropological Interpretation." *Der Islam* 68 (1991): 193–231.

Drompp, Michael R. "The Uighur-Chinese Conflict of 840–848." In Di Cosmo, *Warfare,* 73–103.

Duby, Georges. *The Early Growth of the European Economy: Warriors and Peasants from the Seventh to the Twelfth Century.* Translated by Howard B. Clarke. London, 1974. Originally published as *Guerriers et paysans, VII–XIIe siècle: Premier essai de l'économie européenne* (Paris, 1973).

———. *L'économie rurale et la vie des campagnes dans l'Occident médiéval: Essai de synthèse, perspectives de recherches.* 2 vols. Paris, 1962. Translated by Cynthia Postan as *Rural Economy and Country Life in the Medieval West* (Columbia, SC, 1986).

———. "Medieval Agriculture 900–1500." In *The Middle Ages,* edited by Carlo Cipolla, 175–220. The Fontana Economic History of Europe 1. London, 1973.

———. *La société aux XIe et XIIe siècles dans la région mâconnaise.* Paris, 1953.

———. *The Three Orders: Feudal Society Imagined.* Translated by Arthur Goldhammer. Chicago, 1980. Originally published as *Les trois ordres; ou, L'imaginaire du féodalisme* (Paris, 1978).

Duby, Georges, and Jacques Le Goff, eds. *Famille et parenté dans l'Occident médiéval.* Rome, 1977.

Ducellier, Alain, et al., eds. *Byzance et le monde orthodoxe.* Paris, 1986.

Dümmler, Ernst. *Geschichte des ostfränkischen Reiches.* 3 vols. Darmstadt, 1960.

Düpmann, Hans-Dieter. *Die Russische Orthodoxe Kirche in Geschichte und Gegenwart.* Vienna, 1977.

Dyer, Christopher. "Medieval farming and technology: Conclusion." In Astill and Langdon, *Medieval Farming,* 293–312.

Eastman, Lloyd E. *Family, Fields and Ancestors: Constancy and Change in China's Social and Economic History, 1550–1949.* New York, 1988.

Ebel, Wilhelm. "Zur Rechtsgeschichte der Gemeinde in Ostfriesland." In Konstanzer Arbeitskreis, *Die Anfänge der Landgemeinde,* 1:305–24.

Ebrey, Patricia Buckley. *Confucianism and Family Rituals in Imperial China: A Social History of Writing about Rites.* Princeton, 1991.

Edelmayer, Friedrich, ed. *Die Geschichte des europäischen Welthandels und der wirtschaftliche Globalisierungsprozeß.* Vienna, 2001.

Edwards, Elwyn Hartley. *Horses: Their Role in the History of Man.* London, 1987.

Eglauer, Martina. *Familie und Haushalt im China der späten Kaiserzeit*. Der europäische Sonderweg 7. Stuttgart, 2001.

Ehmer, Josef, Tamara K. Haraven, and Richard Wall, eds. *Historische Familienforschung: Ergebnisse und Kontroversen*. Frankfurt am Main, 1997.

Ehmer, Josef, and Michael Mitterauer, eds. *Familienstruktur und Arbeitsorganisation in ländlichen Gesellschaften*. Vienna, 1986.

Ehrenkreutz, Andrew S. "The Silent Force behind the Rise of Medieval Islamic Civilization." In Bosworth et al., *The Islamic World*, 121–26.

Eisenstadt, Schmuel N. "The Axial Age: The Emergence of Transcendental Visions and the Rise of Clerics." *European Journal of Sociology* 23, no. 2 (1982): 294–314.

———, ed. *Kulturen der Achsenzeit: Ihre Ursprünge und ihre Vielfalt*. 3 vols. Frankfurt am Main, 1987–92.

Eisenstein, Elizabeth L. "The Impact of Printing on European Education." In *Sociology, History and Education*, edited by P. W. Musgrave, 87–95. London, 1970.

———. *The Printing Press as an Agent of Change: Communications and Cultural Transformations in Early Modern Europe*. 2 vols. Cambridge, 1979.

———. *The Printing Revolution in Early Modern Europe*. Cambridge, 1983.

Eisenstein, Herbert. "Mensch und Tier im Islam." In Münch and Walz, *Tiere und Menschen*, 121–46.

Elvin, Mark. "China as a Counterfactual." In Baechler et al., *Europe and Capitalism*, 101–13.

———. *The Pattern of the Chinese Past*. Stanford, 1973.

———. "Why China Failed to Create an Endogenous Capitalism: A Critique of Max Weber's Explanation." *Theory and Society* 13, no. 3 (1984): 379–91.

Emmrich, Thomas. *Tabu und Meidung im antiken China: Aspekte des Verpönten*. Bad Honnef, 1992.

Endress, Gerhard. *Islam: An Historical Introduction*. 2nd ed. Translated by Carole Hillenbrand. New York, 2002. Originally published as *Der Islam: Eine Einführung in seine Geschichte*, 3rd ed. (Munich, 1997).

Ennen, Edith. *Die europäische Stadt des Mittelalters*. Göttingen, 1972.

Erdmann, Carl. "Die Fortbildung des populären Kreuzzugsgedankens." In Borst, *Das Rittertum*, 47–83.

Erdmann, Carl. *The Origin of the Idea of Crusade*. Translated by Marshall W. Baldwin and Walter Goffart. Princeton, 1977. Originally published as *Die Entstehung des Kreuzzugsgedankens* (Stuttgart, 1935).

Ertman, Thomas. *Birth of the Leviathan: Building States and Regimes in Medieval and Early Modern Europe*. Cambridge, 1997.

Faith, Rosamond. *The English Peasantry and the Growth of Lordship*. London, 1997.

Faroqhi, Suraya. *Kultur und Alltag im Osmanischen Reich: Vom Mittelalter bis zum Anfang des 20. Jahrhunderts*. Munich, 1995.

Fasoli, Gina. "Grundzüge einer Geschichte des Rittertums" (1958). In Borst, *Das Rittertum*, 198–211. Darmstadt, 1976.

Faulstich, Werner. *Medien zwischen Herrschaft und Revolte: Die Medienkultur der frühen Neuzeit.* Göttingen, 1998.

Feldbauer, Peter. *Herren und Ritter.* Vol. 1 of Bruckmüller et al., *Herrschaftsstruktur und Ständebildung.*

———. *Die islamische Welt 600–1250.* Vienna, 1995.

Feldbauer, Peter, Gottfried Liedl, and John Morrissey, eds. *Vom Mittelmeer zum Atlantik: Die mittelalterlichen Anfänge der europäischen Expansion.* Vienna, 2001.

Feldbauer, Peter, Michael Mitterauer, and Wolfgang Schwentker, eds. *Die vormoderne Stadt: Asien und Europa im Vergleich.* Querschnitte: Einführungstexte zur Sozial-, Wirtschafts- und Kulturgeschichte 10. Munich, 2002.

Feldbauer, Peter, and John Morrissey. "Italiens Kolonialexpansion—östlicher Mittelmeerraum und die Küsten des Schwarzen Meeres." In Feldbauer et al., *Vom Mittelmeer zum Atlantik*, 83–102.

Feldbauer, Peter, and John Morrissey. *Venedig, 800–1600: Wasservögel als Weltmacht.* Vienna, 2002.

Fichtenau, Heinrich. *Lebensordnungen des 10. Jahrhunderts: Studien über Denkart und Existenz im einstigen Karolingerreich.* Munich, 1984.

Fine, Agnès. *Parrains, marraines: La parenté spirituelle en Europe.* Paris, 1994.

Formanek, Susanne. *Denn dem Alter kann keiner entfliehen: Altern und Alten im Japan der Nara- und Heian-Zeit.* Beiträge zur Kultur- und Geistesgeschichte Asiens 13. Vienna, 1994.

———. "Etoki: Mittelalterliche religiöse Welten erklärt in Bildern." In Formanek and Linhart, *Buch und Bild*, 11–44.

Formanek, Susanne und Sepp Linhart, eds. *Buch und Bild als gesellschaftliche Kommunikationsmittel in Japan einst und jetzt.* Vienna, 1995.

Fößel, Amalie. "'Europa—aber was ist es'—Aspekte einer kontrovers geführten Diskussion." In Schlumberger and Segl, *Europa—aber was ist es?* 285–302.

Fouracre, Paul. "Cultural Conformity and Social Conservation in Early Medieval Europe." *History Workshop Journal* 33, no. 1 (1992): 152–61.

Franconie, Hélène. "Le seigle à travers les atlas linguistiques et ethnographiques romans." In Devroey et al., *Le seigle*, 51–82.

Frank, Andre Gunder. *ReOrient: Global Economy in the Asian Age.* Berkeley, 1998.

Frank, Isnard Wilhelm. *Kirchengeschichte des Mittelalters.* Düsseldorf, 1984.

Frank, Karl Suso. *Geschichte des christlichen Mönchtums.* 5th ed. Darmstadt, 1993.

Franke, Herbert. "Der Mönch in China und sein Verhältnis zur politischen Macht." In "Versuch einer 'Historischen Anthropologie,'" edited by Oskar Köhler. Special issue, *Saeculum* 25, nos. 2–3 (1974): 201–2.

Franke, Herbert, and Rolf Trauzettel. *Das Chinesische Kaiserreich.* Fischer-Weltgeschichte 19. Frankfurt am Main, 1968.

Frasch, Tilman. "Die Welt des Buddhismus im Jahre 1000." *Periplus: Jahrbuch für außereuropäische Geschichte* 10 (2000): 56–72.

Frauenstädt, Paul. *Blutrache und Totschlagsühne im deutschen Mittelalter.* Leipzig, 1881.

Freedman, Maurice, ed. *Family and Kinship in Chinese Society.* Stanford, 1970.

Freedman, Maurice. "Ritual Aspects of Chinese Kinship and Marriage." In Freedman, *Family and Kinship,* 163–87.

Friedländer, Max J. *Der Holzschnitt.* Berlin, 1970.

Friedrich, Paul. "An Evolutionary Sketch of Russian Kinship." In *Proceedings of the Annual Spring Meeting of the American Sociological Society,* 1–26. N.p., 1963.

Fritze, Wolfgang. "Probleme der abodritischen Stammes- und Reichsverfassung und ihrer Entwicklung vom Stammesstaat zum Herrschaftsstaat." In *Siedlung und Verfassung der Slawen zwischen Elbe, Saale und Oder,* edited by Herbert Ludat, Herbert Jankuhn, Walter Schlesinger, and Ernst Schwarz, 141–219. Gießen, 1960.

Fumagalli, Vito. *Mensch und Umwelt im Mittelalter.* Translated by Walter Kögler and Dagmar Zerbst. Berlin, 1992. Originally published as *L'uomo e l'ambiente nel Medioevo* (Rome, 1992).

Gabrieli, Francesco. *Muhammad and the Conquests of Islam.* Translated by Virginia Luling and Rosamund Linell. London, 1968. Originally published as *Maometto e le grandi conquiste arabe* (Milan, 1967).

Ganshof, François L. "L'armée sous les Carolingiens." *Settimane di studio del Centro Italiano di Studi sull'Alto Medioevo* 15, no. 1 (1968): 109–30.

Garcin, Jean-Claude. "The Mamlūk Military System and the Blocking of Medieval Moslem Society." In Baechler et al., *Europe and Capitalism,* 113–30.

Gaunt, David. "The Property and Kin Relationships of Retired Farmers in Northern and Central Europe." In Wall et al., *Family Forms,* 249–79.

Gdoura, Wahid. *Le début de l'imprimerie arabe à Istanbul et en Syrie: Évolution de l'environnement culturel (1706–1787).* Tunis, 1985.

Gellner, Ernest. "The Distinctiveness of the Muslim State." In *Islam et politique au Maghreb,* edited by Ernest Gellner and Jean-Claude Vatin, 163–74. Paris, 1980.

———. "Introduction." In Baechler et al., *Europe and Capitalism,* 1–5.

———. *Muslim Society.* Cambridge, 1981.

Gerhard, Dietrich. "Assemblies of Estates and the Corporate Order." In Rausch, *Die geschichtlichen Grundlagen,* 1:303–24.

Gernet, Jacques. *A History of Chinese Civilization.* 2nd ed. Cambridge, 1996.

Gestrich, Andreas, Jens-Uwe Krause, and Michael Mitterauer. *Geschichte der Familie.* Europäische Kulturgeschichte 1. Stuttgart, 2003.

Giesecke, Michael. *Der Buchdruck in der frühen Neuzeit.* Frankfurt am Main, 1998.

Gilmont, Jean-François. "Protestant Reformations and Reading." In Cavallo and Chartier, *Reading in the West,* 213–37.

Gimpel, Jean. *The Medieval Machine: The Industrial Revolution of the Middle Ages.* 2nd ed. Aldershot, 1988.

Glick, Thomas F., and Helena Kirchner. "Hydraulic Systems and Technologies of Islamic Spain: History and Archeology." In Squatriti, *Working with Water*, 267–329.

Goehrke, Carsten. "Die Anfänge des mittelalterlichen Städtewesens in eurasischer Perspektive." *Saeculum* 31 (980): 194–239.

———. *Frühzeit des Ostslaventums.* Darmstadt, 1992.

Goitein, S. D. *A Mediterranean Society: The Jewish Communities of the Arab World as Portrayed in the Documents of the Cairo Ganiza.* 3 vols. Berkeley, 1978.

Golden, Peter P. *An Introduction to the History of the Turkic Peoples: Ethnogenesis and State-Formation in Medieval and Early Modern Eurasia and the Middle East.* Turcologica 9. Wiesbaden, 1992.

Goody, Jack. *The Development of the Family and Marriage in Europe.* Cambridge, 1983.

———. *The East in the West.* Cambridge, 1996.

———. *The European Family: An Historico-Anthropological Essay.* Oxford, 2000.

———. *The Logic of Writing and the Organization of Society.* New York, 1986.

———. *The Oriental, the Ancient and the Primitive: Systems of Marriage and the Family in the Pre-Industrial Societies of Eurasia.* Cambridge, 1990.

Gorski, Karól. "Die Anfänge des Ständewesens in Nord- und Ostmitteleuropa im Mittelalter." *Anciens Pays et Assemblées d'États* 40 (1966): 43–59.

———. "Institutions représentatives et émancipation de la noblesse: Pour une typologie des assemblées d'États au XVIème siècle." *Études présentées à la CIHAE* 52 (1975), 133–47.

———. "The Origins of the Polish Sejm." *Slavonic and East European Review* 44 (1965–66): 122–38.

Graham, Brian, and Lindsay J. Proudfoot. *An Historical Geography of Ireland.* London, 1993.

Greyerz, Kaspar von. *Religion und Kultur: Europa, 1500–1800.* Göttingen, 2000.

Grigg, David. *Population Growth and Agrarian Change: An Historical Perspective.* Cambridge, 1980.

Greyerz, Kaspar von. *Religion und Kultur: Europa 1500–1800.* Göttingen, 2000.

Gronke, Monika. "Auf dem Weg von der geistlichen zur weltlichen Macht: Schlaglichter zur frühen Safawiya." *Saeculum* 42 (1991): 164–83.

Gründer, Horst. *Welteroberung und Christentum.* Gütersloh, 1992.

Guerreau, Alain. *L'avenir d'un passé incertain.* Paris, 2001.

———. "L'étude de l'économie médiévale: Genèse et problèmes actuels." In *Le Moyen Âge aujourdhui*, 31–82. Cahiers du Léopard d'Or 7. Paris, 1998.

Guerreau-Jalabert, Anita. "La désignation des relations et des groupes de parenté en latin médiéval." *Archivum Latinitatis Medii Aevi* 46 (1988): 65–108.

———. "Sur les structures de parenté dans l'Europe médiévale." *Annales, Économies, Sociétés, Civilisations* 36, no. 6 (1981): 1028–49.

Guichard, Pierre, and Jean-Pierre Cuvillier. "Barbarian Europe." In *Distant Worlds, Ancient Worlds*, vol. 1 of *A History of the Family*, edited by André Burguière, Christiane Klapisch-Zuber, Martine Segalen, and Françoise Zonabend; translated by Sarah Hanbury Tenison, Rosemary Morris, and Andrew Wilson, 318–78. Cambridge, MA, 1996.

Gurevitch, Aaron. *Das Individuum im europäischen Mittelalter*. Translated by Erhard Glier. Munich, 1994.

Haarmann, Harald. *Universalgeschichte der Schrift*. Frankfurt am Main, 1990.

Haase, Felix. *Volksglaube und Brauchtum der Ostslaven*. Wrocław, 1939.

Hägermann, Dieter. "Technik im frühen Mittelalter zwischen 500 und 1000." In Hägermann and Schneider, *Landbau und Handwerk*, 317–523.

Hägermann, Dieter, and Helmuth Schneider, eds. *Landbau und Handwerk: 750 v. Chr. bis 1000 n. Chr.* Propyläen Technikgeschichte 1. Berlin, 1991.

Hahn, Alois. "Sakramentale Kontrolle." In Schluchter, *Max Webers Sicht des okzidentalen Christentums*, 229–53.

Hajnal, John. "European Marriage Patterns in Perspective." In *Population in History: Essays in Historical Demography*, edited by D. V. Glass and D. E. C. Eversley, 101–43. London, 1965.

———. "Two Kinds of Pre-industrial Household Formation System." In Wall et al., *Family Forms*, 65–104.

Haldon, John. *Warfare, State and Society in the Byzantine World, 565–1204*. London, 1999.

Hall, John A. *Powers and Liberties: The Causes and Consequences of the Rise of the West*. Oxford, 1985.

———. "Religion and the Rise of Capitalism." *European Journal of Sociology* 26 (1985): 193–223.

———. "States and Societies: The Miracle in Comparative Perspective." In Baechler et al., *Europe and Capitalism*, 20–38.

———, ed. *States in History*. Oxford, 1986.

Hallinger, Kassius. *Gorze—Kluny: Studien zu den monastischen Lebensformen und Gegensätzen im Hochmittelalter*. 2 vols. Rome, 1950–51.

Halm, Heinz. "Die 'Regierung der Rechtsgelehrten': Die Schia an der Macht." In *Die Welten des Islam*, edited by Gernot Rotter, 60–66. Frankfurt am Main, 1993.

Hamesse, Jacqueline. "The Scholastic Model of Reading." In Cavallo and Chartier, *Reading in the West*, 103–19.

Hamm, Frank R. "Buddhismus und Jinismus: Zwei Typen indischer Religiosität und ihr Weg in die Geschichte." *Saeculum* 15 (1964): 41–56.

Hammer, Carl I. "Family and *familia* in Early-Medieval Bavaria." In Wall et al., *Family Forms*, 217–48.

Hannig, Jürgen. *Consensus fidelium: Frühfeudale Interpretationen des Verhältnisses von Königtum und Adel am Beginn des Frankenreiches*. Monographien zur Geschichte des Mittelalters 27. Stuttgart, 1982.

Hardt, Matthias. "Das 'slawische Dorf' und seine kolonisationszeitliche Umformung nach schriftlichen und historisch-geographischen Quellen."
Siedlungsforschung: Archäologie—Geschichte—Geographie 17 (1999): 269–91.

Hartmann, Angelika. "Islamisches Predigtwesen im Mittelalter: Ibn al-Gauzi
und sein 'Buch der Schlußreden' (1186 n. Chr.)." *Saeculum* 38 (1978):
336–65.

Hartwell, Robert. "A Revolution in the Chinese Iron and Coal Industries during the Northern Sung, 960–1126 A.D." *Journal of Asian Studies* 21, no. 2
(1962): 153–62.

Harva, Uno. "Der Bau des Verwandtschaftssystems und der Verwandschafts-
verhältnisse bei den Fenno-Ugriern." *Finnisch-Ugrische Studien* 26 (1939):
91–120.

Hastrup, Kirsten. *Island of Anthropology: Studies in Past and Present Iceland.* Studies in Northern Civilization 5. Odense, 1990.

Haude, Rüdiger. "Alphabet und Demokratie." *Saeculum* 50 (1999): 1–28.

Haverkamp, Alfred, ed. *Haus und Familie in der spätmittelalterlichen Stadt.* Cologne, 1984.

Haversath, Johann-Bernhard. "Ländliche Siedlungen in hessischen Altsiedelräumen." *Siedlungsforschung: Archäologie—Geschichte—Geographie* 17 (1999):
29–46.

Heine, Peter. *Ethnologie des Nahen und Mittleren Ostens: Eine Einführung.* Berlin,
1989.

Hellmann, Manfred. "Zum Problem der ostslawischen Landgemeinde." In Konstanzer Arbeitskreis, *Die Anfänge der Landgemeinde,* 2:255–72.

Hering, Gunnar. "Die Juden von Saloniki." *Südostforschungen* 58 (1999), 23–39.

Herlihy, David. *Medieval Households.* Studies in Cultural History. Cambridge,
MA, 1985.

Herrmann, Joachim. "Die Slaven der Völkerwanderungszeit." In *Welt der
Slaven: Geschichte, Gesellschaft, Kultur,* edited by Joachim Herrmann,
19–40. Munich, 1986.

Hintze, Otto. *Staat und Verfassung: Gesammelte Abhandlungen zur allgemeinen
Verfassungsgeschichte.* Göttingen, 1970.

———. "Typologie der ständischen Verfassungen des Abendlandes" (1930). In
Staat und Verfassung, 120–39.

———. "Weltgeschichtliche Bedingungen der Repräsentativverfassung" (1931).
In *Staat und Verfassung,* 140–85.

———. "Wesen und Verbreitung des Feudalismus" (1929). In *Staat und Verfassung,* 84–119.

Hlawitschka, Eduard. *Franken, Alemannen, Bayern und Burgunder in Oberitalien
(774–962).* Freiburg, 1960.

Hourani, Albert. *Die Geschichte der arabischen Völker.* Frankfurt am Main, 1992.

Hsia, R. Po-Chia. *The Myth of Ritual Murder: Jews and Magic in Reformation Germany.* New Haven, 1988.

Hudemann, Rainer, Harmut Kaelble, and Klaus Schwabe, eds. "Europa im Blick der Historiker: Europäische Integration im 20. Jahrhundert: Bewusstsein und Institutionen." Beiheft 21. *Historische Zeitschrift* (1995).

Huff, Toby. *The Rise of Early Modern Science: Islam, China, and the West.* Cambridge, 1993.

Huntington, Samuel. *The Clash of Civilizations and the Remaking of World Order.* New York, 1996.

Hyde, J. K. *Society and Politics in Medieval Italy.* London, 1973.

Hyland, Ann. *The Horse in the Middle Ages.* Stroud, UK, 1999.

———. *The Warhorse, 1250–1600.* Stroud, UK, 1998.

Janssen, Walter, and Dietrich Lohrmann, eds. *Villa—Curtis—Grangia: Landwirtschaft zwischen Loire und Rhein von der Römerzeit zum Hochmittelalter; Économie rurale entre Loire et Rhin de l'époque gallo-romaine au XIIe–XIIIe siècle.* Supplementary volume 11. *Francia* (1983).

Jeremias, Joachim. *Jerusalem zur Zeit Jesu.* Göttingen, 1958.

Jockenhövel, Albert. "Agrargeschichte der Bronzezeit und vorrömischen Eisenzeit." In Lüning et al., *Deutsche Agrargeschichte*, 141–262.

Johanek, Peter, ed. *Einungen und Bruderschaften in der spätmittelalterlichen Stadt.* Cologne, 1993.

Johansen, Paul. "Einige Funktionen und Formen mittelalterlicher Landgemeinden in Estland und Finnland." In Konstanzer Arbeitskreis, *Die Anfänge der Landgemeinde*, 2:273–306.

Jones, Eric L. *The European Miracle: Environments, Economies and Geopolitics in the History of Europe and Asia.* 2nd ed. Cambridge, 1987.

———. *Growth Recurring: Economic Change in World History.* Oxford, 1988.

Jussen, Bernhard. *Patenschaft und Adoption im frühen Mittelalter.* Göttingen, 1991.

Kaelble, Hartmut. "Europabewusstsein, Gesellschaft und Geschichte: Forschungsstand und Forschungschancen." In Hudemann et al., "Europa im Blick der Historiker," 1–29.

Kagay, Donald J., and L. J. Andrew Villalon, eds. *The Circle of War in the Middle Ages: Essays in Medieval Military and Naval History.* Woodbridge, UK, 1999.

Kampmann, Christoph. "Universalismus und Staatenvielfalt: Zur europäischen Identität in der frühen Neuzeit." In Schlumberger and Segl, *Europa—aber was ist es?* 45–76.

Kaplan, Michel. *Les hommes et la terre à Byzance du VIe au XIe siècle: Propriété et exploitation du sol.* Paris, 1992.

Kappeler, Andreas. "Die Bedeutung der Geschichte Osteuropas für ein Gesamteuropäisches Geschichtsverständnis." In Stourzh et al., *Eine europäische Geschichtsschreibung*, 43–56.

———. "Osteuropäische Geschichte'." In *Räume*, vol. 2 of *Aufriß der historischen Wissenschaften*, edited by Michael Maurer, 198–265. Stuttgart, 2001.

Kaser, Karl. *Familie und Verwandtschaft auf dem Balkan.* Vienna, 1995.

————. *Macht und Erbe: Männerherrschaft, Besitz und Familie im östlichen Europa (1500–1900)*. Vienna, 2000.

Kaser, Karl, Siegfried Gruber, and Robert Pichler, eds. *Historische Anthropologie im südöstlichen Europa: Eine Einführung*. Vienna, 2003.

Keen, Maurice. *Chivalry*. New Haven, 1984.

Kehrer, Günter. *Einführung in die Religionssoziologie*. Darmstadt, 1988.

Keller, Hagen. "Die Entstehung der italienischen Stadtkommunen als Problem der Sozialgeschichte." *Frühmittelalterliche Studien* 10 (1976): 169–211.

Kern, Fritz. *Gottesgnadentum und Widerstandsrecht im frühen Mittelalter: Zur Entwicklungsgeschichte der Monarchie*. Leipzig, 1914.

Khuri, Fuad. "Parallel Cousin Marriage Reconsidered: A Middle Eastern Practice that Nullifies the Effects of Marriage on the Intensity of Family Relationships." *Man*, n.s. 5, no. 4 (1970): 597–618.

Kiesewetter, Hubert. *Das einzigartige Europa: Zufällige und notwendige Faktoren der Industrialisierung*. Göttingen, 1996.

Kindermann, Heinz. *Theatergeschichte Europas*. 10 vols. Salzburg, 1957.

Kiple, Kenneth F., and Kriemhild Coneè Ornelas, eds. *The Cambridge World History of Food*. 2 vols. Cambridge, 2000.

Klengler, Horst. *Handel und Händler im alten Orient*. Vienna, 1979.

Klewitz, Hans-Walter. "Königtum, Hofkapelle und Domkapitel im 10. und 11. Jahrhundert." *Archiv für Urkundenforschung* 16 (1939): 102–56.

Knittler, Herbert. *Städte und Märkte*. Vol. 2 of Bruckmüller et al., *Herrschaftsstruktur und Ständebildung*.

Koch, Ursula. "Damaszieren von Waffen." In Lindgren, *Europäische Technik*, 217–20.

Koenigsberger, Helmut G. "Dominium regale or dominium politicum et regale? Monarchies and Parliaments in Early Modern Europe." In Bosl and Möckl, *Der moderne Parlamentarismus*, 43–68.

————. "Zusammengesetzte Staaten, Repräsentativversammlungen und der amerikanische Bürgerkrieg." *Zeitschrift für historische Forschung* 18 (1991): 399–423.

Konstanzer Arbeitskreis für mittelalterliche Geschichte, ed. *Die Anfänge der Landgemeinde und ihr Wesen*. 2 vols. Vorträge und Forschungen 7–8. Sigmaringen, 1986.

The Koran Interpreted. Translated by A[rthur] J[ohn] Arberry. New York, 1955.

Koranyi, Karol. "Zum Ursprung des Anteils der Städte an den ständischen Versammlungen und Parlamenten des Mittelalters." In Album Helen Maud Cam 1, *Études présentées à la CIHAE* 23 (1960): 37–54.

Körber-Grohne, Udelgard. *Nutzpflanzen in Deutschland: Kulturgeschichte und Biologie*. Stuttgart, 1988.

Kornicki, Peter. *The Book in Japan: A Cultural History from the Beginnings to the Nineteenth Century*. Leiden, 1998.

Köster, Fritz. *Religiöse Erziehung in den Weltreligionen: Hinduismus, Buddhismus, Islam*. Darmstadt, 1986.

Krader, Lawrence. "Principles and Structures in the Organization of the Asiatic Steppe-Pastoralists." *Southwestern Journal of Anthropology* 11, no. 2 (1955): 67–92.

Krüger, Kersten. "Die ständischen Verfassungen in Skandinavien in der frühen Neuzeit: Modelle einer europäischen Typologie?" *Zeitschrift für historische Forschung* 10 (1983): 129–48.

Kuchenbuch, Ludolf. *Bäuerliche Gesellschaft und Klosterherrschaft im 9. Jahrhundert.* Wiesbaden, 1978.

———. "Die Klostergrundherrschaft im Frühmittelalter: Eine Zwischenbilanz." *Herrschaft und Kirche: Beiträge zur Entstehung und Wirkungsweise episkopaler und monastischer Organisationsformen*, edited by Friedrich Prinz, 297–343. Monographien zur Geschichte des Mittelalters 33. Stuttgart, 1988.

Kuhn, Dieter. *Die Song-Dynastie (960–1279): Eine neue Gesellschaft im Spiegel ihrer Kultur.* Weinheim, 1987.

Kulke, Hermann. "Einleitung." In "Asien im Jahr 1000," edited by Hermann Kulke. Special issue, *Periplus: Jahrbuch für außereuropäische Geschichte* 10 (2000): 1–12.

Kulke, Hermann, and Dietmar Rothermund. *A History of India.* London, 1998. Originally published as *Geschichte Indiens von der Induskultur bis heute* (Munich, 1998).

Kunczik, Michael. *Geschichte der Öffentlichkeitsarbeit in Deutschland.* Cologne, 1997.

Küng, Hans. *Christianity: Essence, History, Future.* Translated by John Bowden. New York, 1995. Originally published as *Das Christentum: Wesen und Geschichte* (Munich, 1994).

Küng, Hans, and Julia Ching. *Christentum und Weltreligionen: Chinesische Religion.* Munich, 1999.

Kunze, Konrad. *dtv-Atlas Namenkunde: Vor- und Familiennamen im deutschen Sprachgebiet.* Munich, 1998.

Küster, Hansjörg. "Rye." In Kiple and Ornelas, *The Cambridge World History of Food*, 1:149–52.

Lancaster, Lewis. "Buddhism and Family in East Asia." In De Vos and Sofue, *Religion and Family*, 139–54.

Lane, Frederic C. *Venice: A Maritime Republic.* Baltimore, 1973.

Lang, Bernhard. *Heiliges Spiel: Eine Geschichte des christlichen Gottesdienstes.* Munich, 1998.

Lapidus, Ira M. "Die Institutionalisierung der frühislamischen Gesellschaften." In Schluchter, *Max Webers Sicht des Islams*, 125–41.

Laslett, Peter. "Characteristics of the Western Family Considered over Time." In Laslett, *Family Life*, 12–49.

———. "The European Family and Early Industrialization." In Baechler et al., *Europe and Capitalism*, 234–41.

―――. "Family and Household as Work Group and Kin Group: Areas of Traditional Europe Compared." In Wall et al., *Family Forms*, 513–63.

―――. *Family Life and Illicit Love in Earlier Generations: Essays in Historical Sociology.* Cambridge, 1977.

―――. Introduction to *Household and Family in Past Time*, edited by Peter Laslett and Richard Wall, 1–90. Cambridge, 1972.

Laslett, Peter, and Richard Wall, eds. *Household and Family in Past Time.* Cambridge, 1972.

Lechner, Karl. "Leistungen und Aufgaben siedlungskundlicher Forschung in den österreichischen Ländern mit besonderer Berücksichtigung von Niederösterreich." In *Ausgewählte Schriften.* Vienna, 1947.

Le Goff, Jacques. *Das Hochmittelalter.* Fischer-Weltgeschichte 11. Frankfurt am Main, 1965.

―――. "The Making of Europe." Introduction to several volumes of the collaborative series The Making of Europe [published in German, English, Italian, Spanish, French]. Munich, 1993–.

―――. *La naissance du Purgatoire.* Paris, 1981. Translated by Arthur Goldhammer as *The Birth of Purgatory* (Chicago, 1984).

―――. *Pour un autre Moyen Age: Temps, travail et culture en Occident: 18 essais* (Paris. 1977). Translated by Arthur Goldhammer as *Time, Work, and Culture in the Middle Ages* (Chicago, 1980).

Lehmann, Leonhard. "Franziskaner und Klarissen," in Dinzelbacher and Hogg, *Kulturgeschichte der christlichen Orden*, 143–92.

Levin, Eve. *Sex and Society in the World of the Orthodox Slavs, 900–1700.* Ithaca, 1989.

Lévi-Strauss, Claude. *The Elementary Structures of Kinship.* Translated by James Harle Bell, John Richard von Sturmer, and Rodney Needham. Boston, 1969. Originally published as *Les structures élémentaires de la parenté* (Paris, 1949).

Lewis, Archibald. "Mediterranean Maritime Commerce, A.D. 300–1100: Shipping and Trade." *Settimane di studio del Centro Italiano di Studi sull'Alto Medioevo* 25, no. 2 (1978): 481–501.

Lewis, Bernard. *The Jews of Islam.* Princeton, 1984.

Linck, Gudula. *Frau und Familie in China.* Munich, 1988.

Lindgren, Uta, ed. *Europäische Technik im Mittelalter, 800–1400: Tradition und Innovation, ein Handbuch.* 3rd ed. Berlin, 1998.

Linhart, Sepp. "Kawaraban—die ersten japanischen Zeitungen." In Formanek and Linhart, *Buch und Bild*, 139–66.

Livi Bacci, Massimo. *The Population of Europe: A History.* Translated by Cynthia De Nardi Ipsen and Carl Ipsen. Oxford, 1999. Originally published as *La popolazione nella storia d'Europa* (Bari, 1998).

Lohrmann, Dietrich. "Antrieb von Getreidemühlen." In Lindgren, *Europäische Technik*, 221–32.

———. "Bedarf und Angebot von Wasserkraft in frühen Siedlungen und Städten." *Saeculum* 42 (1991): 262–65.

———. "Le moulin à eau dans le cadre de l'économie rurale de la Neustrie." In *La Neustrie: Les pays au nord de la Loire de 650 à 850*, edited by Hartmut Atsma, 367–404. Sigmaringen, 1989.

Lohrum, Meinolf. "Dominikaner." In Dinzelbacher and Hogg, *Kulturgeschichte der christlichen Orden*, 117–42.

Lombard, Maurice. *L'Islam dans sa première grandeur (VIIIe–XIe siècle)*. Paris, 1971. Translated by Joan Spencer as *The Golden Age of Islam* (Princeton, 2005).

Löwenthal, Richard. "Kontinuität und Diskontinuität: Zur Grundproblematik des Symposiums." In Bosl and Möckl, *Der moderne Parlamentarismus*, 341–56.

Ludwig, Karl-Heinz. "Technik im hohen Mittelalter zwischen 1000 und 1350/1400." In Ludwig and Schmidtchen, *Metalle und Macht*, 11–205, 601–6.

Ludwig, Karl-Heinz, and Völker Schmidtchen, eds. *Metalle und Macht: 1000 bis 1600*. Propyläen Technikgeschichte 2. Berlin, 1992.

Lüning, Jens, Albrecht Jockenhövel, Helmut Bender, and Torsten Capelle, eds. *Deutsche Agrargeschichte: Vor- und Frühgeschichte*. Stuttgart, 1997.

Lutterbach, Hubertus. *Sexualität im Mittelalter: Eine Kulturstudie anhand von Bußbüchern des 6. bis 12. Jahrhunderts*. Cologne, 1999.

Luven, Yvonne. *Der Kult der Hausschlange: Eine Studie zur Religionsgeschichte der Letten und Litauer*. Cologne, 2001.

Lynch, Joseph H. *Godparents and Kinship in Early Medieval Europe*. Princeton, 1986.

Macfarlane, Alan. "The Cradle of Capitalism: The Case of England." In Baechler et al., *Europe and Capitalism*, 185–203.

———. "The Mystery of Property: Inheritance and Industrialization in England and Japan." In *Property Relations: Renewing the Anthropological Tradition*, edited by C. M. Hann, 104–23. Cambridge, 1998.

———. *The Origins of English Individualism: The Family, Property and Social Transition*. Oxford, 1978.

———. *The Riddle of the Modern World: Of Liberty, Wealth and Equality*. London, 2000.

Madelung, Wilferd. *The Succession to Muhammad: A Study of the Early Caliphate*. Cambridge, 1997.

Maenchen-Helfen, Otto J. *Die Welt der Hunnen*. Vienna, 1978.

Mager, Johannes, Günter Meissner, and Wolfgang Orf. *Die Kulturgeschichte der Mühlen*. Tübingen, 1989.

Magnusson, Roberta, and Paolo Squatriti. "The Technologies of Water in Medieval Italy." In Squatriti, *Working with Water*, 217–66.

Maier, Johann. *Grundzüge der Geschichte des Judentums im Altertum*. Darmstadt, 1981.

Makdisi, George. "Authority in the Islamic Community." In *History and Politics in Eleventh-Century Baghdad*, sect. 8, 117–26. Aldershot, 1990.

Makdisi, George, Dominique Sourdel, and Janine Sourdel-Thomine, eds. *Prédication et propagande au Moyen Age: Islam, Byzance, Occident*. Paris, 1983.

Mann, Michael. "European Development: Approaching a Historical Explanation." In Baechler et al., *Europe and Capitalism*, 6–19.

———. *A History of Power from the Beginning to A.D. 1760*. Vol. 1 of *The Sources of Social Power*. 2 vols. Cambridge, 1986.

———. "States, Ancient and Modern." *Archives Européennes de Sociologie* 18 (1977): 262–98.

Marker, Gary. *Publishing, Printing, and the Origins of Intellectual Life in Russia, 1700–1800*. Princeton, 1985.

Martin, Jochen. *Spätantike und Völkerwanderung*. Oldenbourg Grundriß der Geschichte 4. Munich, 1987.

———. "Zwei Alte Geschichten: Vergleichende historisch-anthropologische Betrachtungen zu Griechenland und Rom." *Saeculum* 48 (1997): 1–20.

Martin, Jochen, and August Nitschke, eds. *Zur Sozialgeschichte der Kindheit*. Freiburg, 1986.

Martin, Jochen, and Renate Zoeppfel, eds. *Aufgaben, Rollen und Räume von Frau und Mann*. 2 vols. Freiburg, 1989.

May, Ekkehard. "Buch und Buchillustration im vormodernen Japan." In Formanek and Linhart, *Buch und Bild*, 45–74.

Mayer, Ernst. *Deutsche und französische Verfassungsgeschichte vom 9. bis zum 14. Jahrhundert*. Vol. 1. Leipzig, 1899.

Mayer, Hans-Eberhard. *Geschichte der Kreuzzüge*. Stuttgart, 1965.

McIlwain, C. H. "Medieval Estates." In *The Cambridge Medieval History*, 7:664–715. Cambridge, 1958.

McNeill, William. *The Age of Gunpowder Empires, 1450–1800*. Washington, D.C., 1989.

———. "The Eccentricity of Wheels, or Eurasian Transportation in Historical Perspective." *American Historical Review* 92, no. 5 (1987): 1111–26.

———. "'The Rise of the West' after Twenty-Five Years." *Journal of World History* 1, no. 1 (1990): 1–21.

———. *The Rise of the West: A History of the Human Community*. Chicago, 1963.

Menzel, Michael. "Predigt und Predigtorganisation im Mittelalter." *Historisches Jahrbuch* 111 (1991): 337–84.

Metz, Wolfgang. *Das karolingische Reichsgut*. Berlin, 1960.

Meyer, Ulrich. *Soziales Handeln im Zeichen des "Hauses": Zur Ökonomik in der Spätantike und im frühen Mittelalter*. Göttingen, 1998.

Michaels, Axel. *Der Hinduismus: Geschichte und Gegenwart*. Munich, 1998.

Miller, Constance R. *Technical and Cultural Prerequisites for the Invention of Printing in China and the West*. San Francisco, 1983.

Mitteis, Heinrich. *Lehnrecht und Staatsgewalt*. Weimar, 1933.

———. *Der Staat im hohen Mittelalter*. Berlin, 1941.

Mitterauer, Michael. *Ahnen und Heilige: Namengebung in der europäischen Geschichte.* Munich, 1993.

———. "Die Anfänge der Universität im Mittelalter: Räume und Zentren der Wissenschaftsentwicklung" in *Phänomenologie des europäischen Wissenschaftssystems,* edited by Wolfgang Mantl, 1–43. Vienna, 2009.

———. "Christentum und Endogamie." In Mitterauer, *Historisch-anthropologische Familienforschung,* 41–86.

———. *Dimensionen des Heiligen: Annäherungen eines Historikers.* Vienna, 2000.

———. *Die Entwicklung Europas—ein Sonderweg? Legitimationsideologien und die Diskussion der Wissenschaft.* Vienna, 1999.

———. "Entwicklungstendenzen von Verwandtschaft und Familie im Mittelalter." In Gestrich, *Geschichte der Familie,* 160–263.

———, ed. "Ein europäischer Sonderweg? Mittelalterliche Grundlagen der Gesellschaftsentwicklung." Special issue, *Beiträge zur historischen Sozialkunde* 27, no. 1 (1997).

———. "Formen der ländlichen Familienwirtschaft im österreichischen Raum." In Ehmer and Mitterauer, *Familienstruktur und Arbeitsorganisation,* 185–324.

———. "Gesindedienst und Jugendphase im europäischen Vergleich." *Geschichte und Gesellschaft* 11 (1985): 177–204.

———. "Grundlagen politischer Berechtigung im mittelalterlichen Ständewesen." In Bosl and Möckl, *Der moderne Parlamentarismus,* 11–42.

———. "Herrenburg und Burgstadt." In Mitterauer, *Markt und Stadt,* 192–234. Originally published in *Bayerische Geschichte als Tradition und Modell,* Festschrift für Karl Bosl. *Zeitschrift für bayerische Landesgeschichte* 36 (1972): 470–521.

———. "'Heut' ist eine heilige Samstatnacht.'" In Mitterauer, *Dimensionen des Heiligen,* 80–121.

———. *Historisch-anthropologische Familienforschung: Fragestellungen und Zugangsweisen.* Kulturstudien 15. Vienna, 1990.

———. *A History of Youth: Family, Sexuality and Social Relations in Past Times,* translated by Graeme Dunphy. Oxford, 1992. Originlly published as Sozialgeschichte der Jugend (Frankfort am Main, 1986).

———. "Une intégration féodale? La dénomination, expression des relations de service et de vasallité." In *L'anthroponymie: Document de l'histoire sociale des mondes médiévaux méditerranéens,* edited by Monique Bourin, Jean-Marie Martin, and François Menant, 295–311. Rome, 1996.

———. "Jahrmärkte in Nachfolge antiker Zentralorte." In Mitterauer, *Markt und Stadt,* 68–153.

———. "Der Krieg des Papstes." In "Kreuzzüge." Special issue, *Beiträge zur historischen Sozialkunde* 26, no. 3 (1996): 116–28.

———. "Die Landwirtschaft und der 'Aufstieg Europas': Jared Diamonds Thesen als Forschungsimpuls." *Historische Anthropologie* 8 (2000): 423–31.

———. *Markt und Stadt im Mittelalter: Beiträge zur historischen Zentralitätsforschung.* Monographien zur Geschichte des Mittelalters 21. Stuttgart, 1980.

———. "Ostkolonisation und Familienverfassung." In *Vilfanov zbornik: Pravo—zgodovin—narod*, edited by Vincenc Rajšp and Ernst Bruckmüller, 203–22. Ljubljana, 1999.

———. *Parlament und Schura: Ratsversammlungen und Demokratieentwicklung in Europa und der Islamischen Welt*. Wiener Vorlesungen im Rathaus 144. Vienna, 2009.

———. "Predigt—Holzschnitt—Buchdruck." In "Geschichte und Kommunikation." Special issue, *Beiträge zur historischen Sozialkunde* 28, no. 2 (1998): 69–78.

———. "Produktionsweise, Siedlungsstruktur und Sozialformen im österreichischen Montanwesen des Mittelalters und der Frühen Neuzeit." In *Österreichisches Montanwesen*, edited by Michael Mitterauer, 234–315. Vienna, 1974.

———. "Religionen." In Kaser et al., *Historische Anthropologie*, 345–75.

———. "Roggen, Reis und Zuckerrohr: Drei Agrarrevolutionen des Mittelalters im Vergleich." *Saeculum* 52 (2001): 245–65.

———. "Schreibrohr und Druckerpresse: Transferprobleme einer Kommunikationstechnologie." In *Plus ultra: Die Welt der Neuzeit: Festschrift für Alfred Kohler zum 65. Geburtstag*, edited by Friedrich Edelmayer et al., 383–406. Münster, 2008.

———. "'Senioris sui nomine': Zur Verbreitung von Fürstennamen durch das Lehenswesen." *Mitteilungen des Instituts für österreichische Geschichtsforschung* 96 (1988): 275–330.

———. "Sozialgeschichte der Familie als landesgeschichtlicher Forschungsgegenstand." In Mitterauer, *Historisch-anthropologische Familienforschung*, 191–232.

———. "Städte als Zentren im mittelalterlichen Europa." In Feldbauer et al., *Die vormoderne Stadt*, 60–78.

———. "Standortfaktor Wasserkraft: Zwei europäische Eisenregionen im Vergleich," in *Erfahrung der Moderne: Festschrift für Roman Sandgruber*, edited by Michael Pammer et al., 59–78. Stuttgart, 2007.

———. "Die Terminologie der Verwandtschaft: Zu mittelalterlichen Grundlagen von Wandel und Beharrung im europäischen Vergleich." *Ethnologia Balkanica* 4 (2000): 11–43.

———. "'Und sie ließen ihren Vater zurück . . .': Die Schwäche der Ahnenbindung im Christentum als Voraussetzung des europäischen Sonderwegs der Familien- und Gesellschaftsentwicklung." In Mitterauer, *Dimensionen des Heiligen*, 214–27.

———. "Von der antiken zur mittelalterlichen Stadt." In Mitterauer, *Markt und Stadt*, 52–67.

———. "Die Witwe des Bruders: Levieratsehe und Familienverfassung." *Otium* 3 (1995): 53–70.

———. "Zur Familienstruktur in ländlichen Gebieten Österreichs im 17. Jahrhundert." In *Familie und Arbeitsteilung: Historisch vergleichende Studien*, 149–213. Vienna, 1992.

Mitterauer, Michael, and John Morrissey. *Pisa: Seemacht und Kulturmetropole.* Essen, 2007.

Mitterauer, Michael, and Reinhard Sieder. *The European Family: Patriarchy to Partnership from the Middle Ages to the Present,* translated by Karla Oosterveen and Manfred Hörzinger. Chicago, 1982. Originally published as *Vom Patriarchat zur Partnerschaft: Zum Strukturwandel der Familie* (Munich, 1977).

Mokyr, Joel. *The Lever of Riches: Technological Creativity and Economic Progress.* Oxford, 1990.

Montanari, Massimo. *The Culture of Food.* Translated by Carl Ipsen. Oxford, 1993. Originally published as *La fame e l'abbondanza: Storia dell'alimentazione in Europa.* (Bari, 1997).

Moore, Barrington. *Social Origins of Dictatorship and Democracy: Lord and Peasant in the Making of the Modern World.* Boston, 1993.

Moore, Robert I. *The First European Revolution, c. 970–1215.* Oxford, 2000.

Mor, Carlo Guido. "Das Rittertum." In Borst, *Das Rittertum,* 247–65.

Morenz, Siegfried. "Entstehung und Wesen der Buchreligion." *Theologische Literaturzeitung* 75 (1950): 709–16.

Morillo, Stephen. "The 'Age of Cavalry' Revisited." In *The Circle of War in the Middle Ages: Essays in Medieval Military and Naval History,* edited by Donald J. Kagay and L. J. Andrew Villalon, 45–58. Woodbridge, UK, 1999.

Moring, Beatrice. "Marriage and Social Change in South-Western Finland 1700–1870." *Continuity and Change* 11, no. 1 (1996): 91–113.

Mörke, Olaf, and Michael North, eds. *Die Entstehung des modernen Europa 1600–1900.* Cologne, 1998.

Morrissey, John. "Die italienischen Seerepubliken." In Feldbauer et al., *Vom Mittelmeer zum Atlantik,* 61–82.

Motzki, Harald. "Dann macht er daraus die beiden Geschlechter, das männliche und das weibliche." In Martin and Zoeppfel, *Aufgaben, Rollen und Räume,* 2:607–42.

———. "Die Entstehung des Rechts." In Noth and Paul, *Der islamische Orient,* 151–72.

———. "Geschlechtsreife und Legitimation zur Zeugung im frühen Islam." In *Geschlechtsreife und Legitimation zur Zeugung,* edited by Wilhelm E. Müller, 479–550. Munich, 1985.

———. "Das Kind und seine Sozialisation in der islamischen Familie des Mittelalters." In Martin and Nitschke, *Zur Sozialgeschichte der Kindheit,* 391–442.

Mühlbacher, Engelbert. *Deutsche Geschichte unter den Karolingern.* Stuttgart, 1959.

Mühlen, Heinz von zur. "Autonomie und Selbstbehauptung der baltischen Stände von der Reformation bis zum Nordischen Krieg." In Weczerka, *Stände und Landesherrschaft,* 39–48.

Müller, C. Detlef. *Geschichte der orientalischen Nationalkirchen.* Göttingen, 1981.

Müller, Johannes. *Kulturlandschaft China: Anthropogene Gestaltung der Landschaft durch Landnutzung und Siedlung.* Gotha, 1997.

Müller-Karpe, Hermann. *Grundzüge antiker Menschheitsreligion: 1. Jahrhundert v. Chr. bis 5. Jahrhundert.* Stuttgart, 2000.

Münch, Paul, and Rainer Walz, eds. *Tiere und Menschen: Geschichte und Aktualität eines prekären Verhältnisses.* Paderborn, 1998.

Muñoz, Maria Rosa, and Regina Pinilla. "Les municipalités et leur participation dans les Cortès valenciennes de l'époque forale." *Parliaments, Estates and Representation* 13 (1993): 1–15.

Musallam, Basim. "The Ordering of Muslim Societies." In Robinson, *Islamic World,* 164–207.

Museum für Völkerkunde in Hamburg, ed. *Das gemeinsame Haus Europa: Handbuch zur europäischen Kulturgeschichte.* Munich, 1999.

Musper, Heinrich Theodor. *Der Holzschnitt in fünf Jahrhunderten.* Stuttgart, 1964.

Mutel, Jacques. "The Modernization of Japan: Why Has Japan Succeeded in its Modernization?" Translated by W. D. Halls. In Baechler et al., *Europe and Capitalism,* 136–58.

Nagel, Tilman. *Staat und Glaubensgemeinschaft im Islam.* Vol. 1. Zurich, 1981.

Needham, Joseph. *Science and Civilisation in China.* 7 vols. Cambridge, 1954–2004.

Nikolaou, Theodor. *Askese, Mönchtum und Mystik in der Orthodoxen Kirche.* St. Ottilien, 1995.

Nippa, Annegret. *Haus und Familie in arabischen Ländern: Vom Mittelalter bis zur Gegenwart.* Munich, 1991.

Nitschke, August. "Das Tier in der Spätantike, im Frühen und Hohen Mittelalter." In Münch and Walz, *Tiere und Menschen,* 227–46.

Nitz, Hans Jürgen. "Introduction from Above: Intentional Spread of Common-Field Systems by Feudal Authorities through Colonization and Reorganization." In Hans Jürgen Nitz, *Allgemeine und vergleichende Siedlungsgeographie,* 290–306. Berlin, 1998.

———. "Siedlungsstrukturen der königlichen und adeligen Grundherrschaft der Karolingerzeit—der Beitrag der historisch-genetischen Siedlungsgeographie." In Rösener, *Strukturen der Grundherrschaft,* 411–82.

———. "Zur Erforschung der frühmittelalterlichen Besiedlung im Raum zwischen Ostharz und jenseits der Saale, mit einem Ausblick auf Thüringen." *Siedlungsforschung: Archäologie—Geschichte—Geographie* 15 (1997): 249–303.

North, Douglas C., and Robert Paul Thomas. *The Rise of the Western World: A New Economic History.* Cambridge, 1973.

Noth, Albrecht. "Von den medinensischen 'Umma' zu einer muslimischen Ökumene." In Noth and Paul, *Der islamische Orient,* 81–135.

Noth, Albrecht, and Jürgen Paul, eds. *Der islamische Orient: Grundzüge seiner Geschichte.* Würzburg, 1998.

Obst, Erich. *Allgemeine Wirtschafts- und Verkehrsgeographie.* Berlin, 1959.

Oesterdieckhoff, Georg W. *Familie, Wirtschaft und Gesellschaft in Europa: Die historische Entwicklung von Familie und Ehe im Kulturvergleich.* Stuttgart, 2000.

Oexle, Otto Gerhard. "Die funktionale Dreiteilung der 'Gesellschaft' bei Adalbero von Laon: Deutungsschemata der sozialen Wirklichkeit im früheren Mittelalter." *Frühmittelalterliche Studien* 12 (1978): 1–54.

Orzechowski, Kazimierz. "Les systèmes des assemblées d'état: Origines, évolution, typologie." *Parliaments, Estates and Representation* 6 (1986): 105–111.

Osterhammel, Jürgen. *Kolonialismus: Geschichte—Formen—Folgen.* Munich, 1995.

———. "Sozialgeschichte im Zivilisationsvergleich: Zu künftigen Möglichkeiten komparativer Geschichtswissenschaft." *Geschichte und Gesellschaft* 22 (1996): 143–64.

———. "Transkulturell vergleichende Geschichtswissenschaft." In *Geschichte und Vergleich: Ansätze und Ergebnisse international vergleichender Geschichtsschreibung,* edited by Heinz-Gerhard Haupt and Jürgen Kocka, 271–313. Frankfurt am Main, 1996.

Ostrogorsky, Georg. *Byzantinische Geschichte, 324–1453.* Munich, 1996.

Ozaki, Masaharu. "The Taoist Priesthood: From Tsai-chia to Ch'u-chia." In De Vos and Sofue, *Religion and Family,* 97–109.

Parker, Geoffrey. *The Military Revolution: Military Innovation and the Rise of the West, 1500–1800.* Cambridge, 1988.

Parker, William N. "Agrarian and Industrial Revolutions." In *Revolution in History,* edited by Roy Porter and Mikuláš Teich, 167–85. Cambridge, 1986.

Partner, Peter. *God of Battles: Holy Wars of Islam and Christianity.* Princeton, 1997.

Patai, Raphael. *The Arab Mind.* New York, 1973.

———. "Cousin-Right in the Middle Eastern Marriage." *Southwestern Journal of Anthropology* 11 (1955): 325–50.

———. *The Jewish Mind.* New York, 1977.

Patterson, Nerys Thomas. *Cattle-Lords and Clansmen: The Social Structure of Early Ireland.* 2nd ed. Notre Dame, 1994.

Patzelt, Erna, and Herbert Patzelt. *Schiffe machen Geschichte: Beiträge zur Kulturentwicklung im vorchristlichen Schweden.* Vienna, 1981.

Pauli, Rainer. *Sardinien: Geschichte—Kultur—Landschaft.* Cologne, 1978.

Pedersen, Johannes. "The Islamic Preacher: wa' iz, mudhakkir, gass." In *Ignace Goldziher Memorial Volume,* edited by Samuel Löwinger and Joseph Somogyi, 1:226–51. Budapest, 1948.

Pelzel, John C. "Japanese Kinship: A Comparison." In Freedman, *Family and Kinship,* 227–48.

Pertusi, Agostino. "Ordinamenti militari, guerre in occidente e teorie di guerra dei Bizantini (secc. VI–X)." *Settimane di studio del Centro Italiano di Studi sull'Alto Medioevo* 15, no. 2 (1968): 631–700.

Peterka, Otto. *Rechtsgeschichte der böhmischen Länder.* Vol. 1. Reichenberg, 1923.

Peters, Joris. *Römische Tierhaltung und Tierzucht.* Rahden, Westphalia, 1998.

Petri, Franz. "Territorienbildung und Territorialstaat des 14. Jahrhunderts im Nordwestraum." *Vorträge und Forschungen* 13 (1970): 383–483.

Petrikovits, Harald von. "L'économie rurale à l'époque romaine en Germanie inférieure et dans la région de Trèves." In Janssen and Lohrmann, *Villa—Curtis—Grangia*, 1–16.

Peyfuss, Maximilian. "Die Druckerei von Moschopolis, 1731–1769: Buchdruck und Heiligenverehrung im Erzbistum Achrida." *Habilitations-Schrift*, University of Vienna, 1988.

Pieper, Renate. "Die Anfänge der europäischen Partizipation am weltweiten Handel: Die Aktivitäten der Portugiesen und Spanier im 15. und 16. Jarhhundert." In *Die Geschichte des europäischen Welthandels und der wirtschaftliche Globalisierungsprozeß*, edited by Friedrich Edelmayer, Bernd Hausberger, and Barbara Potthast, 33–53. Vienna, 2001.

Pillorget, René. "The European Tradition in Movements of Insurrection." In Baechler et al., *Europe and Capitalism*, 204–19.

Pitz, Ernst. *Europäisches Städtewesen und Bürgertum: Von der Spätantike bis zum hohen Mittelalter.* Darmstadt, 1991.

———. *Die griechisch-römische Ökumene und die drei Kulturen des Mittelalters: Geschichte des mediterranen Weltteils zwischen Atlantik und dem Indischen Ozean, 270–812.* Berlin, 2001.

Planhol, Xavier de. *L'Islam et la mer: La mosquée et le matelot: VIIe–XXe siècle.* Paris, 2000.

Pleiner, Radomir. "Vom Rennfeuer zum Hochofen: Die Entwicklung der Eisenverhüttung, 9.–14. Jahrhundert." In Lindgren, *Europäische Technik*, 249–56.

Pleterski, Andrej. "Die Methode der Verknüpfung der retrogressiven Kataster-analyse mit schriftlichen und archäologischen Quellen." *Siedlungsforschung: Archäologie—Geschichte—Geographie* 13 (1995): 251–81.

Pomeranz, Kenneth. *The Great Divergence: China, Europe, and the Making of the Modern World Economy.* Princeton, 2000.

Post, Gaines. "Plena Potestas and Consent in Medieval Assemblies: A Study in Romano-Canonical Procedure and the Rise of Representation, 1150–1325." In Rausch, *Die geschichtlichen Grundlagen*, 1:30–114.

Potter, Jack M. "Land and Lineage in Traditional China." In Freedman, *Family and Kinship*, 121–38.

Powelson, John P. *Centuries of Economic Endeavor: Parallel Paths in Japan and Europe and Their Contrast with the Third World.* Ann Arbor, 1994.

Prestwich, Michael. *Armies and Warfare in the Middle Ages: The English Experience.* New Haven, 1996.

Prinz, Friedrich, ed. *Mönchtum und Gesellschaft im Frühmittelalter.* Darmstadt, 1976.

———. "Vasallität und Stiftsvasallität: Die Rolle der Kirche im karolingischen und ottonischen Herrschaftssystem." *Settimane di studio del Centro Italiano di Studi sull'Alto Medioevo* 47 (2000): 851–72.

Ptak, Roderich. *Pferde auf See: Chinas Pferdeimporte von den Riukiu-Inseln und den Ländern Südostasiens und des Indischen Ozeans (1368–1435)*. Kleine Beiträge zur europäischen Überseegeschichte 8. Bamberg, 1991.

Radtke, Berend, "Die tanzenden Derwische." In *Die Welten des Islam*, edited by Gernot Rotte, 46–51. Frankfurt am Main, 1993.

Raepsaet, Georges. "The Development of Farming Implements between the Seine and the Rhine from the Second to the Twelfth Centuries." In Astill and Langdon, *Medieval Farming*, 41–68.

Rausch, Heinz. Introduction to *Die geschichtlichen Grundlagen der modernen Volksvertretung: Die Entwicklung von den mittelalterlichen Korporationen zu den modernen Parlamenten*, edited by Heinz Rausch. 2 vols. Darmstadt, 1974–80.

Reinhard, Wolfgang. "Die Europäisierung der Erde und ihre Folgen." In Schlumberger and Segl, *Europa—aber was ist es?* 77–93.

———. "Frühmoderner Staat—moderner Staat." In Mörke and North, *Entstehung des modernen Europa*, 1–10.

———. *Geschichte der europäischen Expansion*. 4 vols. Stuttgart, 1983–90.

———. *Geschichte der Staatsgewalt: Eine vergleichende Verfassungsgeschichte Europas von den Anfängen bis zur Gegenwart*. Munich, 2000.

———. "Die lateinische Variante von Religion und ihre Bedeutung für die politische Kultur Europas: Ein Versuch in historischer Anthropologie." *Saeculum* 43 (1992): 231–55.

———, ed. *Verstaatlichung der Welt? Europäische Staatsmodelle und außereuropäische Machtprozesse*. Schriften des Historischen Kollegs 47. Munich, 1999.

Reynolds, Susan. *Fiefs and Vassals: The Medieval Evidence Reinterpreted*. Oxford, 1994.

———. *Kingdoms and Communities in Western Europe, 900–1300*. Oxford, 1984.

Reynolds, Terry S. *Stronger than a Hundred Men: A History of the Vertical Water Wheel*, Baltimore, 1983.

Reynolds, Terry S., and Stephen H. Cunliffe, eds. *Technology and the West: A Historical Anthology from Technology and Culture*. Chicago, 1997.

Richards, Donald S. "Mamluk Amirs and Their Families and Households." In *The Mamluks in Egyptian Politics and Society*, edited by Thomas Philipp and Ursula Haarmann, 32–54. Cambridge, 1998.

Richter, Michael. *Irland im Mittelalter*. Stuttgart, 1983.

Rill, Bernd. *Sizilien im Mittelalter: Das Reich der Araber, Normannen und Staufer*. Darmstadt, 1995.

Robinson, Francis, ed. *The Cambridge Illustrated History of the Islamic World*. Cambridge, 1996.

Rodinson, Maxime. *Islam et Capitalisme*. Paris, 1966. Translated by Brian Pearce as *Islam and Capitalism* (New York, 1972).

Rogers, Randall. *Latin Siege Warfare in the Twelfth Century*. Oxford, 1997.

Rösener, Werner. *Agrarwirtschaft, Agrarverfassung und ländliche Gesellschaft im Mittelalter*. Enzyklopädie Deutscher Geschichte 13. Munich, 1992.

———. *Die Bauern im Mittelalter*. Munich 1985. Translated by Alexander Stützer as *Peasants in the Middle Ages* (Urbana, 1992).

———. *Die Bauern in der europäischen Geschichte*. Munich, 1993. Translated by Thomas M. Barker as *The Peasantry of Europe* (Oxford, 1994).

———. *Einführung in die Agrargeschichte*. Darmstadt, 1997.

———. *Grundherrschaft im Wandel: Untersuchungen zur Entwicklung geistlicher Grundherrschaften im südwestdeutschen Raum vom 9.–14. Jahrhundert*. Veröffentlichungen des Max-Planck-Instituts für Geschichte 102. Göttingen, 1991.

———. *Strukturen der Grundherrschaft im frühen Mittelalter*. Veröffentlichungen des Max-Planck-Instituts für Geschichte 92. Göttingen, 1989.

———. "Strukturen und Wandlungen des Dorfes in Altsiedellandschaften." *Siedlungsforschung: Archäologie—Geschichte—Geographie* 17 (1999): 9–26.

Rosenwein, Barbara. "Reformmönchtum und der Aufstieg Clunys: Webers Bedeutung für die Forschung heute." In Schluchter, *Max Webers Sicht des okzidentalen Christentums*, 276–311.

Rotter, Gernot. "Der Islam hat die Demokratie erfunden." In Rotter, *Welten des Islam*, 173–77.

———, ed. *Die Welten des Islam: Neunundzwanzig Vorschläge, das Unvertraute zu verstehen*. Frankfurt am Main, 1993.

Rudolph, Kurt. *Die Gnosis*. Leipzig, 1977.

Ruipérez, Germán. *Die strukturelle Umschichtung der Verwandtschaftsbezeichnungen im Deutschen: Ein Beitrag zur historischen Lexikologie, diachronen Semantik und Ethnolinguistik*. Marburg, 1984.

Runciman, Steven. *The Great Church in Captivity: A Study of the Patriarchate of Constantinople from the Eve of the Turkish Conquest to the Greek War of Independence*. Cambridge, 1968.

———. *A History of the Crusades*. 3 vols. Cambridge, 1951–54.

Russell, J. C. "Die Bevölkerung Europas, 500–1500." In Cipolla and Borchardt, *Europäische Wirtschaftsgeschichte*, 1:13–44. Originally published as "Population in Europe, 500–1500," in *The Middle Ages*, edited by Carlo Cipolla, the Fontana Economic History of Europe 1 (London, 1973), 25–70.

Saberwal, Satish. "On the Making of Europe: Reflections from Delhi." *History Workshop* 33 (1992): 145–51.

Sachs, Hannelore, Ernst Badstübner, and Helga Neumann. *Erklärendes Wörterbuch zur christlichen Kunst*. Hanau, 1983.

Saenger, Paul. "Reading in the Later Middle Ages." In Cavallo and Chartier, *Reading in the West*, 120–48.

Sanderson, Stephen K. *Social Transformations: A General Theory of Historical Development*. Oxford, 1995.

Sandgruber, Roman. *Ökonomie und Politik: Österreichische Wirtschaftsgeschichte vom Mittelalter bis zur Gegenwart*. Vienna, 1995.

Sanz, Porfirio. "The Cities in the Aragonese Cortes in the Medieval and Early Modern Periods." *Parliaments, Estates and Representation* 14 (1994): 95–108.

Saperstein, Marc, ed. and trans. *Jewish Preaching, 1200–1800: An Anthology*. New Haven, 1989.

Sarnowsky, Jürgen. "Hospitalorden." In Dinzelbacher and Hogg, *Kulturgeschichte der christlichen Orden*, 193–204.

Scheibelreiter, Georg. *Tiernamen und Wappenwesen*. Vienna, 1992.

Schimmel, Annemarie. *Der Islam*. Stuttgart, 1990.

Schimmelpfennig, Bernhard. *Das Papsttum: Von der Antike bis zur Renaissance*. Darmstadt, 1984.

Schippmann, Klaus. *Grundzüge der Geschichte des sasanidischen Reiches*. Darmstadt, 1990.

Schluchter, Wolfgang, ed. *Max Webers Sicht des antiken Christentums: Interpretation und Kritik*. Frankfurt am Main, 1981.

———, ed. *Max Webers Sicht des Islams: Interpretation und Kritik*. Frankfurt am Main, 1987.

———, ed. *Max Webers Sicht des okzidentalen Christentums: Interpretation und Kritik*. Frankfurt am Main, 1988.

———, ed. *Max Webers Studie uber das antike Judentum: Interpretation und Kritik*. Frankfurt am Main, 1981.

———. *Religion und Lebensführung*. 2 vols. Frankfurt am Main, 1988.

Schlumberger, Jörg A. "Europas antikes Erbe." In Schlumberger and Segl, *Europa—aber was ist es?* 1–20.

Schlumberger, Jörg A., and Peter Segl, eds. *Europa—aber was ist es? Aspekte einer Identität in interdisziplinärer Sicht*. Cologne, 1994.

Schmale, Wolfgang. "Die Komponenten der historischen Europäistik." In Stourzh et al., *Eine europäische Geschichtsschreibung*, 119–39.

Schmaus, Alois. "Zur altslavischen Religionsgeschichte." *Saeculum* 4 (1953): 206–30.

Schmid, Heinrich Felix. "Die Burgbezirksverfassung bei den slavischen Völkern in ihrer Bedeutung für die Geschichte ihrer Siedlung und ihrer staatlichen Organisation." *Jahrbücher für Kultur und Geschichte der Slaven*, n.s. 2, no. 2 (1926): 81–132.

Schmidt, Hans-Joachim. *Kirche, Staat, Nation: Raumgliederung der Kirche im mittelalterlichen Europa*. Weimar, 1999.

Schmidtchen, Völker. "Technik im Übergang zur Neuzeit zwischen 1350 und 1600." In Ludwig and Schmidtchen, *Metalle und Macht*, 299–600.

Schmidt-Glintzer, Helwig. "Der Buddhismus im frühen chinesischen Mittelalter und der Wandel der Lebensführung bei der Gentry im Süden." *Saeculum* 23 (1972): 269–94.

Schmitthenner, Paul. *Krieg und Kriegsführung im Wandel der Weltgeschichte*. Potsdam, 1930.

Schneider, Fedor. *Die Entstehung von Burg und Landgemeinde in Italien*. Berlin, 1924.

Schneider, Helmut. "Die Gaben des Prometheus: Technik im antiken Mittelmeerraum zwischen 750 v. Chr und 500 n. Chr." In Hägermann and Schneider, *Landbau und Handwerk*, 19–313.

Schottenhammer, Angela. "China und Ostasien im Jahre 1000." *Periplus: Jahrbuch für Außereuropäische Geschichte* 10 (2000): 13–55.

Schrader, Erich. *Das Befestigungsrecht in Deutschland von den Anfängen bis zum Beginn des 14. Jahrhunderts.* Göttingen, 1909.

Schramm, Percy Ernst. *Der König von Frankreich: Das Wesen der Monarchie vom 9. bis zum 16. Jahrhundert.* Darmstadt, 1960.

Schreiner, Klaus. "'Consanguinitas'—'Verwandtschaft' als Strukturprinzip religiöser Gemeinschafts- und Verfassungsbildung in Kirche und Mönchtum des Mittelalters." In *Beiträge zur Geschichte und Struktur der mittelalterlichen Germania Sacra,* edited by Irene Crusius, 176–305. Veröffentlichungen des Max-Planck-Instituts für Geschichte 93. Göttingen, 1989.

———. "Laienfrömmigkeit—Frömmigkeit von Eliten oder Frömmigkeit des Volkes? Zur sozialen Verfaßtheit laikaler Frömmigkeitspraxis im späten Mittelalter." In *Laienfrömmigkeit im späten Mittelalter,* edited by Klaus Schreiner, with Elisabeth Müller-Luckner, 1–78. Munich, 1992.

Schulz, Knut. *"Denn sie lieben die Freiheit so sehr . . .": Kommunale Aufstände und Entstehung des europäischen Bürgertums im Hochmittelalter.* Darmstadt, 1992.

Schulze, Hagen. *Staat und Nation in der europäischen Geschichte.* Munich, 1994.

Schwarz, Gabriele. *Allgemeine Siedlungsgeographie.* Berlin, 1966.

Schwentker, Wolfgang. "Die 'vormoderne' Stadt in Europa und Asien: Überlegungen zu einem strukturgeschichtlichen Vergleich." In Feldbauer et al., *Die vormoderne Stadt,* 259–87.

Segl, Peter. "Europas Grundlegung im Mittelalter." In Schlumberger and Segl, *Europa—aber was ist es?* 21–44.

Seibt, Ferdinand. *Die Begründung Europas: Ein Zwischenbericht über die letzten tausend Jahre.* Frankfurt am Main, 2002.

———. "Landesherr und Stände in Westmitteleuropa am Ausgang des Mittelalters." In Weczerka, *Stände und Landesherrschaft,* 11–21.

Shiga, Shuzo. "Family Property and the Law of Inheritance in Traditional China." In Buxbaum, *Chinese Family Law,* 109–50.

Sieferle, Rolf Peter. "Der europäische Sonderweg: Ursachen und Faktoren." In *Der europäische Sonderweg: Ein Projekt der Breuninger Stiftung.* Vol. 1. Stuttgart, 2000.

———. *Rückblick auf die Natur: Eine Geschichte des Menschen und seiner Umwelt.* Munich, 1997.

———. *Der unterirdische Wald: Energiekrise und Industrielle Revolution.* Munich, 1982.

Sigaut, François. "De l'écobuage au pain d'épice: Quelques questions sur l'histoire du seigle." In Devroey et al., *Le seigle,* 211–50.

Silber, Ilana Friedrich. *Virtuosity, Charisma, and the Social Order: A Comparative Sociological Study of Monasticism in Theravada Buddhism and Medieval Catholicism.* Cambridge, 1995.

Silberman, Alphons. "Massenkommunikation." In *Handbuch der empirischen Sozialforschung,* edited by René König, 10:146–250. Stuttgart, 1977.

Sogner, Solvi, and Jacques Dupâquier. Introduction to *Marriage and Remarriage in Populations of the Past*, edited by Jacques Dupâquier, Etienne Hélin, Peter Laslett, Massimo Livi Bacci, and Solvi Sogner, 3–10. London, 1981.

Sokoll, Thomas. *Bergbau im Übergang zur Neuzeit*. Idstein, 1994.

Sourdel, Dominique. *Medieval Islam*. Translated by J. Montgomery Watt. London, 1983. Originally published as *L'Islam médiéval* (Paris, 1979).

Spieß, Karl-Heinz. *Familie und Verwandtschaft im deutschen Hochadel des Spätmittelalters: 13. bis Anfang des 16. Jahrhunderts*. Supplementary volume 111, *Vierteljahrschrift für Sozial- und Wirtschaftsgeschichte* (1993).

Sprandel, Rolf. *Das Eisengewerbe im Mittelalter*. Stuttgart, 1968.

———. *Mentalitäten und Systeme: Neue Zugänge zur mittelalterlichen Geschichte*. Stuttgart, 1972.

———. "Zu den Funktionen des Mönchtums." *Saeculum* 25 (1974): 211–14.

Spuler, Bertold. "The Arab Expansion and the Crusades." In Spuler, *Gesammelte Aufsätze*, 63–76.

———. "Die Bedeutung der Derwische im Islam." *Saeculum* 25 (1974): 214–16.

———. *Gesammelte Aufsätze*. Leiden, 1980.

———. "Die Ostgrenze des Abendlandes und die orthodoxe Kirche." In Spuler, *Gesammelte Aufsätze*, 99–108.

Squatriti, Paolo. *Water and Society in Early Medieval Italy: AD 400–1000*. Cambridge, 1998.

———, ed. *Working with Water in Medieval Europe: Technology and Resource-Use*. Leiden, 2000.

Stadtmüller, Georg. "Bemerkungen zu den Unterschieden des Mönchtums im Osten und im Abendland." *Saeculum* 25 (1974): 209–11.

Steindorf, Ludwig. *Memoria in Altrussland: Untersuchungen zu den Formen christlicher Totensorge*. Stuttgart, 1994.

Steininger, Hans. "Der Buddhismus in der chinesischen Geschichte des Mittelalters." *Saeculum* 13 (1962): 132–65.

Stemberger, Günter. *Juden und Christen im Heiligen Land*. Munich, 1987.

Stevenson, W. H. "Trinoda necessitas." *English Historical Review* 29 (1914): 689–703.

Stietencron, Heinrich von. "Die Wertmotivation der religiösen Aussonderungen in Indien." In "Versuch einer 'Historischen Anthropologie,'" edited by Oskar Köhler. Special issue, *Saeculum* 25, nos. 2–3 (1974): 202–5.

Stock, Brian. "Schriftgebrauch und Rationalität im Mittelalter." In Schluchter, *Max Webers Sicht des okzidentalen Christentums*, 165–83.

Stökl, Günther. "Das frühneuzeitliche Ständewesen im östlichen Europa." In Weczerka, *Stände und Landesherrschaft*, 193–200.

Stoob, Heinz. "Landesausbau und Gemeindebildung an der Nordseeküste im Mittelalter." In Konstanzer Arbeitskreis, *Die Anfänge der Landgemeinde*, 1:365–422.

Stourzh, Gerald, with Barbara Haider and Ulrike Harmat, eds. *Annäherungen an eine europäische Geschichtsschreibung*. Archiv für österreichische Geschichte 137. Vienna, 2002.

Stourzh, Gerald. "Statt eines Vorworts: Europa, aber wo liegt es?" In Stourzh et al., *Eine europäische Geschichtsschreibung*, ix–xx.

Stradal, Helmuth. "Die Prälaten." In Bruckmüller et al., *Herrschaftsstruktur und Ständebildung*, 3:53–114.

Struve, Tilman. "Die mittelalterlichen Grundlagen des modernen Europa." *Saeculum* 41 (1990): 100–114.

Suenari, Michio. "The 'Religious Family' among the Chinese of Central Taiwan." In De Vos and Sofue, *Religion and Family*, 169–84.

Suhling, Lothar. "Verhüttung silberhaltiger Kupfererze." In Lindgren, *Europäische Technik*, 269–76.

Surdich, Francesco. "Le città marinare tra rivoluzione commerciale e crociate fino all'inizio del Duecento." In *La società comunale e il policentrismo*, edited by Anna Benvenuti et al., 13–52. Storia della Società Italiana 6. Milan, 1986.

Swartz, Merlin L. "The Rules of the Popular Preaching in Twelfth-Century Bagdad, according to Ibn al-Jawzî." In Makdisi, *Prédication et propagande*, 223–40.

Sweeney, Del, ed. *Agriculture in the Middle Ages: Technology, Practice, and Representation*. Philadelphia, 1995.

Szücs, Jenö. *Die drei historischen Regionen Europas*. Frankfurt am Main, 1994.

Tangheroni, Marco. *Politica, commercio, agricoltura a Pisa nel Trecento*. Pisa, 1973.

Thornton, Arland, and Hui-Sheng Lin. *Social Change and the Family in Taiwan*. Chicago, 1994.

Thrupp, Sylvia L. "Das mittelalterliche Gewerbe, 1000–1500." In Cipolla and Borchardt, *Europäische Wirtschaftsgeschichte*, 1:141–76.

Tibi, Bassam. *Kreuzzug und Djihad: Der Islam und die christliche Welt*. Munich, 1999.

———. *Der wahre Imam: Der Islam von Mohammed bis zur Gegenwart*. Munich, 1996.

Todorova, Maria. "The Balkans as Category of Analysis: Borders, Space, Time." In Stourzh et al., *Eine europäische Geschichtsschreibung*, 57–84. Abbreviated version of "Der Balkan als Analysekategorie: Grenzen, Raum, Zeit," *Geschichte und Gesellschaft* 28, no. 3 (2002): 470–92.

———. "Zum erkenntnistheoretischen Wert von Familienmodellen: Der Balkan und die 'europäische Familie.'" In *Historische Familienforschung: Ergebnisse und Kontroversen*, edited by Josef Ehmer, Tamara Hareveen, and Richard Wall, 283–300. Frankfurt am Main, 1997.

Treadgold, Warren. *Byzantium and Its Army, 284–1081*. Stanford, 1995.

Tworuschka, Monika, and Udo Tworuschka, eds. *Religionen der Welt: Grundlagen, Entwicklung und Bedeutung in der Gegenwart*. Munich, 1996.

Udovitch, Abraham L. "Time, Sea and Society: Duration of Commercial Voyages on the Southern Shores of the Mediterranean during the High Middle Ages." *Settimane di studio del Centro Italiano di Studi sull'Alto Medioevo* 25, no. 2 (1978): 503–47.

Uslar, Rafael von. *Studien zu frühgeschichtlichen Befestigungsanlagen zwischen Nordsee und Alpen*. Cologne, 1964.

Vallone, Giancarlo. "La 'curia regis' tra ammistrazione e giuridizione." In *Contributi alla storia parlamentare Europea (secoli XIII–XX)*, edited by Maria Sofia Corciulo, 100–109. Atti del 43° Congresso ICHRPI. Camerino, 1996.

Verbruggen, J. F. *The Art of Warfare in Western Europe during the Middle Ages: From the Eighth Century to 1340*. 2nd ed. Translated by Sumner Willard and S. C. M. Southern. Woodbridge, UK, 1997.

Verhulst, Adriaan. "Die Binnenkolonisation und die Anfänge der Landgemeinde in Seeflandern." In Konstanzer Arbeitskreis, *Die Anfänge der Landgemeinde*, 1:447–60.

———. "La genèse du régime domanial classique en France au haut moyen âge." *Settimane di studio del Centro Italiano di Studi sull'Alto Medioevo* 13 (1966): 135–60.

Vetters, Herman. "Von der spätantiken zur frühmittelalterlichen Festungsbaukunst." *Settimane di studio del Centro Italiano di Studi sull'Alto Medioevo* 15, no. 2 (1968): 929–60.

Vogt, Joseph. "Die Ausbildung des frühen Mönchtums und seine exemplarische Bedeutung in der Spätantike." In "Versuch einer 'Historischen Anthropologie,'" edited by Oskar Köhler. Special issue, *Saeculum* 25, nos. 2–3 (1974): 206–8.

Volz, Paul. *Die biblischen Altertümer* (1914). Reprint, Wiesbaden, 1989.

Wall, Richard, with Jean Robin and Peter Laslett, eds. *Family Forms in Historic Europe*. Cambridge, 1983.

Waltner, Ann. *Getting an Heir: Adoption and the Construction of Kinship in Late Imperial China*. Honolulu, 1990.

Watson, Andrew M. *Agricultural Innovation in the Early Islamic World: The Diffusion of Crops and Farming Techniques, 700–1100*. Cambridge, 1983.

———. "The Arab Agricultural Revolution and Its Diffusion, 700–1100." *Journal of Economic History* 34, no. 1 (1974): 8–35.

———. "Arab and European Agriculture in the Middle Ages: A Case of Restricted Diffusion." In Sweeney, *Agriculture*, 62–75.

Weber, Max. *Economy and Society: An Outline of Interpretive Sociology*, edited by Guenther Roth and Claus Wittich. Translated by Ephraim Fischoff et al. 2 vols. New York, 1968.

———. *Gesammelte Aufsätze zur Religionssoziologie*. 3 vols. Tübingen, 1920–21.

Weczerka, Hugo, ed. *Stände und Landesherrschaft in Ostmitteleuropa in der frühen Neuzeit*. Historische und landeskundliche Ostmitteleuropa-Studien 16. Marburg, 1995.

Weiss, Bernard G., and Arnold H. Green. *A Survey of Arab History*. Cairo, 1998.

Wenskus, Reinhard. "Kleinverbände und Kleinräume bei den Prußen des Samlandes." In Konstanzer Arbeitskreis, *Die Anfänge der Landgemeinde*, 2:201–54.

———. *Stammesbildung und Verfassung: Das Werden der frühmittelalterlichen gentes*. 2nd ed. Cologne, 1977.

Wenzel, Horst. *Hören und Sehen: Kultur und Gedächtnis im Mittelalter*. Munich, 1995.

Werner, Karl Ferdinand, "Heeresorganisation und Kriegführung im deutschen Königreich des 10. und 11. Jahrhunderts." *Settimane di Studi del Centro Italiano di Studi sull'Alto Medioevo* 15, no. 2 (1968): 791–843.

———. "Political and Social Structures of the West." In Baechler et al., *Europe and Capitalism*, 169–84.

White, Colin. *Russia and America: The Roots of Economic Divergence*. London, 1987.

White, Lynn, Jr. "Cultural Climates and Technological Advance in the Middle Ages." In *Medieval Religion and Technology: Collected Essays*, 241–46. Berkeley, 1978.

———. "The Expansion of Technology, 500–1500." In *The Middle Ages*, edited by Carlo Cipolla, 143–74. The Fontana Economic History of Europe 1. London, 1973.

———. *Medieval Technology and Social Change*. Oxford, 1962.

———. "What Accelerated Technological Progress in the Western Middle Ages." In *Scientific Change: Historical Studies in the Intellectual, Social and Technical Conditions for Scientific Discovery and Technical Invention, from Antiquity to the Present*, edited by A. C. Crombie, 272–91. Oxford, 1963.

Wickham, Chris. "The Uniqueness of the East." In Baechler et al., *Europe and Capitalism*, 66–100. Originally published in "Feudalism and Non-European Societies," edited by T. J. Byres and H. Mukhia. Special issue, *Journal of Peasant Studies* 12, nos. 2–3 (1985): 166–96.

Wiesehöfer, Josef. *Das antike Persien*. Düsseldorf, 1998.

Winter, Carsten. *Predigen unter freiem Himmel: Die medienkulturellen Funktionen der Bettelmönche und ihr geschichtlicher Hintergrund*. Bardowick, 1996.

Wischermann, Clemens. "Institutionenökonomische Theorien und die Erklärung der Wirtschaftsentwicklung Europas in der Neuzeit." In Mörke and North, *Entstehung des modernen Europa*, 81–92.

Wolfram, Herwig. *Die Germanen*. Munich, 1995.

———. *History of the Goths*. Translated by Thomas J. Dunlap. Rev. from the 2nd German ed. Berkeley, 1988. Originally published as *Die Goten: Von den Anfängen bis zur Mitte des sechsten Jahrhunderts: Entwurf einer historischen Ethnographie* (Munich 1979).

———. *Salzburg, Bayern, Österreich: Die Conversio Bagoariorum et Carantanorum und die Quellen ihrer Zeit*. Mitteilungen des Instituts für Österreichische Geschichtsforschung, Ergänzungsband 31. Vienna, 1995.

Wong, R. Bin. *China Transformed: Historical Change and the Limits of European Experience*. Ithaca, 1997.

Zerfaß, Rolf. *Der Streit um die Laienpredigt: Eine pastoralgeschichtliche Untersuchung zum Verständnis des Predigeramts und zu seiner Entwicklung im 12. und 13. Jahrhundert*. Freiburg, 1974.

Zernack, Klaus. "Staatsmacht und Ständefreiheit: Politik und Gesellschaft in der Geschichte des östlichen Mitteleuropa." In Weczerka, *Stände und Landesherrschaft*, 1–10.

Ziehr, Wilhelm. *Das Kreuz: Symbol—Gestalt—Bedeutung*. Darmstadt, 1997.

Zöllner, Erich. *Geschichte der Franken bis zur Mitte des sechsten Jahrhunderts: Auf der Grundlage des Werkes von Ludwig Schmidt unter Mitwirkung von Joachim Werner neu bearbeitet*. Munich, 1970.

Index

Abbasids, 52, 124, 159, 163, 164, 168
absolutism, 142, 193
Abu Bekr, 257
Adalhard (abbot of Corbie), 11
Admonitio generalis, 247
adoption, 85–86, 90
affined relationships, 70
agrarium, 30
agriculture: agrarian revolution in early Middle Ages, 1–27, 273–74; in British Isles, 10, 44–45; burn-beating cultivation, 9; in Byzantine Empire, 12–13, 51–52; in China, 2, 3, 17–20, 22, 52–53; Cistercians as agricultural innovators, 277; core Europe defined in terms of, 54, 294; in eastern Europe, 45–49, 191; ecological limits of medieval revolution, 293; in Europe's special path, xvii, xviii; family system and agrarian system, 58; feudalism requires agrarian base, 105, 110; and growth of trades, 21–24, 284; integrating farming with animal husbandry, 5–6, 19, 21, 22, 24–26, 35, 273; in Islamic world, 2, 3, 13–17, 22, 52; lordship expands with expansion of, 100; manorialism as social framework for agrarian revolution, 8, 26, 30, 32, 34, 35, 37, 274, 276; military based on,
25–26; in mining's development, 277, 278–79; on monasteries, 40; new cultural areas and innovations, 2; northern versus Mediterranean region, 10–12, 293; and settlement patterns, 25; slash-and-burn economy, 8, 48, 78, 81; social system influenced, 28; and trade, 24–25; western versus eastern, 9. *See also* animal husbandry; cerealization; imported crops; peasants; plows; three-field system
Albigensian Crusade, 204
Alexander II, Pope, 198, 199
Alexios, Emperor, 204
Alfred the Great, King, 44
almonds, 11
alphabetic writing, 258, 259, 267, 268
altars, 183, 290–91
Amalfi, 190, 199, 221, 223, 224, 225
ancestors: naming children after, 90. *See also* ancestor worship
ancestor worship: in China, 82–86, 89, 90, 92; Christianity and, 79–80, 81–82, 88, 91, 93; in eastern Europe, 79–80, 81–82; family's significance, 292; Islamic world and, 88; kinship terms and, 84; seniority and, 96; sons and, 79, 85, 96
anchorites, 155, 190

Islamic structures contrasted, 26, 52;
life-cycle servants, 64–65; and lineage
system as in conflict, 68; lordship, 26,
55–57, 63, 100; lord's right to decide
succession, 66–67; in Mediterranean
region, 49–50, 293; monastic, 39–40,
59, 191; papal church's range as greater
than, 192; peasant retirement, 65–66;
plowing service as initial force, 30,
34–35, 50; points of contact with other
forms, 32–35; Roman *villa* as precursor,
29–30, 33–34, 35; royal manors, 37–39,
49; in settlement formation, 284; as social framework for agrarian revolution,
8, 26, 30, 32, 34, 35, 37, 274, 276; stud
farms, 32; the trades and, 21, 35–36;
transformations of classic system,
40–41; tribal structures supplanted,
54–55; unfree people, 30–31, 55;
uniqueness, 53–54; universal religious
orders influenced, 277
Mansur, al-, Caliph, 165
maritime republics, Italian, 217–31;
communal autonomy, 226, 285; in
Crusades, 195, 212; as exceptional,
228, 231; independence as condition of
being colonial power, 225–26; navies,
223–25, 227, 228; possessions in Holy
Land, 213–14; protocolonialism, 194,
195, 223, 228, 230, 293; shipbuilding,
224; trade with Islamic world, 195,
222–23, 229; in western Mediterranean, 195, 217–23. *See also* Genoa; Pisa;
Venice
markets: as appurtenances of royal manors, 37; at castles, 121
Markward von Annweiler, 206
marriage: age at, 63, 65, 90, 94, 95;
Chinese rules of, 84–85, 92; choice of
spouse, 95; in Christianity, 72–73, 93,
95–96; congregational context of rite,
73; by consent, 93, 95, 277; eastern
versus western patterns, 60–62; fertility, 95–96; in Islamic world, 88, 91–93;
levirate, 85–86, 91; lord of manor
influences, 63, 101; for love, 95; low
rate, 95; origins of European patterns,
xvii; polygamy, 90; between relatives
banned, 72–73, 93; relatives by, 70;
as sacrament, 88, 93, 95, 181. *See also*
remarriage

Martin, Jochen, 180
martyrdom, cult of, 202
Mass. *See* Eucharist (Mass)
mass communication: based on images,
235, 276; based on literacy, 234, 239,
276; based on orality, 233, 239, 276;
commonalities created, 268; conditions
required, 232; in East Asia, 267–68;
in integration of general public into
state organization, 270; nonconform-
ism and heterodoxy benefit from, 269;
woodcuts in, 234. *See also* preaching;
printing
Master of Flémalle, 244
Master of the Vienna Schottenstift, 290
Mauritius, Saint, 210
meat, 21
medicinal plants, 40
Mediterranean region: Atlantic colonialism's roots in eastern, 217; Crusades
conquer lands in eastern, 193; Islamic
expansionism, 195, 201; manorialism,
49–50, 293; maritime republics in western, 195, 217–23; northern agriculture
versus, 10–12, 293; *oppida*, 116; papal
church, 192; Phoenician and Greek
cities, 229; regions occupied in "Fourth
Crusade," 214–15. *See also* Italy; *and
islands by name*
mendicant orders: as geographically congruent with Western Church, 248, 261;
and lay piety, 262; lay sermon controversy and founding, 245–46; poverty
movement reflected, 208; preaching,
240, 247, 248, 249, 268; printing as
geographically congruent with, 261;
silent reading, 263
mercenaries, 123–24, 133
Mercurius, Saint, 201
metal cuts, 241, 255
Middle Ages: agrarian revolution in
early, 1–27; the church, 144–93;
conjugal family and bilateral kinship,
58–98; mass communication in early,
232–71; population growth, 20–21;
settlement patterns, 25; social evolutionary forces shift to northwest, 1–3,
13, 145, 156, 180, 227. *See also* Carolingian Empire; Crusades; feudalism;
manorialism
miles Christianus, 182, 208–11